EDWARD AUGUSTUS FREEMAN

THE GROWTH

OF THE

ENGLISH CONSTITUTION

FROM THE EARLIEST TIMES

Elibron Classics
www.elibron.com

Elibron Classics series.

ISBN 1-4021-5982-X (paperback)
ISBN 1-4212-7884-7 (hardcover)

This Elibron Classics Replica Edition is an unabridged facsimile of the edition published in 1872 by Macmillan and Co., London.

THE GROWTH

OF

THE ENGLISH CONSTITUTION

FROM THE EARLIEST TIMES.

THE GROWTH

OF THE

ENGLISH CONSTITUTION

FROM THE EARLIEST TIMES.

BY

EDWARD A. FREEMAN, M.A., HON. D.C.L.,

LATE FELLOW OF TRINITY COLLEGE, OXFORD.

'Concedis justas leges et consuetudines esse tenendas, et promittis eas per te esse protegendas et ad honorem Dei roborandas, *quas vulgus elegerit*, secundum vires tuas ?'—ANCIENT CORONATION OATH.

'Rex habet superiorem, Deum. Item Legem, per quam factus est Rex. Item curiam suam.'—BRACTON.

'Igitur communitas regni consulatur,
Et quid universitas sentiat sciatur.'
POLITICAL POEM, *XIII. Cent.*

London:

MACMILLAN AND CO.

1872.

LONDON:
R. CLAY, SONS, AND TAYLOR, PRINTERS,
BREAD STREET HILL.

PREFACE.

THE proverb "*qui s'excuse s'accuse*" is so regularly turned against any author who gives any account of the origin of his work that it may be well to prevent its quotation by quoting it oneself. I have to ask that these three Chapters and their accompanying notes may not be judged by the standard of a book. If I were to write a book on the English Constitution, it would be different in form and, in many points, different in style. What the reader has here is a somewhat extended form of two Lectures given at Leeds and Bradford last January. I had thought that they might be worth printing in the shape of two magazine-papers; others thought that they might do good in their present shape. I therefore expanded the latter part of the second Lecture, which had to be cut very short in delivery, so as to make a third Chapter, and I added such notes and references as seemed to be needed.

I say all this, in order that what I have now written may be judged by the standard of lectures, not by the standard of a book. In a popular lecture it is impossible to deal with everything with which it is desirable to deal; it is impossible to go to the bottom of those things which one picks out to deal with. It is enough—because it is all that can be done—if the choice of subjects is fairly well made, and if the treatment of those that are chosen, though necessarily inadequate, is accurate as far as it goes. Many things must be left out altogether; many things must be treated very imperfectly; the attention of the hearers must be caught by putting some things in a more highly wrought shape than one would choose at another time. The object is gained, if the lecturer awakens in his hearers a real interest in the subject on which he speaks, and if he sends them to the proper sources of more minute knowledge. If I can in this way send every one who wishes to understand the early institutions of his country to the great work of Professor Stubbs—none the less great because it lies in an amazingly small compass—my own work will be effectually done. In Mr. Stubbs'

"Documents Illustrative of English History," the ordinary student will find all that he can want to learn, while he who means to write a book, or to carry out his studies in a more minute way, will find the best of guidance towards so doing. The great documents of early English history, hitherto scattered far and wide, are now for the first time brought together, and their bearing is expounded in a continuous narrative worthy of the unerring learning and critical power of the first of living scholars.

For my own part, my object has been to show that the earliest institutions of England and of other Teutonic lands are not mere matters of curious speculation, but matters closely connected with our present political being. I wish to show that, in many things, our earliest institutions come more nearly home to us, and that they have more in common with our present political state, than the institutions of intermediate ages which at first sight seem to have much more in common with our own. As the continuity of our national life is to many so hard a lesson to master, so the continuity of our political life, and the way in which we have so often fallen back on the very earliest principles of our race, is a lesson which many find specially hard. But the holders of Liberal principles in modern politics need never shrink from tracing up our political history to it's earliest beginnings. As far at least as our race is concerned, freedom is everywhere older than bondage; we may add that toleration is older than intolerance. Our ancient history is the possession of the Liberal, who, as being ever ready to reform, is the true Conservative, not of the self-styled Conservative who, by refusing to reform, does all he can to bring on destruction. One special point on which I have dwelt is the way in which our constitutional history has been perverted at the hands of lawyers. It is perfectly true that the history of England must be studied in the Statute-Book, but it must be in a Statute-Book which begins at no point later than the Dooms of Æthelberht.

As I have often had need to take facts and doctrines for granted which I believe myself to have proved in my larger works, I have in the Notes given frequent references to those works, instead of bringing in the evidence for the same things over again. And in the more modern part of the subject, I have given several extracts at full length, even from very familiar authors, because I know that a reader is often well pleased to have a striking passage set before him at once, without having to seek for it in the original. On the other hand, I have given at full length several extracts from statutes and other documents which most readers are not likely to have at hand. The historical portions of any Act of Parliament can be studied only in the Acts themselves, and not in the summaries of lawyers. Legal writers and speakers seem constantly to repeat what has been said before them, without any reference to the original sources. A memorable example is to be found in the assertion of Blackstone and of a crowd of lawyers after him, in Parliament and out of Parliament, that the King or Queen is by Law Head of the Church. I need hardly say that that title was used by Henry, Edward, and Mary, but that it was given up by Mary, and was not taken up again by any later Sovereign.

SOMERLEAZE, WELLS,
March 25, 1872.

CONTENTS.

CHAPTER I.

CHAPTER II.

CHAPTER III.

THE GROWTH OF

THE ENGLISH CONSTITUTION

FROM THE

EARLIEST TIMES.

CHAPTER I.

YEAR by year, on certain spots among the dales and the mountain-sides of Switzerland, the traveller who is daring enough to wander out of beaten tracks and to make his journey at unusual seasons may look on a sight such as no other corner of the earth can any longer set before him. He may there gaze and feel, what none can feel but those who have seen with their own eyes, what none can feel in its fulness more than once in a life-time, the thrill of looking for the first time face to face on freedom in its purest and most ancient form. He is there in a land where the oldest institutions of our race, institutions which may be traced up to the earliest times of which history or legend gives us any glimmering, still live on in their primæval freshness. He is in a land where an immemorial freedom, a freedom only less eternal than the rocks that guard it, puts to shame the boasted antiquity of kingly dynasties, which, by its side, seem but as innovations of yesterday. There year by year, on some bright morning of the springtide, the Sovereign People, not entrusting its rights to a few of its own number, but discharging them itself in the majesty of its corporate person, meets in the open market-place or in the green meadow at the mountain's foot, to frame the laws to which it yields obedience as its own work, to choose the rulers whom it can afford to greet with reverence as drawing their commission from itself. Such a sight there are but few Englishmen who have seen; to be among those few I reckon among the highest privileges of my life. Let me ask you to follow me in spirit to the very home and birth-place of freedom, to the land where we need not myth and fable to add aught to the fresh and gladdening feeling with which we for the first time tread the soil and drink in the air of the immemorial democracy of Uri (1). It is one of the opening days of May; it is the morning of Sunday; for men there deem that the better the day the better the deed; they deem that the Creator cannot be more truly honoured than in using, in His fear and in His presence, the highest of the gifts which

He has bestowed on man. But deem not that, because the day of Christian worship is chosen for the great yearly assembly of a Christian commonwealth, the more direct sacred duties of the day are forgotten. Before we, in our luxurious island, have lifted ourselves from our beds, the men of the mountains, Catholic and Protestant alike, have already paid the morning's worship in God's temple. They have heard the mass of the priest or they have listened to the sermon of the pastor, before some of us have awakened to the fact that the morn of the holy day has come. And when I saw men thronging the crowded church, or kneeling, for want of space within, on the bare ground beside the open door, and when I saw them marching thence to do the highest duties of men and citizens, I could hardly forbear thinking of the saying of Holy Writ, that "where the Spirit of the Lord is, there is liberty." From the market-place of Altdorf, the little capital of the Canton, the procession makes its way to the place of meeting at Bözlingen. First marches the little army of the Canton, an army whose weapons never can be used save to drive back an invader from their land([2]). Over their heads floats the banner, the bull's head of Uri, the ensign which led men to victory on the fields of Sempach and Morgarten And before them all, on the shoulders of men clad in a garb of ages past, are borne the famous horns, the spoils of the wild bull of ancient days, the very horns whose blast struck such dread into the fearless heart of Charles of Burgundy (3). Then, with their lictors before them, come the magistrates of the commonwealth on horseback (4), the chief magistrate, the Landammann, with his sword by his side. The people follow the chiefs whom they have chosen to the place of meeting, a circle in a green meadow, with a pine forest rising above their heads and a mighty spur of the mountain range facing them on the other side of the valley. The multitude of freemen take their seats around the chief ruler of the commonwealth, whose term of office comes that day to an end. The Assembly opens; a short space is first given to prayer, silent prayer offered up by each man in the temple of God's own rearing. Then comes the business of the day. If changes in the law are demanded, they are then laid before the vote of the Assembly, in which each citizen of full age has an equal vote and an equal right of speech. The yearly magistrates have now discharged all their duties; their term of office is at an end, the trust which has been placed in their hands falls back into the hands of those by whom it was given, into the hands of the sovereign people. The chief of the commonwealth, now such no longer, leaves his seat of office and takes his place as a simple citizen in the ranks of his fellows. It rests with the free will of the Assembly to call him back to his chair of office, or to set another there in his stead. Men who have neither looked into the history of the past, nor yet troubled themselves to learn what happens year by year in their own age, are fond of declaiming against the caprice and ingratitude of the people, and of telling us that under a democratic government neither men nor measures can remain for an hour unchanged. The witness alike of the present and of the past is an answer to baseless theories like these. The spirit which made democratic Athens year by year bestow her highest offices on the patrician Periklês and the reactionary Phôkiôn([5]) still lives in the democracies of Switzerland, alike in the Landesgemeinde of Uri and in the Federal Assembly at Bern. The ministers of Kings, whether despotic or constitutional, may vainly envy the sure tenure of office which falls to the lot of those who are chosen to rule by the voice of the people. Alike in the whole Confederation and in the single Canton re-election is the rule; the rejection of the out-going magistrate is the rare exception ([6]). The Landammann of Uri, whom his countrymen have raised to the seat of honour, and who has done nothing to lose their confidence, need not fear that when he has gone to the place of meeting in the pomp of office, his place in the march homeward will be transferred to another against his will.

Such is the scene, which, save for a moment, when the world was turned upside down by the inroads of revolutionary France(7), has gone on year by year as far as history goes back in the most unchanged of European states. Let me ask you to follow me yet again to the place of assembly of a younger member of the same noble band of commonwealths (8), to pass from Uri to Appenzell, from the green meadows of Bözlingen to the hill-side market-place of Trogen. Somewhat of the pomp and circumstance which marks the assembly of Catholic and pastoral Uri is lacking in the assembly of the Protestant and industrial population of the Outer Rhodes of Appenzell. But the stamp of antiquity, the stamp of immemorial freedom, is impressed alike on the assembly and on the whole life of either commonwealth. We miss in Appenzell the solemn procession, the mounted magistrates, the military pomp, of Uri, but we find in their stead an immemorial custom which breathes perhaps more than any other the spirit of days when freedom was not a thing of course, but a thing for which men had to give their toil, and, if need be, their blood. Each man who makes his way to the Landesgemeinde of Trogen, bears at his side the sword which the law at once commands him to carry and forbids him to draw (ᵍ). And in the proceedings of the assembly itself, the men of Appenzell have kept one ancient rite, which surpasses all that I have ever seen or heard of in its heart-stirring solemnity. When the newly chosen Landammann enters on his office, his first duty is to bind himself by an oath to obey the laws of the commonwealth over which he is called to rule. His second duty is to administer to the multitude before him the same oath by which he has just bound himself. To hear the voice of thousands of freemen pledging themselves to obey the laws which they themselves have made is a moment in one's life which can never be forgotten, a moment for whose sake it would be worth while to take a far longer and harder journey than that which leads us to Uri or Appenzell.

And now I may be asked why I have begun a discourse on the constitution of England with a picture of the doings of two small commonwealths whose political and social state is so widely different from our own. I answer that I have done so, because my object is, not merely to speak of the constitution of England in the shape which the changes of fourteen hundred years have at last given it, but to trace back those successive changes to the earliest times which either history or tradition sets before us. In the institutions of Uri and Appenzell, and in those others of the Swiss Cantons which have never departed from the primæval model, we may see the institutions of our own forefathers, the institutions which were once common to the whole Teutonic race, institutions whose outward form has necessarily passed away from greater states, but which contain the germs out of which every free constitution in the world has grown. Let us look back to the earliest picture which history can give us of the political and social being of our own forefathers. In the Germany of Tacitus we have the picture of the institutions of the Teutonic race before one branch of that race sailed from the mouths of the Elbe and the Weser to seek new homes by the Humber and the Thames. There, in the picture of our fathers and brethren seventeen hundred years back, the free Teutonic Assembly, the armed Assembly of the whole people, is set before us, well-nigh the same, in every essential point, as it may still be seen in Uri, Unterwalden, Glarus, and Appenzell. One point however must be borne in mind. In the assemblies of those small Cantons it is only the most democratic side of the old Teutonic constitution which comes prominently into sight. The commonwealth of Uri, by the peculiar circumstances of its history, grew into an independent and sovereign state. But in its origin it was not a nation, it was not even a tribe(10). The Landesgemeinden of which I have been speaking are the Assemblies, not of a nation but of a district; they answer in our own land, not to the Assemblies of the whole Kingdom, but to the lesser Assemblies of the shire or the hundred. But they are not on that account any the less worthy of our notice, they do not on that account throw any the less light on that common political heritage which belongs alike to Swabia and to England. In every Teutonic land which still keeps any footsteps of its ancient institutions, the local divisions are not simply administrative districts traced out for convenience on the map. In fact, they are not divisions at all; they are not divisions of the Kingdom, but the earlier elements out of whose union the Kingdom grew. Yorkshire, by that name, is younger than England, but Yorkshire, by its elder name of Deira, is older than England(11). And Yorkshire or Deira itself is younger than the smaller districts of which it is made up, Craven, Cleveland, Holderness, and others. The Landesgemeinde of Uri answers, not to an Assembly of all England, not to an Assembly of all Deira, but to an Assembly of Holderness or Cleveland. But in the old Teutonic system the greater aggregate was simply organized after the model of the lesser elements out of whose union it was formed.

In fact, for the political unit, for the atom which joined with its fellow atoms to form the political whole, we must go to areas yet smaller than those of Holderness or Uri. That unit, that atom, the true kernel of all our political life, must be looked for in Switzerland in the *Gemeinde* or *Commune;* in England—smile not while I say it—in the parish vestry (12).

The primitive Teutonic constitution, the constitution of the Germans of Tacitus, the constitution which has lingered on in a few remote corners of the old German realm, is democratic, but it is not purely democratic. Or rather it is democratic, purely democratic, in the truer, older, and more honourable sense of that much maligned word; it is not purely democratic in that less honourable, but purely arbitrary, sense which is often put upon it in modern controversy. Democracy, according to Periklês, is a government of the whole people, as opposed to oligarchy, a government of only a part of the people (13). A government which vests all power in any one class, a government which shuts out any one class, whether that class be the highest or the lowest, does not answer the definition of Periklês; it is not a government of the whole but only of a part; it is not a democracy but an oligarchy (14). Democracy, in the sense of Periklês, demands that every freeman shall have a voice in the affairs of the commonwealth; it does not necessarily demand that every freeman should have an equal voice. It does not forbid the existence of magistrates clothed with high authority and held in high reverence, nor does it forbid respect for ancient birth or even an attachment to an hereditary line of rulers. The older school of English constitutional writers delighted to show that the English Constitution contained a monarchic, an aristocratic, and a democratic element, the three being wrought together in such true and harmonious proportion that we could enjoy the good side of all the three great forms of government without ever seeing the evil side of any of them. These worthy speculators were perhaps a little Utopian in their theories; still there is no doubt that, in every glimpse we get of old Teutonic politics, we see what we may fairly call a monarchic, an aristocratic, and a democratic element. Those earliest glimpses set before us three classes of men as found in every Teutonic society, the noble, the common freeman, and the slave([15]). The existence of the slave, harshly as the name now grates on our ears, is no special shame or blame to our own forefathers. Slavery, in some shape or other, has unhappily been the common law of most nations in most ages; it is a mere exception to the general rule that, partly through the circumstances of most European countries, partly through the growth of humanity and civilization, the hateful institution has, during a few centuries past, gradually disappeared from a certain portion of the earth's surface. And we must not forget that, in many states of society, the doom of slavery may have been thankfully received as an alleviation of his lot by the man whose life was forfeited either as a prisoner in merciless warfare or as a wrong-doer sentenced for his crimes(16). But I mention the existence of slavery only that we may remember that when we speak of freedom, freemen, democracy, and the like, we are after all speaking of the rights of a privileged class—that, whether in Athens, in Rome, or in the early Teutonic communities, there was always a large mass of human beings who had no share in the freedom, the victory, or the glory of their masters. We are now more closely concerned with the distinctions which, from the earliest times, we find among the freemen themselves. In the Germany of Tacitus, as at this day in the democratic Cantons, the sovereign power is vested in the whole people, acting directly in their own persons. But if the sovereignty of the popular Assembly is plainly set before us, we have also no less plainly set before us the existence of a Council smaller than the popular Assembly, and also the existence of a class of nobles, the nature and extent of whose privileges is not very well defined, but who clearly had privileges of some kind or other, and whose privileges passed on by hereditary descent. Here we have an aristocratic element as distinctly marked as the democratic element which is supplied by the popular assembly. And at the head of all we see personal chiefs of tribes and nations, chiefs bearing different titles, Kings, Dukes, or Ealdormen, who in most cases drew their title to rule from an union of birth and election, rulers whom the nation chose and whom the nation could depose, but who still were the personal leaders of the nation, its highest magistrates in peace, its highest leaders in war. Here then, besides the democratic and the aristocratic elements, we have a distinct monarchic element standing out clearly in our earliest glimpses of Teutonic political life. King, Lords, and Commons, in their present shapes, are something comparatively recent, but we may see something which may fairly pass as the germ of King, Lords, and Commons, from the very beginning of our history.

I will even go a step further. The Constitution which I have just sketched is indeed the common possession of the Teutonic race, but it is something more. We should perhaps not be wrong if we were to call it a common possession of the whole Aryan family of mankind. It is possible that we may even find traces of it beyond the bounds of the Aryan family (17). But I will put speculations like these aside. It is enough for me that the Constitution which was the common heritage of the Teutonic race, was an heritage which the Teuton shared with his kinsfolk in Greece and Italy. Turn to the earliest records of European civilization. In the Homeric poems we see a constitution essentially the same as that which is set before us in the Germany of Tacitus, established alike in the Achaian camp before Ilios, in the island realm of Ithakê, and even among the Gods on Olympos. Zeus is the King of all; but he has around him his Council of the greater Gods, and there are times when he summons to his court the whole Assembly of the Divine nation, when Gods of all ranks gather together in the court of their chief, when, save old Ocean himself, even all the River-gods were there, and when we are specially told—a fact which might perhaps be pressed into the service of very recent controversies—that not one of the Nymphs stayed away (18). If we come down to earth, we find the King of Men as the common leader of all, but we find him surrounded by his inner Council of lesser princes and captains. And on great occasions, Agamemnôn on earth, like Zeus in heaven, gathers together the general Assembly of freeborn warriors, an assembly in which, if debate was mainly confined to a few eloquent leaders, the common freeman, the undistinguished citizen and soldier, had at least the right of speaking his mind as to the proposals of his chiefs, by loud applause or by emphatic silence([19] Nor is this picture confined to the host in battle array beneath the walls of Ilios; we must remember that in all early societies the distinction between soldier and civilian is unknown; the army is the nation, and the nation is the army. The same picture which the Iliad sets before us as the constitution of the Achaian army, the glimpses of more peaceful life which we find in the Odyssey set before us as being no less the constitution of every Hellenic commonwealth on its own soil. Everywhere we find the same three elements, the supreme leader or King, the lesser chiefs who form his Council, and the final authority of all, the general Assembly of the freemen([20]). We see the same in every glimpse which history or legend gives us of the political state of Rome and the other old Italian commonwealths ([21]). Everywhere we find the King, the Senate, the Assembly of the people, and the distribution of powers is not essentially changed when the highest personal authority is transferred from the hands of a King chosen for life to the hands of Consuls chosen for a year(22). The likeness between the earliest political institutions of the Greek, the Italian, and the Teuton is so close, so striking in every detail, that we can hardly fail to see in it possession handed on from the earliest times, a possession which Greek, Italian, and Teuton already had in the days before the separation, in those unrecorded but still authentic times when Greek, Italian, and Teuton were still a single people speaking a single tongue.

I have referred more than once to the picture of our race in its earliest recorded times, as set before us by the greatest of Roman historians in the Germany of Tacitus. Let me now set before you some special points of his description in his own words as well as I am able to clothe them in an English dress (23).

"They choose their Kings on account of their nobility, their leaders on account of their valour. Nor have the Kings an unbounded or arbitrary power, and the leaders rule rather by their example than by the right of command; if they are ready, if they are prominent, if they are forward in leading the van, they hold the first place in honour. . . . On smaller matters the chiefs debate, on greater matters all men; but so that those things whose final decision rests with the whole people are first handled by the chiefs. . . . The multitude sits armed in such order as it thinks good; silence is proclaimed by the priests, who have also the right of enforcing it. Presently the King or chief, according to the age of each, according to his birth, according to his glory in war or his eloquence, is listened to, speaking rather by the influence of persuasion, than by the power of commanding. If their opinions give offence, they are thrust aside with a shout; if they are approved, the hearers clash their spears. It is held to be the most honourable kind of applause to use their weapons to signify approval. It is lawful also in the assembly to bring matters for trial and to bring charges of capital crimes. . . . In the same assembly chiefs are chosen to administer justice through the districts and villages. Each chief in so doing has a hundred companions of the commons assigned to him, as at once his counsellors and his authority. Moreover they do no matter of business, public or private, except in arms."

Here we have a picture of a free commonwealth of warriors, in which each freeman has his place in the state, where the vote of the general Assembly is the final authority on all matters, but where both hereditary descent and elective office are held in high honour. We see also in a marked way the influence of personal character and of the power of speech;

we see the existence of local divisions, local assemblies, local magistrates; in a word, we see in this picture of our forefathers in their old land, seventeen hundred years ago, the germs of all the institutions which have grown up step by step among ourselves in the course of ages. And a Swiss of the democratic Cantons would see in it, not merely the germs of his constitution, but the living picture of the thing itself.

This immemorial Teutonic constitution was thus the constitution of our forefathers in their old land of Northern Germany, before they made their way into the Isle of Britain. And that constitution, in all its essential points, they brought with them into their new homes, and there, transplanted to a new soil, it grew and flourished, and brought forth fruit richer and more lasting than it brought forth in the land of its earlier birth. On the Teutonic mainland, the old Teutonic freedom, with its free assemblies, national and local, gradually died out before the encroachments of a brood of petty princes (24). In the Teutonic island it has changed its form from age to age; it has lived through many storms and it has withstood the attacks of many enemies, but it has never utterly died out. The continued national life of the people, notwithstanding foreign conquests and internal revolutions, has remained unbroken for fourteen hundred years. At no moment has the tie between the present and the past been wholly rent asunder; at no moment have Englishmen sat down to put together a wholly new constitution in obedience to some dazzling theory. Each step in our developement has been the natural consequence of some earlier step; each change in our law and constitution has been, not the bringing in of anything wholly new, but the developement and improvement of something that was already old. Our progress has in some ages been faster, in others slower; at some moments we have seemed to stand still, or even to go back; but the great march of political developement has never wholly stopped; it has never been permanently checked since the day when the coming of the Teutonic conquerors first began to change Britain into England. New and foreign elements have from time to time thrust themselves into our law; but the same spirit which could develope and improve whatever was old and native has commonly found means sooner or later to cast forth again whatever was new and foreign. The lover of freedom, the lover of progress, the man who has eyes keen enough to discover identity under a garb of outward unlikeness, need never shrink from tracing up the political institutions of England to their earliest shape. The fourteen hundred years of

English history are the possession of those who would ever advance, not the possession of those who would stand still or go backwards. The wisdom of our forefathers was ever shown, not in a dull and senseless clinging to things as they were at any given moment, but in that spirit, the spirit alike of the true reformer and the true conservative, which keeps the whole fabric standing, by repairing and improving from time to time, whatever portions of it stand in need of repair or improvement. Let ancient customs prevail(25); let us ever stand fast in the old paths. But the old paths have in England ever been the paths of progress; the ancient custom has ever been to shrink from mere change for the sake of change, but fearlessly to change whenever change was really needed. And many of the best changes of later times, many of the most wholesome improvements in our Law and Constitution, have been only the casting aside of innovations which have crept in in modern and evil times. They have been the calling up again, in an altered garb, of principles as old as the days when we get our first sight of our forefathers in their German forests. Changed as it is in all outward form and circumstance, the England in which we live, has, in its true life and spirit, far more in common with the England of the earliest times than it has with the England of days far nearer to our own. In many a wholesome act of modern legislation, we have gone back, wittingly or unwittingly, to the earliest principle of our race. We have advanced by falling back on a more ancient state of things; we have reformed by calling to life again the institutions of earlier and ruder times, by setting ourselves free from the slavish subtleties of Norman lawyers, by casting aside as an accursed thing the innovations of Tudor tyranny and Stewart usurpation.

I have said that the primæval Teutonic constitution was brought with them by our Teutonic forefathers when they came as conquerors into the Isle of Britain. I will not again go into the details of the English Conquest, the settlement which gave us a new home in a new land, nor into all the questions and controversies to which the details of the English Conquest have given rise. I have spoken of them over and over again with my voice and with my pen, and I hope I may now take for granted what I have already argued out elsewhere ([26]). I hope that I may be allowed to assume the plain facts of the case, without going through the details of every point. I will assume then—for it is that to which the question really comes—that England is England and that Englishmen are Englishmen. I will assume that we are not Romans or Welshmen, but that we are the descendants of the Angles, Saxons, and Jutes who came hither in the fifth and sixth centuries, of the Danes and Northmen who came hither in the ninth. I will assume that we are a people, not indeed of unmixed Teutonic blood—for no people in the world is of absolutely unmixed blood — but a people whose blood is not more mixed than that of any other nation; that Englishmen are as truly Englishmen as Welshmen are Welshmen or as High-Germans are High-Germans. I will assume that what is Teutonic in us is not merely one element among others, but that it is the very life and essence of our national being; that whatever else we may have in us, whatever we have drawn from those whom we conquered or from those who conquered us, is no co-ordinate element, but a mere infusion into our Teutonic essence; in a word I will assume that Englishmen are Englishmen, that we are ourselves and not some other people. I assume all this; if any man disputes it, if any man chooses not to be an Englishman but to be a Welshman or a Roman, I cannot argue with him now; I can only ask him to turn to the arguments which I have urged on all those points in other times and places. I assume that, as we have had one national name, one national speech, from the beginning, we may be fairly held to have an unbroken national being. And when we find a Teutonic-speaking people in Britain living under the same political and social forms as the Teutonic-speaking people of the mainland, it is surely no very rash or far-fetched inference that the tongue and the laws which they have in common are a common possession drawn from a common source; that the island colony in short came itself and brought its laws and language with it from the elder mother-land beyond the sea.

Our fathers then came into Britain, and they brought with them the same primæval political system, the same distinctions of rank, the same division of political power, which they had been used to in their elder Anglian and Saxon homes. The circumstances of the Conquest would no doubt bring about some changes. It would probably tend to increase the numbers of the class of slaves. Such of the natives as were neither slain nor driven out would of course pass into that class. Especially, though there is no doubt that our forefathers brought their women with them from their own homes, there is no doubt that many British women passed into bondage, so much so that one of the common Old-English names for a female slave is *Wylne* or *Welsh-woman* (27). And we may infer that this increased familiarity with slavery would tend to strengthen the custom by which freemen guilty of crimes were reduced to slavery by sentence of law. Again, I suspect that the circumstances of the Conquest did something to raise the position both of the common freeman and of the King or leader, as compared with the intermediate class of nobles. No two things are more levelling than colonization and successful warfare. The levelling effect of colonization is obvious; the levelling effect of warfare is not so obvious in modern times. In modern armies, where there is a strictly defined system of military ranks, where the distinction of officer and private is broadly drawn, where the private soldier is little more than a machine in the hands of his commander, the effect may even be the other way. But in an earlier state of things, where victory depends on the individual prowess of each man, nothing can be more levelling than warfare. Honour and profit fall to the lot of the stoutest heart and the strongest arm, whether their owner be noble or peasant in his own land. And this would be still more the case when war and colonization went hand in hand, when success brought not only victory but conquest, when men fought, not to go back loaded with glory and plunder to their old homes, but to win for themselves new homes as the reward of their valour. On the other hand, in an early state of things personal influence is almost everything; a vigorous and popular ruler is practically absolute, because no one has the wish to withstand his will, but a weak or unpopular rule can exercise no authority whatever. In such a state of things as this no one can so easily gain the authority of unbounded influence as the military chief who leads his tribe to victory. And again, that influence would be increased tenfold when the successful chief led them not only to victory but to conquest, when he was not only a ruler but a founder, the man who had led his people to win for themselves a new land, to create a new state, the prize of his sword and of theirs. Mere nobility of birth, however highly honoured, would be but a feeble influence compared with either of these influences above and below it. I think that we may trace something of the results of these influences in the position of the oldest English nobility. That there was a difference between the noble and the common freeman, in Old-English phrase between the *Eorl* and the *Ceorl* (28), is shown by countless allusions to the distinction in our earliest records. But it is by no means easy to say what the distinction really was. And, as we shall presently see that this primitive nobility gradually gave way to a nobility of quite another kind and founded on quite another principle, we may perhaps be inclined to think that, at least after the settlement of the English in Britain, the privileges of the *Eorlas* were little more than honorary. I need hardly say that a traditional deference for high birth, a traditional preference for men of certain families in the disposal of elective offices, may go on when birth carries with it no legal privilege whatever. Nowhere has this been more strikingly shown than in those democratic Cantons of Switzerland of which I have already spoken. In a commonwealth where magistrates were chosen yearly, where every freeman had an equal vote in their choice, it still happened that, year after year, the representatives of certain famous houses were chosen as if by hereditary right. Such were the Barons of Attinghausen in Uri and the house of Tschudi in Glarus(29). And, whatever we say of such a custom in other ways, it was surely well suited to have a good effect on the members of these particular families; it was well suited to raise up in them a succession of men fitted to hold the high offices of the commonwealth. A man who knows that, if he be at all worthy of a certain post of honour, he will be chosen to it before any other man, but who also knows that, if he shows himself unworthy of it, he may either fail to attain it at all or be peacefully removed at the end of any twelvemonth, is surely under stronger motives to make himself worthy of the place which he hopes to fill than either the man who has to run the chance of an unlimited competition or the man who succeeds to honour and authority by the mere right of his birth.

Our fathers then came into Britain, bringing with them the three elements of the primitive constitution which we find described by Tacitus; but, as I am inclined to think, the circumstances of the Conquest did something, for a while at least, to strengthen the powers both of the supreme chief and of the general body of the people at the expense of the intermediate class of *Eorlas* or nobles. Let us first trace the origin and growth of the power of the supreme leader, in other words, the monarchic element, the kingly power. What then is a King? The question is much more easily asked than answered. The name of King has meant very different things in different times and places; the amount of authority attached to the title has varied greatly in different times and places. Still a kind of common idea seems to run through all its different uses; if we cannot always define a King, we at least generally know a King when we see him. The King has, in popular sentiment at least, a vague greatness and sanctity attaching to him which does not attach to any mere magistrate, however high in rank and authority. I am not talking of the reason of the thing, but of what, as a matter of fact, has at all times been the popular feeling. Among the heathen

Swedes, it is said that, when public affairs went wrong, in the state of things when we should now turn a Minister out of office and when our forefathers some generations back would have cut off his head, they despised any such secondary victims, and offered the King himself in sacrifice to the Gods(30). Such a practice certainly implies that our Scandinavian kinsfolk had not reached that constitutional subtlety according to which the responsibility of all the acts of the Sovereign is transferred to some one else. They clearly did not, like modern constitution-makers, look on the person of the King as inviolable and sacred. But I suspect that the very practice which shows that they did not look on him as inviolable shows that they did look on him as sacred. Surely the reason why the King was sacrificed rather than any one else was because there was something about him which there was not about any one else, because no meaner victim would have been equally acceptable to the Gods. On the other hand—to stray for a moment beyond the range of Teutonic and of Aryan precedent—we read that the ancient Egyptians forestalled the great device of constitutional monarchy, that their priests, in a yearly discourse, dutifully attributed all the good that was done in the land to the King personally and all the evil to his bad counsellors (31).

These may seem two exactly opposite ways of treating a King; but the practice of sacrificing the King, and the practice of treating the King as one who can do no wrong, both start from the same principle, the principle that the King is, somehow or other, inherently different from everybody else. Our own Old-English Kings, like all other Teutonic Kings, were anything but absolute rulers; the nation chose them and the nation could depose them; they could do no important act in peace or war without the national assent; yet still the King, as the King, was felt to hold a rank differing in kind from the rank held by the highest of his subjects. Perhaps the distinction mainly consisted in a certain religious sentiment which attached to the person of the King, and did not attach to the person of any inferior chief. In heathen times, the Kings traced up their descent to the Gods whom the nation worshipped; in Christian times, they were distinguished from lesser rulers by being admitted to their office with ecclesiastical ceremonies; the chosen of the people became also the Anointed of the Lord. The distinction between Kings and rulers of any other kind is strictly immemorial; it is as old as anything that we know of the political institutions of our race. The distinction is clearly marked in the description which I read to you from Tacitus. He distinguishes in a marked way *Reges* and *Duces,* Kings and Leaders; Kings whose claim to rule rested on their birth, and leaders whose claim to rule rested on their personal merit. But from the same writer we learn that, though the distinction was so early established and so well understood, it was still not universal among all the branches of the Teutonic race. Of the German nations described by Tacitus, some, he expressly tells us, were governed by Kings, while others were not (32). That is to say, each tribe or district had its own chief, its magistrate in peace and its leader in war, but the whole nation was not united under any one chief who had any claim to the special and mysterious privileges of kingship. That is to say, though we hear of kingship as far back as our accounts will carry us, yet kingship was not the oldest form of government among the Teutonic tribes. The King and his Kingdom came into being by the union of several distinct tribes or districts, which already existed under distinct leaders of their own, and in our own early history we can mark with great clearness the date and circumstances of the introduction of kingship. We should be well pleased to know what were the exact Teutonic words which Tacitus expressed by the Latin equivalents *Rex* and *Dux.* As for the latter at least, we can make a fair guess. The Teutonic chief who was not a King bore the title of *Ealdorman* in peace and of *Heretoga* in war. The former title needs no explanation. It still lives on among us, though with somewhat less than its ancient dignity. The other title of *Heretoga*, army-leader, exactly answering to the Latin *Dux*, has dropped out of our own language, but it survives in High-German under the form of *Herzog*, which is familiarly and correctly translated by *Duke* (33). The *Duces* of Tacitus, there can be no doubt, were *Ealdormen* or *Heretogan*. It is less clear what the title was which he intended by *Rex*. Our word *Cyning*, *King*, is common to all the existing Teutonic tongues, and we find it as far back as we can trace the English language (34). But it is not the only, nor seemingly the oldest, word to express the idea. In the oldest monument of Teutonic speech, the Gothic translation of the Scriptures, the word *King*, in any of its forms, is not found. The word there used is *Thiudans* (35). And there is a third word *Drihten*, which in English is most commonly used in a religious sense (36). I would ask you to bear with me while I plunge for a moment into some obsolete Teutonic etymologies, as I think that the analogies of these three words are not a little interesting. All three names come from, or are closely connected with, words meaning the race or people. One of those words, *Cyn* or *Kin*, we still keep in modern English with no change of sound and with very little change of meaning. Now, the word *Cyning*, in its shortened form *King*, either comes straight from the substantive *Cyn*, or else from a closely connected adjective *Cyne*, noble, just like the Latin *generosus* from *Genus*, which, let me add, is the same word as our English *Cyn*. Let no one delude you into thinking that *King* has anything to do with the *canning* or *cunning* man. The man who first said that it had had simply not learned his Old-English grammar (37). It has to do with *Cyn* and *Cyne*, and it may be taken as "the noble one," or, as *ing* is the Teutonic patronymic, any one that chooses may thus form *Cyning* from *Cyn*, and make the King not the father of his people, but their offspring (38). Now the other two names, *Thiudans* or *Theoden*, and *Drihten*, have dropped out of our language, and so have the two words with which they are connected, just as *Cyning* is connected with *Cyn*. *Thiudans* or *Theoden* comes from *Thiuda* or *Theod*, also meaning *people*, a word which you will recognize in many of the old Teutonic names, *Theodric*, *Theodberht*, *Theodbald*, and the like. So *Drihten* either comes straight from *Driht*, a family or company, or else, just like *Cyn* and *Cyne*, from an adjective *driht* meaning noble or lordly. All these three names expressing kingship have thus to do with words meaning the race or people. They imply the chief of a people, something more than the chief of a mere tribe or district. Now in our Old-English Chronicles, when they tell how the first English conquerors, Hengest and Horsa, settled in Kent, they do not call them *Cyningas* but *Heretogan,* Leaders or Dukes. It is not till after some victories over the Britons that we hear that Hengest took the *rice* or kingdom, and that his son Æsc is called *King.* So in Wessex, the first conquerors Cerdic and Cynric are called *Ealdormen* when they land; but, when they have established a settled dominion at the expense of the Welsh, we read that they too took the *rice,* and the leaders of the West-Saxons are henceforth spoken of as Kings (39). It is plain then that the first leaders of the English settlements in Britain, when they came over, bore only the lowlier title of *Heretoga* or *Ealdorman;* it was only when they had fought battles and found themselves at the head of a powerful and victorious settlement on the conquered soil that they were thought worthy of the higher title of Kings. And we may further believe that, with all their exploits, they would not have been thought worthy of it, if they had not been held to come of the blood of the Gods, of the divine stock of Woden.

We thus see that kingship, in the strict sense of

the word, as distinguished from the government of Dukes or Ealdormen, had its beginning among the English in Britain, not in the very first moment of the Conquest, but in the years which immediately followed it, within the life-time of the first generation of conquerors. The same distinction which we find among the Angles and Saxons we find also among the kindred nations of Scandinavia. When the Danes and Northmen began those invasions which led to such important settlements in Northern and Eastern England, we always find two marked classes of leaders, the Kings and the *Jarls*, the same word as *Eorl.* Of these the *Jarls* answer to the English *Ealdormen* (40). The distinction is again clearly marked, when we read that the Old-Saxons, the Saxons of the mainland, were ruled, not by Kings, but by what our Latin writer is pleased to call *Satraps*—that is, of course, *Dukes* or *Ealdormen* (41). But it is most strongly marked of all in several accounts where we read of nations which had been united under Kings falling back again upon the earlier dominion of these smaller local chiefs. Thus the Lombards in Italy, who had been led by Kings to their great conquest, are said for a while to have given up kingly government, and to have again set up a rule of independent Dukes. So the West-Saxons in our own island are said at one time to have cast away kingly government, and to have in the like sort fallen back on the rule of independent *Ealdormen* (42). In all these cases, we should be glad to know more clearly than we do what was the exact distinction between the *King* and the *Duke* or *Ealdorman*. But it is plain that the King was the representative of a closer national unity, while the Ealdorman represented the tendency on the part of each tribe or district to claim independence for itself. The government of the Ealdorman may not have been less effective than that of the King. If we remember the distinction drawn by Tacitus as to the respective qualifications for the two offices, we may even believe that the rule of the Ealdorman may have been the more effective. But we may be sure that the Ealdorman was felt to be, in some way or other, less distant from the mass of his people than the King was; the place of King could be held only by one of the stock of Woden; the place of Ealdorman, it would seem, was open to any man who showed that he possessed the gifts which were needed in a leader of men.

Kingship thus became the law of all the Teutonic tribes which settled in Britain and whose union made up the English nation. That union, we must always remember, was very gradual. Step by step, smaller Kings or independent Ealdormen admitted the supremacy of a more powerful King. Then, in a second stage, the smaller state was absolutely incorporated with the greater. Its ruler now, if he continued to rule at all, ruled no longer as an independent or even as a vassal sovereign, but as a mere magistrate, acting by the deputed authority of the sovereign of whom he held his office (43). The settlement made by Cerdic and Cynric on the southern coast grew, step by step, by the incorporation of many small kingdoms and independent Ealdormanships, into the lordship of the whole Isle of Britain, into the immediate kingship of all its English inhabitants. The Ealdorman of a corner of Hampshire thus grew step by step into the King of the West-Saxons, the King of the Saxons, the King of the English, the Emperor of all Britain, the lord, in later times, of a dominion reaching into every quarter of the world (44). But the point which now concerns us is that, with each step in the growth of the King's territorial dominion, his political authority within that dominion has grown also. The change from an Ealdorman to a King, the change from a heathen King to a Christian King crowned and anointed, doubtless did much to raise the power and dignity of the ruler who thus at each change surrounded himself with new titles to reverence. But this was not all. The mere increase in the extent of territorial dominion would at each step work most powerfully to increase the direct power of the King, and still more powerfully to increase the vague reverence which everywhere attaches to kingship. In Homer we read of Kings, some of whom were "more kingly," more of Kings, than others. So it was among ourselves. A King who reigned over all Wessex was more of a King than a King who reigned only over the Isle of Wight, and a King who reigned over all England was more of a King than a King who reigned only over Wessex ([45]). The greater the territory over which a King reigns, he becomes of necessity less familiar to the mass of his people; he becomes more and more shrouded in a mysterious awe, more and more looked on as a being of a different nature from other men, of a different nature even from other civil magistrates and military leaders, however high their authority and however illustrious their personal character. Such a separation of the King from the mass of his people may indeed, in some states of things, lead, not to the increase, but to the lessening of his practical power. He may become in popular belief too great and awful for the effectual exercise of power, and, by dint of his very greatness, his practical authority may be transferred to his representatives who govern in his name. He may be surrounded with a worship almost more than earthly, while the reality of power passes to a Mayor of the Palace, or is split up among the satraps of distant provinces (46). But, with a race of vigorous and politic Kings ruling over a nation whose tendencies are to unity and not to wider separation, each step in the territorial growth of the kingdom is also a step in the growth, not only of the formal dignity, but of the practical authority of the King. The King of the English, who in the eleventh century held the direct sovereignty of all England, the over-lordship of all Britain, was a very different person from his forefather, who in the sixth century deemed that another victory over the Briton, the acquisition of another strip of British territory, another hundred, it may be, of modern Hampshire, had made him great enough to change his title of Ealdorman to that of King. Such a King was every inch a King; his personal character was of the highest moment for the good or evil fortune of his kingdom. His will counted for much in the making of the laws by which his people were to be governed, and in the disposal of honours and offices among those who were to govern under him. But yet he was not a despot; men never forgot that the King was what his name implied, the representative, the impersonation, the offspring of the people. It was from the choice of the people that he received his authority to rule over them, a choice limited under all ordinary circumstances to the royal house, but which, within that house, was not tied down by a blind regard to any particular law of succession. It was a choice which at any time could fix itself on the worthiest man of the royal house, and which, when the royal house failed to supply a fitting candidate, could boldly fix itself on the worthiest man of the whole people(47). And those from whom the King first drew his power ever shared with him in its exercise. The laws, the grants, the appointments to offices, which the King made, needed the assent of the people in their national Assembly, the gathering of the Wise Men of the whole land (48). And those who gave him his power and who guided him in its exercise could also, when need so called, take away the power which they had given. At rare intervals —for it is only at rare intervals that so great a step is likely to be taken—has the English nation exercised its highest power by taking away the Crown from Kings who were unworthy to wear it. I speak not of acts of violence or murder, or of processes which, though clothed under legal form, were without precedent in our history. I speak not of the secret death of Henry the Sixth or of the open execution of Charles the First. I speak of the regular process of the Law. In Northumberland the right of deposition was exercised with special frequency (49). But I will speak only of that direct and unbroken line of Kings who from Kings of the West-Saxons grew into Kings of the English. Six times at least, in the space of nine hundred years, from Sigeberht of Wessex to James the Second, have the Witan or the Parliament thus put forth the last and greatest of their powers ([50]). The last exercise of this power has made its future exercise needless. All that in old times was to be gained by the deposition of a King can now be gained by a vote of censure on a Minister, or, in the extremest case, by his impeachment.

But, besides that growth of the King's power which followed naturally on the growth of the King's dominions, another cause was busily at work which clothed him with a personal influence which was of almost greater moment than his political authority. To a large portion of his subjects, to all the men of special wealth or power, the King gradually became, not only King but *lord;* his subjects gradually became, not only his subjects but his *men.* These names may need some explanation, and I will again go back to Tacitus as our starting-point. Side by side with the political community, the King, the nobles, the popular Assembly, all of them strictly political powers, he describes another institution, a relation in itself not political but purely personal, but which gradually became of the highest political moment. This was the institution of the *comitatus*, the system of personal relation between a man and his lord, a relation of faithful service on one side, of faithful protection on the other. Let us again hear the words of the great Roman interpreter of our own earliest days (51).

"It is no shame among the Germans to be seen among the companions (*comites*) of a chief. And there are degrees of rank in the companionship (*comitatus*), according to the favour of him whom they follow; and great is the rivalry among the companions which shall stand highest in the favour of his chief, and also among the chiefs which shall have the most and the most valiant companions. . . . When they come to battle, it is shameful for the chief to be surpassed in valour; it is shameful for his companions not to equal the valour of their chief. It is even a badge of disgrace for the remainder of life if a man comes away alive from the field on which his chief has fallen. To guard, to defend him, to assign their own valiant deeds to his credit, is their first religious duty. The chiefs fight for victory; the companions fight for their chief."

This is the description given by a Roman historian of the second century; let me set beside it the words of an English poet of the tenth. He is describing the battle of Maldon in 991, which was fought by the East-Saxons under their Ealdorman

Brihtnoth against the invading Northmen. The Ealdorman has been killed; two of his followers have fled, one of them on the Ealdorman's horse, and every word that is put into the mouth of his faithful companions turns upon the personal tie between them and their lord (52).

> " Thereon hewed him
> The heathen soldiers;
> And both the warriors
> That near him by-stood;
> Ælfnoth and Wulfmær both
> Lay there on the ground
> By their lord;
> Their lives they sold.
> There bowed they from the fight
> That there to be would not;
> There were Odda's bairns
> Erst in flight;
> Godric from battle went,
> And the good man forsook
> That to him ofttimes
> Horses had given.
> He leapt on the horse
> That his lord had owned,
> On the housings
> That it not right was."

Presently we read of the exploits done by his Thegns over his body;

> " There was fallen
> The folk's Elder,
> Æthelred's Earl;
> All there saw

Of his hearth's comrades
That their lord lay dead.
Then there went forth
The proud Thanes,
The undaunted men
Hastened gladly;
They would there all
One of two things,
Either life forsake,
Or the loved one wreak."

Then one of the Thegns speaks;

"Neither on that folk
Shall the Thanes twit me
That I from this host
Away would go
To seek my home,
Now mine Elder lieth
Hewn down in battle;
To me is that harm most;
He was both my kinsman
And my lord."

Then another speaks in answer;

"How thou, Ælfwine, hast
All our Thanes
In need-time cheered.
Now our lord lieth,
The Earl on the earth,
That of us each one
Others should embolden
Warmen to the war,
That while we weapons may
Have and hold
The hard falchion
Spear and good sword."

Then another speaks;

> "I this promise
> That I hence nill
> Flee a footstep,
> But will further go,
> To wreak in the fight
> My lord and comrade.
> Nor by Stourmere
> Any steadfast hero
> With words need twit me
> That I lordless
> Homeward should go,
> And wend from the fight."

The story goes on a little later;

> "Rath was in battle
> Offa hewn down,
> Yet had he furthered
> That his lord had pledged,
> As he ere agreed
> With his ring-giver
> That they should both
> To the borough ride
> Hale to home,
> Or in the host cringe
> On the slaughter place,
> Of their wounds die.
> He lay thane-like
> His lord hard by."

Lastly another Thegn speaks;

> "Mind shall the harder be,
> Heart shall the keener be,
> Mood shall the more be,
> As our main lessens.
> Here lies our Elder,
> All down hewn,

A good man in the dust;
Ever may he groan
Who now from this war-play
Of wending thinketh.
I am old of life;
Hence stir will I not,
And I by the half
Of my lord,
By such a loved man
To lie am thinking."

This institution of military companionship seems to have struck Tacitus with some amazement. He says that this kind of personal relation was among the Germans not thought shameful. This was the natural feeling of a Roman. The duty of a Roman citizen was wholly towards the state. The state might be represented either by a responsible magistrate or an irresponsible Emperor; in either case obedience was due to the representative of the state; but there was no personal relation to the man. The old Roman institution of patron and client, which was so like the German *comitatus*, had pretty well died out by the time of Tacitus, and it had at no time been entered into by men of high rank (53). What amazed Tacitus was that among the Germans the noblest in birth and exploits were not looked on as dishonoured by entering the service of a personal lord. To Tacitus himself Trajan was the chief magistrate of the Roman commonwealth, the chief commander of the Roman army; he was a personal master to none but his slaves and freedmen (54). It was only in a much later stage of the Roman Empire that personal service in the court and household of the Emperor began to be looked on as honourable(55). But among the Teutonic nations the personal relation coloured everything; personal service towards a King or other chief was honourable from the beginning; the proudest nobles of Europe have down to this day thought themselves honoured by filling offices about the persons of Emperors, Kings, and other princes which Tacitus would have deemed beneath the dignity of any Roman citizen. We are now accustomed to see this kind of service paid in the case of royal personages only; a few centuries back men of any rank deemed themselves honoured by paying the like service to men of the rank next above their own, or even to men of their own rank who had the start of them in age and reputation. The knight was served by his esquire and the master by his scholar; and the same principle, laid aside everywhere else, lingers on in what is undoubtedly a trace of the Teutonic *comitatus*, the fagging of our public schools. Now the political effect of the existence of the principle of personal service, the institution of the *comitatus*, alongside of the primitive political community, was most important in our early history. The personal relation went far to swallow up the purely political one. To enter the service of a chief became so established a practice that at last it was deemed that it was the part of every man to "seek a lord," as the phrase was, to commend himself, to put himself under the protection of some man more powerful than himself ([56]). The *man* owed faithful service to his *lord;* the lord owed faithful protection to his man. The very word *Lord,* in its older and fuller form *Hlaford,* implies the rewards which the lord bestowed on his faithful man. The word is in some sort a puzzling one; but there can be no doubt that it is connected with *hlaf, loaf,* and that its general meaning is *the giver of bread* ([57]). Now herein lurks something which has greatly affected all later political and social arrangements. The institution of the *comitatus* in its first state had nothing whatever to do with the holding of land. But the *man* looked for reward of his faithful service at the hands of his *lord;* he looked for the bread of which his lord's title proclaimed him as the giver. There was of course no form of reward, no form of *bread,* so convenient or so honourable as that of a grant of land to be held as the reward of past and the condition of future service. Moreover the custom of granting out lands to be held by the tenure of military service had become common in the later days of Roman power(58). Such lands were of course held, not of the Emperor as a personal lord, but of the Roman Commonwealth of which he was the head and representative. But the custom of holding lands by military service fell in well with the Teutonic institution of personal service, and the union of the two in the same person produced that feudal relation which has had such an important bearing on all political and social life through the whole of the middle ages and down to our own time. The land granted by the lord to his man, or the land which the man agreed to hold as if it had been so granted, might be a kingdom held of the Emperor or the Pope, or it might be the smallest estate held of a more powerful neighbour. In either case, such a holding by military service was a *fief*, and from the institution of such fiefs the so-called Feudal System, with all its manifold workings for good and for evil, had its rise. But so far as the Feudal System existed, either in England or in any other country, it existed wholly as a system which had grown up by the side of an earlier system which it wholly or partially displaced. The feudal tenant, holding his land of a lord by military service, gradually supplanted, wholly or partially, in most countries of Europe, the *allodial* holder who held his land of no other man, and who knew no superior but God and the Law (59). In England this change took place only gradually and partially; it was through the Norman Conquest, or, more accurately, through the subtle legal theories which came in with the Norman Conquest, that it was finally established. And, after all, it was rather in theory than in fact that it was established. The Feudal System, as something spreading into every corner of the land, and affecting every relation of life, never obtained the same complete establishment in England which it did in some continental countries.

But it is only indirectly that my subject has anything to do with the Feudal System, and especially with its social working. I have to do with the *comitatus*, out of which the feudal relation grew, mainly in another aspect equally indirect, namely, the way in which it affected our earliest political institutions. It gave us a new form of nobility, a nobility of office and of personal relation to the King, instead of a nobility founded on birth only. It gave us a nobility of *Thegns*, which gradually supplanted the earlier nobility of the *Eorls*. As the royal power and dignity grew, it came to be looked on as the highest honour to enter into the personal service of the King. Two results followed; service towards the King, a place, that is, in the King's *comitatus*, became the badge and standard of nobility ([60]). And it greatly strengthened the power of the King that he stood to all the chief men of his kingdom in the relation, not only of a political ruler, but of a personal lord, a lord to whose service they were bound by a personal tie, and of whom they held their lands as the gift of his personal bounty. It marks perhaps a decline from the first idea of the *comitatus* that the old word *Gesith*, *companion*, answering exactly to the Latin *Comes* used by Tacitus, was supplanted by the name *Thegn*, literally *servant* ([61]). But when personal service was deemed honourable, the name of servant was no degradation, and the name *Thegn* became equivalent to the older *Eorl*. The King's Thegns, the men who held their land of the King and who were bound to him by the tie of personal service, formed the highest class of nobility. The Thegns of inferior lords, of Bishops and Ealdormen, formed a secondary class. A nobility of this kind, there can be no doubt, was so far more liberal than the elder nobility of birth that admission to it was not forbidden to men of lower degree. The *Ceorl*, the ordinary freeman, could not in strictness become an *Eorl*, for the simple reason that he could not change his forefathers; but he might, and he often did, become a *Thegn* ([62]). But, on the other hand, such a nobility, while it made it easier for the common freeman to rise, tended to lower the condition of the common freemen who did not rise. For the very reason that the barrier of birth is one which cannot be passed, it is in some respects less irksome than the barrier of wealth or office. The privileges of a strictly hereditary class are much more likely to sink into mere honorary distinctions than the privileges of a nobility whose rank is backed by the solid advantages of office and of a personal relation to the sovereign.

The tendency then of the first six hundred years after the settlement of the English in Britain was to increase the power of the Crown, to depress the lower class of freemen, to exchange a nobility of birth for a nobility of personal service to the King. That is to say, England had, before the Norman Conquest, already begun to walk, though with less speed than most other nations, in the path which led to the general overthrow of liberty throughout Europe. The foreign invasion which for a moment seemed to have created her freedom for ever did in truth only lead to its new birth, to its fresh establishment in forms better fitted to the altered state of things, forms better fitted to be handed on to later times, forms better fitted to preserve the well-being of a great nation, than those forms of the old Teutonic community which still linger on in those remote corners of the world which

I spoke of at my beginning. That momentary overthrow, that lasting new birth, will be the subject of my second chapter. I will now only call you to bear in mind that England has never been left at any time without a National Assembly of some kind or other. Be it Witenagemót, Great Council, or Parliament, there has always been some body of men claiming, with more or less of right, to speak in the name of the nation. And bear too in mind that, down to the Norman Conquest, the body which claimed to speak in the name of the nation was, in legal theory at least, the nation itself. This is a point on which I mean again to speak more fully; I would now simply suggest the thought, new perhaps to many, that there was a time when every freeman of England, no less than every freeman of Uri, could claim a direct voice in the councils of his country. There was a time when every freeman of England could raise his voice or clash his weapon in the Assembly which chose Bishops and Ealdormen and Kings, when he could boast that the laws which he obeyed were laws of his own framing, and that the men who bore rule over him were rulers of his own choosing. Those days are gone, nor need we seek to call them back. The struggles of ages on the field and in the Senate have again won back for us the selfsame rights in forms better suited to our times than the barbaric freedom of our fathers. Yet it is well that we should look back to the source whence comes all that we boast of as our own possession, all that we have handed on to our daughter commonwealths in other continents. Let us praise famous men and our fathers that begat us. Let us look to the rock whence we were hewn and to the hole of the pit whence we were digged. Freedom, the old poet says, is a noble thing [63]; it is also an ancient thing. And those who love it now in its more modern garb need never shrink from tracing back its earlier forms to the first days when history has aught to tell us of the oldest life of our fathers and our brethren.

CHAPTER II.

In my first chapter I dealt mainly with those political institutions of the earliest times, institutions common to our whole race, institutions which still live on untouched among some small primitive communities of our race, out of which the still living Constitution of England grew. It is now my business, as the second part of my subject, to trace the steps by which that Constitution grew out of a political state with which at first sight it seems to have so little in common. My chief point is that it did thus, in the strictest sense, grow out of that state. Our English Constitution was never made, in the sense in which the Constitutions of many other countries have been made. There never was any moment when Englishmen drew out their political system in the shape of a formal document, whether as the carrying out of any abstract political theories or as the imitation of the past or present system of any other nation. There are indeed certain great political documents, each of which forms a landmark in our political history. There is the Great Charter, the Petition of Right, the Bill of Rights. But not one of these gave itself out as the enactment of anything new. All claimed to set forth, with new strength, it might be, and with new clearness, those rights of Englishmen which were already old. In all our great political struggles the voice of Englishmen has never called for the assertion of new principles, for the enactment of new laws; the cry has always been for the better observance of the laws which were already in force, for the redress of grievances which had arisen from their corruption or neglect (1). Till the Great Charter was wrung from John, men called for the laws of good King Eadward. And when the tyrant had unwillingly set his seal to that ground-work of all our later Law, men called for the stricter observance of a Charter which was deemed to be itself only the laws of Eadward in a newer dress (2). We have made changes from time to time; but they have been changes which have been at once conservative and progressive—conservative because progressive, progressive because conservative. They have been the application of ancient principles to new circumstances; they have been the careful repairs of an ancient building, not the pulling down of an old building and the rearing up of a new. The life and soul of English law has ever been precedent; we have always held that what our fathers once did their sons have a right to do again. When the Estates of the Realm declared the throne of James the Second to be vacant, they did not seek to justify the act by any theories of the right of resistance, or by any doctrines of the rights of man. It was enough that, three hundred years before, the Estates of the Realm had declared the throne of Richard the Second to be vacant (3). By thus walking in the old paths, by thus hearkening to the wisdom of our forefathers, we have been able to change whenever change has been needed, and we have been kept back from changing out of the mere love of abstract theory. We have thus been able to advance, if somewhat slowly, yet the more surely; and when we have made a false step, we have been able to retrace it. On this last power, the power of undoing whatever has been done amiss, I wish specially to insist. In tracing the steps by which our Constitution has grown into its present shape, I shall try specially to show in how many cases the best acts of modern legislation have been, wittingly or unwittingly, a falling back on the principles of our earliest times.

In my first chapter I tried to show how our fathers brought with them into the Isle of Britain those primæval institutions which were common to them with the whole Teutonic race. I tried to show how those institutions were modified in the course of time by the circumstances of the English Conquest of Britain, and by the events which followed the Conquest. I showed how the kingly power grew with every increase of the territorial extent of the kingdom; how the old nobility of birth gave way to a new nobility of personal relation to the sovereign: and how the effect of these changes seems to have been to make it easier for the individual freeman of the lower rank to rise, but at the same time to lower the position of the ordinary freemen as a class. This last change was still more largely brought about as an independent result of the same changes which tended to increase the kingly power. In a state of things where representation is unknown, where every freeman is an elector and a lawgiver, but where, if he exercises his elective and legislative rights, he must exercise them directly in his own person—in such a state of things as this every increase of the national territory makes those rights of less practical value, and causes the actual powers of government to be shut up in the hands of a smaller body. There is no doubt that in the earliest Teutonic assemblies every freeman had his place. There is no doubt that in England every freeman kept it in the smaller local assemblies of the *mark*, the *hundred*, and the *shire* (4). He still, where modern legislation has not wholly swept it away, keeps, as I hinted in my former lecture, some faint shadow of the old right when he gives a vote in the assembly which still continues the assembly of the mark, that is, in the vestry of his parish. But how as to the great assembly of all, the Assembly of the Wise, the Witenagemót of the whole realm? No ancient record gives us any clear or formal account of the constitution of that body. It is commonly spoken of in a vague way as a gathering of the wise, the noble, the great men (5). But, alongside of passages like these, we find other passages which speak of it in a way which implies a far more popular constitution. King Eadward is said to be chosen King by "all folk." Earl Godwine "makes his speech before the King and all the people of the land." Judicial sentences and other acts of authority are voted by the army, that is by the people under arms. Sometimes we find direct mention of the presence of large and popular classes of men, as the citizens of London or Winchester (6). The inference from all this is obvious. The right of the ordinary freeman to attend, to vote—it might perhaps be nearer the truth to say to shout (7)—in the general Assembly of the whole realm was never formally taken away. But it freely chosen representative body may, without much straining of language, be said to be done by the whole people. But acts done by a body not representative could never be called the acts of the whole people, unless the whole people had an acknowledged right to attend its meetings, though that right might, under all ordinary circumstances, be exercised only by a few of their number.

Out of this body, whose constitution, by the time of the Norman Conquest, had become not a little anomalous and not a little fluctuating, our Parliament directly grew. Of one House of that Parliament we may say more; we may say, not that it grew out of the ancient Assembly but that it is absolutely the same by personal identity. The House of Lords not only springs out of, it actually is, the ancient Witenagemót. I can see no break between the two. King William summoned his Witan as King Eadward had summoned them before him. In one memorable assembly of the Conqueror's reign, we read that the great men of the realm were reinforced by the presence of the whole body of the landholders of England, whose number tradition handed down as sixty thousand ([9]). But, as a rule, the Great Councils after the Norman Conquest bear the same uncertain and fluctuating character as the Gemóts of earlier days. In the constitution of the House of Lords I can see nothing mysterious or wonderful. Its hereditary character came in, like other things, step by step, by accident rather than by design. And it should not be forgotten that, as long as the Bishops keep their seats in the House, the hereditary character of the House does not extend to all its members. To me it seems simply that two classes of men, the two highest classes, the Earls and the Bishops, never lost or disused that right of attending in the National Assembly which was at first common to them with all other freemen. Besides these two classes, the King summoned other men to our early Parliaments, pretty much, it would seem, at his own pleasure. The right of the King so to do could not be denied; when all had an abstract right to attend, we cannot blame the King for specially summoning those for whose attendance he specially wished. But it would almost naturally follow that such a special summons would gradually be held to confer an exclusive right, and that those who were not specially summoned would soon be looked upon as having no part or lot in the matter. But it is certain that it was long before such a summons was held to confer a hereditary, or even a lasting personal right. The King did not always summon the same men to every Parliament. Besides the Earls and the Bishops, others both of the laity and the clergy were always was a right which, in its own nature, most men could hardly ever exercise. None but men of wealth would have the means, none but men of some personal importance would have any temptation, to take long journeys for such a purpose. It is not likely that any great multitude would, under ordinary circumstances, set off from Northern England to attend meetings which were habitually held at Westminster, Winchester, and Gloucester. It is plain that the habitual attendance would not go beyond a small body of chief men, Earls, Bishops, Abbots, the officers of the King's court, the Thegns of the greatest wealth or the highest personal influence. But it is plain that, when the heart of the nation was specially stirred by some overwhelming interest, many men would find their way who would not find their way in ordinary times. And, when the Assembly was held in a town, the citizens of that town at once formed a popular element ready on the spot. Hence we can account for the seemingly contradictory way in which the Assembly is spoken of, sometimes in language which would imply an aristocratic body, sometimes in language which would imply a body highly democratic. It was in fact a body, democratic in ancient theory, aristocratic in ordinary practice, but to which any strong popular impulse could at any time restore its ancient democratic character ([8]). Acts done by a summoned, but the list of those who were summoned, both of the laity and of the lesser ecclesiastical dignitaries, constantly varies from Parliament to Parliament (10). That the personal summons conveyed an exclusive hereditary right was one of those devices of lawyers of which so many have crept into our constitution. When the notion of hereditary right had once established itself, the formal creation of peerages by patent was a natural stage. Looking at the matter from this historical point of view, it seems to me simply wonderful how any one can doubt the power of the Crown to create life-peerages, or to regulate the tenure or succession of a peerage in any way in which it thinks good.

The House of Lords then, I do not hesitate to say, represents, or rather is, the ancient Witenagemót. An assembly in which at first every freeman had a right to appear has, by the force of circumstances, step by step, without any one moment of sudden change, shrunk up into an Assembly wholly hereditary and official, an Assembly to which the Crown may summon any man, and to which, it is now strangely held, the Crown cannot refuse to summon the representatives of any man whom it has once summoned. As in most other things, the tendency to shrink up into a body of this kind began to show itself before the Norman Conquest, and was finally confirmed and established through the results of the Norman Conquest. But the special function of the body into which the old national Assembly has changed, the function of "another House," an Upper House, a House of Lords as opposed to a House of Commons, could not show itself till a second House of a more popular constitution had arisen by its side. Like everything else in our English polity, both Houses in some sort came of themselves. Neither of them was the creation of any ingenious theorist, though we need not doubt that many of the several steps in the growth of each were, each in its own time, the work of practical statesmanship. Our forefathers had no theories; but men, each in his own generation, had eyes keen enough to see that such and such a change in detail would get rid of such and such an immediate evil, or would bring with it such and such an immediate advantage. Nay more, it has sometimes happened that a change which was brought in with an evil intent has in the end worked for good. Measures which were taken with a view of strengthening the power of the Crown have come in the end to widen the rights of the people. On the other hand, institutions which once answered a good and needful purpose have sometimes, through change of times, changed their nature and have become instruments of evil instead of good. But in neither case were the institutions of our fathers the work of abstract theory. They have therefore lived on, and they have borne good fruit. Our national Assembly has changed its name and its constitution, but its corporate identity has lived on unbroken. We can therefore at any moment reform without destroying. In France, on the other hand, institutions have been the work of abstract theory; they have been the creations, for good or for evil, of the minds of individual men. The English Parliament is immemorial; it grew step by step out of the older order of things. In France the older order of things utterly vanished; the ground lay open for the creation of a wholly new institution, and the States-General were called into being at the bidding of Philip the Fair (11). Englishmen in the fourteenth and fifteenth centuries had no theories of the rights of man or of universal humanity. But when they saw a practical grievance, they called for its redress. Frenchmen in the fourteenth and fifteenth centuries had theories as magnificent as any that have been put forth in the eighteenth or the nineteenth. And they had even then already learned to do deeds of blood in the name of freedom and philanthropy (12). Therefore French institutions have not lasted. The States-General lived but a fitful life from century to century, and they perished for ever in the Great Revolution. Since that time no French institution, no form either of the legislative or of the executive power, has been able to keep up a continuous being of twenty years. This difference has not been owing to any lack of great men or of noble purposes on the part of our continental neighbours. It has been owing, partly, we may believe, to differences in the inborn character of the two nations, partly to differences in the course taken by their several histories. In France the Kings gradually swept away all traces of older free institutions, and established a simple despotism in the Crown (13). The French therefore have been left without any traditional foundation to build on. In all their changes for good or for evil they have been driven to build afresh from the beginning. Our Kings never wholly wiped out our free institutions; they found means to turn them to their own purposes, and to establish a practical despotism without destroying the outward forms of freedom. The forms thus lived on, and in better times they could again be clothed with their substance. We ever had traditional principles to fall back upon, a traditional basis to build upon. It would be hard to reckon up the number of Assemblies, Conventions, Chambers of Deputies, and Legislative Bodies, which have risen and fallen in France, while the House of Lords and the House of Commons have lived on, with their powers, their duties, their relations to the Crown, to the Nation, and to one another, ever silently changing, but with their continuous being remaining throughout unbroken.

But I would again point out that, while the growth of English institutions has thus gone on almost in obedience to a natural law, the wisdom, the foresight, the patriotism, of individual statesmen is never to be put out of our reckoning. There was a given state of things, and some man had keenness of sight to see what was the right thing to do in that state of things. Our Constitution has no founder; but there is one man to whom we may give all but honours of a founder, one man to whose wisdom and self-devotion we owe that English history has taken the course which it has taken for the last six hundred years. It might no doubt have taken that course without him; things might have come about as they did without any one man coming so prominently to the front; or, if he had not arisen, some other man might have arisen to do his work. But we need not speculate as to what might have been; it is enough that one man did arise to do the work, that there is one man to whom we owe that the wonderful thirteenth century, the great creative and destructive age throughout the world (14), was to us an age of creation and not of destruction. That man, the man who finally gave to English freedom its second and more lasting shape, the hero and martyr of England in the greatest of her constitutional struggles, was Simon of Montfort, Earl of Leicester. If we may not call him the founder of the English Constitution, we may at least call him the founder of the House of Commons (15). It was in his age that the new birth of English freedom began to show itself; it was mainly by his work that that new birth was not stifled before it had brought forth lasting fruits. Strange it may at first sight seem that the founder of the later liberties of England was not an Englishman. Simon of Montfort, a native of France, did for the land of his adoption what even he might not have been able to do for the land of his birth. And why? The land of his birth was—shall I say flourishing or suffering?—under the baleful virtues of the most righteous of Kings. Saint Lewis reigned in France, Saint Lewis the just and holy, the man who never swerved from the path of right, the man who sware to his neighbour and disappointed him not, though it were to his own hindrance. Under his righteous rule there could be no ground for revolt or disaffection. By surrounding the Crown with the reflected glory of his own virtues, he did more than any other man to strengthen its power. He thus did more than any other man to pave the way for that foul despotism of his successors whose evil deeds would have daily vexed his righteous soul. In England, on the other hand, we had the momentary curse, the lasting blessing, of a succession of evil Kings. We had Kings who had no spark of English feeling in their breasts, but from whose follies and necessities our fathers were able to wring their freedom, all the more lastingly because it was bit by bit that it was wrung. A Latin poet once sang that freedom never flourishes more brightly than it does under a righteous King (16). And so it does while that righteous King himself tarries among men. But to win freedom as an heritage for ever there are times when we have more need of the vices of Kings than of their virtues. The tyranny of our Angevin masters woke up English freedom from its momentary grave. Had Richard and John and Henry been Kings like Ælfred and Saint Lewis, the crosier of Stephen Langton, the sword of Robert Fitzwalter, would never have flashed at the head of the Barons and people of England; the heights of Lewes would never have seen the mightiest triumph of her freedom; the pavement of Evesham choir would never have closed over the mangled relics of her noblest champion (17).

The career of Simon of Montfort is the most glorious in our later history. Cold must be the heart of every Englishman who does not feel a thrill of reverence and gratitude as he utters that immortal name. But, fully to understand his work, we must go back somewhat before his own time, we must go back and trace how the sway of foreign invaders first made the path ready for the course of the foreign deliverer. I have shown in what state our Constitution stood at the time of the Norman Conquest. In that Constitution, be it ever remembered, the Norman Conquest made no formal change whatever. Nothing has had a more lasting effect on all later English history than the personal character and position of the Norman Conqueror. But it was not in the character of a legislator that the main work of William was done. His greatest work of all was to weld together the still imperfectly united kingdoms of our ancient England into one indivisible body, a body which, since his day, no man has ever dreamed of rending asunder. But this was not the work of any formal legislative enactment; it was the silent result of the compression of foreign conquest. So it was with William's whole policy and position. He was in truth a Conqueror, King by the edge of the sword, but it was his aim in everything to disguise the fact. He claimed the Crown by legal right; he received it by the formal election of the English people, and he was consecrated to his kingly office by the hands of an English Primate. He professed to rule, not according to his own will, not according to any laws of his own devising, but according to the laws of his predecessor and kinsman King Eadward (18). The great immediate change which was wrought under him was not any formal legislative change; it was the silent revolution implied in the transfer—the wary and gradual transfer—of all the greatest estates and highest offices in England to the hands of foreign holders. The momentary effect was to make Englishmen on their own soil the subjects of foreign conquerors. The lasting effect was to change those foreign conquerors into Englishmen, and to call forth the spirit of English freedom in a more definite and antagonistic shape than it had ever before put on. What was the real position of a landowner of Norman descent within a generation or two after the Conquest? He held English lands according to English law; in all but the highest rank he lived on equal terms with other landowners of English birth; he was himself born on English soil, often of an English mother; he was called on in endless ways to learn, to obey, and to administer, the laws of England. Such a man soon became in feeling, and before long in speech also, as good an Englishman as if he had come of the male line of Hengest or Cerdic. There was nothing to hinder even one of the actual conquerors from thoroughly throwing in his lot with his new country and with its people. His tongue was French, but in truth he had far more in common with the Englishman than with the Frenchman. He was but a near kinsman slightly disguised. The Norman was a Dane who, in his sojourn in Gaul, had put on a slight French varnish, and who came into England to be washed clean again. The blood of the true Normans, in the real Norman districts of Bayeux and Coutances, differs very little from the blood of the inhabitants of the North and East of England (19). See a French soldier and a Norman farmer side by side, and you feel at once that the Norman is nothing but a long parted kinsman. The general effect of him is that of a man of Yorkshire or Lincolnshire who has somehow picked up a bad habit of talking French. Such men readily became Englishmen. We have the distinct assertions of contemporary writers, and every incidental notice bears out their assertions, that, among all classes between the highest and the lowest, among all between the great noble and the villain, the distinction of Norman and Englishman had been forgotten within little more than a hundred years after the time when King William came into England (20). And presently other causes came to make all the sons of the soil draw nearer and nearer together. A new dynasty filled the throne, a dynasty which claimed by female descent to be at once Norman and English, but which, in origin and feeling, was neither Norman nor English (21). Henry the Second, Count of Anjou through his father, Duke of Aquitaine through his wife, inherited also his mother's claims on Normandy and England, but under him Normandy and England alike were but parts of a vast dominion which stretched from the Orkneys to the Pyrenees. Under the mighty, and on the whole the righteous, sway of the great Henry the worst side of this state of things did not show itself (22). Under his sons and grandson England felt to the full the bitterness and the blessings of the Conquest. The land was overrun by utter strangers; the men of Old-English birth and the descendants of the first Norman settlers both saw the natives of other lands placed over the heads of both alike. Places of trust and honour and wealth were handed over to foreign favourites, and every man in the land was exposed to a yet heavier scourge, to the violence and insolence of foreign mercenaries. Under John Normandy was lost (23), and England again became the chief possession of the King of England. But neither John nor Henry learned the lesson. The personal vices of the father, the personal virtues of the son, worked to the same end as far as their kingdom was concerned. The King whose wickedness became a proverb, who surrounded himself with the kindred ruffians of every nation, and the King whose chief fault was that he could never say No to his wife or his mother, helped alike to call forth the spirit of resistance, to draw all Englishmen of whatever origin nearer together, and thereby to work out the great work of giving England a free and lasting Constitution. For such Kings we may well be thankful, but to such Kings we owe no thanks. Our feelings of personal thankfulness towards any of our later Kings begin only when a King arose who joined the political skill of Henry the Second to the personal virtues of Henry the Third, and who added to both a feeling of English patriotism, a ruling sense of right in public affairs, of which neither Henry ever felt the slightest spark in his bosom. Edward the First, the first of our later Kings who bore an English name and an English heart, was the first round whose name can gather any feelings of personal thankfulness. In him we see the first of our Kings of foreign blood who did aught for the growth of our constitutional rights in some other way than that of calling forth the spirit of opposition to his rule.

Thus it was that the misgovernment of our Angevin Kings called forth among all the natives of the land an universal spirit of revolt against the domination of strangers within the realm. And they called forth the spirit of revolt in another way, a way hardly less important, by their base subserviency to a foreign power in ecclesiastical matters. I have here nothing to do with theological dogmas, with their truth or their falsehood, but the ecclesiastical position of the nation forms a most important aspect of its history throughout these times. In Old-English times there can be no doubt as to the existence of an effective supremacy in ecclesiastical matters on the part of the Crown. The King was the Supreme Governor of the Church, because he was the Supreme Governor of the Nation. The Church and the Nation were absolutely the same; the King and his Witan dealt with ecclesiastical questions and disposed of ecclesiastical offices by the same right by which they dealt with temporal questions and disposed of temporal offices ([24]). The Bishop and the Ealdorman, each appointed by the same authority, presided jointly in the assembly of the shire, and the assembly over which they presided dealt freely both with ecclesiastical and with temporal causes. One of the few formal changes in our Law which took place in the days of the Conqueror was the separation of the two jurisdictions of the Bishop and the Ealdorman. One of William's extant laws ordained the establishment, according to continental models, of distinct ecclesiastical courts for the trial of ecclesiastical causes ([25]).

But more important than this formal change was the practical result of the Conquest in bringing England into closer connexion than before with the See of Rome. The enterprise of the Conqueror was approved by Hildebrand, and it was blessed by the Pope in whose name Hildebrand already ruled (26). While William lived, the royal supremacy remained untouched, and, allowing for his position in a conquered land, we may fairly say that it was not abused. But in meaner hands the ancient power of the Crown as the representative of the nation was often abused and often disputed. Quarrels arose as to the limits of the ecclesiastical and the civil power such as had never been heard of in the old times. And we must remember that claims which seem utterly monstrous now were far from seeming monstrous in a state of things so wholly unlike our times. Even the claim of the clergy to an exemption from temporal jurisdiction in criminal cases had a very different look then from what it has now. The privilege thus claimed was by no means confined to the priesthood; it took in a large part of those among the people who were least able to defend themselves (27). And when we think of the horrible punishments, death and mutilations worse than death, which the courts of our Angevin Kings freely inflicted for very slight offences, we can understand that men looked favourably on the courts of the Bishops, where the heaviest penalties were stripes and imprisonment. In the disputes between the Crown and the Church, from William Rufus to Henry the Second, we always find popular feeling enlisted on the ecclesiastical side (28). Nor need we wonder at this, when we find among the Constitutions of Clarendon, which King Henry strove to enforce and which Archbishop Thomas withstood, one which forbad the ordination of villains without the consent of their lords. That is to say, it cut off from the lowest class the only path by which they had any hope of rising to posts of honour and authority (29). But from the reign of John onwards we get a new state of things. A foreign power stepped in, a power which had as yet meddled but little in the strictly internal affairs of England, and which, so far as it had meddled at all, had on the whole taken the popular side. In the latter days of John and through the whole reign of Henry the Third, we find the Pope and the King in strict alliance against the English Church and Nation. The last good deed done by a Pope towards England was when Innocent the Third sent us Stephen Langton (30). Ever afterwards we find Pope and King leagued together to back up each other's oppressions and exactions. The Papal power was always ready to step in on behalf of the Crown, always ready to hurl spiritual censures against the champions of English freedom. The Great Charter was denounced at Rome; so was its author the patriot Primate (31); Earl Simon died excommunicate; but, in the belief of Englishmen, the excommunications of Rome could not hinder an English Earl from working countless signs and wonders (32)—a pretty convincing argument, one might deem, that the Bishop of Rome hath no jurisdiction in this realm of England. Against King and Pope the whole nation stood united; clergy and laity, nobles and commons, men of Norman and men of Old-English birth, all stood together alike against the King's foreign favourites and against the aggressions of Rome. The historians of the age, all of them churchmen, most of them monks, are all but unanimous on the popular side. Prelates like the Primate Stephen, like Robert Grosseteste of Lincoln and Walter of Cantelupe of Worcester, were foremost in the good cause; the two latter were among the closest friends and counsellors of the patriot Earl (33). We see how old distinctions and old enmities had been wiped out, how all the sons of the soil were banded together in one fellowship, when we read the letter denouncing the abuses of the Roman See which was sent to that See in the name of no less a body than the whole Nobility, Clergy, and Commons of the English realm. In that letter, an out-spoken and truly English document, which has been preserved by an historian who well appreciated it, the writers set forth that, as the Nobles, Clergy, and Commons in whose name it is written have no common seal, they have, for the signature of their document, borrowed the seal of the city of London (34).

This last fact brings me round to what I first spoke of long ago, what I may perhaps seem to have forgotten, but what I have in truth had constantly before my eyes, the distinctly constitutional reforms which we owe to Earl Simon of Montfort. The fact that a document which professed to speak in the name of all classes of the whole nation could not be so fittingly signed as with the seal of the city of London marks the place which that city held in the political estimation of the time. But London held that position only as the greatest member of an advancing class, as the foremost among the cities and boroughs of England. Now the great work of Earl Simon was to give those cities and boroughs their distinct place as one of the elements of the body politic. Let us trace the steps by which that great work was done. When we reach the thirteenth century, we may look on the old Teutonic constitution as having utterly passed away. Some faint traces of it indeed we may find here and there in the course of the twelfth century, as when both sides in the wars of Stephen and Matilda acknowledged the right of the citizens of London to a voice in the disposal of the Crown ([35]). But the regular Great Council, the lineal representatives of the ancient *Mycel Gemót* or *Witenagemót*, was shrinking up into a body not very unlike our House of Lords. Its constitution, as I have already hinted, was far more fluctuating, far less strictly hereditary than the modern body, but it was almost as far from being in any sense a representation of the people. The Great Charter secures the rights of the nation and of the national Assembly as against arbitrary legislation and arbitrary taxation on the part of the Crown. But it makes no change in the constitution of the Assembly itself. The greater Barons were to be summoned personally; the lesser tenants in chief, the representatives of the *landsittende menn* of Domesday, by a general summons ([36]). The Great Charter in short is a Bill of Rights, but not what, in modern phrase, we understand by a Reform Bill. But, during the reigns of John and Henry the Third, a popular element was fast making its way into the national Councils in a more practical form. The right of the ordinary freeman to attend in person had long been a shadow; that of the ordinary tenant-in-chief was becoming hardly more practical; it now begins to be exchanged for what had by this time become the more practical right of choosing representatives to act in his name. Like all other things in England, this right has grown up by degrees and as the result of what we might almost call a series of happy accidents. Both in the reign of John and in the former part of the reign of Henry, we find several instances of knights from each county being summoned(37). Here we have the beginning of our county members and of the title which they still bear, of knights of the shire. Here is the beginning of popular representation, as distinct from the gathering of the people in their own persons; but we need not think that those who first summoned them had any conscious theories of popular representation. The first object was probably a fiscal one; it was a safe and convenient way of getting money. The notion of summoning a small number of men to act on behalf of the whole was doubtless borrowed from the practice in judicial proceedings and in inquests and commissions of various kinds, in which it was usual for certain select men to swear on behalf of the whole shire or hundred. We must not forget, though it is a matter on which I have no time to insist here, that our judicial and our parliamentary institutions are closely connected, that both sprang out of the primitive Assemblies, that things which now seem so unlike as our popular juries and the judicial powers of the House of Lords are in truth both of them fragments of the judicial powers which Tacitus speaks of as being vested in those primitive Assemblies. It was only step by step that the functions of judge, juror, witness, and legislator became the utterly distinct functions which they are now ([38]).

Thus we find the beginnings of the House of Commons, as we might have expected, in that class of its members which, for the most part, has most in common with the already established House of Lords. Thus far the developement of the Constitution had gone on in its usual incidental way. Each step in advance, however slight, was doubtless the work of the discernment of some particular man, even though his views may not have gone beyond the compassing of some momentary advantage. But now we come to that great change, that great measure of Parliamentary Reform, which has left to all later reformers nothing to do but to improve in detail. We come to that great act of the patriot Earl which made our popular Chamber really a popular Chamber. A House of knights, of county members, would have been comparatively an aristocratic body; it would have left out one of the most healthy and vigorous, and by far the most progressive, element in the nation. When, after the fight of Lewes, Earl Simon, then master of the kingdom with the King in his safe keeping, summoned his famous Parliament, he summoned, not only two knights from every county, but also two citizens from every city and two burgesses from every borough (39). The Earl had long known the importance and value of the growing civic element in the political society of his age. When, in an earlier stage of his career, he held the government of Gascony, he had, on his return to England, to answer charges brought against him by the Archbishop of Bourdeaux and the nobles of the province. The Earl's answer was to bring forward a writing giving him the best of characters signed with the common seal of the city of Bourdeaux (40). As it was in Gascony, so it was in England. The Earl was always a reformer, one who set himself to redress practical grievances, to withstand the royal favourites, to put a check on the oppressions of Pope and King. But his first steps in the way of reform were made wholly on an aristocratic basis. He tried to redress the grievances of the nation by the help of his fellow nobles only. Step by step he learned that no true reform could be wrought for so narrow a platform, and step by step he took into his confidence, first the knights of the counties, and lastly the class to whose good will he had owed so much in his earlier trial, the citizens and burgesses. Through the whole struggle they stood steadily by him; London was as firm in his cause as Bourdeaux had been, and its citizens fought and suffered and triumphed with him on the glorious day of Lewes(41). By a bold and happy innovation, he called a class which had done so much for him and for the common cause to take their place in the councils of the nation. It was in Earl Simon's Parliament of 1265 that the still abiding elements of the popular chamber, the Knights, Citizens, and Burgesses, first appeared side by side. Thus was formed that newly developed Estate of the Realm which was, step by step, to grow into the most powerful of all, the Commons' House of Parliament.

Such was the gift which England received from her noblest champion and martyr. Nor should it sound strange in our ears that her champion and martyr was by birth a stranger. We boast ourselves that we have led captive our conquerors, and that we have made them into sons of the soil as faithful as ourselves. What we have done with conquerors we have also done with peaceful settlers. In after days we welcomed every victim of oppression and persecution, the Fleming, the Huguenot, and the Palatine. And what we welcomed we adopted and assimilated, and strengthened our English being with all that was worthiest in foreign lands. So can we honour, along with the men of English birth, those men of other lands who have done for England as sons for their own mother. The Danish Cnut ranks alongside of the worthiest of our native Kings. Anselm of Aosta ranks alongside of the worthiest of our native Prelates. And so alongside of the worthiest of our native Earls we place the glorious name of Simon the Righteous. A stranger, but a stranger who came to our shores to claim lands and honours which were his lawful heritage, he became our leader against strangers of another mould, against the adventurers who thronged the court of a King who turned his back on his own people. The first noble of England, the brother-in-law of the King, he threw in his lot, not with princes or nobles, but with the whole people. He was the chosen leader of England in his life, and in death he was worshipped as her martyr. In those days religion coloured every feeling; the patriot who stood up for right and freedom was honoured alongside of him who suffered for his faith. We fill our streets and market-places with the statues of worthies of later days; Peel and Herbert and Lewis and Cobden yet live among us in bronze or marble. In those days honour to the statesman was not well distinguished from worship to the saint, and Waltheof and Simon and Thomas of Lancaster ([42]) were hailed as sainted patrons of England, and wonders were held to be wrought by their relics or at their tombs. The poets of three languages vied in singing the praises of the man who strove and suffered for right, and Simon, the guardian of England on the field and in the senate, was held to be her truer guardian still in the heavenly places from which our fathers deemed that the curse of Rome had no power to shut him out (43).

The great work of the martyred Earl had a strange destiny. His personal career was cut short, his political work was brought to perfection, by a rival and a kinsman only less to be honoured than himself. On the field of Evesham Simon died and Edward triumphed. But it was on Edward that Simon's mantle fell; it was to his destroyer that he handed on the torch which fell from his dying grasp. For a moment his work seemed to have died with him; for some years Parliaments were still summoned which were not after the model of the great Assembly which answered to the writs of the captive Henry. But the model still lived in men's hearts, and presently the wisdom of the great Edward saw that his uncle's gift could no longer be denied to his people. Parliaments after Simon's model have been called together in unbroken succession from Edward's day to our own (44). Next to the name of Simon we may honour the name of Edward himself and the names of the worthies who withstood him. To Roger Bigod of Norfolk and Humfrey Bohun of Hereford we owe the crowning of the work (45). The Parliament of England was now wrought into the fulness of its perfect form, and the most homely, but not the least important, of its powers was now fully acknowledged. No tax or gift could the King of England claim at the hands of Englishmen save such as the Lords and Commons of England had granted him of their free will (46).

Thus we may say that, in the time of Edward the First, the English Constitution definitely put on the same essential form which it has kept ever since. The germs of King, Lords, and Commons we had brought with us from our older home eight hundred years before. But, from King Edward's days onwards, we have King, Lords, and Commons themselves, in nearly the same outward shape, with nearly the same strictly legal powers, which they still keep. All the great principles of English freedom were already firmly established. There is indeed a wide difference between the political condition of England under Edward the First and the political condition of England in our own day. But the difference lies far more in the practical working of the Constitution than in its outward form. The changes have been many; but a large portion of those changes have not been formal enactments, but those silent changes whose gradual working has wrought out for us a conventional Constitution existing alongside of our written Law. Other changes have been simple improvements in detail; others have been enactments made to declare more clearly, or to secure more fully in practice, those rights whose existence was not denied. But, speaking generally, and allowing for the important class of conventional understandings which have never been clothed with the form of written enactments, the main elements of the English Constitution remain now as they were fixed then. From that time English constitutional history is not merely an inquiry, however interesting and instructive, into something which has passed away. It is an inquiry into something which still lives; it is an inquiry into laws which, whenever they have not been formally repealed, are in full force at this day. Up to the reign of Edward the First English history is strictly the domain of antiquaries. From the reign of Edward the First it becomes the domain of lawyers([47]).

We find then—it will be understood with what qualifications I am speaking—the English Constitution full grown by the end of the thirteenth century, and we find it to be, in the shape which it then took, the work of Earl Simon of Montfort and of King

Edward the First. Now there are several points in which the shape which our Constitution thus finally took differed from the shapes which were taken by most of the kindred Constitutions on the Continent. The usual form taken by a national or provincial assembly in the middle ages was that of an Assembly of *Estates*. That is to say, it consisted of representatives of all those classes in the nation which were possessed of political rights. These in most countries were three, Nobles, Clergy, and Commons. And the name of the Three Estates, that is the Nobles, Clergy, and Commons, is equally well known in England, though the meaning of the three names differs not a little in England from what it meant elsewhere. In England we never had, unless it were in the old days of the *Eorlas*, a Nobility such as is understood by that name in other countries. Elsewhere the nobles formed a distinct class, a class into which it was perhaps not absolutely impossible for those who were beneath it to be raised, but from which it was at least absolutely impossible for any of its members to come down. Whatever the privileges of the noble might be, they extended to all his children and their children for ever and ever. In some countries his titles descend in this way to all his descendants; all the children of a Duke, for instance, are Dukes and Duchesses. In France, and in most other countries where the system of Estates existed, the Estate of the Nobles in the National Assembly was a representation, in some shape or other, of the whole class of nobles as a distinct body. How different this is from our House of Lords I need not point out. In strictness, I repeat, we have no nobility. The seats in our Upper Chamber go by descent and not by election or nomination; but no political privilege attaches to the children of their holders. Even the eldest son of the peer, the future holder of the peerage, is a commoner as long as his father lives. Whatever titles he bears are simply titles of courtesy which carry with them no political privileges above other commoners. Nay, we may go higher still. As the children of the peer have no special advantage, so neither have the younger children of the King himself. The King's wife, his eldest son, his eldest daughter, his eldest son's wife, all have special privileges by Law. His other children are simple commoners, unless their father thinks good to raise them, as he may raise any other of his subjects, to the rank of peerage ([48]). There is perhaps no feature in our Constitution more important and more beneficial than this, which binds all ranks together, and which has hindered us from suffering at any time under the curse of a noble caste. Yet this marked distinction between our own Constitution and that of most other countries is purely traditional. We cannot say that it was enacted by any particular man or in any particular Assembly. But it is easy to see that the fact that in England our national Assemblies always went on in some shape or other, that the right of all freemen to attend in person was never formally abolished, that the King kept the right of specially summoning whom he would, all helped to hinder the growth of an exclusive noble caste. The aristocratic sentiment, the pride of birth, has doubtless been very strong at all times. But it has been merely a sentiment, resting on no legal foundation. The Crown could always ennoble any one; but the nobility so granted belonged to one only of the family at the time, to the actual owner of the peerage. All ranks could at all times freely intermarry; all offices were open to all freemen; and England, unlike Germany, never saw ecclesiastical foundations whose members were bound to be of noble birth.

The position of the second Estate, that of the Clergy, was also widely different in England from what it was in other countries. In fact the political position of the Clergy has, ever since Edward the First, been something utterly anomalous and inconsistent. Elsewhere the representatives of the Clergy, just like those of the Nobles, formed one distinct

Estate in the Assembly. In England the great Prelates had seats in the House of Lords, where the Bishops keep them still. But there also existed the anomalous body called Convocation, whose character has always fluctuated between that of an ecclesiastical Synod and that of a parliamentary Estate of the realm ([49]). The Clergy are still summoned along with every Parliament; and one distinctly parliamentary function they held down to the reign of Charles the Second, which was then taken away without any formal enactment. It was one of our great constitutional principles established in King Edward's days that no tax could be granted to the King except by those who had to pay it. But for a long time the Lords and the Commons taxed themselves separately, and the Clergy in their Convocation taxed themselves also. And, till this power was given up, an ecclesiastical benefice gave no right to vote in the election of members of the House of Commons ([50]).

The Commons too themselves bear a name which had a far different meaning in England from what it bore elsewhere. The usage by which the Knights of the shire and the Citizens and Burgesses were brought together in a single House, whatever was its origin, whether it were at first the result of design or of happy accident, has been an usage no less wholesome, no less needful to our full constitutional developement, than that which decreed that the children of peers should be commoners. In most other countries the class of men who were returned as representatives of the counties, the Knights of the Shire, would have been members of the Estate of the Nobles. In France the words *nobleman* and *gentleman* had the same meaning, that of the members of an exclusive aristocratic caste. The Commons, the Third Estate, consisted of the citizens of the privileged towns only (51). But in England the middle class was not confined to the towns; it spread itself, in the form of a lesser gentry and a wealthy yeomanry, over the whole face of the land. That class, the smaller landowners, was for a long time the strength of the country, and the happiest results came from the union of their representatives in a single chamber with those of the cities and boroughs. Each class gained strength from its fellowship with the other, and the citizen class gained, from their union on equal terms with the landed gentry, a consideration which otherwise they might never have reached. In short, the union of the two, the union of all classes of freemen except the clergy and the actual members of the peerage, of all classes from the peer's eldest son to the smallest freeholder or burgess, made the House of Commons a real representation of the whole nation, and not of any single order in the nation.

Mark again that the form of government which political writers call *bi-cameral*, that is to say, where the Legislative Assembly consists of two Chambers or Houses, arose out of one of the accidents of English History. The merits of that form of government are now freely under discussion, but it is assumed on both sides that the only choice lies between one chamber and two; no one proposes to have three or four([52]). But most of the continental bodies of Estates consisted, as we have seen, of three Houses; in Sweden, where the peasants, the small freeholders, were important enough to be separately represented alongside of the Nobles, Clergy, and Citizens, there were till lately four([53]). The number two became the number of our Houses of Parliament, not out of any conviction of the advantages of that number, but because it was found impossible to get the Clergy in England habitually to act, as they did elsewhere, as a regular member of the parliamentary body. They shrank from the burthen, or they deemed secular legislation inconsistent with their profession. Thus, instead of the Clergy forming, as they did in France, a distinct Estate of the Legislature, we got a Parliament of two Houses, Lords and Commons, attended by a kind of ecclesiastical shadow of the Parliament in the shape of the two Houses of the ecclesiastical Convocation. Thus, for all practical purposes, there were only two Estates in the English Parliament, Lords and Commons. Thus the phrase of the Three Estates, which had a meaning in France, became meaningless in England. For centuries back there has been no separate Estate of the Clergy; some of their highest members have belonged to the Estate of the Lords, and the rest to the Estate of the Commons. Hence has arisen a common but not unnatural misconception, a misconception as old as the days of the Long Parliament, as to the meaning of the phrase of the Three Estates. Men constantly use those words as if they meant the three elements among which the legislative power is divided, King, Lords, and Commons. But an Estate means a class or order or rank of men, like the Lords, the Clergy, or the Commons. The King is not an Estate, because there is no class or order of Kings, the King being one person alone by himself. The proper phrase is the King and the three Estates of the Realm. But in England, as I have already shown, the phrase is meaningless, as we have in truth two Estates only (54).

We thus had in England, not an Estate of Nobles, forming a distinct class from the people, but an Upper House of hereditary and official Lords, whose privileges were purely personal, and whose children had no political privilege above other men. Our Bishops and some other of our ecclesiastical dignitaries had seats in the Upper House, but there was no distinct Estate of the Clergy, having its distinct voice in legislation. Our Lower House, lower in name, but gradually to become upper in real power, came to represent, not merely the inhabitants of privileged towns, but the whole nation, with the single exception of the personal holders of hereditary or official seats in the Upper House. That such an Assembly should gradually draw to itself all the real powers of the state was in the nature of things, but it was only gradually that it did so. Few things in our parliamentary history are more remarkable than the way in which the two Houses have for the most part worked together. I am not talking of very modern times, but of times when the two Houses were really coordinate powers in the state. During the six hundred years that the two Houses have lived side by side, serious disputes between them have been very rare, and those disputes which have happened have generally had to do with matters of form and privilege which were chiefly interesting to members of the two Houses themselves, not with questions which had any great importance for the nation at large ([55]). For a while the Commons followed the lead of the Lords; then the Lords came gradually to follow the lead of the Commons; but open and violent breaches between the Houses have been rare indeed. From the days of Earl Simon onwards both the power of Parliament as a whole, and the special power of the House of Commons, was constantly growing. The Parliaments of the fourteenth century exercised all the powers which our Parliament exercised now, together with some which modern Parliaments shrink from exercising. That is to say, the Parliaments of those days were obliged either to do directly or to leave undone many things which the developement of political conventionality enables a modern Parliament to do indirectly. The ancient Parliaments demanded the dismissal of the King's ministers; they regulated his personal household; they put his authority into commission; if need be, they put forth their last and greatest power and deposed him from his kingly office. In those days a change of government, a change of policy, the getting rid of a bad minister and the putting a better in his place, were things which never could be done without an open struggle between King and Parliament; often they could not be done without the bondage, the imprisonment, or the death, perhaps only of the minister, perhaps even of the King himself. The same ends can now be gained by a vote of censure in the House of Commons; in many cases they can be gained even without a vote of censure, by the simple throwing out of a measure by which a Ministry has given out that it will stand or fall ([56]).

The fifteenth century, as compared with the thirteenth and fourteenth, was in some respects a time in which things went back. It is plain that the Parliaments of that day were bodies which were much less independent than the Parliaments of earlier times. During the Wars of the Roses each successive military victor found a Parliament ready to confirm his claim to the Crown and to decree the condemnation of his enemies (57). And it was a Parliament of Henry the Sixth which passed the most reactionary measure which any Parliament ever did pass, that by which the qualification for a county elector was narrowed to those freeholders whose estates were of the yearly value of forty shillings (58). In this case time and the change in the value of money have redressed the wrong; there may be freeholders whose estates are under the value of forty shillings, but I cannot think that they are now a very large or important class. But, to understand the meaning of the restriction in the fifteenth century, for forty shillings we may fairly read forty pounds; and certainly, if we struck off the register all those electors whose qualification is a freehold—much more those whose qualification is an estate less than a freehold—under the value of forty pounds, the lessening of the constituencies of our counties would not be small. On the other hand, during the revolutionary times which followed, we more than once hear of direct appeals to the people which remind us of days far earlier. Edward the Fourth and Richard the Third were chosen Kings, or at least had their claims to the Crown acknowledged, by gatherings of the citizens of London which remind us of the wars of Stephen and Matilda (59). Still even in this age, the power of Parliament was advancing (60); the anxiety of every pretender to get a parliamentary sanction for his claims was a sign of the growing importance of Parliament, and we get incidental notices showing that a seat in the House of Commons, and that not as a knight of a shire, but as a burgess of a borough, was now an object of ambition for men of the class from which knights of the shire were chosen, and even for the sons of members of the Upper House (61).

At last came the sixteenth century, the time of trial for parliamentary institutions in so many countries of Europe. Not a few assemblies which had once been as free as our own Parliament were, during that age, either utterly swept away or reduced to empty formalities. Then it was that Charles the Fifth and Philip the Second overthrew the free constitutions of Castile and Aragon; then it was that the States-General of France met for the last time before their last meeting of all on the eve of the great Revolution (62). In England parliamentary institutions were not swept away, nor did Parliament sink into an empty form. But, for a while, Parliaments, like all our other institutions, became perverted into instruments of tyranny. Under Henry the Eighth, Parliaments, like Judges, Juries, and ecclesiastical Synods, decreed whatever seemed good to the caprice of the despot. Why had they so fallen away from what they had been in a past age, from what they were to be again? The reason is plain; the Commons had not yet gained strength enough to act without the Lords, and the Lords had ceased to be an independent body. The old nobility had been cut off at Towton and Barnet, and the new nobility were the abject slaves of the King to whom they owed their honours. A century later, the new nobility had inherited the spirit of the old, and the Commons had grown to the fulness of their power. Thus it came that we find in the Parliaments of the sixteenth century an abject submission to a tyrant's will, of which we find no sign in the Parliaments either of the fourteenth or of the seventeenth. Very different indeed from the Parliaments which overthrew Richard the Second and Charles the First were the Parliaments which, almost without a question, passed bills of attainder against any man against whom Henry's caprice had turned, the Parliaments which, in the great age of religious controversy, were ever ready to enforce by every penalty that particular shade of doctrine which for the moment commended itself to the Defender of the Faith, to his son or to his daughters. Why, it may be asked, in such a state of things, did not parliamentary institutions perish in England as they perished in so many other lands? It might be enough to say that no ruler had an interest in destroying institutions which he found that he could so conveniently turn to his own purposes. But why did not those institutions sink into mere forms, which they certainly did not do, even in the worst times? One reason undoubtedly is that special insular position of our country which has in so many other ways given a peculiar turn to our history. The great foe of parliamentary institutions was the introduction of standing armies. But the sovereign of England, shut up within his island, had far less need of a standing army than the sovereigns of the Continent, engaged as they were in their ceaseless wars with neighbours on their frontiers. But I believe that the personal character of Henry the Eighth had a great deal to do with the final preservation of our liberties. Do not for a moment fancy that I belong to that school of paradox which sets up Henry the Eighth as a virtuous and beneficent ruler. Do not think that I claim for him any feelings of direct thankfulness such as I do claim for Earl Simon and King

Edward. The position of Henry is more like the position of William the Conqueror, though I certainly hold that the Conqueror was in everything the better man of the two. Both served the cause of freedom indirectly, and both served it by means of features in the personal character of each. In one respect indeed William and Henry stood in utterly different positions towards England. William was a stranger, and it was largely because he was a stranger that he was able to do us indirect good. Henry, with all his crimes, was a thorough Englishman; throughout his reign there was a sympathy between him and the mass of his subjects, who, after all, did not greatly suffer by the occasional beheading of a Queen or a Duke. But the despotism of William and the despotism of Henry agreed in this, that each, even in his worst deeds, retained a scrupulous regard for the letter of the Law. In the case of William this is not hard to see for any one who carefully studies the records of his age ([63]); in the case of Henry it stands boldly proclaimed in the broadest facts of English history. While his fellow-tyrants abroad were everywhere overthrowing free institutions, Henry was in all things showing them the deepest outward respect. Through his reign he took care to do nothing except in outward and regular legal form, nothing for which he could not shelter himself under the sanction either of precedent or of written Law. In itself, this perversion of Law, this clothing of wrong with the garb of right, is really worse—at all events it is more corrupting—than deeds of open violence against which men are tempted openly to revolt. But such a tyranny as Henry's is one form of the homage which vice pays to virtue; the careful preservation of the outward forms of freedom makes it easier for another and happier generation again to kindle the form into its ancient spirit and life. Every deed of wrong done by Henry with the assent of Parliament was in truth a witness to the abiding importance of Parliament; the very degradation of our ancient Constitution was a step to its revival with new strength and in a more perfect form (64).

A like witness to the importance of Parliament in this age was shown in two other very remarkable ways, whereby the power and importance of the House of Commons was acknowledged in the very act of corrupting it. One was the active interference of the Government in parliamentary elections; the other was the creation of boroughs in order to be corrupt. One needs no stronger proofs than these of the importance of the body which it was found needful thus to pack and to manage. The Crown still kept the power of summoning members from any boroughs which it thought fit, and throughout the Tudor reigns the power was freely abused by sending writs to places which were likely to return members who would be subservient to the Court ([65]). Thus arose many of the wretched little boroughs in Cornwall and elsewhere which were disfranchised by our successive Reform Bills. These boroughs, which always were corrupt, and which were created in order to be corrupt, must be carefully distinguished from another class which perished with them. Many towns to which Earl Simon and King Edward sent writs decayed in process of time; sometimes they decayed positively; more commonly they decayed relatively, by being utterly outstripped by younger towns and so losing the importance which they had once had. The disfranchisement of both classes was equally just; but the different history of the two classes should be carefully borne in mind. It was right to take away its members from Old Sarum, but there had been a time when it was right to give Old Sarum members. In the case of a crowd of Cornish boroughs, it not only was right to take away their members, but they never ought to have had members at all ([66]).

It was in the days of Elizabeth that something of the ancient spirit again breathed forth. It is then that we come to the beginning of that long line of parliamentary worthies which stretches on in unbroken order from her days to our own. A few daring spirits in the Commons' House now began once more to speak in tones worthy of those great Assemblies which had taught the Edwards and the Richards that there was a power in England mightier than their own (67). Under the puny successor of the great Queen the voice of freedom was heard more loudly (68). In the next reign the great strife of all came, and a King of England once more, as in the days of Henry and Simon, stood forth in arms against his people to learn that the power of his people was a greater power than his. But in the seventeenth century, just as in the thirteenth, men did not ask for any rights and powers which were admitted to be new; they asked only for the better security of those rights and powers which had been handed on from days of old. Into the details of that great struggle and of the times which followed it is not my purpose to enter. I have traced at some length the origin and growth of our Constitution from the earliest times to its days of special trial in the days of Tudor and Stewart despotism. Our later constitutional history rather belongs to an inquiry of another kind. It is mainly a record of silent changes in the practical working of institutions whose outward and legal form remained untouched.

I will therefore end my consecutive historical sketch—if consecutive it can claim to be—at the point which we have now reached. Instead of carrying on any regular constitutional narrative into times nearer to our own, I will rather choose, as the third part of my subject, the illustration of one of the special points with which I set out, namely the power which our gradual developement has given us of retracing our steps, of falling back, whenever need calls for falling back, on the principles of earlier, often of the earliest, times. Wittingly or unwittingly, much of our best modern legislation has, as I have already said, been a case of advancing by the process of going back. As the last division of the work which I have taken in hand, I shall try to show in how many cases we have, as a matter of fact, gone back from the cumbrous and oppressive devices of feudal and royalist lawyers to the sounder, freer, and simpler principles of the days of our earliest freedom.

CHAPTER III.

In my two former chapters I have carried my brief sketch of the history of the English Constitution down to the great events of the seventeenth century. I chose that point as the end of my consecutive narrative, because the peculiar characteristic of the times which have followed has been that so many and such important practical changes have been made without any change in the written Law, without any re-enactment of the Law, without any fresh declaration of its meaning. The movements and revolutions of former times, as I have before said, seldom sought any acknowledged change in the Law, but rather its more distinct enactment, its more careful and honest administration. This was the general character of all the great steps in our political history, from the day when William of Normandy renewed the Laws of Eadward to the day when William of Orange gave his royal assent to the Bill of Rights. But, though each step in our progress took the shape, not of the creation of a new right, but of the firmer establishment of an old one, yet each step was marked by some formal and public act which stands enrolled among the landmarks of our progress. Some Charter was granted by the Sovereign, some Act of Parliament was passed by the Estates of the Realm, setting forth in legal form the nature and measure of the rights which it was sought to place on a firmer ground. Since the seventeenth century things have in this respect greatly altered. The work of legislation, of strictly constitutional legislation, has never ceased; a long succession of legislative enactments stand out as landmarks of political progress no less in more recent than in earlier times. But alongside of them there has also been a series of political changes, changes of no less moment than those which are recorded in the statute-book, which have been made without any legislative enactment whatever. A whole code of political maxims, universally acknowledged in theory, universally carried out in practice, has grown up, without leaving among the formal acts of our legislature any trace of the steps by which it grew. Up to the end of the seventeenth century, we may fairly say that no distinction could be drawn between the Constitution and the Law. The prerogative of the Crown, the privilege of Parliament, the liberty of the subject, might not always be clearly defined on every point. It has indeed been said that those three things were all of them things to which in their own nature no limit could be set. But all three weie supposed to rest, if not on the direct words of the Statute Law, yet at least on that somewhat shadowy yet very practical creation, that mixture of genuine ancient traditions and of recent devices of lawyers, which is known to Englishmen as the Common Law. Any breach either of the rights of the Sovereign or of the rights of the subject was a legal offence, capable of legal definition and subjecting the offender to legal penalties. An act which could not be brought within the letter either of the Statute or of the Common Law would not then have been looked upon as an offence at all. If lower courts were too weak to do justice, the High Court of Parliament stood ready to do justice even against the mightiest offenders. It was armed with weapons fearful and rarely used, but none the less regular and legal. It could smite by impeachment, by attainder, by the exercise of the greatest power of all, the deposition of the reigning King. But men had not yet reached the more subtle doctrine that there may be offences against the Constitution which are no offences against the Law. They had not learned that men in high office may have a responsibility practically felt and acted on, but which no legal enactment has defined, and which no legal tribunal can enforce. It had not been found out that Parliament itself has a power, now practically the highest of its powers, in which it acts neither as a legislature nor as a court of justice, but in which it pronounces sentences which have none the less practical force because they carry with them none of the legal consequences of death, bonds, banishment, or confiscation. We now have a whole system of political morality, a whole code of precepts for the guidance of public men, which will not be found in any page of either the Statute or the Common Law, but which are in practice held hardly less sacred than any principle embodied in the Great Charter or in the Petition of Right. In short, by the side of our written Law, there has grown up an unwritten or conventional Constitution. When an Englishman speaks of the conduct of a public man being constitutional or unconstitutional, he means something wholly different from what he means by conduct being legal or illegal. A famous vote of the House of Commons, passed on the motion of a great statesman, once declared that the then Ministers of the Crown did not possess the confidence of the House of Commons, and that their continuance in office was therefore at variance with the spirit of the Constitution ([1]). The truth of such a position, according to the traditional principles on which public men have acted for some generations, cannot be disputed; but it would be in vain to seek for any trace of such doctrines in any page of our written Law. The proposer of that motion did not mean to charge the existing Ministry with any illegal act, with any act which could be made the subject either of a prosecution in a lower court or of impeachment in the High Court of Parliament itself. He did not mean that they, Ministers of the Crown, appointed during the pleasure of the Crown, committed any breach of the Law of which the Law could take cognizance, by retaining possession of their offices till such time as the Crown should think good to dismiss them from those offices. What he meant was that the general course of their policy was one which to a majority of the House of Commons did not seem to be wise or beneficial to the nation, and that therefore, according to a conventional code as well understood and as effectual as the written Law itself, they were bound to resign offices of which the House of Commons no longer held them to be worthy. The House made no claim to dismiss those Ministers from their offices by any act of its own; it did not even petition the Crown to remove them from their offices. It simply spoke its mind on their general conduct, and it was held that, when the House had so spoken, it was their duty to give way without any formal petition, without any formal command, on the part either of the House or of the Sovereign (2). The passing by the House of Commons of such a resolution as this may perhaps be set down as the formal declaration of a constitutional principle. But though a formal declaration, it was not a legal declaration. It created a precedent for the practical guidance of future Ministers and future Parliaments, but it neither changed the Law nor declared it. It asserted a principle which might be appealed to in future debates in the House of Commons, but it asserted no principle which could be taken any notice of by a Judge in any Court of Law. It stands therefore on a wholly different ground from those enactments which, whether they changed the Law or simply declared the Law, had a real legal force, capable of being enforced by a legal tribunal. If any officer of the Crown should levy a tax without the authority of Parliament, if he should enforce martial law without the authority of Parliament, he would be guilty of a legal crime. But, if he merely continues to hold an office conferred by the Crown and from which the Crown has not removed him, though he hold in teeth of any number of votes of censure passed by both Houses of Parliament, he is in no way a breaker of the written Law. But the man who should so act would be universally held to have trampled under foot one of the most undoubted principles of the unwritten but universally accepted Constitution.

The remarkable thing is that, of these two kinds of hypothetical offences, the latter, whose guilt is purely conventional, is almost as unlikely to happen as the former, whose guilt is a matter established by Law. The power of the Law is so firmly established among us that the possibility of breaches of the Law on the part of the Crown or its Ministers hardly ever comes into our heads. And conduct sinning against the broad lines of the unwritten Constitution is looked on as almost as unlikely. Political men may debate whether such and such a course is or is not constitutional, just as lawyers may debate whether such a course is or is not legal. But the very form of the debate implies that there is a Constitution to be observed, just as in the other case it implies that there is a Law to be observed. Now this firm establishment of a purely unwritten and conventional code is one of the most remarkable facts in history. It is plain that it implies the firmest possible establishment of the power of the written Law as its groundwork. If there were the least fear of breaches of the written Law on the part of the Crown or its officers, we should be engaged in finding means to getting rid of that more serious danger, not in disputing over points arising out of a code which has no legal existence. But it is well sometimes to stop and remember how thoroughly conventional the whole of our received system is. The received doctrine as to the relations of the two Houses of Parliament to one another, the whole theory of the position of the body known as the Cabinet and of its chief the Prime Minister, every detail in short of the practical working of government among us, is a matter belonging wholly to the unwritten Constitution and not at all to the written Law. The limits of the royal authority are indeed clearly defined by the written Law. But I suspect that many people would be amazed at the amount of power which the Crown still possesses by Law, and at the many things, which in our eyes would seem utterly monstrous, but which might yet be done by royal authority without any law being broken. The Law indeed secures us against arbitrary legislation, against the repeal of any old laws, or the enactment of any new ones, without the consent of both Houses of Parliament. But it is the unwritten Constitution alone which makes it practically impossible for the Crown to refuse its assent to measures which have passed both Houses of Parliament, and which in many cases makes it almost equally impossible to refuse the prayer of an address sent up by one of those Houses only. The written Law leaves to the Crown the choice of all its ministers and agents, great and small; their appointment to office and their removal from office, as long as they commit no crime which the Law can punish, is a matter left to the personal discretion of the Sovereign. The unwritten Constitution makes it practically impossible for the Sovereign to keep a Minister in office whom the House of Commons does not approve, and it makes it almost equally impossible to remove from office a Minister whom the House of Commons does approve (3). The written Law and the unwritten Constitution alike exempt the Sovereign from all ordinary personal responsibility (4). They both transfer the responsibility from the Sovereign himself to his agents and advisers. But the nature and extent of their responsibility is widely different in the eyes of the written Law and in the eyes of the unwritten Constitution. The written Law is satisfied with holding that the command of the Sovereign is no excuse for an illegal act, and that he who advises the commission of an illegal act by royal authority must bear the responsibility from which the Sovereign himself is free. The written Law knows nothing of any responsibility but such as may be enforced either by prosecution in any of the ordinary Courts or by impeachment in the High Court of Parliament. The unwritten Constitution subjects the agents and advisers of the Crown to a responsibility of quite another kind. What we understand by the responsibility of Ministers is that they are liable to have all their public acts discussed in Parliament, not only on the ground of their legal or illegal character, but on the vaguest grounds of their general tendency. They may be in no danger of prosecution or impeachment; but they are no less bound to bow to other indications of the will of the House of Commons; the unwritten Constitution makes a vote of censure as effectual as an impeachment, and in many cases it makes a mere refusal to pass a ministerial measure as effectual as a vote of censure. The written Law knows nothing of the Cabinet or the Prime Minister; it knows them as members of one or the other House of Parliament, as Privy Councillors, as holders each man in his own person of certain offices, but, as a collective body bound together by a common responsibility, the Law never heard of them ([5]). But in the eye of the unwritten Constitution the Prime Minister and the Cabinet of which he is the head form the main feature of our system of government. It is plain at a moment's glance that the practical power of the Crown is not now what it was in the reign of William the Third or even in that of George the Third. But the change is due, far less to changes in the written Law than to changes in the unwritten Constitution. The Law leaves the powers of the Crown untouched, but the Constitution requires that those powers should be exercised by such persons, and in such a manner, as may be acceptable to a majority of the House of Commons. In all these ways, in a manner silent and indirect, the Lower House of Parliament, as it is still deemed in formal rank, has become the really ruling power in the nation. There is no greater contrast than that which exists between the humility of its formal dealings with the Crown, and even with the Upper House (6), and the reality of the irresistible power which it exercises over both. It is so conscious of the mighty force of its indirect powers that it no longer cares to claim the direct powers which it exercised in former times. There was a time when Parliament was directly consulted on questions of War and Peace. There was a time when Parliament claimed directly to appoint several of the chief officers of state. There were much later times when it was no unusual thing to declare a man in power to be a public enemy, or directly to address the Crown for his removal from office and from the royal presence. No such direct exercises of parliamentary power are needed now, because the whole machinery of government may be changed by the simple process of the House refusing to pass a measure on which the Minister has made up his mind to stake his official being.

Into the history of the stages by which this most remarkable state of things has been brought about I do not intend here to enter. The code of our unwritten Constitution has, like all other English things, grown up bit by bit, and, for the most part, silently and without any acknowledged author. Yet some stages of the developement are easily pointed out, and they make important landmarks. The beginning may be placed in the reign of William the Third, when we first find anything at all like a *Ministry* in the modern sense. Up to that time the servants of the Crown had been servants of the Crown, each man in the personal discharge of his own office. The holder of each office owed faithful service to the Crown, and he was withal responsible to the Law; but he stood in no special fellowship towards the holder of any other office. Provided he discharged his own duties, nothing hindered him from being the personal or political enemy of any of his fellow-servants. It was William who first saw that, if the King's government was to be carried on, there must be at least a general agreement of opinions and aims among the King's chief agents in his government (7). From this beginning a system has gradually grown up which binds the chief officers of the Crown to work together in at least outward harmony, to undertake the defence of one another, and on vital points to stand and fall together. Another important stage happened in much later times, when the King ceased to take a share in person in the deliberations of his Cabinet. And I may mark a change in language which has happened within my own memory, and which, like other changes of language, is certainly not without its meaning. We now familiarly speak, in Parliament and out of Parliament, of the body of Ministers actually in power, the body known to the Constitution but wholly unknown to the Law, by the name of "the Government." We speak of "Mr. Gladstone's Government" or "Mr. Disraeli's Government." I can myself remember the time when such a form of words was unknown, when "Government" still meant "Government by King, Lords, and Commons," and when the body of men who acted as the King's immediate advisers were spoken of as "Ministers" or "the Ministry" (8).

This kind of silent, I might say stealthy, growth, has, without the help of any legislative enactment, produced that unwritten and conventional code of political rules which we speak of as the Constitution. This process I have spoken of as being characteristic of the days since the Revolution of 1688, as distinguished from earlier times. And so it undoubtedly is. At no earlier time have so many important changes in constitutional doctrine and practice won universal acceptance without being recorded in any written enactment. Yet this tendency of later times is, after all, only a further developement of a tendency which was at work from the beginning. It is simply another application of the Englishman's love of precedent. The growth of the unwritten Constitution has much in common with the earlier growth of the unwritten Common Law. I have shown in earlier chapters that some of the most important principles of our earlier Constitution were established silently and by the power of precedent, without resting on any known written enactment. If we cannot show any Act of Parliament determining the relations in which the members of the Cabinet stand to the Crown, to the House of Commons, and to one another, neither can we show the Act of Parliament which decreed, in opposition to the practice of all other nations, that the children of the hereditary Peer should be simple Commoners. The real difference is that, in more settled times, when Law was fully supreme, it was found that many important practical changes might be made without formal changes in the Law.

It was also found that there is a large class of political subjects which can be better dealt with in this way of tacit understandings than they can be in the shape of a formal enactment by Law. We practically understand what is meant by Ministers having or not having the confidence of the House of Commons; we practically recognize the cases in which, as not having the confidence of the House, they ought to resign office and the cases in which they may fairly appeal to the country by a dissolution of Parliament. But it would be utterly impossible to define such cases beforehand in the terms of an Act of Parliament. Or again, the Speaker of the House of Commons is an officer known to the Law. The Leader of the House of Commons is a person as well known to the House and the country, his functions are well understood, as those of the Speaker himself. But of the Leader of the House of Commons the Law knows nothing. It would be hopeless to seek to define his duties in any legal form, and the House itself has, before now, shrunk from recognizing the existence of such a person in any shape of which a Court of Law could take notice ([9]).

During a time then which is now not very far short of two hundred years, the silent and extra-legal growth of our conventional Constitution has been at least as important as the actual changes in our written Law. With regard to these last, the point on which I wish chiefly to dwell is the way in which not a few pieces of modern legislation have been—whether wittingly or unwittingly I do not profess to know—a return to the simpler principles of our oldest constitution. I trust to show that, in many important points, we have cast aside the legal subtleties which grew up from the thirteenth century to the seventeenth, and that we have gone back to the plain common sense of the eleventh or tenth, and of times far earlier still. In those ancient times we had already laws, but we had as yet no lawyers. We hear in early times of men who were versed above others in the laws of the land, but such special knowledge is spoken of as the attribute of age or experience in public business, not as the private possession of a professional class ([10]). The class of professional lawyers grew up along with the growth of a more complicated and technical jurisprudence under our Norman and Angevin Kings. Now I mean no disrespect to a profession which in our present artificial state of society we certainly cannot do without, but there can be no kind of doubt that lawyers' interpretations and lawyers' ways of looking at things have done no small mischief, not only to the true understanding of our history but to the actual course of our history itself. The lawyer's tendency is to carry to an unreasonable extent that English love of precedent which, within reasonable bounds, is one of our most precious safeguards. His virtue is that of acute and logical inference from given premisses; the premisses themselves he is commonly satisfied to take without examination from those who have gone before him. It is often wonderful to see the amazing ingenuity with which lawyers have piled together inference upon inference, starting from some purely arbitrary assumption of their own. Each stage of the argument, taken by itself, is absolutely unanswerable; the objection must be taken earlier, before the argument begins. The argument is perfect, if we only admit the premisses; the only unlucky thing is that the premisses will constantly be found to be historically worthless. Add to this that the natural tendency of the legal mind is to conservatism and deference to authority. This will always be the case, even with thoroughly honest men in an age when honesty is no longer dangerous. But this tendency will have tenfold force in times when an honest setting forth of the Law might expose its author to the disfavour of an arbitrary government. We shall therefore find that the premisses from which lawyers' arguments have started, but which historical study shows to be unsound, are commonly premisses devised in favour of the prerogative of the Crown, not in favour of the rights of the people. Indeed the whole ideal conception of the Sovereign, as one, personally at least, above the Law, as one personally irresponsible and incapable of doing wrong, the whole conception of the Sovereign as the sole fountain of all honour, as the original grantor of all property, as the source from which all authority of every kind issues in the first instance, is purely a lawyer's conception, and rests upon no ground whatever in the records of our early history ([11]). In later times indeed the evil has largely corrected itself; the growth of our unwritten Constitution under the hands of statesmen has done much practically to get rid of these slavish devices of lawyers. The personal irresponsibility of the Sovereign becomes practically harmless when the powers of the Crown are really exercised by Ministers who act under a twofold responsibility, both to the written Law and to the unwritten Constitution. Yet even now small cases of hardship sometimes occur, in which some traditional maxim of lawyers, some device devised in favour of the prerogative of the Crown, stands in the way of the perfectly equal administration of justice. But in several important cases the lawgiver has directly stepped in to wipe out the inventions of the lawyer, and modern Acts of Parliament have brought things back to the simpler principles of our earliest forefathers. I will wind up my sketch of our constitutional history by pointing out several cases in which this happy result has taken place.

For many ages it was a legal doctrine universally received that Parliament at once expired at the death of the reigning King. The argument by which the lawyers reached this conclusion is, like most of their arguments, altogether unanswerable, provided only we admit their premisses. According to the lawyer's conception, whatever might be the powers of Parliament when it actually came together, however much the King might be bound to act by its advice, consent, and authority, the Parliament itself did nevertheless derive its being from the authority of the King. Parliament was summoned by the King's writ. The King might indeed be bound to issue the writs for its summons; still it was from the King's writ that the Parliament actually derived its being and its powers. By another legal assumption, the force of the King's writ was held to last only during the lifetime of the King who issued it. It followed therefore that Parliament, summoned by the King's writ and deriving its authority from the King's writ, was dissolved *ipso facto* by the death of the King who summoned it. Once admit the assumptions from which this reasoning starts, and the reasoning itself is perfect. But what is the worth of the assumptions? Let us see how this mass of legal subtlety would have looked in the eyes of a man of the eleventh century, in the eyes of a man who had borne his part in the elections of Eadward and of Harold, and who had raised his voice and clashed his arms in the great Assembly which restored Godwine to his lands and honours ([12]). To such an one the doctrine that a national Assembly could be gathered together only by the King's writ, and the consequent doctrine that the national Assembly ceased to exist when the breath went out of the King's body, would have seemed like the babble of a madman. When was the gathering together of the national Assembly more needed, when was it called upon to exercise higher and more inherent powers, than when the throne was actually vacant, and when the Assembly of the nation came together to determine who should fill it? And how could the Assembly be gathered together by the King's writ when there was no King in the land to issue a writ? The King's writ would be, in his eyes, a convenient way in ordinary times for fixing a time and place for the meetings of the Assembly, but it would be nothing more. It would be in no sense the source of the powers of the Assembly, powers which he would look upon as derived from the simple fact that the Assembly was itself the nation. In his eyes it was not the King who created the Assembly, but the Assembly which created the King. The doctrine that the King never dies, that the throne never can be vacant, would have seemed gibberish to one who had seen the throne vacant and had borne his part in filling it. The doctrine that the King can do no wrong would have seemed no less gibberish to one who knew that he might possibly be called on to bear his part in deposing a King. Three of the most famous Assemblies in English history have ever been puzzles in the way of mere legal interpreters; to the man of the eleventh century they would have seemed to be perfectly legal and regular, alike in their constitution and in their acts. The Assembly which in 1399 deposed Richard the Second and elected Henry the Fourth, though summoned by the King's writ, was not opened by his commission, and it seems to have shrunk from taking the name of Parliament, and to have acted only by the name of the Estates of the Realm. As an Assembly which was in some sort irregular, it seems to have shrunk from going through the usual forms of a regular Parliament, and, though it did in the end exercise the greatest of parliamentary powers, it seems to have been afraid to look its own act in the face. Richard was deposed, but his deposition was mixed up with a resignation of the Crown on his part, and with a challenge of the Crown on the part of Henry. Then, as a demise of the Crown had taken place, it was held that the same legal consequences followed as if that demise had been caused by the death of the King. It was held that the Parliament which had been summoned by the writ of King Richard ceased to exist when Richard ceased to be King, and, as it was not thought good to summon a new Parliament, the same Parliament was, by a legal fiction, summoned again under the writ of King Henry ([13]). All these doubts and difficulties, all these subtleties of lawyers, would have been wholly unintelligible to a man of the eleventh century. In his eyes the Witan would have come together, whether by King Richard's writ or not it mattered little; having come together, they had done the two greatest of national acts by deposing one King and choosing another; having done this, if there was any other national business to be done, there was no reason on earth why they should not go on and do it. Take again another Assembly of equal importance in our history, the Convention which voted the recall of Charles the Second. That Assembly succeeded a Parliament which had ventured on a still stronger step than deposing a King, that of sending a reigning King to trial and execution (14). It was not held in 1649 that the Long Parliament came to an end when the axe fell on the neck of Charles the First, but the doctrine that it ought to have done so was not forgotten eleven years later (15). And the Convention which was elected, as freely as any Parliament ever was elected (16), in answer to the vote of the expiring Long Parliament, was, because it was so elected and not in answer to the King's writ, looked on as an Assembly of doubtful validity. It acted as a Parliament; it restored the King; it granted him a revenue; and it did a more wonderful work than all, for it created itself, and passed an Act declaring itself to be a lawful Parliament (17). Yet, after all, it was deemed safer that all the Acts of the Convention Parliament should be confirmed by its successor which was summoned in due form by the King's writ. These fantastic subtleties also, subtleties worthy of the kindred device by which the first year of Charles' reign was called the twelfth, would again have been wholly unintelligible to our man of the eleventh century. He might have remembered that the assembly which restored Æthelred—which restored him on conditions, while Charles was restored without conditions—did not scruple to go on and pass a series of the most important decrees that were passed in any of our early Assemblies (18). Once more again, the Convention which deposed James and elected William, seemed, like that which deposed Richard and elected Henry, to doubt its own existence and to shrink from its own act. James was deposed; but the Assembly which deposed him ventured not to use the word, and, as an extorted abdication was deemed expedient in the case of Richard, so a constructive abdication was imagined in the case of James (19). And the Assembly which elected William, like the Assembly which elected Henry and that which recalled Charles, prolonged its own existence by the same transparent fiction of voting itself to be a lawful Parliament. Wise men held at the time that, at least in times of revolution, a Parliament might be called into being by some other means than that of the writ of a King. Yet it was deemed that some additional security was given to the existence of the Assembly and to the validity of its acts by this second exercise of the mysterious power of self-creation (20). Once more in the same reign the question was brought forward whether a Parliament summoned by the joint writ of William and Mary did not expire when Mary died and William reigned alone. This subtlety was suggested only to be contemptuously cast aside; yet it may be fairly doubted whether it was not worth at least as much as any of the kindred subtleties which on the three earlier occasions were deemed of such vast importance ([21]). The untutored wisdom of Englishmen, in the days when we had laws but when those laws had not yet been made the sport of the subtleties of lawyers, would have seen as little force in the difficulties which it was deemed necessary to get over by solemn parliamentary enactments as in the difficulty which neither House of Parliament thought worthy of any serious discussion.

And now what has modern legislation done towards getting rid of all these pettifogging devices, and towards bringing us back to the simpler doctrines of our forefathers? Parliament is still summoned by the writ of the Sovereign; in settled times no other way of bringing it together can be so convenient. But, if times of revolution should ever come again, we, who do even our revolutions according to precedent, shall probably have learned something from the revolutionary precedents of 1399, of 1660, and of 1688. In each later case the subtlety is one degree less subtle than in the former. The Estates of the Realm which deposed Richard were changed into a Parliament of Henry by the transparent fiction of sending out writs which were not, and could not be, followed by any real elections. The Convention which recalled—shall we rather say which elected?

—Charlés the Second did indeed turn itself into a Parliament, but it was deemed needful that its acts should be confirmed by another Parliament. The acts of the Convention of 1688 were not deemed to need any such confirmation. Each of these differences marks a stage in the return to the common-sense doctrine, that, convenient as it is in all ordinary times that Parliament should be summoned by the writ of the Sovereign, yet it is not from that summons, but from the choice of the people, that Parliament derives its real being and its inherent powers. As for the other end of the lawyers' doctrine, the inference that Parliament is *ipso facto* dissolved by a demise of the Crown, from that a more rational legislation has set us free altogether. Though modern Parliaments are no longer called on to elect Kings, yet experience and common sense have taught us that the time when the Sovereign is changed is exactly the time when the Great Council of the Nation ought to be in full life and activity. By a statute only a few years later than the raising of the question whether a Parliament of William and Mary did or did not expire by the death of Mary, all such subtleties were swept away, and it became the Law that the Parliament which was in being at the time of a demise of the Crown should remain in being for six months, unless specially dissolved by the new sovereign. And it is now deemed so needful that a new Sovereign should have a Parliament ready to act with him that a later statute provides that, if a demise of the Crown should take place during the short interval when there is no Parliament in being, the last Parliament shall *ipso facto* revive, and shall continue in being, unless a second time dissolved, for six months more ([22]). Thus the event which, by the perverted ingenuity of lawyers, was held to have the power of destroying a Parliament is now, by the wisdom of later legislation, clothed with the power of calling a Parliament into being. Truly this is a case where the letter killeth and the spirit giveth life. The doctrine which had been inferred by unanswerable logic from an utterly worthless premiss has been cast aside in favour of the dictate of common sense. We have learned that the moment when the State has lost its head is the last moment to choose for depriving it of its body also.

Here then is a notable instance of the way in which the latest legislation of England has fallen back upon the principles of the earliest. Here is a point on which the eleventh century and the nineteenth are of one mind, and on which the fanciful scruples of the fourteenth and the seventeenth centuries are no longer listened to. Let us take another instance. In the old Teutonic Constitution, just as in the old Roman Constitution, large tracts of land were the property of the State, the *ager publicus* of Rome, the *folkland* of England. As the royal power grew, as the King came to be more and more looked on as the impersonation of the nation, the land of the people came to be more and more looked on as the land of the King, and the *folkland* of our old English charters gradually changed into the *Terra Regis* of Domesday ([23]). Like other changes of the kind, the Norman Conquest only strengthened and brought to its full effect a tendency which was already at work; but there can be no doubt that, down to the Norman Conquest, the King at least went through the form of consulting his Witan, before he alienated the land of the people to become the possession of an individual—in Old-English phrase, before he turned *folkland* into *bookland* ([24]). After the Norman Conquest we hear no more of the land of the people; it has become the land of the King, to be dealt with according to the King's personal pleasure. From the days of the first William to those of the Third, the land which had once been the land of the people was dealt with without any reference to the will of the people. Under a conscientious King it might be applied to the real service of the state, or bestowed as the reward of really faithful servants of the State. Under an unconscientious King it might be squandered broadcast among his minions or his mistresses ([25]). Now this wrong too is redressed. A custom as strong as law now requires that, at the beginning of each fresh reign, the Sovereign shall, not by an act of bounty but by an act of justice, restore to the nation the land which the nation lost so long ago. The royal demesnes are now handed over to be dealt with like the other revenues of the State, to be disposed of by Parliament for the public service ([26]). That is to say, the people have won back their own; the usurpation of the days of foreign rule has been swept away. We have in this case too gone back to the sound principles of our forefathers; the *Terra Regis* of the Norman has once more become the *folkland* of the days of our earliest freedom.

I will quote another case, a case in which the return from the fantasies of lawyers to the common sense of antiquity has been distinctly to the profit, if not of the abstraction called the Crown, yet certainly to that of its personal holder. As long as the *folkland* remained the land of the people, as long as our monarchy retained its ancient elective character, the King, like any other man, could inherit, purchase, bequeath, or otherwise dispose of, the lands which were his own private property as much as he lands of other men were theirs. We have the wills of several of our early Kings which show that a King was in this respect as free as any other man ([27]). But as the lawyers' figment of hereditary right took root, as the other lawyers' figment also took root by which the lands of the people were held to be at the personal disposal of the King, a third figment grew up, by which it was held that the person and the office of the King were so inseparably fused into one that any private estates which the King may have held before his accession to the throne became *ipso facto* part and parcel of the royal demesne. As long as the Crown remained an elective office, the injustice of such a rule would have made itself plain; it would have been at once seen to be as unreasonable as if it had been held that the private estates of a Bishop should merge in the estates of his see. As long as there was no certainty that the children or other heirs of the reigning King would ever succeed to his Crown, it would have been the height of injustice to deprive them in this way of their natural inheritance. The election of a King would have carried with it the confiscation of his private estate. But when the Crown was held to be hereditary, when the *folkland* was held to be *Terra Regis*, this hardship was no longer felt. The eldest son was provided for by his right of succession to the Crown, and the power of disposing of the Crown lands at pleasure gave the King the means of providing for his younger children. Still the doctrine was none the less unreasonable; it was a doctrine founded on no ground either of natural justice or of ancient law; it was a mere inference which had gradually grown up out of the arbitrary theories about the King's powers and prerogatives. And, as the old state of things gradually came back again, as men began to feel that the demesnes of the Crown were not the private possession of the reigning King, but were the true possession of the people—that is, as the *Terra Regis* again came back to its old state of *folkland*—it was felt to be unreasonable to debar the Sovereign from a natural right which belonged to every one of his subjects. The land which, to put it in the mildest form, the King held in trust for the common service of the nation was now again employed to its proper use. It was therefore reasonable that a restriction which belonged to a past state of things should be swept away, and that Sovereigns who had surrendered an usurped power which they ought never to have held should be restored to the enjoyment of a natural right which ought never to have been taken from them. As our present Sovereign in so many other respects holds the place of Ælfred rather than the place of the Richards and Henries of later times, so she again holds the right which Ælfred held, of acquiring and disposing of private property like any other member of the nation (28).

These examples are, I hope, enough to make out my case. In each of them modern legislation has swept away the arbitrary inferences of lawyers, and has gone back to those simpler principles which the untutored wisdom of our forefathers never thought of calling in question. I could easily make the list much longer. Every act which has restrained the arbitrary prerogative of the Crown, every act which has secured or increased either the powers of Parliament or the liberty of the subject, has been a return, sometimes to the letter, at all times to the spirit, of our earliest Law. But I would enlarge on one point only, the most important point of all, and a point in which we may at first time seem, not to have come nearer, but to have gone away further from the principles of early times. I mean with regard to the succession to the Crown. The Crown was of old, as I have already said, elective. No man had a right to be King till he had been called to the kingly office by the choice of the Assembly of the nation. No man actually was King till he had been admitted to the kingly office by the consecration of the Church. The doctrines that the King never dies, that the throne never can be vacant, that there can be no interregnum, that the reign of the next heir begins the moment the reign of his predecessor is ended, are all figments of later times. No traces of such doctrines can be found at any time earlier than the accession of Edward the First (29). The strong preference which in early times belonged to members of the kingly house, above all to the born son of a crowned King (30), gradually grew, under the influences which the Norman Conquest finally confirmed, into the doctrine of absolute hereditary right. That doctrine grew along with the general growth of the royal power; it grew as men gradually came to look on kingship as a possession held by a single man for his own profit, rather than as an office bestowed by the people for the common good of the realm. It might seem that, in this respect at least, we have not gone forward, but that we rather have gone back. For nothing is more certain than that the Crown is more strictly and undoubtedly hereditary now than it was in the days of Normans, Angevins, or Tudors. But a little thought will show that, in this case also, we have not gone back but have gone forward. That is to say, we have gone forward by going back, by going back, in this case, not to the letter, but assuredly to the spirit of earlier times. The Crown is now more undoubtedly hereditary than it was in the fifteenth or sixteenth century; but that is because it is now hereditary by Law, because its powers are distinctly defined by Law. The will of the people, the source of all Law and of all power, has been exercised, not in the old form of personally choosing a King at every vacancy of the Crown, but by an equally lawful exercise of the national will, which has thought good to entail the Crown on a particular family. It was in the reign of our last elective King that the Crown first became legally hereditary. The doctrine may seem a startling one, but it is one to which an unbiassed study of our history will undoubtedly lead us. Few things are more amusing than the treatment which our early history has met with at the hands of purely legal writers. There is something almost pitiable in the haltings and stumblings of such a writer as Blackstone, unable to conceive that his lawyer's figment of hereditary right was anything short of eternal, and yet coming at every moment across events which showed that in early times any such figment was utterly unknown (31). In early times the King was not only elected, but he went through a twofold election. I have already said that the religious character with which most nations have chosen to invest their Kings took in England, as in most other Christian lands, the form of an ecclesiastical consecration to the kingly office. That form we still retain; but in modern times it has become a mere form, a pageant impressive no doubt and instructive, but still a mere pageant, which invests the crowned King with no powers which he did not equally hold while still uncrowned. The death of the former King at once puts his successor in possession of every kingly right and power; his coronation in no way adds to his legal authority, however much it may increase his personal responsibility towards God and his people. But this was not so of old time. The election of the national Assembly gave the King so chosen the sole right to become King, but it did not make him King. The King-elect was like a Bishop-elect. The recommendation of the Crown, the election of the Chapter, and the confirmation of the Archbishop, give a certain man the sole right to a certain see, but it is only the purely religious rite of consecration which makes him actually Bishop of it (32). So it was of old with a King. The choice of the Witan made him King-elect, but it was only the ecclesiastical crowning and anointing which made him King. And this ecclesiastical ceremony involved an election. Chosen already to the civil office by the Nation in its civil character, he was again chosen by the Church—that is, by the Nation in its religious character, by the Clergy and People assembled in the church where the crowning rite was to be done (33). This second ecclesiastical election must always have been a mere form, as the choice of the nation was already made before the ecclesiastical ceremony began. But the ecclesiastical election survived the civil one. The state of things which lawyers dream of from the beginning is a law of strict hereditary succession, broken in upon by occasional interruptions. These interruptions, which, in the eye of history, are simply exercises of an ancient right, are, in the eyes of lawyers, only revolutions or usurpations. Now this state of things, a state in which a fixed rule was sometimes broken, which Blackstone dreams of in the tenth and eleventh centuries, really did exist from the thirteenth century onwards. From the accession of Edward the First, the first King who reigned before his coronation, hereditary succession became the rule in practice. The son, or even the grandson, of the late King(34) was commonly acknowledged as a matter of course, without anything which could fairly be called an election. But the right of Parliament to settle the succession was constantly exercised, and ever and anon we come across signs which show that the ancient notion of an election of a still more popular kind had not wholly passed away out of men's minds. Two Kings were formally deposed, and on the deposition of the second the Crown passed, as it might have done in ancient times, to a branch of the royal house which was not the next in lineal succession. Three Kings of the House of Lancaster reigned by a good parliamentary title, and the doctrine of indefeasible hereditary right, the doctrine that there was some virtue in a particular line of succession which the power of Parliament itself could not overthrow, was first brought forward as the formal justification of the claims of the House of York (35). Those claims in truth could not be formally justified on any showing but that of the most slavish doctrine of divine right, but it was not on any such doctrine as that that the cause of the House of York really rested. The elaborate list of grandmothers and great-grandmothers which was brought to show that Henry the Fifth was an usurper would never have been heard of if the government of Henry the Sixth had not become utterly unpopular, while Richard Duke of York was the best beloved man of his time. Richard accepted a parliamentary compromise, which of course implied the right of Parliament to decide the question. Henry was to keep the Crown for life, and Richard was to displace Henry's son as heir-apparent. That is to say, according to a custom common in Germany, though rare in England, Richard was chosen to fill a vacancy in the throne which had not yet taken place (36). Duke Richard fell at Wakefield; in the

Yorkist reading of the Law the Crown was presently forfeited by Henry, and Edward, the heir of York, had his claim acknowledged by a show of popular election which carries us back to far earlier times. The claim of Richard the Third, whatever we make of it on other grounds, was acknowledged in the like sort by what had at least the semblance of a popular Assembly (37). In short, though the hereditary principle had now taken firm root, though the disputes between the pretenders to the Crown were mainly disputes as to the right of succession, yet the remembrance of the days when the Crown had been truly the gift of the people had not wholly passed away.

The last King who could bring even the shadow of a claim to have been chosen by the voice of the people beneath the canopy of heaven was no other than Richard the Third. The last King who could bring a better claim to have been chosen by the same voice beneath the vault of the West Minster was no other than Henry the Eighth. Down to his time the old ecclesiastical form of choosing the King remained in the coronation-service, and it was not wholly out of character that Henry should issue a *congé d'élire* for his own election. The device for Henry's coronation survives in his own handwriting, and, while it contains a strong assertion of his hereditary right, it also contains a distinct provision for his election by the people in ancient form [38]. The claim of Henry was perfectly good, for a Parliament of his father's reign had declared that the Crown should abide in Henry the Seventh and the heirs of his body [39]. But it was in his case, that the hereditary and parliamentary claim was confirmed by the ancient rite of ecclesiastical election for the last time in our history. His successor was not thus distinctly chosen. This was perhaps, among other reasons, because in his case the form was specially needless. For the right of Edward the Sixth to succeed his father was beyond all dispute. By an exercise of parliamentary power, which we may well deem strange, but which was none the less lawful, Henry had been entrusted with the power of bequeathing and entailing the Crown as he thought good. That power he exercised on behalf of his own children in order, and, failing them and their issue, on the issue of his younger sister [40]. Edward, Mary, Elizabeth, therefore all reigned lawfully by virtue of their father's will. A moment's thought will show that Mary and Elizabeth could not both reign lawfully according to any doctrine of hereditary succession. On no theory, Catholic or Protestant, could both be the legitimate daughters of Henry. Parliament indeed had declared both to be illegitimate; on any theory one or the other must have been so (41). But each reigned by a perfectly lawful title, under the provisions of the Act which empowered their father to settle the succession according to his pleasure. While Elizabeth reigned, almost divine as she might be deemed to be in her own person, it was at least not held that there was any divine right in any other person to succeed her. The doctrine which came into vogue under her successors was in her day looked upon as treasonable (42). Elizabeth knew where her strength lay, and the Stewarts knew where their strength, such as it was, lay also. In the eye of the Law the first Stewart was an usurper; he occupied the Crown in the teeth of an Act of Parliament still in force, though he presently procured a fresh Act to salve over his usurpation (43). There can be no doubt that, on the death of Elizabeth, the lawful right to the Crown lay in the house of Suffolk, the descendants of Henry's younger sister Mary. But the circumstances of the time were unfavourable to their pretensions; by a tacit agreement, politically convenient, but quite in the teeth of the existing Law, the Crown silently passed to the King of Scots, the descendant of Henry's elder sister Margaret. She had not been named in Henry's entail; her descendants therefore, lineal heirs of William and Cerdic as they were, had no legal claim to the Crown, but it was passed after James was already in possession. They were therefore driven, like the Yorkists at an earlier time, to patch up the theory of the divine right of hereditary succession, in order to justify an occupation of the throne which had nothing to justify it in English Law (44).

On one memorable day a Stewart King was reminded that an English King received his right to reign from the will of the people. Whatever else we say of the nature or the acts of the tribunal before which Charles the First was arraigned, it did but assert the ancient Law of England when it told how "Charles Stewart was admitted King of England, and therein trusted with a limited power, to govern by and according to the laws of the land and not otherwise." It did but assert a principle which had been acted on on fitting occasions for nine hundred years, when it told its prisoner that "all his predecessors and he were responsible to the Commons of England." Forgetful of the fate of Sigeberht and Æthelred, of Edward and of Richard, Charles ventured to ask for precedents, and told his judges that "the Kingdom of England was hereditary and not successive" (45). After a season, the intruding dynasty passed away, on that great day when the English people exercised for the last time its ancient right of deposing and electing Kings. The

Convention of which we have so often spoken, that great Assembly, irregular in the eyes of lawyers, but in truth all the more lawful because no King's writ had summoned it, cast all fantasies and subtleties to the winds by declaring that the throne was vacant. A true Assembly of the nation once more put forth its greatest power, and chose William of Orange, as, six hundred years before, another Assembly of the nation had chosen Harold the son of Godwine. The cycle had come round, and the English people had won back again the rights which their fathers had brought with them from their old home beyond the sea. Nor was it without fitness that their choice went back to those kindred lands, and that a new William crossed the sea to undo, after so many ages, the wrongs which England had suffered from his namesake. And now, under the rule of an elective King, England could at last afford to make her Crown strictly and permanently hereditary. The Act of Settlement, as we all know, entailed the Crown on the Electress Sophia and her heirs (46). Therefore no Kings have ever reigned by a better right than those who, by virtue of that Act, have been called to reign by the direct operation of the Law. They are in truth Kings—*Cyningas* in the most ancient sense—whose power flows directly from the will of the nation. In the existing state of our institutions, the hereditary character of our modern kingship is no falling away from ancient principles; it in truth allows us to make a fuller application of them in another shape. In an early state of things no form of government is so natural as that which we find actually prevailed among our forefathers. A feeling which was not wholly sentimental demanded that the King should, under all ordinary circumstances, be the descendant of former Kings. But a sense that some personal qualification was needed required as a rule that the electors should have the right of freely choosing within the royal house. In days when Kings governed as well as reigned, such a choice, made with some regard to the personal qualities of the King chosen, was the best means for securing freedom and good government. Under the rule of a conventional constitution, when Kings reign but do not govern, when it is openly professed in the House of Commons that it is to that House that the powers of government have passed ([47]), the objects which were once best secured by making kingship elective are now best secured by making kingship hereditary. It is as the Spartan King said; by lessening the powers of the Crown, its possession has become more lasting ([48]). A political system like ours would be inconsistent with an elective kingship. An elective King could not be trusted simply to reign; he would assuredly govern, or try to govern. We need not suppose that he would attempt any breaches of the written Law. But those powers which the written Law attaches to the Crown, he would assuredly try to exercise according to his own personal views of what was right and expedient. And he would assuredly be justified in so doing. For the personal choice of a certain man to be King would in all reason be held to imply that he was personally fit for the work of government. He would be a President or Prime Minister chosen for life, and whom there would be no means of removing from office except by the most extreme and most unusual exercise of the powers of Parliament. There are states of society in which an elective Monarchy is a better kind of government than either a Commonwealth or an hereditary Monarchy. But, under the present circumstances of the civilized states of Europe and America, the choice lies between the hereditary Monarchy and the Commonwealth. The circumstances of our history have made us an hereditary Monarchy, just as the circumstances of the history of Switzerland have made that country a Federal Commonwealth. And no reasonable person will seek to disturb an institution which, like other English institutions, has grown up because it was wanted ([49]). Our unwritten Constitution, which gives us an hereditary Sovereign, but which requires his government to be carried on by Ministers who are practically chosen by the House of Commons, does in effect attain the same objects which were sought to be attained by the elective kingship of our forefathers. Our system gives the state a personal chief, a personal embodiment of the national being, which draws to itself those feelings of personal homage and personal duty which a large class of mankind find it hard to look upon as due to the more abstract ideas of Law and Commonwealth. And, when the duties of constitutional royalty are discharged as our own experience tells us that they may be discharged, the feeling awakened is more than a mere sentiment; it is a rational feeling of genuine personal respect. But widely as the hereditary kingship of our latest times differs in outward form from the hereditary kingship of our earliest times, the two have points of likeness which are not shared by kingship in the form which it took in the ages between the two. In our earliest and in our latest system, the King exists for the sake of the people; in the intermediate times it sometimes seemed that the people existed for the sake of the King. In our earliest and in our latest system, the King is clothed with an office, the duties of which are to be discharged for the common good of all. In the intermediate times it sometimes seemed as if the King had been made master of a possession, which was to be enjoyed for his personal pleasure and profit. In the intermediate times we constantly hear of the rights and powers of the Crown as something distinct from, and almost hostile to, the common rights of the people. In our earliest and in our latest times, the rights of the Crown and the rights of the people are the same, for it is allowed that the powers of the Crown are to be exercised for the welfare of the people by the advice and consent of the people or their representatives. Without indulging in any Utopian dreams, without picturing to ourselves the England of a thousand years back as an earthly paradise, the voice of sober history does assuredly teach us that those distant times have really much that is in common with our own, much in which we are really nearer to them than to times which, in a mere reckoning of years, are far less distant from us. Thus it is that the cycle has come round, that the days of foreign rule have been wiped out, and that England is England once again. Our present Sovereign reigns by as good a right as Ælfred or Harold, for she reigns by the same right by which they reigned, by the will of the people, embodied in the Act of Parliament which made the crown of Ælfred and Harold hereditary in her ancestress. And, reigning by the same right by which they reigned, she reigns also for the same ends, for the common good of the nation of which the Law has made her the head. And we can wish nothing better for her kingdom than that the Crown which she so lawfully holds, which she has so worthily worn among two generations of her people, she may, like Nestor of old, continue to wear amid the well-deserved affection of a third ([50]).

NOTES.

CHAPTER I.

(1) What I say of Uri and the other democratic Cantons must not be misunderstood, as if I all accepted the now exploded dreams which made out the *Waldstädte* or Forest Cantons to have had some special origin, and some special independence, apart from the rest of Germany. The researches of modern scholars have shown, not only that the Forest Cantons were members of the Empire like their neighbours, but that various lesser lords, spiritual and temporal, held different rights within them. Their acquisition of perfect independence, even their deliverance from other lords and promotion to the state of *Reichsunmittelbarkeit* or immediate dependence on the Empire, was a work of time. Thus Uri itself, or part of it, was granted in 853 by Lewis the German to the Abbey of Nuns (*Fraumünster*) in Zürich, and it was not till 1231 that its independence of any lord but the Emperor was formally acknowledged. But the universal supremacy of the Empire in no way interfered with the internal constitution of any district, city, or principality; nor was such interference necessarily implied even in subjection to some intermediate lord. The rule of a female monastery especially would be very light. And from the earliest times we find both the men of Uri in general and the men of

particular parts of the district (*Gemeinden*, *Communes*, or parishes) spoken of as communities capable of acting together, and even of treating with those who claimed to be their masters. ("Nos inhabitantes Uroniam" appear in a deed of 955 as capable of making an agreement with the officer of the Abbey at Zürich.) All this is in no way peculiar to the Forest Cantons; it is no more than what we find everywhere; what is peculiar is that, whereas elsewhere the old local communities gradually died out, in the Forest Cantons they lived and flourished, and gained new rights and powers till they grew into absolutely independent commonwealths. I think therefore that I have a right to speak of the democracy of Uri as immemorial. It is not immemorial in its fully developed shape, but that fully developed shape grew step by step out of earlier forms which are strictly immemorial and common to the whole Teutonic race.

On the early history of the democratic Cantons, a subject than which none has been more thoroughly misunderstood, I am not able to point to any one trustworthy work in English. Among the writings of Swiss scholars—shut up for the most part from readers of other nations in the inaccessible Transactions of local Societies—there is a vast literature on the subject, of the whole of which I am far from pretending to be master. But I may refer to the *Essai sur l'Etat des Personnes et la Condition des Terres dans le Pays d'Ury au XIIIe Siècle*, by the Baron Frederick de Gingins-la-Sarraz, in the *Archiv für schweizerische Geschichte*, i. 17; to Dr. J. R. Burckhardt's *Untersuchungen über die erste Bevölkerung des Alpengebirgs* in the same collection, iv. 3; to the early chapters of the great work of Bluntschli, *Geschichte des schweizerischen Bundesrechtes* (Zürich, 1849), and of Blumer's *Staats- und Rechtsgeschichte der schweizerischen*

Demokratien (St. Gallen, 1850); to Dr. Alfons Huber, *Die Waldstaette* (Innsbruck, 1861), and Dr. Wilhelm Vischer, *Die Sage von der Befreiung der Waldstädte* (Leipzig, 1867). Dr. H. von Liebenau, in *Die Tell-Sage zu dem Jahre* 1230, takes a line of his own. The results of the whole inquiry will be found in the most accessible form in M. Albert Rilliet's *Les Origines de la Confédération Suisse* (Genève et Bâle, 1868).

(2) Individual Swiss mercenaries may doubtless still be found in foreign armies, as Italy some years back knew to her cost. But the Federal Constitution of 1848 altogether swept away the system of military capitulations which used to be publicly entered into by the Cantons.

(3) See Johannes von Müller, *Geschichte der schweizerische Eidgenossenschaft*, Book v., c. 1 (vol. xvi. p. 25, of his *sämmtliche Werke*, Stuttgart und Tübingen, 1832, and the note in vol. xxii. p. 14; or the French translation, vol. viii. p. 35: Paris and Geneva, 1840). The description in Peterman Etterlin's Chronicle, p. 204 (Basel, 1752), is worth quoting in the original. "Dann do der Hertzog von Burgunn gesach den züg den berg ab züchen, schein die sunn gerad in sy, und glitzet als wie ein spiegel, des gelichen lüyet das horn von Ury, ouch die harschorne von Lutzern, und was ein sölich toffen, das des Hertzogen von Burgunn lüt ein grusen darab entpfiengent, und trattent hinder sich."

(4) The magistrates rode when I was present at the Landesgemeinden of 1863 and 1864. I trust that so good a custom has not passed away.

(5) On the character and position of Phôkiôn, see Grote, xi. 382, xii. 481; and on the general question of the alleged fickleness of the Athenian people, see iv. 496.

(6) Some years ago I went through all the elections to the *Bundesrath* or Executive Council in Switzerland, and found that in eighteen years it had only twice happened that a member of the Council seeking re-election had failed to obtain it. I therefore think that I was right in congratulating a member of the Federal Council, whom I had the pleasure of meeting last year, on being a member of the most permanent government in Europe.

(7) Under the so-called Helvetic Republic of 1798, the Cantons ceased to be sovereign States, and became mere divisions, like counties or departments. One of the earliest provisions of this constitution abolishes the ancient democracies of the Forest Cantons. "Die Regierungsform, wenn sie auch sollte verändert werden, soll allezeit eine repräsentative Demokratie sein." (See the text in Bluntschli, ii. 305. The "repräsentative Demokratie" thus forced on these ancient commonwealths by the sham democrats of Paris was meant to exclude the pure democracy of Athens and Uri.

The Federal system was in some sort restored by the Act of Mediation (*Vermittlungsakte*) of Napoleon Buonaparte, when First Consul in 1803. See the text in Bluntschli, ii. 322.

(8) Appenzell, though its history had long been connected with that of the Confederates, was not actually admitted as a Canton till December 1513, being the youngest of the thirteen Cantons which formed the Confederation down to 1798. See Zellweger, *Geschichte des Appenzellischen Volkes,* ii. 366, and the text in his *Urkunden,* ii. part 2, p. 481, or in the older *Appenzeller Chronick* of Walser (Saint Gallen, 1740), 410, and the Act in his *Anhang,* p. 18. The frontispiece of this volume contains a lively picture of a *Landesgemeinde.* In 1597 the Canton was divided into the two Half-

cantons of *Ausser-Rhoden*, Protestant, and *Inner-Rhoden*, Catholic. See Zellweger, iii. part 2, p. 160; Walser, 553.

(9) On armed assemblies see Norman Conquest, ii. 331.

(10) I perhaps need hardly insist on this point after the references given in my first note; but I find it constantly needful to explain that there is no such thing as a Swiss *nation* in any but a political sense. The Cantons were simply members of the Empire which gradually won a greater independence than their fellows. And the Forest Cantons, and the German-speaking Swiss generally, do not even form a distinct part of the German nation; they are simply three settlements of the Alemanni, just as the three divisions of Lincolnshire are three settlements of the Angles.

(11) The earliest instance that I know of the use of the word *Englaland* is in the Treaty with Olaf and Justin in 991. Its earliest use in the English Chronicles is in 1014. See Norman Conquest, i. 78, 276, 605, 629. The oldest use that I know of the name Yorkshire (*Eoforwicscīr*) is in the Chronicles under 1065. See Norman Conquest, ii. 478. Deira is, of course, as old as Gregory the Great's pun.

(12) The real history of English parishes has yet to be worked out. I feel sure that they will be found to have much more in common with the continental *Gemeinden* than would seem at first sight. Some hints may be found in a little pamphlet which I lately came across, called "The Parish in History."

(13) The nature of democracy is set forth by Periklês in the Funeral Oration, Thucydides, ii. 37: ὄνομα μὲν διὰ τὸ μὴ ἐς ὀλίγους ἀλλ' ἐς πλείονας οἰκεῖν δημοκρατία κέκληται· μέτεστι δὲ κατὰ μὲν τοὺς νόμους πρὸς τὰ ἴδια διάφορα πᾶσι τὸ ἴσον, κατὰ δὲ τὴν ἀξίωσιν ὡς ἕκαστος ἐν τῷ εὐδοκιμεῖ. It is set

forth still more clearly by Athênagoras of Syracuse, vi. 39, where the functions of different classes in a democracy are clearly distinguished: *ἐγὼ δέ φημι πρῶτα μὲν δῆμον ξύμπαν ὠνομάσθαι, ὀλιγαρχίαν δὲ μέρος, ἔπειτα φύλακας μὲν ἀρίστους εἶναι χρημάτων τοὺς πλουσίους, βουλεῦσαι δ' ἂν βέλτιστα τοὺς ξυνετοὺς, κρῖναι δ' ἂν ἀκούσαντας ἄριστα τοὺς πολλοὺς, καὶ ταῦτα ὁμοίως καὶ κατὰ μέρη καὶ ξύμπαντα ἐν δημοκρατίᾳ ἰσομοιρεῖν.* Here a distinct sphere is assigned both to wealth and to special intelligence. Nearly the same division is drawn by a writer who might by comparison be called aristocratic. Isokratês (Areop. 29) holds that the management of public affairs should be immediately in the hands of the men of wealth and leisure, who should act as servants of the People, the People itself being their master—or, as he does not scruple to say, *Tyrant*—with full power of reward and punishment: *ἐκεῖνοι διεγνωκότες ἦσαν ὅτι δεῖ τὸν μὲν δῆμον ὥσπερ τύραννον καθιστάναι τὰς ἀρχὰς καὶ κολάζειν τοὺς ἐξαμαρτάνοντας καὶ κρίνειν περὶ τῶν ἀμφισβητουμένων, τοὺς δὲ σχολὴν ἄγειν δυναμένους καὶ βίον ἱκανὸν κεκτημένους ἐπιμελεῖσθαι τῶν κοινῶν ὥσπερ οἰκέτας, καὶ δικαίους μὲν γενομένους ἐπαινεῖσθαι καὶ στέργειν ταύτῃ τῇ τιμῇ, κακῶς δὲ διοικήσαντας μηδεμιᾶς συγγνώμης τυγχάνειν, ἀλλὰ ταῖς μεγίσταις ζημίαις περιπίπτειν.* This he elsewhere (Panath 166) calls democracy with a mixture of aristocracy—not oligarchy (*τὴν δημοκρατίαν τὴν ἀριστοκρατίᾳ μεμιγμένην*).

The unfavourable meaning which is often attached to the word democracy, when it does not arise from simple ignorance, probably arises from the use of the word by Aristotle. He makes (Politics, iii. 7) three lawful forms of government, *kingship* (*βασιλεία*), *aristocracy* (*ἀριστοκρατία*), and what he calls specially *πολιτεία* or *commonwealth.* Of these he makes three corruptions *tyranny, oligarchy,* and *democracy* (*τυραν-*

νίς, ὀλιγαρχία, δημοκρατία), defining *democracy* to be a government carried on for the special benefit of the poor (πρὸς τὸ συμφέρον τὸ τῶν ἀπόρων). In this there is something of a philosopher's contempt for all popular government, and it is certain that Aristotle's way of speaking is not that which is usual in the Greek historians. Polybios, like Herodotus and Thucydides, uses the word democracy in the old honourable sense, and he takes (ii. 38) as his special type of democracy the constitution of the Achaian League, which certainly had in it a strong element of practical aristocracy (see History of Federal Government, cap. v.): ἰσηγορίας καὶ παρρησίας καὶ καθόλου δημοκρατίας ἀληθινῆς σύστημα καὶ προαίρεσιν εἰλικρινεστέραν οὐκ ἂν εὕροι τις τῆς παρὰ τοῖς Ἀχαιοῖς ὑπαρχούσης. In short, what Aristotle calls πολιτεία Polybios calls δημοκρατία; what Aristotle calls δημοκρατία Polybios calls ὀχλοκρατία.

(14) It follows that, when the commonwealth of Florence disfranchised the whole of the noble families, it lost its right to be called a democracy. See the passing of the Ordinance of Justice in Sismondi, Républiques Italiennes, iv. 65; Chroniche di Giovanni Villani, viii. 1.

(15) On Slavery in England, see Norman Conquest, i. 81, 333, 368, 432, iv. 385. For fuller accounts, see Kemble's Saxons in England, i. 185; Zöpfl, *Geschichte der deutschen Rechtsinstitute*, 62. The three classes of nobles, common freemen, and slaves cannot be better set forth than in the Life of Saint Lebuin (Pertz, ii. 361): "Sunt denique ibi, qui illorum lingua edlingi, sunt qui frilingi, sunt qui lassi dicuntur, quod in Latina sonat lingua, nobiles, ingenuiles, atque serviles."

(16) On the *Wite-þeow*, the slave reduced to slavery for his crimes, see Kemble, Saxons in England, i. 200. He

is mentioned several times in the laws of Ine, 24, 48, 54, where, as usual in the West-Saxon laws, a distinction is drawn between the English and the Welsh *wite-þeow.* The second reference contains a provision for the case of a newly enslaved *þeow* who should be charged with a crime committed before he was condemned to slavery.

(17) I wish to leave the details of Eastern matters to Eastern scholars. But there are several places in the Old Testament where we see something very much like a general assembly, combined with distinctions of rank among its members, and with the supremacy of a single chief over all.

(18) Iliad, xx. 4.

Ζεὺς δὲ Θέμιστα κέλευσε θεοὺς ἀγορήνδε καλέσσαι
Κρατὸς ἀπ' Οὐλύμποιο πολυπτύχου· ἡ δ' ἄρα πάντη
Φοιτήσασα κέλευσε Διὸς πρὸς δῶμα νέεσθαι.
Οὔτε τις οὖν Ποταμῶν ἀπέην, νόσφ' Ὠκεανοῖο,
Οὔτ' ἄρα Νυμφάων ταί τ' ἄλσεα καλὰ νέμονται,
Καὶ πηγὰς ποταμῶν, καὶ πίσεα ποιήεντα.

Besides the presence of the Nymphs in the divine *Mycel Gemôt,* something might also be said about the important position of Hêrê, Athênê, and other female members of the inner council.

We find the mortal Assembly described at length in the second book of the Iliad, and indeed by implication at the very beginning of the first book.

(19) We hear the applause of the assembly in i. 23 and ii. 333, and in the Trojan Assembly, xviii. 313.

(20) On the whole nature of the Homeric ἀγορή see Gladstone's Homer and the Homeric Age, iii. 14. Mr. Gladstone has to my thinking understood the spirit of the old Greek polity much better than Mr. Grote.

(21) There is no need to go into any speculations as to the early Roman Constitution, as to the origin of the distinction of *patres* and *plebs*, or any of the other points about which controversies have raged among scholars. The three elements stand out in every version, legendary and historical In Livy, i. 8, Romulus first holds his general Assembly and then chooses his Senate. And in c. 26 we get the distinct appeal from the King, or rather from the magistrates acting by his authority, to an Assembly which, whatever might be its constitution, is more popular than the Senate.

(22) It is hardly needful to show how the Roman Consuls simply stepped into the place of the Kings. It is possible, as some have thought, that the revolution threw more power into patrician hands than before, but at all events the Senate and the Assembly go on just as before.

(23) Tacitus, de Moribus Germaniæ, c. 7—13:

"Reges ex nobilitate; Duces ex virtute sumunt. Nec Regibus infinita aut libera potestas; et Duces exemplo potius quam imperio: si prompti, si conspicui, si ante aciem agant, admiratione præsunt. . . . . De minoribus rebus Principes consultant; de majoribus omnes; ita tamen ut ea quoque quorum penes plebem arbitrium est apud Principes pertractentur. . . . . Ut turbæ placuit, considunt armati. Silentium per Sacerdotes, quibus tum et coercendi jus est, imperatur. Mox Rex, vel Princeps, prout ætas cuique, prout nobilitas, prout decus bellorum, prout facundia est audiuntur, auctoritate suadendi magis quam jubendi pote tate. Si displicuit sententia, fremitu adspernantur; sin placuit, frameas concutiunt. Honoratissimum adsensûs genus est, armis laudare. Licet apud concilium adcusare quoque et discrimen capitis intendere. . . . . Eliguntur in iisdem conciliis et Principes, qui jura per pagos vicosque reddant. Centeni singulis ex plebe comites, consilium simul et auctoritas, adsunt. Nihil autem neque publicæ neque privatæ rei nisi armati agunt."

For a commentary, see Zöpfl, *Geschichte der deutschen Rechtsinstitute*, p. 94. See also Allen, Royal Prerogative, 12, 162.

(24) See Norman Conquest, i. 95. The primitive Constitution lasted longest at the other end of the Empire, in Friesland. See Eichhorn, *Deutsche Staats- und Rechtsgeschichte*, ii. 265, iii. 158. Zöpfl, *Geschichte der deutschen Rechtsquellen*, p. 154.

(25) Τὰ ἀρχαῖα ἤθη κρατείτω is an ecclesiastical maxim; rightly understood, it is just as true in politics.

(26) See my papers on "the Origin of the English Nation" and "the Alleged Permanence of Roman Civilization in England" in Macmillan's Magazine, 1870.

(27) See Schmid, *Gesetze der Angel-Sachsen*, on the words "*wealh*" and "*wylne*." Earle, Philology of the English Tongue, 318. On the fact that the English settlers brought their women with them, see Historical Essays, p. 36.

(28) On *Eorlas* and *Ceorlas* I have said something in the History of the Norman Conquest, i. 80. See the two words in Schmid, and the references there given.

(29) On the Barons of Attinghausen, see Blumer, *Staats- und Rechtsgeschichte der schweizerischen Demokratien*, i. 122, 214, 272.

(30) I cannot at this moment lay my hand on my authority for this curious, and probably mythical, custom, but it is equally good as an illustration any way.

(31) This custom is described by Diodôros, i. 70. The priest first recounted the good deeds of the King and attributed to him all possible virtues; then he invoked a curse for whatever has been done wrongfully, absolving the King from all blame and praying that the vengeance might fall on his ministers who had suggested evil things (τὸ τελευταῖον ὑπὲρ τῶν ἀγνοουμένων ἀρὰν ἐποιεῖτο, τὸν μὲν βασιλέα τῶν ἐγκλημάτων ἐξαιρούμενος, εἰς δὲ τοὺς ὑπηρετοῦντας καὶ διδάξαντας τὰ φαῦλα καὶ τὴν βλαβὴν καὶ τὴν τιμωρίαν ἀξιῶν ἀποσκῆψαι). He wound up with some moral and religious advice.

(32) Tacitus (Germ. 25) distinguishes "eæ gentes quæ regnantur" from others. And in 43 he speaks of "erga Reges obsequium" as characteristic of some particular tribes: see Norman Conquest, i. 579.

(33) On the use of the words *Ealdorman* and *Heretoga*, see Norman Conquest, i. 581, and the references there given.

(34) See Norman Conquest, i. 583, and the passages in Kemble and Allen there referred to.

(35) See Kemble's Saxons in England, i. 152, and Massmann's Ulfilas, 744.

(36) See the words *driht, drihten* in Bosworth's Anglo-Saxon Dictionary.

(37) To say nothing of other objections to this derivation, its author must have fancied that *ing* and not *end* was the ending of the Old-English participle. The mistake is as old as Sir Thomas Smith. See his Commonwealth of England, p. 12.

(38) See Norman Conquest, i. 583, and the passages there quoted. I am afraid of meddling with Sanscrit, but it strikes me that the views of Allen and Kemble are not

inconsistent with a connexion with the Sanscrit *Ganaka*. As one of the curiosities of etymology, it is worth noticing that Mr. Wedgwood makes the word "probably identical with Tartar *chan*."

(39) We read in the Chronicles, 449, how, on the first Jutish landing in Kent, "heora *heretogan* wæron twegen gebroðra Hengest and Horsa." It is only in 455, on the death of Horsa, that "æfter þam Hengest feng to *rice* and Æsc his sunu"; and in 488, seemingly on the death of Hengest, "Æsc feng to *rice* and was xxiiii wintra Cantwara *cyning*." So among the West-Saxons, in 495, "coman twegen *ealdormen* on Brytene, Cerdic and Cynric his sunu." It is only in 519 that we read "her Cerdic and Cynric West-Sexena *rice* onfengun."

(40) The distinction between Kings and Jarls comes out very strongly in the account of the battle of Ashdown (Æscesdune) in the Chronicles in 871. The Danes "wæron on twam gefylcum, on oþrum wæs Bagsecg and Healfdene, þa hæðenan *cingas* and on oðrum wæron þa *eorlas*." It may be marked that in the English army King Æthelred is set against the Danish Kings, and his brother the Ætheling Ælfred against the Jarls. So in the Song of Brunanburh we read of the five Kings and seven Jarls who were slain.

"Fife lagon sweordum aswefede,
on ðæm campstede swilce seofone eac
ciningas geonge, eorlas Anlafes."

We may mark that the Kings were young, as if they had been chosen "ex nobilitate;" nothing is said of the age of the Jarls, who were doubtless chosen "ex virtute."

(41) I have quoted the passage from Bæda about the satraps in Norman Conquest, i. 579. The passage in the

Life of Saint Lebuin, quoted in note 15, also speaks of "principes" as presiding over the several *pagi* or *gauen*, but he speaks of no King or other common chief over the whole country. And this is the more to be marked, as there was a "generale concilium" of the whole Old-Saxon nation, formed, as we are told, of twelve chosen men from each *gau*. This looks like an early instance of representation, but it should be remembered that we are here dealing with a constitution strictly Federal.

In the like sort we find the rulers of the West-Goths at the time of their crossing the Danube spoken of as *Judices*. See Ammianus, xxvii. 5, and the notes of Lindenbrog and Valesius. So also Gibbon, c. xxv. (iv. 305, ed. Milman). So Jornandes (26) speaks of "primates eorum, et duces, qui regum vice illis præerant." Presently he calls Fredigern "Gothorum regulus," like the *subreguli* or *under-cyningas* of our own History. Presently in c. 28 Athanaric, the successor of Fredigern, is pointedly called *Rex*.

On all this, see Allen, Royal Prerogative, 163.

(42) See Norman Conquest, i. 75, 580.

(43) The best instance in English History of the process by which a kingdom changed into a province, by going through the intermediate stage of a half-independent Ealdormanship, is to be found in the history of South-Western Mercia under its Ealdorman Æthelred and the Lady Æthelflæd, in the reigns of Ælfred and Eadward the Elder. See Norman Conquest, i. 563.

(44) See Norman Conquest, i. 39, 78.

(45) Iliad, ix. 160 :—

καί μοι ὑποστήτω, ὅσσον βασιλεύτερός εἰμι.

(46) The instances in which a great kingdom has been broken up into a number of small states practically independent, but owning a nominal superiority in the successor of the original Sovereign, are not few. In the case of the Empire I have found something to say about it in my Historical Essays, 151, and in the case of the Caliphate in my History and Conquest of the Saracens, 137. How the same process took place with the Mogul Empire in India is set forth by Lord Macaulay in his Essays on Lord Clive and Warren Hastings. But he should not have compared the great Mogul, with his nominal sovereignty, to "the most helpless driveller among the later Carlovingians," a class whom Sir Francis Palgrave has rescued from undeserved contempt. But the breaking up of the Western Kingdom is none the less an example of the same law. The most remarkable thing is the way, or rather the three different ways, in which the scattered members have been brought together again in Germany, Italy, and France.

This process of dismemberment, where a nominal supremacy is still kept by the original Sovereign, must be distinguished from that of falling back upon Dukes or Ealdormen after a period of kingly rule. In this latter case it would seem that no central sovereignty went on.

(47) At this time of day I suppose it is hardly necessary to prove the elective character of Old-English kingship. I have said what I have to say about it in Norman Conquest, i. 106, 596. But I may quote one most remarkable passage from the report made in 787 to Pope Hadrian the First by George and Theophylact, his Legates in England (Haddan and Stubbs, Councils and Ecclesiastical Documents, iii. 453). "Sanximus ut in ordinatione Regum nullus permittat pravorum prævalere assensum: sed legitime Reges a sacerdotibus et senioribus populi eligantur." One would like to know who

the "pravi" here denounced were. The passage sounds very like a narrowing of the franchise or some other interference with freedom of election, but in any case it bears witness to the elective character of our ancient kingship, and to the general popular character of the constitution.

(48) I have described the powers of the Witan, as I understand them and as they were understood by Mr. Kemble, at vol. i. p. 108, of the History of the Norman Conquest and in some of the Appendices to that volume. With regard to the powers of the Witan, I find no difference between my own views and those of Professor Stubbs in the Introductory Sketch to his Select Charters (p. 11), where the relations between the King and the Witan, and the general character of our ancient constitution, are set forth with wonderful power and clearness. But I find Mr. Stubbs and myself differing altogether as to the constitution of the Witenagemót. I look upon it as an Assembly of the whole kingdom, after the type of the smaller assemblies of the shire and other lesser divisions. Mr. Stubbs fully admits the popular character of the smaller assemblies, but denies any such character to the national gathering. It is dangerous to set oneself up against the greatest master of English constitutional history, but I must ask the reader to weigh what I say in note Q in the Appendix to my first volume.

(49) I have collected some of the instances of deposition in Northumberland in the note following that on the constitution of the Witenagemót. (Norman Conquest, i. 593.) It is not at all unlikely that the report of George and Theophylact quoted above may have a special reference to the frequent changes among the Northumbrian Kings.

(50) I have mentioned all the instances at vol. i. p. 105 of the Norman Conquest. Sigeberht, Æthelred, Harthacnut,

Edward the Second, Richard the Second, James the Second. It is remarkable that nearly all are the second of their respective names; for, besides Æthelred, Edward, Richard, and James, Harthacnut might fairly be called Cnut the Second.

(51) Tacitus, De Moribus Germaniæ, 13, 14:—"Nec rubor inter comites adspici. Gradus quinetiam et ipse comitatus habet, judicio ejus quem sectantur; magnaque et comitum æmulatio quibus primus apud Principem suum locus; et Principum cui plurimi et acerrimi comites. . . . Quum ventum in aciem, turpe Principi virtute vinci, turpe comitatui virtutem Principis non adæquare. Jam vero infame in omnem vitam ac probrosum, superstitem Principi suo ex acie recessisse. Illum defendere, tueri, sua quoque fortia facta gloriæ ejus adsignare, præcipuum sacramentum est. Principes pro victoria pugnant; comites pro Principe." See Allen, Royal Prerogative, 142.

(52) The original text of the Song of Maldon will be found in Thorpe's Analecta Anglo-Saxonica. My extracts are made from the modern English version which I attempted in my Old-English History, p. 192. I went on the principle of altering the Old-English text no more than was actually necessary to make it intelligible. When a word has altogether dropped out of our modern language, I have of course changed it; when a word is still in use, in however different a sense, I have kept it. Many words which were anciently used in a physical sense are now used only metaphorically; thus "cringe" is used in one of the extracts in its primary meaning of bowing or falling down, and therefore of dying.

(53) The history of the Roman clientship is another of those points on which legend and history and ingenious modern

speculation all come to much the same, as far as our present purpose is concerned. Whether the clients were the same as the *plebs* or not, at any rate no patricians entered into the client relation, and this at once supplies the contrast with Teutonic institutions.

(54) The title of *dominus*, implying a master of slaves, was always refused by the early Emperors. This is recorded of Augustus by Suetonius (Aug. 53) and Dion (lv. 12), and still more distinctly of Tiberius (Suetonius, Tib. 27; Dion, lvii. 8). Tiberius also refused the title of *Imperator*, except in its strictly military sense: οὔτε γὰρ δεσπότην ἑαυτὸν τοῖς ἐλευθέροις οὔτε αὐτοκράτορα πλὴν τοῖς στρατιώταις καλεῖν ἐφίει. Caius is said (Aurelius Victor, Cæs. xxxix. 4) to have been called *dominus*, and there is no doubt about Domitian (Suetonius, Dom. 13; Dion, lxvii. 13, where see Reimar's Note). Pliny in his letters constantly addresses Trajan as *dominus*; yet in his Panegyric (45) he draws the marked distinction: "Scis, ut sunt diversa natura dominatio et principatus, ita non aliis esse principem gratiorem quam qui maxime dominum graventur." This marks the return to older feelings and customs under Trajan. The final and formal establishment of the title seems to have come in with the introduction of Eastern ceremonies under Diocletian (see the passage already referred to in Aurelius Victor). It is freely used by the later Panegyrists, as for instance Eumenius, iv. 21, v. 13: "Domine Constanti," "Domine Maximiane, Imperator æterne," and so forth.

(55) Vitellius (Tac. Hist. i. 58) was the first to employ Roman knights in offices hitherto always filled by freedmen; but the system was not fully established till the time of Hadrian (Spartianus, Hadrian, 22).

(56) See Norman Conquest, i. 89, 587, and the passages here quoted.

(57) Both *hláford* and *hlæfdige* (*Lord* and *Lady*) are very puzzling words as to the origin of their later syllables. It is enough for my purpose if the connexion of the first syllable with *hláf* be allowed. Different as is the origin of the two words, *hlaford* always translates *dominus*. The French *seigneur*, and the corresponding forms in Italian and Spanish, come from the Latin *senior*, used as equivalent to *dominus*. This is one of the large class of words which are analogous to our *Ealdorman*.

(58) This is fully treated by Palgrave, English Commonwealth, i. 350, 495, 505.

(59) On the change from the *alod*, *odal*, or *eðel*, a man's very own property, to the land held of a lord, see Hallam, Middle Ages, i. 113.

(60) See Norman Conquest, i. 85—88. I have there chiefly followed Mr. Kemble in his chapter on the Noble by Service, Saxons in England, i. 162.

(61) See the whole history and meaning of the word in the article *þegen* in Schmid's Glossary.

(62) See Norman Conquest, i. 89.

(63) Barbour, Bruce, i. 224:

"A! fredome is A noble thing."

So said Herodotus (v. 78) long before;

ἡ ἰσηγορίη ὡς ἔστι χρῆμα σπουδαῖον.

CHAPTER II.

(1) In the great poetical manifesto of the patriotic party in Henry the Third's reign, printed in Wright's Political Songs of England (Camden Society, 1839), there seems to be no demand whatever for new laws, but only for the declaration and observance of the old. Thus, the passage which I have chosen for my motto, runs on thus :—

"Igitur communitas regni consulatur ;
Et quid universitas sentiat sciatur,
Cui leges propriæ maxime sunt notæ.
Nec cuncti provinciæ sic sunt idiotæ,
Quin sciant plus cæteris regni sui mores,
Quos relinquant posteris hii qui sunt priores.
Qui reguntur legibus magis ipsas sciunt ;
Quorum sunt in usibus plus periti fiunt ;
Et quia res agitur sua, plus curabunt,
Et quo pax adquiritur sibi procurabunt."

(2) On the renewal of the Laws of Eadward by William, see Norman Conquest, iv. 324. Stubbs, Documents, 25. It should be marked that the Laws of Eadward were again confirmed by Henry the First (see Stubbs, 90—99), and, as the Great Charter grew out of the Charter of Henry the First produced by Archbishop Stephen Langton in 1213, the descent of the Charter from the Laws of Eadward is very simple. See Roger of Wendover, iii. 263 (ed. Coxe). The Primate there distinctly says that he had made John swear to renew the Laws of Eadward. "Audistis quomodo, tempore quo apud Wintoniam Regem absolvi, ipsum jurare compulerim,

quod leges iniquas destrueret et leges bonas, videlicet leges Eadwardi, revocaret et in regno faceret ab omnibus observari." It must be remembered that the phrase of the Laws of Eadward or of any other King does not really mean a code of laws of that King's drawing up, but simply the way of administering the Law, and the general political condition, which existed in that King's reign. This is all that would be meant by the renewal of the Laws of Eadward in William's time. It simply meant that William was to rule as his English predecessors had ruled before him. But, by the time of John, men had no doubt begun to look on the now canonized Eadward as a lawgiver, and to fancy that there was an actual code of laws of his to be put in force.

On the various confirmations of the Great Charter, see Hallam, Middle Ages, ii. 111.

(3) Macaulay, ii. 660. "When they were told that there was no precedent for declaring the throne vacant, they produced from among the records of the Tower a roll of parchment, near three hundred years old, on which, in quaint characters and barbarous Latin, it was recorded that the Estates of the Realm had declared vacant the throne of a perfidious and tyrannical Plantagenet." See more at large in the debate of the conference between the Houses, ii. 645.

(4) See Kemble, Saxons in England, ii. 186—194. This, it will be remembered, is admitted by Professor Stubbs. See above, note 48 to Chapter I.

(5) See Kemble, ii. 199, 200, and compare page 187.

(6) I have collected these passages in my History of the Norman Conquest, i. 591.

(7) On the acclamations of the Assembly, see note 19 to Chapter I. I suspect that in all early assemblies, and not in that of Sparta only, κρίνουσι βοῇ καὶ οὐ ψήφῳ (Thuc. i. 87). We still retain the custom in the cry of "Aye" and "No," from which the actual vote is a mere appeal, just as the division ordered by Sthenelaïdas when he professed not to know on which side the shout was.

(8) See Norman Conquest, i. 100, and History of Federal Government, i. 263.

(9) See Norman Conquest, iv. 694. In this case the Chronicler, under the year 1086, distinguishes two classes in the Assembly, "his witan and ealle þa landsittende men þe ahtes wæron ofer eall Engleland." These "landsittende men" were evidently the forerunners of the "libere tenentes," who, whether their holdings were great or small, kept their place in the early Parliaments. See Hallam, ii. 140—146, where will be found many passages showing the still abiding traces of the popular constitution of the Assembly.

(10) The practice of summoning particular persons can be traced up to very early times. See Kemble, ii. 202, for instances in the reign of Æthelstan. On its use in later times, see Hallam, ii. 254—260; and on the irregularity in the way of summoning the spiritual peers, ii. 253.

The bearing of these precedents on the question of life peerages will be seen by any one who goes through Sir T. E. May's summary, Constitutional History, i. 291—298.

(11) Sismondi, Histoire des Français, v. 289: "Ce roi, le plus absolu entre ceux qui ont porté la couronne de France, le moins occupé du bien de ses peuples, le moins consciencieux

dans son observation des droits établis avant lui, est cependant le restaurateur des assemblées populaires de la France, et l'auteur de la représentation des communes dans les états généraux." See Historical Essays, 45.

(12) See the history of Stephen Martel in Sismondi, Histoire des Français, vol. vi. cap. viii. ix., and the account of the dominion of the Butchers, vii. 259, and more at large in Thierry's History of the Tiers-État, capp. ii. iii.

(13) The Parliament of Paris, though it had its use as some small check on the mere despotism of the Crown, can hardly come under the head of free institutions. France, as France, under the old state of things, cannot be said to have kept any free institutions at all; the only traces of freedom were to be found in the local Estates which still met in several of the provinces. See De Tocqueville, Ancien Régime, 347.

(14) The thirteenth century was the time when most of the existing states and nations of Europe took something like their present form and constitution. The great powers which had hitherto, in name at least, divided the Christian and Mahometan world, the Eastern and Western Empires and the Eastern and Western Caliphates, may now be looked on as practically coming to an end. England, France, and Spain began to take something like their present shape, and to show the beginnings of the characteristic position and policy of each. The chief languages of Western Europe assumed something like their present shape. In short, the character of this age as a time of beginnings and endings might be traced out in detail through the most part of Europe and Asia.

(15) Dr. Pauli does not scruple to give him this title in

his admirable monograph, "*Simon von Montfort Graf von Leicester, der Schöpfer des Hauses der Gemeinen.*" The career of the Earl should be studied in this work, and in Mr. Blaauw's "Barons' War."

(16) "Numquam libertas gratior exstat
Quam sub rege pio."—Claudian, ii. Cons. Stil. 114.

(17) Macaulay, i. 15. "England owes her escape from such calamities to an event which her historians have generally represented as disastrous. Her interest was so directly opposed to the interest of her rulers that she had no hope but in their errors and misfortunes. The talents and even the virtues of her six first French Kings were a curse to her. The follies and vices of the seventh were her salvation. . . . England, which, since the battle of Hastings, had been ruled generally by wise statesmen, always by brave soldiers, fell under the dominion of a trifler and a coward. From that moment her prospects brightened. John was driven from Normandy. The Norman nobles were compelled to make their election between the island and the continent. Shut up by the sea with the people whom they had hitherto oppressed and despised, they gradually came to regard England as their country, and the English as their countrymen. The two races so long hostile, soon found that they had common interests and common enemies. Both were alike aggrieved by the tyranny of a bad King. Both were alike indignant at the favour shown by the court to the natives of Poitou and Aquitaine. The great grandsons of those who had fought under William and the great grandsons of those who had fought under Harold began to draw near to each other in friendship; and the

first pledge of their reconciliation was the Great Charter, won by their united exertions, and framed for their common benefit."

(18) I have tried to work out the gradual character of the transfer of lands and offices under William in various parts of the fourth volume of my History of the Norman Conquest; see especially p. 22, et seqq. The popular notion of a general scramble for everything gives a most false view of William's whole character and position.

(19) See Norman Conquest, i. 176.

(20) This is distinctly asserted in the Dialogus de Scaccario (i. 10), under Henry the Second: "Jam cohabitantibus Anglicis et Normannis, et alterutrum uxores ducentibus vel nubentibus, sic permixtæ sunt nationes, ut vix discerni possit hodie, de liberis loquor, quis Anglicus quis Normannus sit genere; exceptis duntaxat ascriptitiis qui villani dicuntur, quibus non est liberum obstantibus dominis suis a sui statûs conditione discedere."

(21) The Angevin family are commonly known as the Plantagenets; but that name was never used as a surname till the fifteenth century. The name is sometimes convenient, but it is not a really correct description, like Tudor and Stewart, both of which were real surnames, borne by the two families before they came to the Crown. In the almanacks the Angevins are called "The Saxon line restored," a name which gives a false idea, though there can be no doubt that Henry the Second was fully aware of the advantages to be drawn from his remote female descent from the Old-English Kings. The point to be borne in mind is that the accession of Henry is the beginning of a distinct dynasty which could not be called either Norman or English in any but the most indirect way.

(22) I do not remember anything in any of the writers of Henry the Second's time to strengthen the popular notions about "Normans and Saxons" as two distinct and hostile bodies. Nor do we as yet hear many complaints of favour being shown to absolute foreigners in preference to either, though it is certain that many high preferments, especially in the Church, were held by men who were not English in either sense. The peculiar position of Henry the Second was something like that of the Emperor Charles the Fifth, that of a prince ruling over a great number of distinct states without being nationally identified with any of them. Henry ruled over England, Normandy, and Aquitaine, but he was neither English, Norman, nor Gascon.

(23) That is the greater, the continental, part of the Duchy. The insular part of Normandy, the Channel Islands, was not lost, and it still remains attached to the English Crown, not as part of the United Kingdom, but as a separate dependancy. See Norman Conquest, i. 187.

(24) See Norman Conquest, i. 310, 367; and on the appointment of Bishops and Abbots, i. 503, ii. 66, 571.

(25) See the Ordinance in Norman Conquest, iv. 392. Stubbs, Select Charters, 81.

(26) See Norman Conquest, iii. 317.

(27) It should be remembered that the clerical immunities which were claimed in this age were by no means confined to those whom we should now call clergymen, but also took in that large class of persons who held smaller ecclesiastical offices without being what we should call in holy orders. The Church also claimed jurisdiction in the causes of widows

and orphans, and in various cases where questions of perjury, breach of faith, and the like were concerned. Thus John Bishop of Poitiers writes to Archbishop Thomas (Giles, Sanctus Thomas, vi. 238) complaining that the King's officers had forbidden him to hear the causes of widows and orphans, and also to hear causes in matters of usury: "prohibentes ne ad querelas viduarum vel orphanorum vel clericorum aliquem parochianorum meorum in causam trahere præsumerem super quacumque possessione immobili, donec ministeriales regis, vel dominorum ad quorum feudum res controversiæ pertineret, in facienda justitia eis defecissent. Deinde ne super accusatione fœnoris quemquam audirem." This gives a special force to the acclamations with which Thomas was greeted on his return as "the father of the orphans and the judge of the widows:" "Videres mox pauperum turbam quæ convenerat in occursum, hos succinctos ut prævenirent et patrem suum applicantem exciperent, et benedictionem præriperent, alios vero humi se humiliter prosternentes, ejulantes hos, plorantes illos præ gaudio, et omnes conclamantes, Benedictus qui venit in nomine Domini, pater orphanorum et judex viduarum! et pauperes quidem sic." Herbert of Bosham, Giles, Sanctus Thomas, vii. 315, cf. 148. See more in Historical Essays, 99.

(28) On the cruel punishments inflicted in the King's courts Herbert of Bosham is very emphatic in more than one passage. He pleads (vii. 101) as a merit of the Bishops' courts that in them no mutilations were inflicted. Men were punished there "absque omni mutilatione vel deformatione membrorum." But he by no means claims freedom from mutilation as a mere clerical privilege; he distinctly condemns it in any case. "Adeo etiam quod ordinis privilegium

excludat cauterium : quam tamen pœnam communiter inter homines etiam jus forense damnat : ne videlicet in homine Dei imago deformetur." (vii. 105.) A most curious story illustrative of the barbarous jurisprudence of the time will be found in Benedict's Miracula Sancti Thomæ, 184.

(29) One of the Constitutions of Clarendon forbade villains to be ordained without the consent of their lords. "Filii rusticorum non debent ordinari absque assensu domini de cujus terra nati dignoscuntur" (Stubbs, Select Charters, 134). On the principles of feudal law nothing can be said against this, as the lord had a property in his villain which he would lose by the villain's ordination. The prohibition is noticed in some remarkable lines of the earliest biographer of Thomas, Garnier of Pont-Sainte-Maxence (La Vie de Saint Thomas le Martyr, Paris, 1859, p. 89), where he strongly asserts the equality of gentleman and villain before God :—

> "Fils à vilains ne fust en nul liu ordenez
> Sanz l'otrei sun seigneur de cui terre il fu nez.
> Et deus à sun servise nus a tuz apelez !
> Mielz valt filz à vilain qui est preux e senez,
> Que ne feit gentilz hum failliz et debutez."

Thomas himself was not the son of a villain, but his birth was such that the King could sneer at him as "plebeius quidam clericus."

(30) We are not inclined to find fault with such an appointment as that of Stephen Langton ; still his forced election at the bidding of Innôcent was a distinct breach of the rights of the King, of the Convent of Christ Church, and of the English nation generally. See the account of his election in Roger of Wendover, iii. 212 ; Lingard, ii. 314 ; Hook's Archbishops, ii. 668.

(31) See the Bulls and Letters by which Innocent professed to annul the Great Charter in Roger of Wendover, iii. 323, 327; the excommunication of the Barons in iii. 336; and the suspension of the Archbishop in iii. 340.

(32) There is a separate treatise on the Miracles of Simon of Montfort, printed along with Rishanger's Chronicle by the Camden Society, 1840.

(33) I think I may safely say that the only royalist chronicler of the reign of Henry the Third is Thomas Wykes, the Austin Canon of Osney. There is also one poem on the royalist side, to balance many on the side of the Barons, among the Political Songs published by the Camden Society, 1839, page 128.

Letters to Earl Simon and his Countess Eleanor form a considerable part of the letters of Robert Grosseteste, published by Mr. Luard for the Master of the Rolls. Matthew Paris also (879, Wats) speaks of him as "episcopus Lincolniensis Robertus, cui comes tamquam patri confessori exstitit familiarissimus." This however was in the earlier part of Simon's career, before the war had broken out. The share of Bishop Walter of Cantilupe, who was present at Evesham and absolved the Earl and his followers, will be found in most of the Chronicles of the time. It comes out well in the riming Chronicle of Robert of Gloucester (ii. 558):—

> "þe bissop Water of Wurcetre asoiled hom alle pere
> And prechede hom, þat hii adde of deþ þe lasse fere."

This writer says of the battle of Evesham:—

> "Suich was þe morþre of Eivesham (vor bataile non it was)."

(34) This letter, addressed in 1247 to Pope Innocent the

Fourth, will be found in Matthew Paris (721, Wats). It is written in the name of "universitas cleri et populi per provinciam Cantuariensem constituti," and it ends, "quia communitas nostra sigillum non habet, præsentes literas signo communitatis civitatis Londinensis vestræ sanctitati mittimus consignatas." Another letter in the same form follows to the Cardinals. There are two earlier letters in 1245 and 1246 (Matthew Paris, 666, 700), the former from the "magnates et universitas regni Angliæ," the other in the name of Richard Earl of Cornwall (afterwards King of the Romans), Simon Earl of Leicester, and other Earls, "et alii totius regni Angliæ Barones, proceres, et magnates, et nobiles portuum maris habitatores, necnon et clerus et populus universus." The distinct mention of the Cinque Ports, whose representatives in Parliament are still called Barons—the "nobiles" of the letter—should be noticed.

(35) The writer of the Gesta Stephani (3) distinctly attributes the election of Stephen to the citizens of London: "Majores igitur natu, consultuque quique provectiores, concilium coegere, deque regni statu, pro arbitrio suo, utilia in commune providentes, ad regem eligendum unanimiter conspiravere." He then goes on with the details of the election. He is borne out by the Chronicle 1135: "Stephne de Blais com to Lundene and te Lundenisce folc him underfeng;" and by William of Malmesbury, Historia Novella, i. 11: "A Londoniensibus et Wintoniensibus in Regem exceptus est." So again when the Legate, Henry Bishop of Winchester, holds a council for the election of the Empress Matilda, the citizens of London were summoned, and it is distinctly said that they held the rank of nobles or barons: "Londonienses (qui sunt quasi optimates, pro magnitudine civitatis, in

Anglia)." "Londonienses, qui præcipui habebantur in Anglia, sicut proceres" (Historia Novella, iii. 45, 46). All his is exactly like the earlier elections of Kings before the Conquest.

(36) The words of the Charter 12—14 (Stubbs, 290) are: "Nullum scutagium vel auxilium ponatur in regno nostro, nisi per commune consilium regni nostri, nisi ad corpus nostrum redimendum, etc. . . . . Et ad habendum commune consilium regni, de auxilio assidendo aliter quam in tribus casibus prædictis, vel de scutagio assidendo, summoneri faciemus archiepiscopos, episcopos, abbates, comites, et majores barones, sigillatim per litteras nostras; et præterea faciemus summoneri in generali, per vicecomites et ballivos nostros, omnes illos qui de nobis tenent in capite." This is exactly like the entry in the Chronicle (1123), describing the summoning of a Witenagemót by Henry the First: "Da sone þæræfter sende se kyng hise write ofer eal Englalande, and bed hise biscopes and hise abbates and hise þeignes ealle þet hi scolden cumen to his gewitenemot on Candelmesse deig to Gleawceastre him togeanes; and hi swa diden."

(37) These first glimmerings of parliamentary representation were carefully traced out by Hallam (Middle Ages, ii. 146—152). They can now be more fully studied in the work of Professor Stubbs. On the summons in 1213 of four men for each shire besides "milites et barones" ("quatuor discretos homines de comitatu tuo illuc venire facias"), the Professor remarks (278). "It is the first writ in which the 'four discreet men' of the county appear as representatives; the first instance of the summoning of the folkmoot to a general assembly by the machinery already used for judicial purposes."

(38) On this subject the eighth chapter of Sir Francis Palgrave's English Commonwealth should be studied.

(39) For the whole career of Simon I must again refer generally to Pauli and Blaauw. The great writ itself, dated at Worcester, December 14th, 1264, will be found in Rymer's Fœdera, i. 449. It has often been noticed how small is the number of Earls and other lay Barons, and how unusually large the number of churchmen, who are summoned to this Parliament. The whole list will be found in Rymer. The parts of the writ which concern us stand thus:

"Item mandatum est singulis vicecomitibus per Angliam; quod venire faciant duos milites de legalioribus, probioribus, et discretioribus militibus singulorum comitatuum, ad Regem London' in octab' prædictis, in formâ supradictâ.

"Item in formâ prædictâ scribitur civibus Ebor', civibus Lincoln', et cæteris burgis Angliæ; quod mittant in formâ prædictâ duos de discretioribus, legalioribus, et probioribus, tam civibus, quam burgensibus suis.

"Item in formâ prædictâ mandatum est baronibus, et probis hominibus Quinque Portuum."

"This is often regarded as the origin of popular representation; but it is not in any sense entitled to that praise. The novelty was simply the assembling the representatives of the towns in conjunction with those of the counties; this was now done for the first time for the purpose of the national council." Stubbs, 401.

(40) The account of this most remarkable trial, held on June 11th, 1252, is given in a letter from Simon's intimate friend the famous Franciscan Adam Marsh (de Marisco) to Bishop Robert Grosseteste. The Latin text is printed in Mr. Brewer's Monumenta Franciscana, p. 122, and there is

an English translation in the Appendix to Mrs. Green's Life of Countess Eleanor, English Princesses, ii. 447. Simon's witnesses, knights and citizens, come "muniti litteris patentibus communitatis Burdegalensis, in quâ quasi totum robur Vasconiæ ad distringendum hostiles et fideles protegendum consistere dignoscitur," setting forth how good Simon's government was in every way, and how those who brought charges against him did it only because his strict justice had put a check on their misdoings. We may compare the words of the great poetical manifesto (Political Songs, 76).

> "Seductorem nominant S. atque fallacem,
> Facta sed examinant probantque veracem."

(41) For the Londoners at Lewes let us take the account of an enemy. Thomas Wykes (148) tells us how the Earl set out, "glorians in virtute sua congregata baronum multitudine copiosa, Londoniensium innumerabili agmine circumcinctus, quia legitur stultorum infinitus est numerus." Presently we read how the "Londoniensium innumera multitudo, bellorum ignara," were put to flight by the Lord Edward very much after the manner of Prince Rupert.

(42) On the religious reverence paid to Earl Waltheof, see Norman Conquest, ii. 602. I have there referred to the office of Thomas of Lancaster, which will be found in Political Songs, 268. Some of the pieces are what we should think most daring parodies of parts of the Church Service, but we may be sure that what was intended was reverence and not irreverence. There is another parody of the same kind in honour of Earl Thomas, a little earlier back in the volume, p. 258. It was a matter of course that Thomas of Lancaster should be likened to Thomas of Canterbury.

" Gaude, Thoma, ducum decus, lucerna Lancastriæ,
Qui per necem imitaris Thomam Cantuariæ ;
Cujus caput conculcatur pacem ob ecclesiæ,
Atque tuum detruncatur causa pacis Angliæ."

(43) Let us take a Latin, a French, and an English specimen of the poems in which Simon's death was lamented and his intercession implored.

" Salve, Symon Montis Fortis,
Totius flos militiæ,
Durus pœnas passus mortis,
Protector gentis Angliæ.
Sunt de sanctis inaudita
Cunctis passis in hac vita,
Quemquam passum talia ;
Manus, pedes, amputari,
Caput, corpus, vulnerari,
Abscidi virilia.
Sis pro nobis intercessor
Apud Deum, qui defensor
In terris exstiteras."—(Political Songs, 124.)

The French poem which follows directly in the collection is too long to copy in full. This is perhaps the most remarkable stanza, in which we again find the comparison with Thomas of Canterbury :—

" Mès par sa mort, le cuens Mountfort conquist la victorie,
Come ly martyr de Caunterbyr, finist sa vie ;
Ne voleit pas li bon Thomas qe perist seinte Eglise,
Le cuens auxi se combati, e morust sauntz feyntise.
Ore est ocys la flur de pris, qe taunt savoit de guerre,
Ly quens Montfort, sa dure mort molt emplorra la terre."

In this poem there is not, as in the Latin one, any direct prayer to the martyred Earl, but in the last stanza we read :—

" Sire Simoun ly prodhom, e sa compagnie,
En joie vont en ciel amount, en pardurable vie."

The only English piece on these wars belongs to an

earlier date, namely, the satirical poem against King Richard, how the one English Augustus

> "Makede him a castel of a mulne post;"

but we get verses on Simon's death in the Chronicle ot Robert of Gloucester (ii. 559):—

> "& sir Simond was aslawe, & is folk al to grounde,
> More murþre are nas in so lute stounde.
> Vor þere was werst Simond de Mountfort aslawe, alas!
> & sir Henri is sone, þat so gentil knizt was.
> * * * * * *
> & among alle oþere mest reuþe it was ido,
> þat sir Simon þe olde man demembred was so."

He then goes on with the details of the dismemberment, of which a picture may be seen opposite p. 254 of Mr. Blaauw's book, and then goes on with the lines which I have before quoted:—

> "Suich was þe morþre of Eivesham (vor bataile non it was),
> And þer wiþ Jesu Crist wel vuele ipaied was,
> As he ssewede bitokninge grisliche and gode,
> As it vel of him sulue, þo he deide on þe rode,
> þat þoru al þe middelerd derk hede þer was inou."

(44) On the occasional and irregular summoning of the borough members between 1265 and 1295 see Hallam, Middle Ages, ii. 160, 165, and more fully in Stubbs, Select Charters, 420, 427, where the gradual developement of parliamentary representation is treated as it has never been treated before, with a full citation of the authorities. The language in which the Chronicles speak of the constitution of the early Parliaments of Edward is as vague as that in which our ancient Gemóts are described. Sometimes they speak only of "proceres" and the like; sometimes they distinctly mention the popular element. Curiously enough, the official language is sometimes more popular than that of the

annalists. Thus the Winchester Annals, recording the Statute of Westminster in 1273, call the Assembly which passed it a "communis convocatio omnium magnatum regni," though it incidentally implies the presence of other persons, "quamplures de regno qui aliqua feoda de corona regia tenuerunt." But the preamble of the Statute itself records the "assentement des erceveskes, eveskes, abbes, priurs, contes, barons, et *la communaute de la tere* ileokes somons." So in the later Parliament of the same year the Annals speak only of the "communis consensus archiepiscoporum, comitum, et baronum," while the official description is "prælati, comites, barones, et alii de regno nostro." But in an earlier Assembly, that held in 1273, before Edward had come back to England, the same Winchester Annals tell us how "convenerunt archiepiscopi et episcopi, comites et barones, et *de quolibet comitatu quatuor milites et de qualibet civitate quatuor.*" This and the summons to the Parliament of 1285, which sat in judgement on David of Wales (Stubbs, 453, 457), seem the most distinct cases of borough representation earlier than 1295, since which time the summoning of the borough members has gone on regularly. See Stubbs, 473. Mr. Stubbs' remarks on the Assemblies of "the transitionary period" in pp. 465, 469 should be specially studied.

(45) The history of the resistance of these two Earls to King Edward, which led to the great Confirmation of the Charters in 1297, will be found in the usual histories of the time, old and new. See also Stubbs, 431, 479. I feel no difficulty in reconciling respect for Edward with respect for the men who withstood him. The case is well put by Stubbs, 34, 35.

(46) The exact value of the document commonly known as the statute "De Tallagio non concedendo" is discussed by Professor Stubbs, p. 487. It is perhaps safest to look on it, like many of the earlier collections of laws, not indeed as an actual statute, but as good evidence of a principle which, from the time of the Confirmation of the Charters, has been universally received. The words are—

"Nullum tallagium vel auxilium per nos vel hæredes nostros de cetero in regno nostro imponatur seu levetur, sine voluntate et assensu communi archiepiscoporum, episcoporum et aliorum prælatorum, comitum, baronum, militum, burgensium, et aliorum liberorum hominum in regno nostro." This, it will be seen, is the same provision which I have already quoted (see above, Note 36) from the Great Charter of John, but which was left out in the Charter in the form in which it was confirmed by Henry the Third. See Stubbs, 330, 332, 336.

(47) I have said this before in Historical Essays, p. 41. On the strongly marked legal character of Edward's age, and especially of Edward's own mind, see Stubbs, 417.

(48) The great statute of treason of 25 Edward the Third (see the Revised Edition of the Statutes, i. 185) secures the life of the King, his wife, and his eldest son, and the chastity of his wife, his eldest daughter, and his eldest son's wife. But the personal privilege extends no further. As the Law of England knows no classes of men except peers and commoners, it follows that the younger children of the King—the eldest is born Duke of Cornwall—are, in strictness of speech, commoners, unless they are personally raised to the peerage. I am not aware that either case has ever risen, but I conceive that there is nothing to hinder a King's son, not being a peer, from voting at an election, or from being chosen

to the House of Commons, and I conceive that, if he committed a crime, he would be tried by a jury. Mere precedence and titles have nothing to do with the matter, though probably a good deal of confusion arises from the very modern fashion—one might almost say the modern vulgarism—of calling all the children of the King or Queen "Princes" and "Princesses." As late as the time of George the Second uncourtly Englishmen were still found who eschewed the foreign innovation, and who spoke of the Lady Caroline and the Lady Emily, as their fathers had done before them.

Another modern vulgarism is that of using the word "royal"—"royal visit," "royal marriage," and so forth—when there is no royalty in the case, the person spoken of being a subject, perhaps a commoner.

(49) On the parliamentary position of the clergy see Hallam, Middle Ages, ii. 263. And as far as the reign of Edward the First is concerned, see the series of summonses in Stubbs, 442.

(50) On this important constitutional change, which was made in 1664, without any Act of Parliament, but by a mere verbal agreement between Archbishop Sheldon and Lord Chancellor Clarendon, see Hallam, Constitutional History, ii. 405.

(51) This is true on the whole, especially at the beginning of the institution of the States General, though there were also *roturiers* who were the immediate burgesses of the King. See Thierry, History of the Tiers État, i. 56 (Eng. trans.). It is in that work that the history of that branch of the States General should be studied.

(52) The question of one or two Chambers in an ordinary

monarchy or commonwealth is altogether different from the same question under a Federal system. In England or France the question between one or two Chambers in the Legislature is simply a question in which of the two ways the Legislature is likely to do its work best. But in a Federal constitution, like that of Switzerland or the United States, the two Chambers are absolutely necessary. The double sovereignty, of the whole nation and of the independent and equal States which have joined together to form it, can be rightly represented only by having two Chambers, one of them, the *Nationalrath* or House of Representatives, directly representing the nation as such, and the other, the *Ständerath* or Senate, representing the separate sovereignty of the Cantons. In the debates which are now going on as to the revision of the Swiss Federal Constitution, a proposal made in the *Nationalrath* for the abolition of the *Ständerath* was thrown out by a large majority.

(53) On the old Constitution of Sweden, see Laing's Tour in Sweden.

(54) This common mistake and its cause are fully explained by Hallam, Middle Ages, ii. 237.

(55) "The two Houses had contended violently in 1675, concerning the appellate jurisdiction of the Lords; they had contended, with not less violence, in 1704, upon the jurisdiction of the Commons, in matters of election they had quarrelled rudely, in 1770, while insisting upon the exclusion of strangers. But upon general measures of public policy, their differences had been rare and unimportant." May's Constitutional History, i. 307. The writer goes on to show why differences between the two Houses on important points have become more common in very recent times.

(56) The share of the Witan in early times in the appointment of Bishops, Ealdormen, and other great officers, need hardly be dwelled upon. For a debate in a Witenagemót of Eadward the Confessor on a question of peace or war, see Norman Conquest, ii. 90. For the like under Henry the Third, see the account in Matthew Paris, in the year 1242, which will be found in Stubbs, 359. The state of the case under Edward the Third is discussed by Hallam, Middle Ages, ii. 184. See also May, ii. 86. But the most remarkable passage of all is one in the great poetical manifesto which I have several times quoted: it is there (Political Songs, 96) made one of the charges against Henry the Third that he wished to keep the appointment of the great officers of state in his own hands. The passage is long, but it is well worth quoting at length.

> "Rex cum suis voluit ita liber esse;
> Et sic esse debuit, fuitque necesse
> Aut esse desineret rex, privatus jure
> Regis, nisi faceret quidquid vellet; curæ
> Non esse magnatibus regni quos præferret
> Suis comitatibus, vel quibus conferret
> Castrorum custodiam, vel quem exhibere
> Populo justitiam vellet, et habere
> Regni cancellarium thesaurariumque.
> Suum ad arbitrium voluit quemcumque,
> Et consiliarios de quacumque gente,
> Et ministros varios se præcipiente,
> Non intromittentibus se de factis regis
> Angliæ baronibus, vim habente legis,
> Principis imperio, et quod imperaret
> Suomet arbitrio singulos ligaret."

(57) Take for example the Act passed after Edward the Fourth's success at Towton. Rot. Parl. v. 466. Among other things, poor Henry the Sixth is not only branded as an usurper, but is charged with personally stirring up the movement in the North, which led to the battle of Wakefield and

the death of Richard Duke of York. "The seid Henry Usurpour, late called Kyng Henry the Sixt, contynuyng in his olde rancour & malice, usyng the fraude & malicious disceit & dissimulacion ayenst trouth & conscience, that accorde not with the honoure of eny Cristen Prynce, ... with all subtill ymaginacions & disceitfull weyes & meanes to hym possible, intended & covertely laboured, excited & procured the fynal destruction, murdre & deth of the seid Richard Duc, and of his Sonnes, that is to sey, of oure seid nowe Soverayne Lord Kyng Edward the fourth, then Erle of Marche, & of the noble Lord Edmund Erle of Ruthlande; & for th' execution of his dampnable & malicious purpose, by writing & other messages, mowed, excited, & stured therunto the Duks of Excestr' & Somerset, & other lordes beyng then in the North parties of this Reame."

(58) This statute was passed in 8 Henry VI. A.D. 1429. The complaint which it makes is well worth notice, and shows the reactionary tendencies of the time. The county elections had been made by "very great, outrageous, and excessive number of people dwelling within the same counties, of which most part was people of small substance, and of no value, whereof every of them pretended a voice equivalent, as to such elections to be made, with the most worthy knights and esquires dwelling within the same counties." To hinder "the manslaughters, riots, batteries, and divisions," which were likely to take place—it is not said that they had taken place—no one is to be allowed to vote who has not "free land or tenement to the value of forty shillings by the year at the least above all charges." It is also provided that both the electors and the elected are to be actually resident in the county. The original French is worth quoting.

"Item come lez eleccions dez Chivalers des Countees esluz a venir as parlements du Roi en plusours Countees Dengleterre, ore tarde ount este faitz par trop̄ graunde & excessive nombre dez gents demurrantz deinz mesmes les Countes, dount lá greindre partie estoit par gentz sinon de petit avoir ou de null valu, dount chescun pretende davoir voice equivalent quant a tielx eleccions faire ove les plius valantz chivalers ou esquiers demurrantz deins mesmes les Countes; dount homicides riotes bateries & devisions entre les gentiles & autres gentz de mesmes les Countees verisemblablement sourdront & seront, si covenable remedie ne soit purveu en celle partie: Notre seigneur le Roy considerant les premisses ad pourveu & ordene par auctorite de cest parlement que les Chivalers des Countes deins le Roialme Dengleterre, a esliers a venir a les parlementz en apres atenirs, soient esluz en chescun Counte par gentz demurrantz & receantz en icelles dount chescun ait frank tenement a le valu de xl s. par an al meins outre les reprises; & que ceux qui seront ensy esluz soient demurrantz & receantz deins mesmes les Countes." Revised Statutes, i. 306.

The necessity of residence in the case of either electors or representatives was repealed by 14 Geo. III. c. 58.

The statute goes on to give the Sheriff power to examine the electors on oath as to the amount of their property. It also gives the Judges of Assize a power foreshadowing that of our present Election Judges, that of inquiring into false returns made by the Sheriff.

Another statute of the same character was passed later in the same reign, 23 Hen. VI. A.D. 1444-5, from which it appears that the knights of the shire were ceasing to be in all cases knights in the strict sense, and that it was beginning to be found needful to fence them about with oligarchic restrictions.

"Issint que lez Chivalers dez Counteez pour le parlement en après a esliers soient notablez Chivalers dez mesmez lez Counteez pour lez queux ils serront issint esluz, ou autrement tielx notablez Esquiers gentils homez del Nativite dez mesmez lez Counteez comme soient ablez destre Chivalers; et null home destre tiel Chivaler que estoise en la degree de vadlet et desouth" (Revised Statutes, i. 346).

Every enactment of this kind bears witness to the growth of the power of the Commons, and to the endeavours of the people to make their representation really popular.

(59) Take for instance the account given by the chronicler Hall (p. 253) of the election of Edward the Fourth.

"After the lordes had considered and weyghed his title and declaracion, they determined by authoritie of the sayd counsaill, for as much as kyng Henry, contrary to his othe, honor and agreement, had violated and infringed, the order taken and enacted in the last Parliament, and also, because he was insufficient to rule the Realme, & inutile to the common wealth, & publique profite of the pore people, he was therefore by the aforesayed authoritie, depriued & deiected of all kyngly honor, & regall souereigntie. And incontinent, Edward erle of Marche, sonne & heyre to Richard duke of Yorke, was by the lordes in the sayd counsaill assembled, named, elected, & admitted, for kyng & gouernour of the realme: on which day, the people of the erles parte, beyng in their muster in sainct Ihons felde, & a great number of the substanciall citezens there assembled, to behold their order: sodaynly the lord Fawconbridge, which toke the musters, wisely declared to the multitude, the offences & breaches of the late agremente done & perpetrated by kyng Henry the vi. & demaunded of the people, whether they woulde haue the sayd kyng Henry to rule & reigne any lenger ouer them: To whome they with a whole voyce, aunswered, nay, nay. Then he asked them, if they would serue, loue, & obey the erle of March as their earthly prince & souereign lord. To which question they aunswered, yea, yea, crieng, king Edward, with many great showtes and clappyng of handes. . . . . The erle, . . . as kyng, rode to the church of sainct Paule, and there offered. And after *Te deum* song, with great solempnitie, he was conueyed to Westmynster, and there set in the hawle, with the scepter royall in his hand, where to all the people which there in a great number were assembled, his title and clayme to the croune of England, was declared by, ii. maner of ways: the firste, as sonne and heyre to duke Richard his father, right enheritor to the same: the second, by aucthoritie of Parliament and forfeiture committed by, kyng Henry. Wherupon it was agayne demaunded of the commons, if they would admitte, and take the sayd erle as their prince and souereigne lord, which al with one voice cried, yea, yea. . . . . On the morow he was proclaymed kyng by the name of kyng Edward the. iiij. throughout the citie."

This was in Lent 1461, before the battle of Towton. Edward was crowned June 29th in the same year. The same chronicler describes the election or acknowledgement of Richard the Third, p. 372.

(60) One especial sign of the advance of the power of Parliament in the fifteenth century was the practice of bringing in bills in the form of Statutes ready made. Hitherto the Acts of the Commons had taken the form of petitions, and it

was sometimes found that, after the Parliament had broken up, the petitions had been fraudulently modified. They now brought in bills, which the King accepted or rejected as they stood. See Hallam, Middle Ages, ii. 222.

(61) Macaulay, i. 38. "The knight of the shire was the connecting link between the baron and the shopkeeper. On the same benches on which sate the goldsmiths, drapers, and grocers who had been returned to Parliament by the commercial towns, sate also members who, in any other country, would have been called noblemen, hereditary lords of manors, entitled to hold courts and to bear coat armour, and able to trace back an honourable descent through many generations. Some of them were younger sons and brothers of great lords. Others could boast even of royal blood. At length the eldest son of an Earl of Bedford, called in courtesy by the second title of his father, offered himself as a candidate for a seat in the House of Commons, and his example was followed by others. Seated in that house, the heirs of the grandees of the realm naturally became as zealous for its privileges as any of the humble burgesses with whom they were mingled."

Hallam remarks (ii. 250) that it is in the reign of Edward the Fourth that we first find borough members bearing the title of Esquire, and he goes on to refer to the Paston Letters as showing how important a seat in Parliament was then held, and also the undue influences which were already brought to bear upon the electors. Since Hallam's time, the authenticity of the Paston Letters has been called in question, but it has, I think, been sufficiently established. Some of the entries are very curious indeed. In one (i. 96), without any date of the year, the Duchess of Norfolk writes to John Paston, Esquire, to use his influence at a county election on behalf of some creatures of the Duke's:

"It is thought right necessarie for divers causes þ^{t} my Lord have at this tyme in the p'lement suche p'sones as longe unto him and be of his menyall S'vaunts wherin we conceyve yor good will and diligence shal be right expedient." The persons to be thus chosen for the convenience of the Duke are described as "our right wel-belovid Cossin and S'vaunts John Howard and Syr Roger Chambirlayn." This is followed by a letter from the Earl of Oxford in 1455, much to the same effect. In ii. 98 we have a letter addressed to the Bailiff of Maldon, recommending the election of Sir John Paston on behalf of a certain great lady not named. The letter is worth giving in full.

"Ryght trusty frend I comand me to yow preyĩg yow to call to yor mynd that lyek as ye and I comonyd of it were necessary for my Lady and you all hyr Serũnts and teñnts to have thys p'lement as for õn of the Burgeys of the towne of Maldon syche a man of worthep and of wytt as wer towardys my seyd Lady and also syche on as is in favor of the Kyng and of the Lords of hys consayll nyghe abought hys p'sone. Sertyfyĩg yow that my seid Lady for her parte and syche as be of hyr consayll be most agreeabyll that bothe ye and all syche as be hyr fermors and teñntys and wellwyllers shold geve your voyse to a worchepfull knyght and on' of my Ladys consayll Sr John Paston whyche standys gretly in favore w^{t} my Lord Chamberleyn and what my seyd Lord Chamberleyn may do w^{t} the Kyng and w^{t} all the Lordys of Inglond I trowe it be not unknowyn to you most of eny on man alyve. Wherefor by the meenys of the seyd Sr John Paston to my seyd Lord Chamberleyn bothe my Lady and ye of the towne kowd not have a meeter man to be for yow in the perlement to have yor needys sped at all seasons. Wherefor I prey yow labor all syche as be my Ladys serũntts tennts and wellwyllers to geve ther voyseys to the seyd Sr John Paston and that ye fayle not to sped my Ladys intent in thys mater as ye entend to do hyr as gret a plesur as if ye gave hyr an C^li [100*l*.]. And God have yow in hys kepīg. Wretyn at Fysheley the xx day of Septebyr.—J. ARBLASTER."

(62) On the effects of the reign of Charles the Fifth in Spain and his overthrow of the liberties of Castile, see the general view in Robertson, iii. 434, though in his narrative (ii. 186) he glorifies the King's clemency. See also the first chapter of the sixth book of Prescott's Philip the Second, and on the suppression of the constitution of Aragon by Philip, Watson, Philip the Second, iii. 223.

The last meeting of the French States-General before the final meeting in 1789, was that in 1614, during the minority of Lewis the Thirteenth. See Sismondi, xiii. 342.

(63) The legal character of William's despotism I have tried to set forth almost throughout the whole of my fourth volume. See especially pp. 8, 617; but it is plain to everyone who has the slightest knowledge of Domesday. No notion can show more utter ignorance of the real character of the man and his times than the idea of William being a mere "rude man of war," as I have seen him called.

(64) On the true aspect of the reign of Henry the Eighth I have said something in the Fortnightly Review, September 1871.

(65) Both these forms of undue influence on the part of the Crown are set forth by Hallam, Constitutional History, i. 45, ii. 203. "It will not be pretended," he says, "that the wretched villages, which corruption and perjury still hardly

keep from famine [this was written before the Reform Bill in 1827], were seats of commerce and industry in the sixteenth century. But the county of Cornwall was more immediately subject to a coercive influence, through the indefinite and oppressive jurisdiction of the stannary court. Similar motives, if we could discover the secrets of those governments, doubtless operated in most other cases."

In the same page the historian, speaking of the different boroughs and counties which received the franchise in the sixteenth century, says, "It might be possible to trace the reason, why the county of Durham was passed over." And he suggests, "The attachment of those northern parts to popery seems as likely as any other." The reason for the omission of Durham was doubtless that it had not wholly lost the character of a separate principality. It was under Charles the Second that Durham city and county, as well as Newark, first sent members to Parliament. Durham was enfranchised by Act of Parliament, as Chester city and county —hitherto kept distinct as being a Palatinate—were by 34 & 35 Hen. VIII. c. 13. (Revised Statutes, i. 522.) Newark was enfranchised by a Royal Charter, the last case of that kind of exercise of the prerogative. Hallam, ii. 204.

(66) I do not know what was the exact state of Old Sarum in 1265 or in 1295, but at a short time before the former date it was still the chief dwelling-place both of the Earl and of the Bishop. But in the reign of Edward the Third it had so greatly decayed that the stones of the Cathedral were used for the completion of the new one which had arisen in the plain.

(67) On the relations between Queen Elizabeth and her Parliaments, and especially for the bold bearing of the two

Wentworths, Peter and Paul, see the fifth chapter of Hallam's Constitutional History, largely grounded on the Journals of Sir Simonds D'Ewes. The frontispiece to D'Ewes' book (London, 1682) gives a lively picture of a Parliament of those days.

(68) On the relations between the Crown and the House of Commons under James the First, see the sixth chapter of Hallam's Constitutional History, and the fifth chapter of Gardner's History of England from 1603 to 1616.

CHAPTER III.

(1) This was the famous motion made by Sir Robert Peel against the Ministry of Lord Melbourne, and carried by a majority of one, June 4, 1841. See May's Constitutional History, i. 158. Irving's Annals of our Times, 86.

(2) This of course leaves to the Ministry the power of appealing to the country by a dissolution of Parliament; but if the new Parliament also declares against them, it is plain that they have nothing to do but to resign office. In the case of 1841 Lord Melbourne dissolved Parliament, and, on the meeting of the new Parliament, an amendment to the address was carried by a majority of ninety-one, August 28, 1841. The Ministry therefore resigned.

(3) How very recent the establishment of these principles is will be seen by any one who studies the history of the reign of George the Third in the work of Sir T. E. May. Mr. Pitt, as is well known, kept office in defiance of repeated votes of the House of Commons, and at last, by a dissolution at a well-chosen moment, showed that the country was on his side. Such conduct would not be deemed constitutional now, but the wide difference between the constitution of the House of Commons then and now should be borne in mind.

(4) Though the command of the Sovereign would be no excuse for any illegal act, and though the advisers of any

illegal act are themselves responsible for it, yet there would seem to be no way provided for punishing an illegal act done by the Sovereign in his own person. The Sovereign may therefore be said to be personally irresponsible.

(5) See Macaulay, iv. 435. It should not be forgotten that writers like Blackstone and De Lolme say nothing about the Cabinet. Serjeant Stephen supplies the omission, ii. 447.

(6) The lowly outward position of the really ruling assembly comes out in some degree at the opening of every session of Parliament. But it is far more marked in the grotesque, and probably antiquated, ceremonies of a conference of the two Houses. This comes out most curiously of all in the conference between the two Houses of the Convention in 1688. See Macaulay, ii. 660.

(7) See Macaulay, iv. 437.

(8) "Ministers" or "Ministry" were the words always used at the time of the Reform Bill in 1831-1832. It would be curious to trace at what time the present mode of speech came into vogue, either in parliamentary debates or in common speech.

(9) In February 1854 Mr. Cayley moved for a "Select Committee to consider the duties of the Member leading the Government business in this House, and the expediency of attaching office and salary thereto." The motion was withdrawn, after being opposed by Sir Charles Wood (now Viscount Halifax), Mr. Walpole, and Lord John Russell (now Earl Russell). Sir Charles Wood described the post of Leader of the House as "an office that does not exist, and

the duties of which cannot be defined." Mr. Walpole spoke of it as "a position totally unknown to the constitution of the country." Yet I presume that everybody practically knew that Lord John Russell was Leader of the House, though nobody could give a legal definition of his position. A discussion then followed between Mr. Walpole and Lord John Russell on the nature of ministerial responsibility. Mr. Walpole said that "members were apt to talk gravely of ministerial responsibility; but responsibility there is none except by virtue of the office that a Minister holds, or possibly by the fact of his being a Privy Councillor. A Minister is responsible for the acts done by him; a Privy Councillor for advice given by him in that capacity. Until the reign of Charles the Second, Privy Councillors always signed the advice they gave; and to this day the Cabinet is not a body recognized by law. As a Privy Councillor, a person is under little or no responsibility for the acts advised by him, on account of the difficulty of proof." Lord John Russell "asked the House to pause before it gave assent to the constitutional doctrines laid down by Mr. Walpole. He unduly restricted the responsibility of Ministers." . . . . "I hold," continued Lord John, "that it is not really for the business the Minister transacts in performing the particular duties of his office, but it is for any advice which he has given, and which he may be proved, before a Committee of this House, or at the bar of the House of Lords, to have given, that he is responsible, and for which he suffers the penalties that may ensue from impeachment."

It is plain that both Mr. Walpole and Lord Russell were here speaking of real legal responsibility, such responsibility as might be enforced by impeachment or other legal process, not of the vaguer kind of responsibility which is commonly meant when we speak of Ministers being "responsible to the House of Commons." This last is enforced, not by legal process, but by such motions as that of Sir Robert Peel in 1841, or that of the Marquess of Hartington in June 1859.

I have made my extracts from the Spectator newspaper February 11, 1854.

(10) We read (Anglia Sacra, i. 335) of Æthelric, Bishop of the South-Saxons at the time of the Conquest, as "vir antiquissimus et legum terræ sapientissimus." So Adelelm, the first Norman Abbot of Abingdon, found much benefit from the legal knowledge of certain of his English monks (Chronicon Monasterii de Abingdon, ii. 2), "quibus tanta secularium facundia et præteritorum memoria eventorum inerat, ut cæteri circumquaque facile eorum sententiam ratam fuisse, quam edicerent, approbarent." The writer adds, "Sed et alii plures de Anglis causidici per id tempus in abbatia ista habebantur quorum collationi nemo sapiens refragabatur." But knowledge of the law was not an exclusively clerical accomplishment; for among the grounds for the election of King Harold himself, we find (de Inventione Sanctæ Crucis Walthamensis, p. 25, Stubbs) that one was "quia non erat eo prudentior in terra, armis strenuus magis, legum terræ sagacior." See Norman Conquest, ii. 538, iv. 366, 478.

(11) On the growth of the lawyers' theory of the royal prerogative, and its utter lack of historical standing-ground, I must refer once for all to Allen's Inquiry into the Rise and Growth of the Royal Prerogative in England.

(12) See Norman Conquest, ii. 330.

(13) The history of this memorable Revolution will be

found in Lingard, iii. 392—405, and the legal points are brought out by Hallam, Middle Ages, ii. 214. He remarks that "In this revolution of 1399 there was as remarkable an attention shown to the formalities of the constitution, allowance made for the men and the times, as in that of 1688;" and, speaking of the device by which the same Parliament was brought together again, he adds, "In this contrivance, more than in all the rest, we may trace the hand of lawyers." The official version entered on the rolls of Parliament by command of Henry will be found in Walsingham, ii. 234—238. Some care seems to be used to avoid using the name of Parliament in the account of the actual proceedings. It is said just before, "Rex perductus est Londonias, conservandus in Turri usque ad Parliamentum proximo celebrandum." And the writs are said to have been sent "ad personas regni qui de jure debeant interesse Parliamento." But when they have come together ("quibus convenientibus") care seems to be taken to give the Assembly no particular name, till in the Act of Richard's deposition the actors are described as "pares et proceres regni Angliæ spirituales et temporales, et ejus regni communitates, omnes status ejusdem regni repræsentantes;" and in the Act of Henry's election they are described as "domini spirituales quam tam temporales, et omnes regni status." In the Act of deposition Richard's resignation of the Crown is recorded, as well as his particular crimes and his general unfitness to wear it, all which are classed together as reasons for his deposition. The actual formula of deposition runs thus:—"propter præmissa, et eorum prætextu, ab omni dignitate et honore regiis, *si quid dignitatis et honoris hujusmodi in eo remanserit*, merito deponendum pronunciamus, decernimus, et declaramus; et etiam simili cautela deponimus." They then declare the throne to be vacant ("ut constabat de præmissis, et eorum occasione, regnum Angliæ, cum pertinentiis suis, vacare"); Henry then makes his challenge, setting forth that strange mixture of titles which is commented on in most narratives of the event, and the Estates, without saying which of Henry's arguments they accept, grant the kingdom to him ("concesserunt unanimiter ut Dux præfatus super eos regnaret"). A more distinct case of deposition and election can hardly be found, only in the words which I have put in italics there seems a sort of anxiety to complete, by the act of deposition, any possible defect in his probably unwilling abdication.

The French narrative by a partisan of Richard (Lystoire de la Traison et Mort du Roy Richart Dengleterre, p. 68) gives, in some respects, a different account. The Assembly is called a Parliament, and the Duke of Lancaster is made to seat himself on the throne at once. Then Sir Thomas Percy "cria 'Veez Henry de Lenclastre Roy Dengleterre.' Adonc crierent tous les seigneurs prelaz et *le commun de Londres*, Ouy Ouy nous voulons que Henry duc de Lencastre soit nostre Roy et nul autre." For "le commun de Londres" there are other readings, "le commun," "le commun Dangleterre et de Londres," and "tout le commun et conseil de Londres."

(14) It should be remembered that Charles the First was not deposed, but was executed being King. He was called King within the indictment at his trial and in the warrant of his beheading.

(15) Monk raised this point in 1660. See Lingard, viii. 607.

(16) Lingard (viii. 612) remarks that at this particular moment "there was no court to influence, no interference of the military to control the elections." The Convention may

therefore be supposed to have been more freely elected than most Parliaments.

(17) The Long Parliament had dissolved itself, and had decreed the election of its successor. By the Act 13 Charles II. (Revised Statutes, i. 733) the Long Parliament is "declared and adjudged to be fully dissolved and determined;" but it is not said when it was dissolved and determined. See also Lingard, ix. 5; Hallam's Constitutional History, ii. 21, where the whole matter is discussed, and it is remarked that "the next Parliament never gave their predecessors any other name in the Journals than 'the late assembly.'"

(18) See Norman Conquest, i. 365, 366.

(19) See the discussion on the famous vote of the Convention Parliament in Hallam, Constitutional History, ii. 260—263. Macaulay, ii. 623. Hallam remarks that "the word 'forfeiture' might better have answered this purpose than 'abdication' or 'desertion,'" and he adds, "they proceeded not by the stated rules of the English government, but by the general rights of mankind. They looked not so much to Magna Charta as the original compact of society, and rejected Coke and Hale for Hooker and Harrington." My position is that there is need to go to what Hallam calls "higher constitutional laws" for the justification of the doings of the Convention, but that they were fully justified by the precedents of English History from the eighth century to the fourteenth.

The Scottish Estates, it should be remembered, did not shrink from using the word "forfeited." Macaulay, iii. 285.

(20) See the Act 1 William and Mary "for removing and preventing all Questions and Disputes concerning the Assembling and Sitting of this Present Parliament" (Revised

Statutes, ii. 1). It decrees, "That the Lords Spiritual and Temporal, and Commons convened at Westminster the two and twentieth day of January, in the year of our Lord one thousand six hundred eighty-eight, and there sitting on the thirteenth day of February following, are the two Houses of Parliament, and so shall be and are hereby declared enacted and adjudged to be to all intents, constructions, and purposes whatsoever, notwithstanding any fault of writ or writs of summons, or any defect of form or default whatsoever, as if they had been summoned according to the usual form." The whole history of the question is given in Macaulay, iii. 27—31. The whole matter is summed up in the words (iii. 27), "It was answered that the royal writ was mere matter of form, and that to expose the substance of our laws and liberties to serious hazard for the sake of a form would be the most senseless superstition. Wherever the Sovereign, the Peers spiritual and temporal, and the Representatives freely chosen by the constituent bodies of the realm were met together, there was the essence of a Parliament." In earlier times it might perhaps have been held that there was the essence of a Parliament even without the Sovereign.

(21) Macaulay, iv. 535. "A paper had been circulated, in which the logic of a small sharp pettifogger was employed to prove that writs, issued in the joint names of William and Mary, ceased to be of force as soon as William reigned alone. But this paltry cavil had completely failed. It had not even been mentioned in the Lower House, and had been mentioned in the Upper only to be contemptuously overruled." From my point of view the cavil is certainly paltry, but it is hard to see how it is more paltry than the others.

(22) This is by the Acts 7 and 8 Will. III. c. 15;

6 Anne, c. 7; and 39 Geo. III. c. 127. See Stephen's Commentaries, ii. 380. Blackstone's reasoning runs thus: "This dissolution formerly happened immediately upon the death of the reigning sovereign; for he being considered in law as the head of the parliament (caput principium, et finis), that failing, the whole body was held to be extinct. But the calling a new parliament immediately on the inauguration of the successor being found inconvenient, and dangers being apprehended from having no parliament in being, in case of a disputed succession, it was enacted," etc.

(23) I have said something on this head in Norman Conquest, i. 94, but the whole thing should be studied in Allen's great section on the Tenure of Landed Property; Royal Prerogative, 125—155. It is to Allen that the honour belongs of showing what *bookland* and *folkland* really were.

(24) I have given a few examples in Norman Conquest, i. 589. Endless examples will be found in Kemble's Codex Diplomaticus.

(25) See the complaints on this head as late as the time of William the Third, in Macaulay, iv. 646. On the Acts by which the power of the Crown in this matter is restrained, see Stephen's Commentaries, ii. 520. See also May's Constitutional History, i. 229.

(26 See May, i. 234—248.

(27) This is discussed in full by Allen, Royal Prerogative, 143—145. The great example is the will of King Ælfred. See Codex Diplomaticus, ii. 112, v. 127.

(28) See May, i. 249; Allen, 154—155, who remarks: "By a singular revolution of policy there was a recurrence in the late reign to the ancient policy of the Anglo-Saxons.

The crown lands were virtually restored to the public, while the King obtained the right of acquiring landed property by purchase, and of bequeathing it by will like a private person."

(29) Edward the First was the earliest King whose reign is dated from a time earlier than his coronation. He was out of the kingdom at his father's death, and his right was acknowledged without opposition. But even in this case there was an interregnum. The regnal years of Edward the First are not reckoned from the day of his father's death, but from the day of his funeral, when Edward was acknowledged King, and when the prelates and nobles swore allegiance to him. See the account in the Worcester Annals, Annales Monastici, iv. 462, and the documents in Rymer, i. part ii. 497. See also the remarks of Allen, 46, 47. The doctrine that there can be no interregnum seems to have been put into shape to please James the First, and it was of course altogether upset by the great vote of 1688. Now of course there is no interregnum; not indeed from any mysterious prerogative of the Crown, but simply because the Act of Settlement has entailed the Crown in a particular way.

(30) On this see Norman Conquest, i. 107, 263, 625. See the same question discussed in quite another part of the world in Herodotus, vii. 3.

(31) The helpless way in which Blackstone himself wrote was perhaps pardonable in the dark times in which he lived. But it is really too bad when lawyer after lawyer, in successive editions, gives again to the world the astounding rubbish which in Blackstone's day passed for early constitutional history. In Kerr's edition of Blackstone, published in 1857, vol. i. p. 180, I find repeated, without alteration or comment,

the monstrous assertion of Blackstone: "I believe there is no instance wherein the Crown of England has ever been asserted to be elective, except by the regicides at the infamous and unparalleled trial of King Charles I." And in Serjeant Stephen's Commentaries (1853), which are not a mere edition of Blackstone, but "New Commentaries partly founded on Blackstone," the same words are found in vol. ii. p. 403, only leaving out the epithet "unparalleled," which might with truth have been allowed to stay. In another place (iv. 481-2) we read how "after the Saxon government was firmly established in this island" came "the subdivision of the kingdom into a heptarchy, consisting of seven independent kingdoms, peopled and governed by different clans and colonies." It seems then that in 1857 there were learned gentlemen who believed in a kingdom subdivided into a heptarchy. But when, in the next page, Blackstone tells us how Ælfred set about "to new-model the constitution, to rebuild it on a plan that should endure for ages," and goes on in the usual style to attribute everything whatever to Ælfred personally, this seems to have been too much, and the editor gives an extract from Kemble by way of correction. One wonders that, if he had read Kemble at all, he had not learned a little more from him. It is amusing again when Blackstone tells us (i. 186, Kerr), "From Egbert to the death of Edmund Ironside, a period of above two hundred years, the Crown descended regularly through a succession of fifteen princes, without any deviation or interruption: save only"—all the cases where it did not descend regularly, according to Blackstone's notions of regularity. But it is almost more amusing when Serjeant Stephen (ii. 410) throws Blackstone's exceptions, which are at least historical facts, into a note, and gives us instead as his own exceptions, the statement, very doubtful and, if true, utterly irrelevant, that Æthelstan and Eadmund Ironside were illegitimate (see Norman Conquest, i. 669—673). We of course get the usual talk about the usurpations of Harold, Stephen, John, and Henry the Fourth, and about the rights of Eadgar and Arthur of Britanny. For the former we get a quotation from Matthew Paris, to whom it would have been more to the purpose to go for the great speech of Archbishop Hubert. The comments on the succession of John (i. 189, Kerr) are singularly amusing, but too long to quote.

One point however must be mentioned. To prove the strictly hereditary nature of the succession, Blackstone (i. 189, Kerr) quotes the Statute of 25 Edward III. "that the law of the Crown of England is, and always hath been, that the children of the King of England, whether born in England or elsewhere, ought to bear the inheritance after the death of their ancestors." We are bound to suppose that these learned lawyers had read through the statute which they quoted; but it is wonderful that they did not see that it had nothing whatever to do with fixing the hereditary succession of the Crown. The original text (Revised Statutes, i. 176) runs thus:—

"La lei de la Corone Dengleterre est, et ad este touz jours tiele, que les enfantz des Rois Dengleterre, *queu part qils soient neez en Engleterre ou aillors*, sont ables et deivent porter heritage, apres la mort lour auncestors."

The object of the statute is something quite different from what any one would think from Blackstone's way of quoting it. The emphatic words are those which are put in italics. The object of the statute is to make the King's children and others born of English parents beyond sea capable of inheriting in England. As far as the succession to the Crown is concerned, its effect is simply to put a child of the King born out of the realm on a level with his brother born in the realm; that is, in the view of our older Law, to give both alike the preference due to an Ætheling.

(32) It is as well to explain this, because most people seem to think that a man becomes a Bishop by virtue of receiving a private letter from the First Lord of the Treasury. We constantly see a man spoken of as Bishop of such a see, and his works advertised as such, before a single ecclesiastical or legal step has been taken to make him so.

(33) See Norman Conquest, iii. 44, 623.

(34) The succession of a grandson, which first took place in England in the case of Richard the Second, marks a distinct stage in the growth of the doctrine of hereditary right. It involves the doctrine of representation, which is a very subtle and technical one, and not nearly so obvious or so likely to occur in an early state of society as the doctrine of nearness of kin. No opposition was made to the accession of Richard the Second, but there seems to have been a strong notion in men's minds that John of Gaunt sought to displace his nephew. In earlier times, as the eldest and most eminent of the surviving sons of Edward the Third, John would probably have been elected without any thought of the claims of young Richard.

(35) In Yorkist official language the three Lancastrian Kings were usurpers, and Duke Richard was *de jure*, though not *de facto*, King. Henry the Sixth is, in the Act of 1461, "Henry Usurpour, late called Kyng Henry the sixt." The claim of the House of York was through an intricate female descent from Lionel Duke of Clarence, a son of Edward the Third older than John of Gaunt. A claim so purely

technical had never been set forth before; but we may be quite sure that it would not have been thought to have much weight, if Duke Richard had not been, by another branch, descended from Edward the Third in the male line, and if he had not been moreover the ablest and most popular nobleman in the country.

(36) A prospective election before the vacancy of course hindered any interregnum. In this case the formula "Le Roi est mort; vive le Roi," was perfectly true. The new King was already chosen and crowned, and he had nothing to do but to go on reigning singly instead of in partnership with his father, just as William went on reigning alone after the death of Mary. In Germany this took place whenever a King of the Romans was chosen in the lifetime of the reigning Emperor. In France, under the early Kings of the Parisian dynasty, the practice was specially common, and the fact that there seldom or never was an interregnum doubtless helped much to make the French Crown become, as it did, the most strictly hereditary crown in Christendom. In England, the only distinct case of a coronation of a son during the lifetime of his father was that of Henry, the son of Henry the Second, known as the younger King, and sometimes as Henry the Third. In earlier times we get something like it in the settlement of the Crown by Æthelwulf, with the consent of his Witan (see Old-English History, 105, 106), but it does not seem clear whether there was any actual coronation during the father's lifetime. If there was not, this would be the case most like that of Duke Richard. The compromise placed the Duke in the same position as if he had been Prince of Wales, or rather in a better one, for it might be held to shut out the need of even a formal election on the King's death.

(37) See note 59 on Chapter II.

(38) See Norman Conquest, iii. 623.

(39) See Hallam's Constitutional History, i. 8. It is to be noticed that the settlement enacts that "the inheritance of the Crown, &c., should remain in Henry the Seventh and the heirs of his body for ever, and in none other." This would seem to bar a great number of contingent claims in various descendants of earlier Kings. As it happens, this Act has been literally carried out, for every later Sovereign of England has been a descendant of the body of Henry the Seventh.

(40) The will of Henry the Eighth is fully discussed by Hallam, i. 34, 288, 294; Lingard, vi. 213. There are two Acts of Henry's reign bearing on the matter. In the earlier one, 28 Henry VIII. c. 7, the Crown is entailed on the King's sons by Jane Seymour or any other wife; then on the King's legitimate daughters, no names being mentioned; the Act then goes on to say, "your Highnes shall have full and plenar power and auctorite to geve despose appoynte assigne declare and lymytt by your letters patentes under your great seale or ells by your laste Will made in wrytynge and signed with your moste gracious hande, at your onely pleasure from tyme to tyme herafter, the imperiall Crowne of this Realme and all other the premisses thereunto belongyng, to be remayne succede and come after your decease and for lack of lawfull heires of your body to be procreated and begoten as is afore lymytted by this Acte, to such person or persones in possession and remaynder as shall please your Highnes and according to such estate and after such maner forme facion ordre and condicion as shalbe expressed declared named and lymitted in your said letters patentes or by your said laste will." The later Act, 35 Henry VIII. c. 1, puts Henry's two daughters, Mary and Elizabeth, into the entail, but in a very remarkable

way. The Acts declaring their illegitimacy are not repealed, nor is the legitimacy of either of them in any way asserted; in fact it is rather denied when the preamble rehearses that "The king's Majesty hath only issue of his body lawfully begotten betwixt his Highness and his said late wife Queen Jane the noble and excellent Prince Edward." The Act then goes on to enact that, although the King had been enabled to "dispose" the Crown "to any person or persons of such estate therein as should please his Highness to limit and appoint," yet that, in failure of heirs of the body of either the King or his son, "the said imperial Crown and all other the premises shall be to the Lady Mary the King's Highness daughter, and to the heirs of the body of the same Lady Mary lawfully begotten, with such conditions as by his Highness shall be limited by his letters patents under his great seal, or by his Majesty's last will in writing signed with his gracious hand." Failing Mary and her issue the same conditional entail is extended to Elizabeth and her issue. The power of creating a remainder after the issue of Elizabeth of course remained with Henry, and he exercised it in favour of the issue of his younger sister Mary. Mary and Elizabeth therefore really reigned, not by virtue of any royal descent, but by virtue of a particular entail by which the Crown was settled on the King's illegitimate daughters, as it might have been settled on a perfect stranger. It was an attempt on the part of Edward the Sixth to do without parliamentary authority what his father had done by parliamentary authority which led to the momentary occupation of the throne by Lady Jane Grey. Mary, on her accession, raked up the whole story of her mother's marriage and divorce, and the Act of the first year of her reign recognized her as inheriting by legitimate succession. The Act passed on the accession of Elizabeth, 1 Eliz. c. 3, is much vaguer. It enacts "that your majestie our sayd Sovereigne Ladye ys and in verye dede and of most meere right ought to bee by the Lawes of God and the Lawes and Statutes of this Realme our most rightfull and lawfull Sovereigne liege Ladie and Quene; and that your Highness ys rightlye lynyallye and lawfully discended and come of the bloodd royall of this Realme of Englande in and to whose princely person and theires of your bodye lawfully to bee begotten after youe without all doubte ambiguitee scruple or question the imperiall and Royall estate place crowne and dignitie of this Reallme withe all honnours stiles titles dignities Regalities Jurisdiccons and preheminences to the same nowe belonging & apperteyning arre & shalbee most fully rightfully really & entierly invested & incorporated united & annexed as rightfully & lawfully to all intentes construccons & purposes as the same were in the said late Henrye theight or in the late King Edwarde the Syxte your Highnes Brother, or in the late Quen Marye your Highnes syster at anye tyme since thacte of parliament made in the xxxvth yere of the reigne of your said most noble father king Henrye theight."

It should be remembered that Sir Thomas More, though he refused to swear to the preamble of the oath of the Act of Supremacy, was ready to swear to the order of succession which entailed the Crown on the issue of Anne Boleyn. On his principles the issue of Anne Boleyn would be illegitimate; but he also held that Parliament could settle the Crown upon anybody, on an illegitimate child of the King's or on a total stranger; to the succession therefore he had no objection to swear.

For a parallel to the extraordinary power thus granted to Henry we have to go back to the days of Æthelwulf.

(41) The position of the daughters of Henry the Eighth was of course practically affected by the fact that each was the child of a mother who was acknowledged as a lawful wife at the time of her birth. There was manifest harshness in ranking children so born with ordinary illegitimate children; but, in strictness of Law, as Henry married Anne Boleyn while Katharine of Aragon was alive, the daughter of Katharine and the daughter of Anne could not both be legitimate. The question was, which marriage was lawful. It should also be remembered that the marriage of Anne Boleyn was declared void, and her daughter declared illegitimate, on grounds—whatever they were—which had nothing to do with the earlier question of the marriage and divorce of Katharine.

(42) See Hallam, i. 129; Lingard, vi. 239, 243. The Act 13 Elizabeth, c. 1, declares it to be treason "yf any person shall in any wyse holde and affyrme or mayntayne that the Common Lawes of this Realme not altred by Parlyament, ought not to dyrecte the Ryght of the crowne of England, or that our said sovrayne Ladye Elizabeth the Quenes Majestie that nowe is, with and by the aucthoritye of the Parlyament of Englande is not able to make Lawes and Statutes of suffycyent force and valyditie to lymit and bynd the Crowne of this Realme, and the Descent Lymitacion Inheritaunce and Government thereof." The like is the crime of "whosoever shall hereafter duryng the Lyef of our said Soveraigne Ladye, by any Booke or Worke prynted or written, dyrectly and expresly declare and affyrme at any tyme before the same be by Acte of Parlyament of this Realme established and affyrmed, that any one particular person whosover it be, is or ought to be the ryght Heire and Successor to the Queenes Majestie that nowe is (whome God longe preserve) except the same be the naturall yssue of her Majesties bodye."

This statute may possibly be taken as setting aside the claims of the House of Suffolk; but, if so, it sets aside the claims of the House of Stewart along with them.

(43) James's right was acknowledged by his own first Parliament, just as the claims of other Kings who entered in an irregular way had been. It should be marked however that he was crowned before he was acknowledged. The Act 1 Jac. I. c. 1, declares that "immediatelie upon the Dissolution and Decease of Elizabeth late Queene of England, the Imperiall Crowne of the Realme of England, and of all the Kingdomes Dominions and Rights belonging to the same, did by inherent Birthright and lawfull undoubted Succession, descend and come to your moste excellent Majestie, as beinge lineallie justly and lawfullie next and sole Heire of the Blood Royall of this Realme as is aforesaid." It is worth noticing that in this Act we get the following definition of Parliament, "this high Court of Parliament, where all the whole Body of the Realm and every particular member thereof, either in Person or by Representation (upon their own free elections), are by the Laws of this Realm deemed to be personally present."

(44) The fact that James the First, a King who came in with no title whatever but what was given him by an Act of Parliament passed after his coronation, was acknowledged without the faintest opposition is one of the most remarkable things in our history. Hallam (i. 294) remarks that "there is much reason to believe that the consciousness of this defect in his parliamentary title put James on magnifying, still more than from his natural temper he was prone to do, the inherent rights of primogenitory succession, as something indefeasible by the legislature; a doctrine which, however it might suit the schools of divinity, was in diametrical opposi-

tion to our statutes." Certainly no opposition can be more strongly marked than that between the language of James's own Parliament, and the words quoted above from 13 Eliz. c. 1. But see the remarks of Hallam a few pages before (i. 288) on the kind of tacit election by which it might be said that James reigned. "What renders it absurd to call him and his children usurpers? He had that which the flatterers of his family most affected to disdain—the will of the people; not certainly expressed in regular suffrage or declared election, but unanimously and voluntarily ratifying that which in itself could surely give no right, the determination of the late Queen's Council to proclaim his accession to the throne."

(45) Whitelocke's Memorials, 367. "The heads of the charge against the King, were published by leave, in this form: That Charles Stuart, being admitted King of England, & therein trusted with a limited power, to govern by, & according to the Laws of the Land, & not otherwise, & by his trust being obliged, as also by his Oath, & office to use the power committed to him, for the good & benefit of the people, & for the preservation of their Rights and Privileges," etc.

At an earlier stage (365) the President had told the King that the Court "sat here by the Authority of the Commons of England: & all your predecessours, & you are responsible to them." The King answered "I deny that, shew me one Precedent." The President, instead of quoting the precedents which were at least plausible, told the prisoner that he was not to interrupt the Court. Earlier still the King had objected to the authority of the Court that "he saw no Lords there which should make a Parliament, including the King; &

urged that the Kingdom of England was hereditary, & not successive." The strong point of Charles's argument undoubtedly was the want of concurrence on the part of the Lords. Both Houses of Parliament had agreed in the proceedings against Edward the Second and Richard the Second.

It is a small point, but it is well to notice that the description of the King as Charles Stewart was perfectly accurate. Charles, the son of James, the son of Henry Stewart Lord Darnley, really had a surname, though it might not be according to Court etiquette to call him by it. The helpless French imitators in 1793 summoned their King by the name of "Louis Capet," as if Charles had been summoned by the name of "Unready," "Bastard," "Lackland," "Longshanks," or any other nickname of an earlier King and forefather.

I believe that many people fancy that Guelph or Welf is a surname of the present, or rather late, royal family.

(46) The Act 1 William and Mary (Revised Statutes, ii. 11) entailed the Crown "after their deceases," "to the heires of the body of the said princesse & for default of such issue to the Princesse Anne of Denmarke & the heires of her body & for default of such issue to the heires of the body of the said Prince of Orange." It was only after the death of "the most hopeful Prince William Duke of Gloucester" that the Crown was settled (12 and 13 Will. III. c. 2; Revised Statutes, ii. 94) on "the most excellent Princess Sophia Electress and Dutchess Dowager of Hannover, daughter of the most excellent Princess Elizabeth, late Queen of Bohemia, daughter of our late sovereign lord King James the First of happy memory," "and the heirs of her body being protestants."

(47) We hardly need assurance of the fact, but if it were needed, something like an assurance to that effect was given by an official member of the House during the present session. At all events we read in Sir T. E. May (ii. 83) that "The increased power of the House of Commons, under an improved representation, has been patent and indisputable. Responsible to the people, it has, at the same time, wielded the people's strength. No longer subservient to the crown, the ministers, and the peerage, it has become the predominant authority in the state." But the following strange remark follows: "But it is characteristic of the British constitution, and *a proof of its freedom from the spirit of democracy*, that the more dominant the power of the House of Commons,—the greater has been its respect for the law, and the more carefully have its acts been restrained within the proper limits of its own jurisdiction." *ὦ δημοκρατία, ταῦτα δῆτ᾽ ἀνασχετά ;* Has Mr. Grote lived and written so utterly in vain that a writer widely indeed removed from the vulgar herd of oligarchic babblers looks on "the spirit of democracy" as something inconsistent with "respect for the law"?

(48) The story is told (Plutarch, Lycurgus, 7), that King Theopompos, having submitted to the lessening of the kingly power by that of the Ephors, was rebuked by his wife, because the power which he handed on to those who came after him would be less than what he had received from those who went before him. *ὃν καί φασιν ὑπὸ τῆς ἑαυτοῦ γυναικὸς ὀνειδιζόμενον ὡς ἐλάττω παραδώσοντα τοῖς παισὶ τὴν βασιλείαν, ἢ παρέλαβε, μείζω μὲν οὖν, εἰπεῖν, ὅσῳ χρονιωτέραν· τῷ γὰρ ὄντι τὸ ἄγαν ἀποβαλοῦσα μετὰ τοῦ φθόνου διέφυγε τὸν κίνδυνον.* Aristotle also (Pol. v. 11) tells the story to the same effect, bringing it in with the comment, *ὅσῳ γὰρ ἂν ἐλαττόνων ὦσι κύριοι, πλείω χρόνον ἀναγκαῖον μένειν πᾶσαν τὴν ἀρχήν·*

αὐτοί τε γὰρ ἧττον γίνονται δεσποτικοὶ καὶ τοῖς ἤθεσιν ἴσοι μᾶλλον, καὶ ὑπὸ τῶν ἀρχομένων φθονοῦνται ἧττον. διὰ γὰρ τοῦτο καὶ ἡ περὶ Μολοττοὺς πολὺν χρόνον βασιλεία διέμεινεν, καὶ ἡ Λακεδαιμονίων διὰ τὸ ἐξ ἀρχῆς τε εἰς δύο μέρη διαιρεθῆναι τὴν ἀρχήν, καὶ πάλιν Θεοπόμπου μετριάσαντος τοῖς τε ἄλλοις καὶ τὴν τῶν ἐφόρων ἀρχὴν ἐπικαταστήσαντος· τῆς γὰρ δυνάμεως ἀφελὼν ηὔξησε τῷ χρόνῳ τὴν βασιλείαν, ὥστε τρόπον τινα ἐποίησεν οὐκ ἐλάττονα ἀλλὰ μείζονα αὐτήν. The kingdom of the Molossians referred to in the extract from Aristotle is one of those states of antiquity of which we should be well pleased to hear more. Like the Macedonian kingdom, it was an instance of the heroic kingship surviving into the historical ages of Greece. But the Molossian kingship seems to have been more regular and popular than that of Macedonia, and to have better deserved the name of a constitutional monarchy. The Molossian people and the Molossian King exchanged oaths not unlike those of the Landesgemeinde and the Landammann of Appenzell-ausserrhoden, the King swearing to rule according to the laws, and the people swearing to maintain the kingdom according to the laws. In the end the kingdom changed into a Federal Republic. See History of Federal Government, i. 151.

(49) It is simply frivolous in the present state of England to discuss the comparative merits of commonwealths and constitutional monarchies with any practical object. Constitutional monarchy is not only firmly fixed in the hearts of the people, but it has some distinct advantages over republican forms of government, just as republican forms of government have some advantages over it. It may be doubted whether the people have not a more real control over the executive when the House of Commons, or, in the last resort, the people itself in the polling booths (as in 1868), can displace a Govern-

ment at any moment, than they have in constitutions in which an executive, however much it may have disappointed the hopes of those who chose it, cannot be removed before the end of its term of office, except on the legal proof of some definite crime. But in itself, there really seems no reason why the form of the Executive Government should not be held to be as lawful a subject for discussion as the House of Lords, the Established Church, the standing army, or anything else. It shows simple ignorance, if it does not show something worse, when the word "republican" is used as synonymous with cut-throat or pickpocket. I do not find that in republican countries this kind of language is applied to the admirers of monarchy; but the people who talk in this way are just those who have no knowledge of republics either in past history or in present times. They may very likely have climbed a Swiss mountain, but they have taken care not to ask what was the constitution of the country at its foot.

I have discussed the three chief forms of executive government, the constitutional King and his Ministry, the President, and the Executive Council, in the last of my Historical Essays.

(50) Iliad, i. 250 :—

> *τῷ δ' ἤδη δύο μὲν γενεαὶ μερόπων ἀνθρώπων*
> *ἐφθίαθ', οἵ οἱ πρόσθεν ἅμα τράφεν ἠδ' ἐγένοντο*
> *ἐν Πύλῳ ἠγαθέῃ, μετὰ δὲ τριτάτοισιν ἄνασσεν.*

R. CLAY, SONS, AND TAYLOR, PRINTERS, BREAD STREET HILL.

October, 1871.

BEDFORD STREET, COVENT GARDEN,
LONDON, W.C.

A CATALOGUE

OF

TRAVELS, FICTION, JUVENILE WORKS, ETC.

PUBLISHED BY

MACMILLAN AND CO.

Alice's Adventures in Wonderland. By LEWIS CARROLL. With Forty-two Illustrations by TENNIEL. Twenty-eighth Thousand. Crown 8vo. cloth gilt. 6*s*.

A GERMAN TRANSLATION OF THE SAME. With TENNIEL'S Illustrations. Crown 8vo. gilt. 6*s*.

A FRENCH TRANSLATION OF THE SAME. With TENNIEL'S Illustrations. Crown 8vo. gilt. 6*s*.

"*Beyond question supreme among modern books for children.*"—SPECTATOR. "*One of the choicest and most charming books ever composed for a child's reading.*"—PALL MALL GAZETTE. "*A very pretty and highly original book, sure to delight the little world of wondering minds, and which may well please those who have unfortunately passed the years of wondering.*"—TIMES.

Baker.—Works by Sir SAMUEL W. BAKER, M.A., F.R.G.S.:—

THE NILE TRIBUTARIES OF ABYSSINIA, AND THE SWORD HUNTERS OF THE HAMRAN ARABS. With Maps and Illustrations. Fourth and Cheaper Edition. Crown 8vo. 6*s*.

"*This charming volume, better written than most essays, and fuller of interest than most novels . . . . . . The best book of sporting adventure it was ever our lot to read.*"—SPECTATOR. "*It abounds in animated tales of exploits, dear to the heart of the British sportsman.*"—TIMES. "*The only disappointment which it can occasion the reader, is that he comes to a close too soon.*"—NEW YORK TRIBUNE. "*He has conquered the secret of the mysterious river.*"—DAILY NEWS.

THE ALBERT N'YANZA GREAT BASIN OF THE NILE, AND EXPLORATION OF THE NILE SOURCES. New and Cheaper Edition. With Maps and Illustrations. One Vol. Crown 8vo. 6*s*.

"*His account of his adventures will probably be the book of the summer. Charmingly written, full of incident, and free from that wearisome reiteration of useless facts which is the drawback to almost all books of African travel.*"—SPECTATOR. "*As a Macaulay arose among the historians, so a Baker has arisen among the explorers.*"—READER.

CAST UP BY THE SEA; OR, THE ADVENTURES OF NED GREY. With Illustrations by HUARD. Third Edition. Crown 8vo. cloth gilt. 7*s*. 6*d*.

"*An admirable tale of adventure, of marvellous incidents, wild exploits and terrible denouements.*"—DAILY NEWS. "*A story of adventure by sea and land in the good old style.*"—PALL MALL GAZETTE.

Baring-Gould.—IN EXITU ISRAEL. An Historical Novel. By S. BARING-GOULD, M.A., Author of "Curious Myths of the Middle Ages." Two Vols. 8vo. 21*s*.

"*Some of its most powerful passages—and prodigiously powerful they are—are descriptions of familiar events in the earlier days of the*

Revolution."—LITERARY CHURCHMAN. "*Full of the most exciting incidents and ably portrayed characters, abounding in beautifully attractive legends, and relieved by descriptions fresh, vivid, and truth-like.*" —WESTMINSTER REVIEW.

Barker.—Works by LADY BARKER :—

STATION LIFE IN NEW ZEALAND. Second and Cheaper Edition. Extra fcap. 8vo. 3*s.* 6*d.*

"*We have never read a more truthful or a pleasanter little book.*"—ATHENÆUM. "*The best, pleasantest, and most encouraging narrative of colonial life to be found among the abundant literature of emigration.*"—CHAMBERS'S JOURNAL.

SPRING COMEDIES. STORIES.

CONTENTS :—A Wedding Story—A Stupid Story—A Scotch Story—A Man's Story. Crown 8vo. 7*s.* 6*d.*

"*Lady Barker is endowed with a rare and delicate gift for narrating stories,—she has the faculty of throwing even into her printed narrative a soft and pleasant tone, which goes far to make the reader think the subject or the matter immaterial, so long as the author will go on telling stories for his benefit.*"—ATHENÆUM.

STORIES ABOUT :— With Six Illustrations. Second Edition. Extra fcap. 8vo. 4*s.* 6*d.*

CONTENTS :—Monkeys—Jamaica—Camp Life—Dogs—Boys, &c.

"*The most entertaining book for children that has been published this season. . . . There is not a tale in the book which can fail to please children as well as their elders.*"—PALL MALL GAZETTE. "*We wager that the book is one a child will read till Nurse comes for the fourth time, and will then beg to have it put under its pillow.*"—TIMES.

A CHRISTMAS CAKE IN FOUR QUARTERS. With Illustrations by JELLICOE. Extra fcap. 8vo. cloth gilt. 4*s.* 6*d.*

Behind the Looking-Glass, and what Alice Saw THERE. By LEWIS CARROLL, Author of "Alice's Adventures in Wonderland." With Fifty Illustrations by TENNIEL. Crown 8vo. 6*s.*

Clemency Franklyn. By the Author of "Janet's Home." Globe 8vo. 2*s.* 6*d.*

"*Full of wisdom and goodness, simple, truthful, and artistic. . . . . . It is capital as a story; better still in its pure tone and wholesome influence.*"—GLOBE.

Clunes.—THE STORY OF PAULINE: an Autobiography. By G. C. CLUNES. Crown 8vo. 6*s.*

"*Both for vivid delineation of character and fluent lucidity of style, 'The Story of Pauline' is in the first rank of modern fiction.*"—GLOBE. "*Told with delightful vivacity, thorough appreciation of life, and a complete knowledge of character.*"—MANCHESTER EXAMINER.

Cox.—RECOLLECTIONS OF OXFORD. By G. V. COX, M.A., late Esquire Bedel and Coroner in the University of Oxford. Second Edition. Crown 8vo. 6*s.*

Mr. Cox's Recollections date from the end of last century to quite recent times. They are full of old stories and traditions, epigrams and personal traits of the distinguished men who have been at Oxford during that period. The TIMES *says that it "will pleasantly recall in many a country parsonage the memory of youthful days."*

Days of Old; STORIES FROM OLD ENGLISH HISTORY. By the Author of "Ruth and her Friends." New Edition. 18mo. cloth, gilt leaves. 3*s.* 6*d.*

"*Full of truthful and charming historic pictures, is everywhere vital with moral and religious principles, and is written with a brightness of description, and with a dramatic force in the representation of character, that have made, and will always make, it one of the greatest favourites with reading boys.*"—NONCONFORMIST.

Dilke.—GREATER BRITAIN. A Record of Travel in English-speaking Countries during 1866-7. (America, Australia, India.) By Sir CHARLES WENTWORTH DILKE, M.P. Fifth and Cheaper Edition. Crown 8vo. 6*s.*

"*It is an entertaining and spirited record of travel in lands which have a fascinating interest for Englishmen.*"—SPECTATOR. "*Mr. Dilke has written a book which is probably as well worth reading as any book of the same aims and character that ever was written.*"—SATURDAY REVIEW. "*A work such as no man who cares for the future of his race can afford to treat with indifference.*"—DAILY NEWS.

Estelle Russell. By the Author of "The Private Life of Galileo." Crown 8vo. 6*s*.

Full of bright pictures of French life. The English family, whose fortunes form the main drift of the story, reside mostly in France, but there are also many English characters and scenes of great interest. It is certainly the work of a fresh, vigorous, and most interesting writer, with a dash of sarcastic humour, which is refreshing and not too bitter.

Fairy Book. The Best Popular Fairy Stories. Selected and Rendered anew by the Author of "John Halifax, Gentleman." With Coloured Illustrations and Ornamental Borders by J. E. ROGERS, Author of "Ridicula Rediviva." Crown 8vo. cloth, extra gilt. 6*s*. (Golden Treasury Edition. 18mo. 4*s*. 6*d*.)

"*A delightful selection, in a delightful external form.*"—Spectator.

Higginson.—MALBONE: An Oldport Romance. By T. W. HIGGINSON. Fcap. 8vo. 2*s*. 6*d*.

This is a story of American life so told as to be interesting and instructive to all English readers. The Daily News *says,* "*Who likes a quiet story, full of mature thought, of clear humorous surprises, of artistic studious design? 'Malbone' is a rare work, possessing these characteristics, and replete, too, with honest literary effort.*"

Keary.—JANET'S HOME. By Miss KEARY. Crown 8vo. 6*s*.

"*Never did a more charming family appear upon the canvas; and most skilfully and felicitously have their characters been portrayed. Each individual of the fireside is a finished portrait, distinct and lifelike. . . . The future before her as a novelist is that of becoming the Miss Austin of her generation.*"—THE SUN.

Keary (A. and E.)—Works by :—

THE LITTLE WANDERLIN, and other Fairy Tales. 18mo. 3*s*. 6*d*.

"*The tales are fanciful and well written, and they are sure to win favour amongst little readers.*"—ATHENÆUM.

THE HEROES OF ASGARD. Tales from Scandinavian Mythology. New and Revised Edition, illustrated by HUARD. Extra fcap. 8vo. 4*s*. 6*d*.

"*Told in a light and amusing style, which, in its drollery and quaintness, reminds us of our old favourite Grimm.*"—TIMES.

Kingsley.—Works by the Rev. CHARLES KINGSLEY, M.A., Rector of Eversley, and Canon of Chester :—

"WESTWARD HO!" or, The Voyages and Adventures of Sir Amyas Leigh. Sixth Edition. Crown 8vo. 6*s*.

No other work conveys a more vivid idea of the surging, adventurous, nobly inquisitive spirit of the generation which immediately followed the Reformation in England. Every reader must find his heart warm with admiration towards the men whose life-like photographs are so clearly and naturally grouped on the author's pages, and whose daring deeds are told with a freshness, an enthusiasm, and a truthfulness that can belong only to one who wishes he had been their leader. His descriptions of the luxuriant scenery of the then new found Western land are acknowledged to be unmatched.

TWO YEARS AGO. Fourth Edition. Crown 8vo. 6*s*.

"*Mr. Kingsley has provided us all along with such pleasant diversions—such rich and brightly tinted glimpses of natural history, such suggestive remarks on mankind, society, and all sorts of topics, that amidst the pleasure of the way, the circuit to be made will be by most forgotten.*"—THE GUARDIAN.

HYPATIA; or, New Foes with an Old Face. Fifth Edition. Crown 8vo. 6*s*.

The work is from beginning to end a series of fascinating pictures of strange phases of that strange primitive society; and no finer portrait has

Kingsley (Rev. C.)—*continued.*

yet been given of the noble-minded lady who was faithful to martyrdom in her attachment to the classical creeds. No work affords a clearer notion of the many interesting problems which agitated the minds of men in those days, and which, in various phases, are again coming up for discussion at the present day.

HEREWARD THE WAKE—LAST OF THE ENGLISH. Crown 8vo. 6*s.*

Mr. Kingsley's power of artistic realization is so great, that here he tells the story of the final conflict of the two races, Saxons and Normans, as if he himself had borne a part in it. While as a work of fiction "Hereward" cannot fail to delight all readers, no better supplement to the dry history of the time could be put into the hands of the young, containing as it does so vivid a picture of the social and political life of the period.

YEAST: A Problem. Fifth Edition. Crown 8vo. 5*s.*

In this production the author shows in an interesting dramatic form, the state of fermentation in which the minds of many earnest men are with regard to some of the most important religious and social problems of the day.

ALTON LOCKE. New Edition. With a New Preface. Crown 8vo. 4*s.* 6*d.*

This novel, which shews forth the evils arising from modern "caste" has done much to remove the unnatural barriers which existed between the various classes of society, and establish a sympathy to some extent between the higher and lower grades of the social scale. Though written with a purpose, it is full of character and interest; the author shows, to quote the SPECTATOR, *"what it is that constitutes the true Christian, God-fearing, man-living gentleman."*

AT LAST: A CHRISTMAS IN THE WEST INDIES. With numerous Illustrations. Two Vols. Crown 8vo. 21*s.*

"In this book Mr. Kingsley revels in the gorgeous wealth of West Indian vegetation, bringing before us one marvel after another, alternately sating and piquing our curiosity. Whether we climb the cliffs with him,

Kingsley (Rev. C.)—*continued.*

or peer over into narrow bays which are being hollowed out by the trade-surf, or wander through impenetrable forests, where the tops of the trees form a green cloud overhead, or gaze down glens which are watered by the clearest brooks, running through masses of palm and banana, and all the rich variety of foliage, we are equally delighted and amazed."—ATHENÆUM.

THE WATER BABIES. A Fairy Tale for a Land Baby. New Edition, with additional Illustrations by Sir NOEL PATON, R.S.A., and P. SKELTON. Crown 8vo. cloth extra gilt. 5*s.*

"*In fun, in humour, and in innocent imagination, as a child's book we do not know its equal.*"—LONDON REVIEW. "*Mr. Kingsley must have the credit of revealing to us a new order of life. . . . There is in the 'Water Babies' an abundance of wit, fun, good humour, geniality,* élan, *go.*"—TIMES.

THE HEROES; or, Greek Fairy Tales for my Children. With Coloured Illustrations. New Edition. 18mo. 4*s.* 6*d.*

"*We do not think these heroic stories have ever been more attractively told. . . . There is a deep under-current of religious feeling traceable throughout its pages which is sure to influence young readers powerfully.*" —LONDON REVIEW. "*One of the children's books that will surely become a classic.*" —NONCONFORMIST.

Kingsley (H.)—Works by HENRY KINGSLEY :—

TALES OF OLD TRAVEL. Re-narrated. With Eight full-page Illustrations by HUARD. Third Edition. Crown 8vo. cloth, extra gilt. 5*s.*

"*We would heartily advise all who wish to place a book in the hands of youth, from which they must derive at once amusement, information, and fine manly sentiments, to select for this purpose Mr. Kingsley's, 'Tales of Old Travel.'*"—ILLUSTRATED TIMES. "*As for the sensational, most novels are tame compared with these articles.*"—ATHENÆUM.

THE LOST CHILD. With Eight Illustrations by FRÖLICH. Crown 4to. cloth gilt. 3*s.* 6*d.*

Knatchbull-Hugessen.—Works by E. H. KNATCHBULL-HUGESSEN, M.P. :—

STORIES FOR MY CHILDREN. With Illustrations. Second Edition. Crown 8vo. 5*s*.

The stories are charming, and full of life and fun."—STANDARD. "*The author has an imagination as fanciful as Grimm himself, while some of his stories are superior to anything that Hans Christian Andersen has written.*"—NONCONFORMIST.

CRACKERS FOR CHRISTMAS. More Stories. With Illustrations by JELLICOE and ELWES. Third Edition. Crown 8vo. 5*s*.

"*A fascinating little volume, which will make him friends in every household in which there are children.*"—DAILY NEWS.

MOONSHINE: Fairy Tales. With Illustrations by W. BRUNTON. Crown 8vo. cloth gilt. 5*s*.

Little Estella, and other Fairy Tales for the Young. Royal 16mo. 3*s*. 6*d*.

"*This is a fine story, and we thank heaven for not being too wise to enjoy it.*"—DAILY NEWS.

Little Lucy's Wonderful Globe. Pictured by FRÖLICH and narrated by CHARLOTTE M. YONGE, Author of "The Heir of Redclyffe." Crown 4to. with 24 Illustrations, 6*s*.

Macmillan.—Works by the Rev. HUGH MACMILLAN :—

BIBLE TEACHINGS IN NATURE. Fifth Edition. Globe 8vo. 6*s*.

"*The writing of the book is most striking, and in many places highly eloquent.*"—LITERARY CHURCHMAN. "*He has made the world more beautiful to us, and unsealed our ears to voices of praise and messages of love that might otherwise have been unheard.*"—BRITISH QUARTERLY REVIEW.

HOLIDAYS ON HIGH LANDS; OR, RAMBLES AND INCIDENTS IN SEARCH OF ALPINE PLANTS. Globe 8vo. 6*s*.

"*Mr. Macmillan's glowing pictures of Scandinavian nature are enough to kindle in every tourist the desire to take the same interesting high lands*

Macmillan (Rev. Hugh)—*continued.*

for the scenes of his own Autumn holidays."—SATURDAY REVIEW. "*With Mr. Macmillan as his guide, the student ought to find a new interest in the Highlands, however dearly he may have loved them before.*" —NONCONFORMIST.

THE TRUE VINE; OR, THE ANALOGIES OF OUR LORD'S ALLEGORY. Globe 8vo. 6*s.*

"*It abounds in exquisite bits of description, and in striking facts clearly stated.*"—NONCONFORMIST.

FOOT-NOTES FROM THE PAGE OF NATURE. With numerous Illustrations. Fcap. 8vo. 5*s.*

"*The naturalist and the botanist will delight in this volume, and those who understand little of the scientific parts of the work will linger over the mysterious page of nature here unfolded to their view.*"—JOHN BULL. "*Although a clergyman, he does not make the marvels of nature an excuse for weak sermons and maudlin reflections. . . . A mild, a liberal spirit breathes throughout.*"—SATURDAY REVIEW.

THE MINISTRY OF NATURE. Extra fcap. 8vo. 6*s.*

Marlitt (E.)—THE COUNTESS GISELA. Translated from the German of E. MARLITT. Crown 8vo. 7*s.* 6*d.*

"*A very beautiful story of German country life.*" —LITERARY CHURCHMAN.

Mitford (A. B.)—TALES OF OLD JAPAN. By A. B. MITFORD, Second Secretary to the British Legation in Japan. With Illustrations drawn and cut on Wood by Japanese Artists. Two Vols. Crown 8vo. 21*s.*

"*These very original volumes have all the value their author claims for them and more. They give us in a pleasant way a vivid insight into the virtues and eccentricities of a doomed civilization. They present us with pictures of Japanese life and manners not worked out in the monotony of minute detail, but dashed in with bold telling touches.*"—PALL MALL GAZETTE. "*We do not venture too high praise when we say that a strange country and people have never been the theme of a more entertaining work than 'Tales of Old Japan.'*"—TIMES.

Nine Years Old. By the Author of "St. Olave's," "When I was a Little Girl," &c. Illustrated by FRÖLICH. Extra fcap. 8vo. cloth gilt, 4*s.* 6*d.*

Norton.—OLD SIR DOUGLAS. By the Hon. Mrs. NORTON. Cheap Edition. Globe 8vo. 2*s.* 6*d.*

"*This varied and lively novel—this clever novel so full of character and of fine incidental remark.*"—SCOTSMAN. "*One of the pleasantest and healthiest stories of modern fiction.*"—GLOBE.

Our Year. A Child's Book, in Prose and Verse. By the Author of "John Halifax, Gentleman." Illustrated by CLARENCE DOBELL. Royal 16mo. 3*s.* 6*d.*

"*It is just the book we could wish to see in the hands of every child.*"—ENGLISH CHURCHMAN.

Palgrave (F. T.)—THE FIVE DAYS' ENTERTAINMENTS AT WENTWORTH GRANGE. A Book for Children. By FRANCIS TURNER PALGRAVE. With Illustrations by ARTHUR HUGHES and Engraved Title-page by JEENS. Small 4to. cloth extra. 6*s.*

"*If you want a really good book for both sexes and all ages, buy this, as handsome a volume of tales as you'll find in all the market.*"—ATHENÆUM. "*Exquisite both in form and substance.*"—GUARDIAN.

Palgrave (W. G.)—A NARRATIVE OF A YEAR'S JOURNEY THROUGH CENTRAL AND EASTERN ARABIA, 1862-3. By WILLIAM GIFFORD PALGRAVE (late of the Eighth Regiment Bombay N.I.) Fifth and Cheaper Edition. With Map, Plans, and Portrait of Author, engraved on Steel by JEENS. Crown 8vo. 6*s.*

"*As amusing as a tale of the Arabian Nights.*"—SPECTATOR. "*A personal narrative of endurance and address, of force of body and of daring courage, such as all the sensational novels in Mudie's shop can never hope to equal in the way of mere sensation; culminating in a tale of shipwreck of absolutely unsurpassed power, such as we might alone expect from Byron, Marryatt, and Sinbad combined.*"—PALL MALL GAZETTE.

Phantasmagoria, and other Poems. By LEWIS CARROLL, Author of "Alice's Adventures in Wonderland." Fcap. 8vo. gilt edges. 6*s*.

"*Those who have not made acquaintance with these poems already, have a pleasure to come. The comical is* so *comical, the grave so really beautiful.*" —LITERARY CHURCHMAN.

Poole.—PICTURES OF COTTAGE LIFE IN THE WEST OF ENGLAND. By MARGARET E. POOLE. Crown 8vo. 6*s*.

"*Charming stories of peasant life, written in something of George Eliot's style. . . . Her stories could not be other than they are, as literal as truth, as romantic as fiction, full of pathetic touches and strokes of genuine humour. . . . All the stories are studies of actual life, executed with no mean art.*"—TIMES.

Population of an Old Pear Tree. From the French of E. VAN BRUYSSEL. Edited by the Author of "The Heir of Redclyffe." With Illustrations by BECKER. Second Edition. Crown 8vo. gilt edges. 6*s*.

"*This is not a regular book of natural history, but a description of all the living creatures that came and went in a summer's day beneath an old pear tree, observed by eyes that had for the nonce become microscopic, recorded by a pen that finds dramas in everything, aud illustrated by a dainty pencil. . . . We can hardly fancy anyone with a moderate turn for the curiosities of insect life, or for delicate French* esprit, *not being taken by these clever sketches.*"—GUARDIAN. "*A whimsical and charming little book.*"—ATHENÆUM.

Puss and Robin, and their Friends Kitty and Bob. Told in Pictures by FRÖLICH, and in Rhymes by TOM HOOD. Crown 4to. cloth gilt, with Thirteen Illustrations. 3*s*. 6*d*.

Realmah. By the Author of "Friends in Council." New and Cheaper Edition. Crown 8vo. 6*s*.

"*Mr. Helps is a master of English, his writing is distinguished by noble thoughts and by high literary culture.*"—DAILY NEWS. "*We have to go back many a day and across a vast tract of print before we reach any work that stands so fair a chance of being preserved.*"—SCOTSMAN. "*We find in it a treasury of graceful thoughts and suggestive ideas.*"—TIMES.

Richardson (Frederika).—THE ILIAD OF THE EAST. A Selection of Legends drawn from Valmiki's Sanskrit Poem, "The Ramayana." By FREDERIKA RICHARDSON. Crown 8vo. 7*s*. 6*d*.

"*It is impossible to read it without recognizing the value and interest of the Eastern epic. It is as fascinating as a fairy tale, this romantic poem of India.*"—GLOBE.

Rogers.—Works by J. E. ROGERS:—

RIDICULA REDIVIVA. Old Nursery Rhymes. Illustrated in Colours, with Ornamental Cover. Crown 4to. 6*s*.

"*The most splendid, and at the same time the most really meritorious of the books specially intended for children, that we have seen.*"—SPECTATOR. "*These large bright pictures will attract children to really good and honest artistic work, and that ought not to be an indifferent consideration with parents who propose to educate their children.*"—PALL MALL GAZETTE.

MORES RIDICULI. Old Nursery Rhymes. Illustrated in Colours, with Ornamental Cover. Crown 4to. 6*s*.

"*These world-old rhymes have never had and need never wish for a better pictorial setting than Mr. Rogers has given them.*"—TIMES. "*Nothing could be quainter or more absurdly comical than most of the pictures, which are all carefully executed and beautifully coloured.*"—GLOBE.

Ruth and her Friends. A Story for Girls. With a Frontispiece. Fourth Edition. Royal 16mo. 3*s.* 6*d.*

"*We wish all the school girls and home-taught girls in the land had the opportunity of reading it.*"—NONCONFORMIST.

Scouring of the White Horse; OR, THE LONG VACATION RAMBLE OF A LONDON CLERK. By the Author of "Tom Brown's School Days." Illustrated by DOYLE. Eighth Thousand. Imp. 16mo. Cheaper Issue. 3*s.* 6*d.*

"*A glorious tale of summer joy.*"—FREEMAN. "*There is a genial hearty life about the book.*"—JOHN BULL. "*The execution is excellent. . . . Like 'Tom Brown's School Days,' the 'White Horse' gives the reader a feeling of gratitude and personal esteem towards the author.*"—SATURDAY REVIEW.

Storehouse of Stories. Edited by CHARLOTTE M. YONGE, Author of "The Heir of Redclyffe." Second Edition, Globe 8vo. 3*s.* 6*d.*

CONTENTS:—History of Philip Quarll—Goody Twoshoes—The Governess—Jemima Placid—The Perambulations of a Mouse—The Village School—The Little Queen—History of Little Jack.

"*Miss Yonge has done great service to the infantry of this generation by putting these eleven stories of sage simplicity within their reach.*"—BRITISH QUARTERLY REVIEW.

A STOREHOUSE OF STORIES. Second Series. Globe 8vo. 3*s.* 6*d.*

CONTENTS:—Family Stories—Elements of Morality—Puzzle for a Curious Girl—Blossoms of Morality.

Tom Brown's School Days. By An OLD BOY.

Golden Treasury Edition, 4*s.* 6*d.* People's Edition, 2*s.*

With Sixty Illustrations, by A. HUGHES and SYDNEY HALL, Square, cloth extra, gilt edges. 10*s.* 6*d.*

With Seven Illustrations by the same Artists, Crown 8vo. 6*s.*

"*We have read and re-read this book with unmingled pleasure. . . . We have carefully guarded ourselves against any tampering with our critical sagacity, and yet have been compelled again and again to exclaim, 'Bene! Optime!'"*—LONDON QUARTERLY REVIEW. *"An exact picture of the bright side of a Rugby boy's experience, told with a life, a spirit, and a fond minuteness of detail and recollection which is infinitely honourable to the author."*—EDINBURGH REVIEW. *"The most famous boy's book in the language."*—DAILY NEWS.

Tom Brown at Oxford. By the Author of "Tom Brown's School Days." New Edition. With Illustrations. Crown 8vo. 6*s*.

"In no other work that we can call to mind are the finer qualities of the English gentleman more happily portrayed."—DAILY NEWS. *"A book of great power and truth."*—NATIONAL REVIEW.

Trench (R. C.)—A HOUSEHOLD BOOK OF ENGLISH POETRY. Selected and Arranged with Notes, by the ARCHBISHOP OF DUBLIN. Second Edition, revised. Extra fcap. 8vo. 5*s*. 6*d*.

"The Archbishop of Dublin has conferred, in this delightful book, an important gift on the whole English-speaking population of the world."—PALL MALL GAZETTE.

Wandering Willie. By the Author of "Effie's Friends," and "John Hatherton." Second Edition. Crown 8vo. 6*s*.

"This is an idyll of rare truth and beauty. . . . The story is simple and touching, the style of extraordinary delicacy, precision, and picturesqueness. . . . A charming gift-book for young ladies not yet promoted to novels, and will amply repay those of their elders who may give an hour to its perusal."—DAILY NEWS.

When I was a Little Girl. STORIES FOR CHILDREN. By the Author of "St. Olave's." Second Edition. Extra fcap. 8vo. 4*s*. 6*d*. With Eight Illustrations by L. FRÖLICH.

"At the head, and a long way ahead of all books for girls, we place 'When I was a Little Girl.'"—TIMES. *"It is one of the choicest morsels of child-biography which we have met with."*—NONCONFORMIST.

Words from the Poets. Selected by the Editor of "Rays of Sunlight." With a Vignette and Frontispiece. Cheaper Edition. 18mo. limp. 1*s.*

"*The selection aims at popularity, and deserves it.*"—GUARDIAN.

Wright.—DAVID, KING OF ISRAEL. By JOSIAH WRIGHT. Readings for the Young. With Six Illustrations. Royal 16mo. cloth gilt. 3*s.* 6*d.*

"*It is the poem of King David's life, represented by thoughts creative, uncommon, and correct, expressed in a graceful felicity of diction uniform but not unvaried, and of which the chastened fertility sustains no impoverishment by redundance, nor waste by excess of ornament.*"—CHURCH OF ENGLAND MONTHLY REVIEW.

Yonge (Charlotte M.) Works by :—

THE HEIR OF REDCLYFFE. Eighteenth Edition. With Illustrations. Crown 8vo. 6*s.*

HEARTSEASE. Eleventh Edition. With Illustrations. Crown 8vo. 6*s.*

THE DAISY CHAIN. Tenth Edition. With Illustrations. Crown 8vo. 6*s.*

THE TRIAL: MORE LINKS OF THE DAISY CHAIN. Fifth Edition. With Illustrations. Crown 8vo. 6*s.*

DYNEVOR TERRACE. Fourth Edition. Crown 8vo. 6*s.*

HOPES AND FEARS. Third Edition. Crown 8vo. 6*s.*

THE YOUNG STEPMOTHER. Third Edition. Crown 8vo. 6*s.*

CLEVER WOMAN OF THE FAMILY. Second Edition. Crown 8vo. 6*s.*

THE DOVE IN THE EAGLE'S NEST. Second Edition. Crown 8vo. 6*s.*

Yonge (Charlotte M.)—*continued.*

THE CAGED LION. Illustrated. Crown 8vo. 6*s.*

THE CHAPLET OF PEARLS; OR, THE WHITE AND BLACK RIBAUMONT. Two Vols. crown 8vo. 12*s.*

THE PRINCE AND THE PAGE. A Tale of the Last Crusade. Illustrated. 18mo. 3*s.* 6*d.*

"*A tale which, we are sure, will give pleasure to many others besides the young people for whom it is specially intended. . . . This extremely prettily-told story does not require the guarantee afforded by the name of the author of 'The Heir of Redclyffe' on the title-page to ensure its becoming a universal favourite.*"—DUBLIN EVENING MAIL.

THE LANCES OF LYNWOOD. New Edition, with Coloured Illustrations. 18mo. 4*s.* 6*d.*

"*The illustrations are very spirited and rich in colour, and the story can hardly fail to charm the youthful reader.*" — MANCHESTER EXAMINER.

THE LITTLE DUKE: RICHARD THE FEARLESS. New Edition. Illustrated. 18mo. 3*s.* 6*d.*

CAMEOS FROM ENGLISH HISTORY. From ROLLO to EDWARD II. Extra Fcap. 8vo. 5*s.* Second Edition, enlarged.

"*They are a series of vivid pictures which will not easily fade from the memory of the young people for whom they are written.*"—GUARDIAN.

CAMEOS FROM ENGLISH HISTORY. Vol. II. THE WARS IN FRANCE. Extra fcap. 8vo. 5*s.*

LITTLE LUCY'S WONDERFUL GLOBE. Pictured by FRÖLICH, and narrated by CHARLOTTE M. YONGE. With Twenty-four Illustrations. Crown 4to. cloth gilt. 6*s.*

A BOOK OF GOLDEN DEEDS OF ALL TIMES AND ALL COUNTRIES. Gathered and Narrated Anew. New Edition, with Twenty Illustrations by FRÖLICH. Crown 8vo. cloth gilt. 6*s.*

GOLDEN TREASURY SERIES.

Uniformly printed in 18*mo. with Vignette Titles by* SIR NOEL PATON, T. WOOLNER, W. HOLMAN HUNT, J.E. MILLAIS, *&c. Engraved on Steel by* JEENS. *Bound in extra cloth*, 4*s*. 6*d*. *each volume. Also kept in various styles of morocco and calf bindings.*

"THE GOLDEN TREASURY SERIES *disputes if it does not carry away the palm of excellence among works in which the taste of the publisher, printer, stationer, engraver, and binder, is jointly exercised to give additional grace to the productions of writers.*"—ILLUSTRATED LONDON NEWS. "*A very noble series of books.*"—BRITISH QUARTERLY REVIEW.

The Golden Treasury of the Best SONGS and LYRICAL POEMS IN THE ENGLISH LANGUAGE. Selected and Arranged, with Notes, by FRANCIS TURNER PALGRAVE.

"*There is no book in the English language which will make a more delightful companion than this.*"—SPECTATOR.

The Book of Praise. From the Best ENGLISH HYMN WRITERS. Selected and Arranged by Sir ROUNDELL PALMER.

"*All previous compilations of this kind must, undeniably, for the present, give place to the 'Book of Praise.'*"—SATURDAY REVIEW. "*It is a book which ought to find a place in every Christian library.*"—RECORD.

The Adventures of Robinson Crusoe. Edited, from the Original Editions, by J. W. CLARK, M.A.

"*Mutilated and modified editions of this English classic are so much the rule, that a cheap and pretty copy of it, rigidly exact to the original, will be a prize to many book buyers.*"—EXAMINER.

The Republic of Plato. Translated into English, with Analysis and Notes, by J. LL. DAVIES, M.A., and D. J. VAUGHAN, M.A.

"*A dainty and cheap little edition.*"—EXAMINER.

The Song Book. Words and Tunes from the best Poets and Musicians. Selected and Arranged by JOHN HULLAH.

"*A choice collection of the sterling songs of England, Scotland, and Ireland, with the music of each prefixed to the words. How much true wholesome pleasure such a book can diffuse, and will diffuse, we trust, through many thousand families.*"—EXAMINER.

The Poetical Works of Robert Burns. Edited, with Biographical Memoir, by ALEXANDER SMITH. Two Vols.

"*This certainly is the handsomest, most convenient, and most accurate pocket edition of Burns.*"—SPECTATOR. "*Beyond all question the most beautiful edition of Burns yet out.*"—EDINBURGH DAILY REVIEW.

La Lyre Francaise. Selected and Arranged, with Notes, by GUSTAVE MASSON.

"*We doubt whether even in France itself so interesting and complete a repository of the best French lyrics could be found.*"—NOTES AND QUERIES.

Bacon's Essays and COLOURS OF GOOD AND EVIL. With Notes and Classical Index, by W. ALDIS WRIGHT, M.A.

"*By far the most complete as well as the most elegant edition we possess.*" —WESTMINSTER REVIEW. "*It is a scholarly edition of Bacon's Essays that has in one or two of its features distinct value for the exact student of English, while it is the best and prettiest of all pocket editions of the text.*" —EXAMINER.

A Book of Golden Deeds OF ALL COUNTRIES AND ALL TIMES. Gathered and Narrated by the Author of "The Heir of Redclyffe."

"*We have seen no prettier gift-book for a long time, and none which, both for its cheapness and the spirit in which it has been compiled, is more deserving of praise.*"—ATHENÆUM.

A Book of Worthies. Gathered from the Old Histories and Written anew by the Author of "The Heir of Redclyffe."

"*It is a golden book of noble deeds, which young and old will equally delight in, and be inspired by.*"—BRITISH QUARTERLY REVIEW. "*An admirable addition to an admirable series.*"—WESTMINSTER REVIEW.

Tom Brown's School Days. By an OLD BOY. With a Vignette by ARTHUR HUGHES.

"*A perfect gem of a book. The best and most healthy book about boys for boys that ever was written.*"—ILLUSTRATED TIMES.

The Sunday Book of Poetry. Selected and Arranged by C. F. ALEXANDER.

"*A well-selected volume of sacred poetry.*"—SPECTATOR.

The Ballad Book. A Selection of the Choicest British Ballads. Edited by WILLIAM ALLINGHAM.

"*The most perfect 'Ballad Book' ever produced, admirable alike for what it contains and what it excludes, and entitled to the hearty gratitude and unrestrained praise of every lover of our pre-Shakespearian song.*"—NONCONFORMIST.

The Children's Garland from the BEST POETS. Selected and Arranged by COVENTRY PATMORE.

"*It has the merit of being the best of its kind, and of having been collected with a definite object and by a competent person.*"—SATURDAY REVIEW. "*It is the richest collection of the best poetry for children.*"—NONCONFORMIST.

The Fairy Book. The Best Popular Fairy Stories. Selected and Rendered anew by the Author of "John Halifax, Gentleman."

"*A delightful selection, in a delightful external form.*"—SPECTATOR.

The Jest Book. The Choicest Anecdotes and Sayings. Selected and Arranged by MARK LEMON, Editor of *Punch.*

"*The fullest and best jest book that has yet appeared.*"—SATURDAY REVIEW.

The Pilgrim's Progress from this World to that which is to Come. By JOHN BUNYAN.

"*A prettier and better edition of the 'Pilgrim's Progress,' and one more exactly suited for use as an elegant and inexpensive Christmas Gift-book, is not to be found.*"—EXAMINER. "*The prettiest possible edition.*"—GUARDIAN.

A Book of Golden Thoughts. By HENRY ATWELL, Knight of the Order of the Oak Crown.

"*Mr. Attwell has produced a book of rare value. Happily it is small enough to be carried about in the pocket, and of such a companion it would be difficult to weary.*"—PALL MALL GAZETTE.

Guesses at Truth. By TWO BROTHERS. New Edition.

"*A new and dainty edition of a work that has taken a sure and lasting place in our literature.*"—DAILY TELEGRAPH.

Other Volumes in Preparation.

MACMILLAN'S GLOBE LIBRARY.

Beautifully printed on toned paper, price 3*s.* 6*d.* each in cloth plain. Cloth elegant, gilt edges, 4*s.* 6*d.* Also kept in various styles of morocco and calf bindings.

"*The Globe Editions are admirable for their scholarly editing, their typographical excellence, their comprehensive form, and their cheapness.*"—SATURDAY REVIEW.

"*A Series unrivalled for its combination of excellence and cheapness.*"—DAILY TELEGRAPH.

The following are now ready :—

Shakespeare's Complete Works. Edited by W. G. CLARK, M.A., and W. ALDIS WRIGHT, M.A. With Glossary.

"*A marvel of beauty, cheapness, and compactness. . . . For the busy man, above all for the working student, this 'Globe' Edition is the best of all existing Shakespeares.*"—ATHENÆUM. "*To have produced the complete works of the world's greatest poet in such a form, and at a price within the reach of every one, is of itself almost sufficient to give the publishers a claim to be considered public benefactors.*"—PALL MALL GAZETTE.

Morte D'Arthur.—Sir THOMAS MALORY'S Book of King Arthur, and of his Noble Knights of the Round Table. The Edition of Caxton, revised for modern use. With an Introduction, Notes, and Glossary, by Sir EDWARD STRACHEY. New Edition.

"*It is with the most perfect confidence that we recommend this edition of the old romance to every class of readers.*"—PALL MALL GAZETTE.

Robert Burns' Complete Works.—The POEMS, SONGS, and LETTERS. Edited, with Glossarial Index, and Biographica Memoir, by ALEXANDER SMITH. New Edition.

"*The works of the bard have never been offered in such a complete form in a single volume.*"—GLASGOW DAILY HERALD. "*Admirable in all respects.*"—SPECTATOR. "*The cheapest, the most perfect, and the most interesting edition which has been ever published.*"—BELL'S MESSENGER.

The Adventures of Robinson Crusoe. Edited after the Original Editions, with Biographical Introduction, by HENRY KINGSLEY.

"*A most excellent and in every way desirable edition.*"—COURT CIRCULAR. "*Macmillan's Globe Robinson Crusoe is a book to have and to keep.*"—MORNING STAR.

Sir Walter Scott's Poetical Works. With Biographical and Critical Essay by FRANCIS TURNER PALGRAVE. New Edition.

"*As a popular edition it leaves nothing to be desired.*"—SPECTATOR. "*We can almost sympathise with a middle-aged grumbler, who, after reading Mr. Palgrave's memoir and introduction, should exclaim 'Why was there not such an edition of Scott when I was a school-boy?'*"—GUARDIAN.

Oliver Goldsmith's Miscellaneous Works. With Biographical Introduction by PROFESSOR MASSON.

"*Cheap, elegant, and complete.*"—NONCONFORMIST. "*We do not know any edition more adapted for popular use.*"—COURT CIRCULAR. "*We do not know a better edition.*"—GLASGOW DAILY HERALD.

Edmund Spenser's Complete Works. Edited with Glossary by R. MORRIS, and Memoir by J. W. HALES.

"*Worthy—and higher praise it needs not—of the beautiful 'Globe Series.' The work is edited with all the care so noble a poet deserves.*"—THE DAILY NEWS. "*The best service the publishers have yet rendered to the lovers of genuine poetry and real English classical scholarship is the issue of this excellent edition.*"—ILLUSTRATED LONDON NEWS.

Alexander Pope's Poetical Works. Edited, with Notes and Introductory Memoir, by PROFESSOR WARD.

"*The book is handsome and handy.*"—ATHENÆUM. "*We are inclined to think this edition not only the cheapest, but the very best that can be put into the hands of a student of English literature.*"—PUBLISHER'S CIRCULAR.

John Dryden's Poetical Works. Edited, with a Revised Text and Notes, by W. D. CHRISTIE, M.A., Trinity College, Cambridge.

"*It is hardly possible that a better and more handy edition of this poet could be produced.*"—ATHENÆUM. "*Probably the most perfect edition yet seen in print.*"—ILLUSTRATED LONDON NEWS.

Cowper's Poetical Works. Edited, with Notes and Biographical Introduction, by W. BENHAM, M.A., Professor of Modern History in Queen's College, London.

"*Mr. Benham's edition of Cowper is one of permanent value. The biographical introduction is excellent, full of information, singularly neat and readable and modest—indeed too modest in its comments. The notes are consise and accurate, and the editor has been able to discover and introduce some hitherto unprinted matter. Altogether the book is a very excellent one.*"—SATURDAY REVIEW.

Virgil's Works rendered into English Prose, with Introductions, running Analysis, and Index by JAMES LONSDALE, M.A., and SAMUEL LEE, M.A.

"*A more complete edition of Virgil in English it is scarcely possible to conceive than the scholarly work before us. The reader will find in its various Introductions an excellent summary of all that is known of the life of Virgil. We recommend the work as a work of high scholarship, refined taste, and worthy of Virgil.*"—GLOBE.

Other Volumes in Preparation.

MACMILLAN'S SUNDAY LIBRARY.

A SERIES OF ORIGINAL WORKS BY EMINENT AUTHORS.

In Crown 8vo. cloth extra, Illustrated, price 4*s.* 6*d.* each Volume; also kept in morocco and calf bindings at moderate prices; and in Ornamental Boxes containing Four Volumes, 21*s.* each.

The following Volumes are now ready:—

The Pupils of St. John the Divine. By the Author of "The Heir of Redclyffe."

"*Young and old will be equally refreshed and taught by these pages, in which nothing is dull, and nothing is far-fetched.*"—CHURCHMAN.

The Hermits. By CANON KINGSLEY.

"*It is from first to last a production full of interest, written with a liberal appreciation of what is memorable for good in the lives of the Hermits, and with a wise forbearance towards legends which may be due to the ignorance, and, no doubt, also to the strong faith of the early chroniclers.*"—LONDON REVIEW.

Seekers after God. By the Rev. F. W. FARRAR.

"*We can heartily recommend it as healthy in tone, instructive, interesting, mentally and spiritually stimulating and nutritious. Mr. Farrar writes as a scholar, a thinker, an earnest Christian, a wise teacher, and a genuine artist.*"—NONCONFORMIST.

England's Antiphon. By GEORGE MACDONALD.

"*Dr. Macdonald has very successfully endeavoured to bring together in his little book a whole series of the sweet singers of England, and makes them raise, one after the other, their voices in praise of God.*"—GUARDIAN.

Great Christians of France: ST. LOUIS AND CALVIN. By M. GUIZOT.

"*A very interesting book.*"—GUARDIAN.

Christian Singers of Germany. By CATHERINE WINKWORTH.

"*Miss Winkworth's volume of this series is, according to our view, the choicest production of her pen.*"—BRITISH QUARTERLY REVIEW.

Apostles of Mediæval Europe. By the Rev. G. F. MACLEAR.

"*Mr. Maclear will have done a great work if his admirable little volume shall help to break up the dense ignorance which is still prevailing among people at large.*"—LITERARY CHURCHMAN.

Alfred the Great. By THOMAS HUGHES, M.P., Author of "Tom Brown's School Days."

"*Mr. Hughes has indeed written a good book, bright and readable we need hardly say, and of a very considerable historical value.*"—SPECTATOR.

Nations Around. By Miss A. KEARY.

"*Miss Keary has skilfully availed herself of the opportunity to write a pleasing and instructive book.*"—GUARDIAN. "*A valuable and interesting volume.*"—ILLUSTRATED TIMES.

St. Anselm. By the Rev. R. W. CHURCH, M.A.

"*It is a sketch by the hand of a master, with every line marked by taste, learning, and real apprehension of the subject.*"—PALL MALL GAZETTE.

Francis of Assisi. By Mrs. OLIPHANT.

"*A valuable volume which cannot fail often to be taken out for its beauty and the freshness and simplicity that bear us away into a region so entirely different from our own.*"—GUARDIAN. "*We are grateful to Mrs. Oliphant for a book of much interest and pathetic beauty, a book which none can read without being the better for it.*"—JOHN BULL.

Pioneers and Founders; OR, RECENT WORKERS IN THE MISSION FIELD. By CHARLOTTE M. YONGE, Author of "The Heir of Redclyffe."

"*Likely to be one of the most popular of the 'Sunday Library' volumes.*" —LITERARY CHURCHMAN.

"*No popular book of the kind has been better executed.*"—DAILY TELEGRAPH.

London: R. Clay, Sons, and Taylor, Printers.

Made in the USA
Monee, IL
13 September 2026

62976973R00148

THE ROLE OF SELF AND ADAPTATION IN LEARNING AND DEVELOPMENT

This book introduces readers to Psychoadaptation—a general model of change that stresses the importance of experiencing disequilibrium in the development of a healthy Self—and applies it to a range of examples across the academic, sport, and health domains.

Built upon his studies of human development and learning, Daniel Rodriguez offers an overview of a model of change with a specific focus on the development of Self and conceptions of Self. The author begins by focusing on academic topics such as conducting research, teaching, and being a student, before highlighting examples from sport and health. With a clear and engaging tone, each chapter highlights how the theory behind Psychoadaptation can be applied across a variety of contexts and in the modern world. The result is a solid balance of scientific theory and practical application that readers can relate to their own circumstances and research.

Offering a unique conceptualization to development, learning, and behavior change, this is a useful resource for students and scholars within these areas, as well as clinicians working in the fields of health and sport. It will also benefit individuals looking to embark upon their own journeys to Self-development.

Daniel Rodriguez, Ph.D., is Professor of Public Health in the Department of Urban Public Health and Nutrition, La Salle University, Philadelphia, PA, USA.

THE ROLE OF SELF AND ADAPTATION IN LEARNING AND DEVELOPMENT

Chasing Excellence

Daniel Rodriguez

Routledge
Taylor & Francis Group
NEW YORK AND LONDON

Cover image: Getty Images © DenisTangneyJr

First published 2024
by Routledge
605 Third Avenue, New York, NY 10158

and by Routledge
4 Park Square, Milton Park, Abingdon, Oxon, OX14 4RN

Routledge is an imprint of the Taylor & Francis Group, an informa business

ISBN: 978-1-032-60856-3 (hbk)
ISBN: 978-1-032-60782-5 (pbk)
ISBN: 978-1-003-46080-0 (ebk)

DOI: 10.4324/9781003460800

Typeset in Galliard
by Newgen Publishing UK

CONTENTS

INTRODUCTION

Introduction to my worldview

Welcome to psychological adaptation, or Psychoadaptation for short! It's my worldview, and I've waited quite some time to finally write this book. Life always seemed to get in the way of me starting this project until the pandemic hit and I was finally able to unleash my writer Self.[1] Since that time (March of 2020), I wrote two textbooks (one for introductory statistics and one for research methods) and then proceeded to work on this book. I recall one day while walking uphill from the beautiful Goodman campus at Lehigh University to the mountaintop campus, I was reviewing the order in which I planned to write my books. It was the height of the pandemic, and almost everything around me was closed as it was for everyone. So, I ventured outdoors to find recreation and tranquility, and to do some thinking. I love to think while walking. It's the activity during which I generally find my best ideas and consolidate my knowledge surrounding the most obfuscating concepts.

At the time, I was in the final stages of writing my introductory statistics textbook and had already agreed with the same publisher to write my research methods textbook. After that, I recall, I planned on writing this book, the one that excited me the most. I went through all of the chapters I planned on writing, in my mind, and essentially had an outline set by the time I made it back down to my car. There would be a chapter on the ideal student. There would be another chapter on Psychoadaptation in tennis and one for skiing. I was at the height of my creativity. I had to wait though, as there was the research methods book to write before I could even think

DOI: 10.4324/9781003460800-1

of starting this book, and the statistics book had not yet been published. Patience is key in achieving one's goals. Thankfully, I have become a master of patience. Without it, it's very difficult to accomplish anything.

Patience was key indeed. One step at a time, I reminded myself. I am really good at focusing on a single task at a time and carrying it out to completion. I wasn't always like that, but I've grown into a patient adult. Carrying out a project to its end is one of the greatest joys I experience, even if I rebel against myself along the way and desire to quit. I always get myself back on track, though. For there is nothing more satisfying for me than moving toward a goal. I'm sure those who quit feel great doing so, as a burden is unloaded from their shoulders. For me, though, overcoming such desires is as euphoric as skiing down the most beautiful slope on a bluebird day. I relish the challenges thrown at me and finding ways to overcome them.

Achieving one's objectives is nice indeed. I do celebrate, thinking about all the sacrifices I made along the way to get from the inception of my pursuit to its conclusion. However, celebrations are not meant to endure as there are other goals to achieve. I guess I became this way from being a researcher for so many years now. There is little time to celebrate when new studies are eagerly awaiting their commencement, and salaries need to be paid by grants. Plus, promotion and tenure in academia favor the productive. Well, here I am being productive again with another project carried out to its completion. Although I already am a full professor with tenure, my motivation this time is more intrinsic. Time sure flies, as the saying goes. It stands still for no one. Indeed, nothing is guaranteed but the passage of time. All pains end and all deadlines come and go. For the strong-minded, that means accomplishments. So, here's my product. I am so proud to introduce it to you, my good reader. I hope you enjoy it.

I wrote this book in four parts. The first part includes two chapters, Chapters 1 and 10.[2] Chapter 1 is the introduction to my worldview. I say worldview instead of theory because I have no pretentions of theory writing. This book is about my uncovering of something that is for me an obvious thread in the developmental process, adaptation. I've appropriated this knowledge and am now sharing what I've learned to the willing reader. I present my worldview along with the theoretical concepts and experiences that were instrumental in its development. I also contrast it to other models I believe are similar to Psychoadaptation. Similarities or differences and the goals of all such worldviews are to better understand human development. With such understanding, we strive to improve the lives of all individuals, from the womb to death. We all have the same goals.

Chapter 10 is about the application of Psychoadaptation in today's world. The world is far more complex now than it was when I was in graduate school and held my first academic jobs post-graduation. The amount of

feedback one is subjected to is far greater than at any time in history. When I was younger, for instance, I could escape evaluation by being alone. In today's world, criticism is everywhere because smartphones connect us to everyone all over the world at every moment in time. Navigating this virtual obstacle course requires the right kind of cognitive development. I believe Psychoadaptation provides some of the best answers for approaching change and researching the cognitive and behavioral processes associated with change in the age of social media and limited privacy.

The remainder of the book is divided into three parts, covering eight chapters. I organized it to allow you, my good reader, to choose the content pertinent to your lives. For instance, in Part I: Academia, I discuss Psychoadaptation as it relates to the academic domain. This section applies to academics, whether you are interested in the student, the instructor, or the researcher. In Chapter 2, I discuss how Psychoadaptation applies to the art of being a successful student, including managing the emotional ebbs and flows within a semester and across one's academic years. In Chapter 3, I discuss Psychoadaptation in the art of teaching. Becoming a successful teacher is one of the most difficult challenges an academic professional can face. Not only must one understand the specific content being delivered in the classroom, but one must also have a deep understanding of the material surrounding the concepts presented and be prepared to respond to questions from sagacious students interested in knowing the whys about what we teach. In Chapter 4, I discuss how Psychoadaptation applies to research. Being a good researcher requires more than good ideas. One must be able to navigate the emotions associated with negative feedback. I don't care how intelligent one believes one's Self to be, there will always be someone smarter and ready to challenge the cocky researcher. Well then, if you are interested in the student, teaching, and research, you should read these chapters. If not, you can skip and read the chapters that interest you.

In Part II: Sport, I discuss Psychoadaptation as it relates to sport and physical fitness. In Chapter 5, I cover exercise. I'm an exercise fanatic, and exercise is critical to physical and mental health. As such, this is an important chapter for any researcher interested in how Psychoadaptation applies to exercise and physical health, and desiring insight into how exercise affects one's self-concept development. I also introduce psychological complexes and discuss how they affect the decisions we make about how and when we exercise. In the next two chapters, I cover two individual sports that I am very familiar with, skiing and tennis. Although these are individual sports and only two of the many sports one may work with or in which one may participate, the application of Psychoadaptation to skiing and tennis mirrors its application to other sports, including team sport. I used these sports as examples because my involvement in both is strong and therefore

my ability to apply the principles of Psychoadaptation in their practice is easy. I focus less on team sport because I have less experience in team sport settings. I've worked with elite tennis players and am a ski instructor at a local ski resort. Thus, I am qualified to discuss these two sports better than other sports I have little or no experience with. Chapter 6 focuses on tennis. Chapter 7 covers skiing. With skiing, I discuss the use of wearable technology to provide instantaneous feedback, and how such feedback is ideal for those seeking to improve performance. Thus, if you are interested in exercise or athletics, these are good chapters to read. You can ignore the others, unless you like my writing style and can't get enough of it. Wishful thinking on my part.

The final part of this book is about health. In Chapter 8 I discuss obesity. This is an important chapter for anyone struggling with weight. It's also perhaps a difficult chapter for those dealing with an eating disorder, such as anorexia or bulimia. I have my style of weight management, but it may not be ideal if one is struggling with an eating disorder, so approach with caution. My experiences around weight and weight management were perhaps the strongest catalysts for my development of Psychoadaptation, so it is an important chapter indeed. Chapter 9 is about cigarette smoking. My career has in large part been shaped by my studies on combustible cigarette smoking, so I discuss how one can quit smoking and the role of Psychoadaptation in the process. Although I have never been a cigarette smoker, my personal experience around cigarette smokers, and the research I have conducted and continue to conduct on the topic, is very strong. This gives me valuable insight into this addictive behavior.

As you read this introduction and weigh the pros and cons of buying this book, or investing your time in reading it, know that I am a regular person who just happened to get a Ph.D. I love what I do because I am a thinker, and thinking is what I derive the greatest pleasure from. My struggles are everyone's struggles. I started from little and made the most out of the little I had. Every day is an adventure for me. I still have relatively few resources, but I have a lot of heart. I never quit and don't allow any barriers to prevent me from moving forward. I laugh at people who tell me that I can't. I do so privately, however, because I am smart enough to not want to offend them. However, I know that I can and will achieve my desires even if those laughing at me continue to say I can't. In this book, I tell you about the process, but I do it from the perspective of a researcher who also wants data to support what I propose and what I do. I also demonstrate how Psychoadaptation applies to different facets of my life relevant to the domains covered. Some researchers do not approve of detailing one's personal experience as it is often said that one cannot generalize from an *n of one*, meaning that what happens to one person (n=1) does not generalize to

others (i.e., the population). I disagree. A good model that aims to explain phenomena should apply widely. As such, readers should attempt to verify theories and theoretical concepts by applying them to what they know. We know ourselves, and we share our humanity with others of our species. A good worldview about human development should be able to account for what we do. Moreover, what happens to one individual happens to others too. We don't share the exact same experiences. Yet, there is much similarity among individuals, particularly those living within similar contexts. I will discuss this in Chapter 1 when I discuss how individuals adapt to contexts. So, we can learn much from an n of one.

My life played an important role in the development of this worldview. However, Psychoadaptation would never have seen the morning light had it not been for my doctoral studies and research thereafter. It is only when one delves into the scholarly work does one learn how to understand thinking and to formulate hypotheses correctly. Learning is about discipline. Without discipline, ideas are like the winds of a storm. They are ephemeral and potentially destructive. Using cognition to construct requires training, and that's what a doctoral program provides students. Further, no one person can explain everything. Therefore, we need the collected knowledge of others to help shape the ways we understand reality. Thus, I not only discuss how Psychoadaptation applies to my experiences but also the experiences of mine that helped shape this worldview. If you decide to read this book, I hope you too will start to examine the validity of the various worldviews you encounter, including Psychoadaptation, by applying their many tenets to your life and the lives of those you know. I hope you find what you like in them and challenge those concepts which you don't like. Perhaps this process will motivate you to go out and write your own book about your own worldview. That's how the world changes. That's how we change the world.

Notes

1 I always capitalize the word Self when it stands alone.

2 Yes, it's odd to have two parts so widely spaced apart. However, the two chapters fit together well, and Chapter 10 doesn't belong in any other part.

1

INTRODUCTION TO PSYCHOADAPTATION

Long ago, just after I graduated from my doctoral studies, I started the process of developing my theoretical beliefs, although I didn't know I was doing so at the time. During my doctoral studies, and my personal studies prior to my return to college in my youth, I read voraciously. Initially, I read about spirituality, focusing heavily on Eastern philosophical teachings and religion. It was what interested me the most then. The *calmness of being* that it released within me was a motivator indeed. At the time, I was struggling with serious anxieties that I couldn't easily alleviate with self-help practices or counseling. Finding a system that included meditation and mindfulness made my life calmer than it otherwise would have been. Apparently, my psychophysiological being wasn't made for Western culture with its competitive ways, at least that's what I felt. I needed something different, and the books I read were perfect for whom I was at the time. They also helped to shape my worldview and were the building blocks for my emerging theoretical beliefs.

In graduate school, I turned my attention to the psychological literature. Before matriculating at the Human Development Ph.D. program at the University of Maryland, I discovered the works of Edward L. Deci and Richard Ryan (Deci & Ryan, 1985). Their work focused on motivational processes. What struck me most was the distinction between intrinsic and extrinsic motivation. As a person who never allowed barriers to hinder my progress, I often wondered what made me the person I am. I endured many painful experiences to achieve my goals. While others would turn away and run headlong into their personal caves, I metaphorically walked directly into the fire. I did not beg for more, as I am not crazy. Instead,

DOI: 10.4324/9781003460800-2

I would yell out in pain and cry like a baby boy, but I kept moving forward. I wanted to understand this, and the psychological literature pointed me to where I needed to go. Plus, there is the bonus that the literature is extremely interesting, and the abstract concepts discussed were ethereal. I think my favorite readings at the time were from C.G. Jung's collected works, especially the more symbolic text. I remember sitting on a bench outside of the Maryland State House in Annapolis on a warm sunny autumn day, reading Jung's work *Mysterium Coniunctionis* (Jung, 1970) and then going for a walk up and down the picturesque streets of that beautiful city thinking about the people I passed, frightening archetypes, and what made people behave as they do.

I read so much. Being in a doctoral program, I was introduced to other works I would have never discovered without the program. I read papers by Susan Harter and Herbert Marsh, my two early academic heroes. I read the works of Robert White and my mentor Allan Wigfield. I also read the works of Dr. Wigfield's longtime colleague Jacquelynne Eccles and fellow University of Maryland professors Stephen Porges and Bradley Hatfield, my other mentor. I read so much and sought out to read even more. My brain was hungry and like any good parent, I nourished it. It grew, and as it did, there emerged a rudimentary understanding of why people develop as they do. I discovered a repeating pattern within the literature I was reading. This pattern was like an average developmental trajectory from a scattering of hundreds of thousands of such trajectories. I was making sense of a scattering of fragments, and what I saw was a beautiful image of human development. That is where Psychoadaptation was born. I did not, nor would I ever, claim that I produced something new. Instead, I found a deeper understanding of the process that I believe leads to change. It may be personal, or it could be within all of us. That I will leave for you my good reader to decide for yourself.

My understanding of the developmental process was indeed quite personal. Yet, what differentiates a non-scholar from a scholar is the ability to translate the complex into the simple. I should say, perhaps, that this is what differentiates the successful scholar from the unsuccessful scholar. I know way too many brilliant scholars who cannot communicate as well as a shy elementary school student. A good scholar must at minimum be able to speak to a non-scholar and do so clearly and without prejudice. I teach academic writing, and I frequently tell my students to *write as if they were doing so for their grandparents*, assuming their grandparents are not scholars too. That may sound crazy, but it should not. There is far too much misunderstanding about human development, and that misunderstanding is often the result of poor communication by the person delivering the

message. Just because one is considered smart, it does not mean one is a good communicator.

When I graduated from the University of Maryland, I deeply felt Psychoadaptation but had no idea how to communicate it. I recall one day when I was at my first post-Ph.D. job, a student of mine asked me to explain this rudimentary theory and I tried, but did so poorly. How good is a theory, I thought, if the theorist himself cannot explain it to a hungry student? It is useless. However, that is where we often are. We feel that we understand something but fail to articulate our understanding to others. For that reason, I love putting myself in demanding situations whereby I am forced to articulate complexities. Indeed, whether it is in teaching how to turn on skis, or the relation between *p*-value and alpha in statistics, I love it when students ask me for specifics, or to further elaborate upon some concept. Actually, I hate it but have come to appreciate the negative feeling of not knowing how to explain something well, for it is the motivator that has driven me to understand and learn to explain a variety of difficult concepts and to do what I never thought I could do previously.

The frustration of not being able to explain my own theory well to a willing listener motivated me. Failure always motivates me. I use this negative *possible self* (Markus & Nurius, 1986) to motivate what I do. While some people see rainbows and bunnies at the end of every tunnel, I see fire and ashes if I make the wrong choice. Others are motivated by chasing the light. I am motivated to escape the dark. They seek success. I seek to not experience catastrophic failures. It may be because I have experienced some unbelievably tough times, including our family being homeless while I was an undergraduate student. Living through difficult experiences taught me to not want to repeat the mistakes of the past. Thus, I study hard to make correct choices, choices with the greatest probabilities of succeeding. Over the past 25 years, I have studied the learning process thoroughly and am now able to explain Psychoadaptation in a way that I hope will make sense to you, my good reader. My goal is for you to take my worldview and use it to guide your own research, teaching, and practice, and your daily life.

Psychoadaptation is the latent process underlying change. I say latent as it is not possible to observe the process directly, although it is knowable through its indicators. An indicator of change could be a new way of understanding (cognitive), such as when one understands how to prove a statistical equation, or physical, such as when one masters the appropriate stance in skiing. Pretty much every construct we read about in fields like psychology, human development, and public health is latent. Even disease is latent. For instance, diabetes and depression are known only through their indicators. Diabetes is known by its symptoms, including blood sugar

levels. Depression is known by one's responses to questions about mood and feelings of self-worth, among other indicators.

Change is learning, although we may not perceive change as positive or an indicator of success when we are in its midst. I love sport and exercise. One of my favorite activities is hiking. I tell people about the trails I hike all the time. My favorite trails are those with steep grades, as they are the most challenging. Challenge means overcoming obstacles. Overcoming obstacles is a manifestation of change. Yet, it is not easy, as each time I try a steeper trail, my body responds in ways that remind me that I have not yet mastered the challenge. I feel the pain of the lactic acid buildup in my quadriceps. There's a saying, *no pain no gain*. When hiking up steeps, that rings true. I also feel my heart racing, and my breathing intensifies, as I struggle to take each additional step. There is a change in my body, and it doesn't feel good. It's even worse when it is hot outside and the sun is bathing my skin with its intense rays. Many people quit when feeling such symptoms. I don't blame them, particularly if they are older or have a medical history that requires caution. For me, though, I know my body and what I can do. Plus, I get regular screenings to ensure that I can exercise hard. Nevertheless, the pain is there, and thoughts race through my mind that aim to defeat my beliefs about my ability. Am I really a good hiker, or am I only fooling myself into believing that I know what I am doing? Am I a fraud? Well, those thoughts are correct, at least in part. They are there to inform me that I am not yet able to do what I am trying to do without struggle. In some cases, these negative thoughts are there to protect us until we can acquire the necessary skills and fitness to hike the steeper grade, to do what we desire to do. As such, the process of negative thoughts telling us that we can't actually isn't bad. Indeed, it is teleological (purposeful). We are wired to know when our way of being, whether physiological or cognitive, doesn't fit the challenges confronting us. It's telling us that we need to change more in order to accomplish our goals. For me, this is very motivating because I desire change. I desire to better myself.

The context and constraints

To understand change, one has to understand the importance of the context. Every behavior takes place within a context, whether physical, social, virtual, or self-constructed. To simplify my presentation, I will include cognition within the rubric behavior. However, I will distinguish the two when necessary for clarity. Bronfenbrenner and colleagues' bioecological model provides the ideal structure to understand the relation between behavior and context (Bronfenbrenner, 1993, 1994; Bronfenbrenner & Ceci, 1994). Indeed, it's the foundation upon which my understanding of the context/

adaptation relation was built. At the most proximal (closest to us) level is the microsystem (Figure 1.1). The microsystem is the face-to-face setting in which all human development occurs. The microsystem is represented by the circles in Figure 1.1, with each circle representing a different microsystem. One of my microsystems, for instance, is the classroom for a specific course taught in a specific semester, such as "Introduction to Statistics." My development as a statistics instructor takes place within this context. Individuals have multiple microsystems (e.g., my classroom, my immediate family, my weekend ski training group). The collection of these microsystems is the mesosystem (same-shade circles within rectangles in Figure 1.1). For instance, my mesosystem includes my immediate family, my different courses and the students, my advisees, the department's faculty, and my fellow ski instructors. It also includes my social media sites and friendships within the various sites. As I will discuss shortly, the consistency of microsystemic values and norms within one's mesosystem is a key to an individual's experience of well-being (Rodriguez et al., 2007).

Just beyond the mesosystem is the exosystem. This is the mesosystem with the addition of at least one microsystem not including the developing

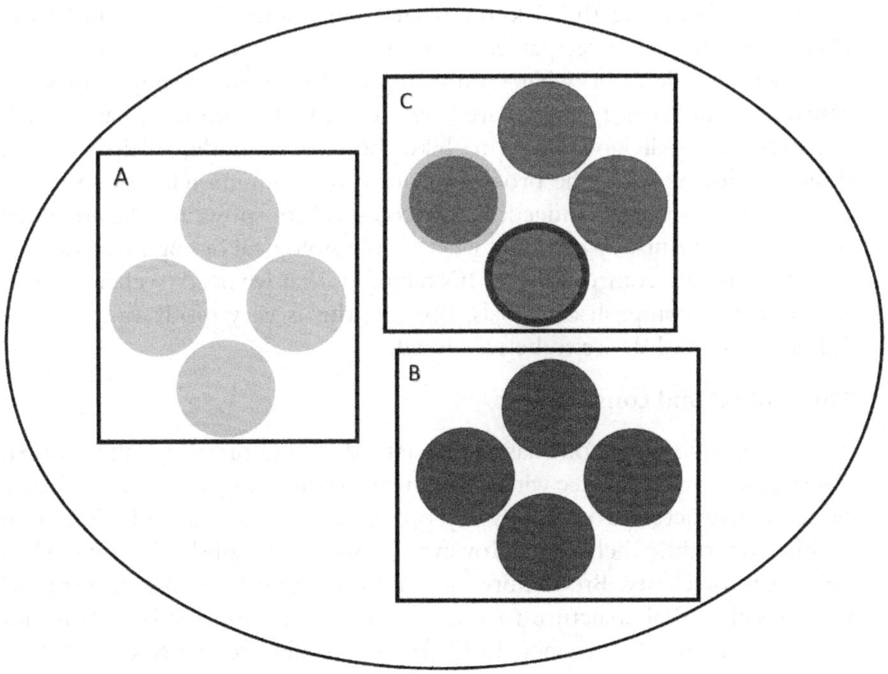

FIGURE 1.1 The mesosystem.

person but that influences the individual's development. In Figure 1.1, I represented these as the circles in mesosystem C with rings matching the shade of the microsystems in mesosystems A or B, depending upon their realm of influence. A simple example is a high school. While classrooms are part of a student's mesosystem, the administration's microsystems influence students' development, even though these microsystems *do not* include the developing adolescent. Similarly, one's supervisors' microsystems impact employee microsystems. If, for instance, a company experiences a financial deficit and decides to reduce employees' salaries, these administrative microsystem behaviors impact the employees' microsystems with little impact from employees' pleas or negotiations.

At the most general and distal[1] (to the developing person) level is the macrosystem (the large oval in Figure 1.1). The macrosystem defines the nature of the microsystems, mesosystems, and exosystems, along with the rules governing each. Macrosystem is synonymous with culture. For instance, the microsystems available to young women living within the United States differ from those available to a young woman in a culture with restrictive beliefs about gender equality and women's rights. A topic of special interest is the placement of subculture within this system. A subculture is similar to a macrosystem in that it has its own micro, meso, and exosystemic structure. For instance, there are subcultures defined by ethnicity and behavior. There are subcultures for athletes and academics. There are illicit drug subcultures too. Nevertheless, the parameters of subcultures are governed by the overall (primary) macrosystem. I'll distinguish the two if and when necessary. However, the mechanisms affecting adaptation in both are the same, as they both are contexts.

Contexts have rules, or norms if you prefer. I like to call these rules *constraints* as they are meant to constrain the range of possible behaviors within a context. Within this range, and with reference to a specific constraint, is a behavioral ideal. Enacting this behavior represents a perfect adaptation to the constraint. Naturally, behaviors vary within any context, with some behaviors more closely approximating the ideal than others. Figure 1.2 presents a probability distribution representing the relation between all possible behaviors within a context and the ideal behavior (Line *a*). For those of you familiar with probability distributions in statistics, this is a normal distribution, with the height of the curve representing the probability associated with some range of behaviors.[2] As such, the probability of behaviors around *b* is lower than the probability of behaviors around the ideal *a*. This makes sense if individuals strive to enact the ideal behavior. Eventually, their behaviors will come to approximate the ideal. With the diversity of behaviors within a context, however, not all behaviors will align with the ideal. Indeed, the further a behavior gets from the mean,

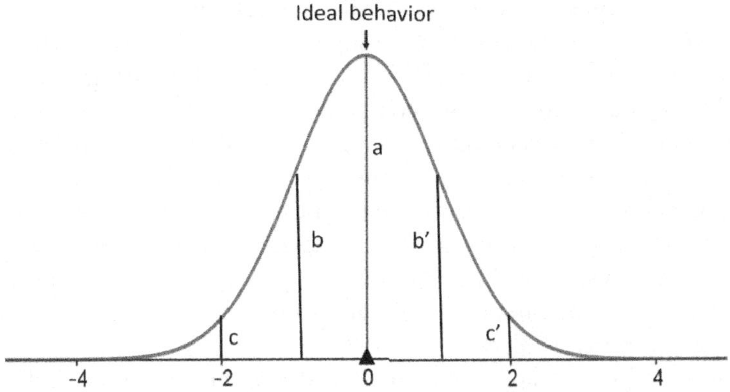

FIGURE 1.2 Probability distribution as it applies to the context.

the lower the probability of that behavior occurring. In addition to line *b*, lines b′ and c and c′ have lower probabilities than line a.

The use of the normal curve and the normal distribution is informative here, although my application isn't the same as modeling a variable's probability distribution in statistics. Moving from left to right in Figure 1.2, we can imagine that behaviors at the left end of the distribution (c and b) are emergent, whereas those at the upper right end (b′ and c′) are those surpassing the context's norms. In other words, we can think of those behaviors on the lower left-hand side as being shaped to adapt to a contextual constraint, whereas those behaviors on the upper right-hand side are indicative of over-mastery of the contextual constraint. I will discuss what I mean by over-mastery later. It suffices for now to imagine these behaviors are too advanced for the constraint and the enactors are either continuing them in an attempt to remain in the context for its rewards or are about to break free and pursue other contexts.[3]

Rewards play a key role in Psychoadaptation and the learning process. Given that each context has an ideal behavior, ***matching one's behavior to the ideal is adaptation***. Rewards can be material or cognitive. In either case, they elicit an emotional response. Most contextual constraints do not involve material reward, although they can, especially when professionals shape behavior. For instance, teachers use token economies to attain desirable student behaviors. One example of a token economy is a listing of names on a poster board with shiny multi-colored stars next to student names for appropriate demonstration (or approximation) of a desirable behavior. In a token economy, these stars can be traded for tangible reinforcers,[4] such as toys, foods, or privileged seating at highly coveted events. Extrinsic rewards such as tokens in a token economy are useful when dealing with a known

set of constraints to which every individual must adapt. In society, however, constraints are less clearly defined, and rewards are more often than not social in nature, not tangible. For instance, adolescents often have unspoken dress codes, including brands of clothing (e.g., a specific type of shoe). When students comply with the dress code, they avoid ridicule (negative reinforcement). If, however they fail to comply, they are socially sanctioned through laughter, negative comments on social media, or isolation (positive punishment).[5]

Interacting with others within a context, one comes to learn the contextual constraints. Applying a Vygotskyan perspective to Psychoadaptation, it's the responsibility of older (or more seasoned in many cases[6]) members of a context to pass cultural knowledge (contextual constraints) to younger (newer) members (Vygotsky, 1980). Constraints govern every possible realm of a context. They govern how one should dress, style one's hair, and how much one should weigh. They govern when one should speak and to whom one is permitted to speak. They govern thought, with those expressing ideas incongruent to the context's norms forbidden. As with a normal (see Figure 1.2) process, there is variation. However, serious deviations from what is considered adaptive behavior (normal within the context) are likely to result in sanctions, with more serious sanctions for behaviors deviating further from the ideal. Therefore, there is pressure for individuals to adapt and stay within a standard deviation of the mean.

In case you are not familiar with statistical language, in a standard normal distribution (depicted in Figure 1.2), 68% of all population values fall within plus or minus one standard deviation of the mean (Rodriguez, 2020), the standard deviation being a unit-less measure of variability about the mean.[7] The further one gets away from the mean (in standard deviation terms) the lower the likelihood a behavior is to occur within a given setting. If we imagine behaviors within a specific context with a specific constraint, behaviors that match the constraint are the most likely to occur because they are the most likely to elicit a positive social response (rewards). Behaviors above one standard deviation from the mean (in either direction) are likely to be sanctioned (punished). The individual exhibiting these nonadaptive (abnormal from the context's perspective) behaviors will not be treated as well as those who are enacting the normative behavior well. It should be noted, though, that there are differences in how non-normative behaviors are treated within any context. Individuals striving to adapt are generally treated better than those refusing to adapt to the contextual constraints. I wrote the qualifier "generally" because, in some contexts, learners are not treated well and are even pressured to leave the context. One such example is seen in individual sport. In skiing, for instance, first-time skiers enrolled in lessons are treated exceedingly well because they interact with instructors

who love teaching and understand the art of learning. Once these individuals leave the learning area and attempt to ski the bigger mountain, however, treatment can change quite drastically, with learners seen as a nuisance to some experienced skiers. This treatment can be especially harsh if the new skier is from a nontraditional skiing group, such as lower-income individuals or ethnic minorities. However, as one more closely approaches the ideal with behavior beginning to match the ideal, praise becomes more common than sanctioning. This occurs because contexts seek adaptation. Adaptation means buying into the constraint, and this is desirable to existing members, regardless of the learner's characteristics.

Individuals at the upper end of the normal distribution (Figure 1.2) are less troubling to the context because they are likely to leave and do so quickly. Thus, although they may disparage the context and its constraints, they do not generally do so for long. The context persists, with or without these individuals. I will spend more time discussing these individuals near the end of the chapter, as they represent an ideal in the development of Self. Indeed, the ability to transcend contexts and constraints is characteristic of what psychologists refer to as the healthy Self (Rodriguez, 2000).

Adapting to the constraint is ideal. When one masters a contextual constraint, one appropriates the constraint into one's Self. Although adapting to a single constraint is key to the Psychoadaptation process, contexts include multiple constraints. However, at this point it's most instructive to focus only on single constraints. Later we'll discuss appropriation of multiple constraints.

Adaptation changes the Self. Indeed, one develops one's conception of Self (self-concept) in this process. The more adaptations one makes, the more diverse the Self becomes. An ideal, as I will discuss in due course, is a Self that has appropriated so many contextual constraints that further adaptation becomes almost unnecessary, even when one enters novel contexts. At that point, one will have achieved true peace and frequently experiences the oceanic feeling; a complete diffusion of the boundary between the Self and non-Self (Rodriguez, 2000). You may know this better, my good reader, as nirvana or a oneness with one's surroundings.

Appropriation is a function of the Self (Masterson, 1985). The Self functions to organize experience. One can imagine the self as composed of two dimensions. The first is the executive. The *executive Self* interacts with the environment and decides upon behavioral enactments. To achieve this, it appeals to stored information from prior experience. The second dimension is *storage*. We store our experience in the self-concept. *The self-concept is the sum total of all experiences, organized hierarchically to make sense of experience and manage its expression to others.* One can imagine the self-concept as a library with an intricate organizational scheme that makes some

content more visible than others and permits others to know who we are (Bramer et al., 1993). Like books on shelves, and a data processing system, one can access different parts of the self-concept as needed. This permits the executive self to withdraw content whenever needed to make the best possible decision. The more *books* one has in the library, the easier it is to make decisions, provided the organizing system is not overly complicated.

Equilibrium and disequilibrium

Every constraint necessitates adaptation, if the individual is indeed motivated to adapt to the constraint. As such, knowing the nature of the constraint is critical. Yet, knowing its nature does not guarantee adaptation. Some constraints are very difficult to adapt to, and not all individuals attempting to adapt have the ability or capability to adapt. For instance, I know what it takes to win a grand slam tournament in tennis, yet even if I work hard to master the constraints required to win the event, practicing hours per day with a top professional and hiring the best possible support staff (e.g., personal trainer, practice partners, and sport psychologist), I won't win, let alone qualify for the event. Heck, I couldn't even qualify for a local satellite tournament if I tried. Not all constraints can be mastered by everyone desiring to master them.

Learning new behaviors can be difficult, particularly when it comes to complex neuromuscular processes such as tennis or learning to drive a car. The task is made more difficult when one does the learning while moving and navigating traffic. Learning to drive is even more difficult if one attempts to master driving a car with a manual transmission. The vast majority of cars in the United States are now automatics, with some automatics having functions that allow drivers to mimic a manual transmission, absent the painful learning process. Yet, manual transmission cars are still found globally. I drive a manual transmission car because I find it entertaining. There is so much involved in driving a stick (shorthand for manual transmission because these cars have stick shifters), the most difficult of which is using the clutch. The clutch is a pedal that one has to depress in order to shift gears. Before I shift, I depress the clutch with my left foot, and while holding it down, I shift from gear to gear with my right hand, making sure to depress the accelerator to avoid too much hesitation or shaking. It's a complicated neuromuscular process that one must perform while paying attention to traffic.

When I first learned to drive a stick, I was a teenager living in Arlington, Virginia, right outside of Washington, DC. My father took me to Georgetown to drive up one of the steep hills from the Potomac River to M street. One of the most difficult skills to learn when adapting to driving a stick is dealing

with hills.[8] While transitioning between gears, one passes through neutral, and the car is free to move. Being on a hill becomes stressful because the car can move backward momentarily during the shifting. It's especially challenging when one is at a stop sign or traffic light, on a hill. Now the driver has to start from scratch. If cars are to the rear, fear can proliferate. What if I back up into the car behind me? What if I stall? Manual transmission cars can stall. If the transition between gears isn't done appropriately, the engine can stall, meaning one has to start up the car again. If one is in a city where people are hyper stressed, harsh words can flow from other drivers feeling burdened by missing an opportunity to go. Pray that stalling doesn't cause someone to miss a green light! Thus, learning to start a stick on a hill is an important constraint to master in adapting to the *driving a stick* context.

In the process of adaptation, there is fear. Fear is not a fun feeling. Even among those who love challenges or claim to experience no fear, there is fear albeit less than for those suffering from severe anxieties. Suppose my goal is to start a manual transmission car parked on a hill and drive one mile to a large parking lot. The first step is to depress the clutch and turn the key. The manual transmission car will not start unless the clutch is depressed while turning the key. Being parked on a hill, the car is left in first gear to keep it in place and to avoid it accidentally rolling down the hill and hurting someone. Thus, my next step is to put the car in neutral and depress the brake. If I were to forget to do this and let go of the clutch, the car would stall, jerking forward in the process. Supposing I made it through this step, I have adapted to one constraint, whose rules were to start the car and put it in neutral. Suppose I am lucky and there are no cars parked either in front of me or behind me, then given the tendency for these types of cars to move while in neutral, having no cars behind or in front of a driver makes learning a bit more pleasant.

The next constraint to adapt to is releasing the parking brake and holding the car in place with the stick in first gear, using the clutch alone. Ah, my friends, this is the holy grail of driving a stick in my view. It's one thing to drive on a highway with only minimal shifting. It is a completely different experience to hold a car in place on a hill using the clutch, the gas pedal, and first gear alone. When I was learning, the goal was to vary pressure on the clutch and gas pedal to have the car rock back and forth. Passing this step, the next is to learn to apply gas appropriately, depressing the gas pedal, and releasing the clutch so that there is a smooth transition between gears. Following that, it would be depressing the clutch again to shift to second gear, again with the intent of a smooth (seamless) transition. This gets easier as one progresses from first to second gear, second to third, and so on.

Each of these adaptations brought me closer to adapting to the *driving a stick* context. However, each adaptation involved a tremendous

amount of failure. Each failure resulted in frustration. Frustration and the associated feelings (e.g., anger, negative mood) are referred to as ***disequilibrium***. Disequilibrium is a very distasteful psychophysiological experience that occurs when one's conceptions do not match the data of experience. A Piagetian concept related to assimilation and accommodation in the cognitive adaptation process, disequilibrium occurs when one's understanding cannot readily assimilate an experience (Piaget, 1951). In Piaget's stage-independent development model, individuals build cognitive structures based on their experiences. These cognitive structures allow us to understand our environments. When we understand our environments (contexts), we are at peace, a trophotropic state (Porges, 2011). When our cognitive structures fail to assimilate experience, there is a potential need for change. Our initial response is to maintain our cognitive structures because they are an intricate part of whom we are. However, if they repeatedly fail to assimilate experiences, the theory (our conception of the reality) needs to change. In other words, there is work to do. When our cognitive structure no longer assimilates experience, and we change it, accommodation occurs. Accommodation is an alteration of the cognitive structures to better fit the data of experience. Disequilibrium occurs when our cognitive structures no longer assimilate experience. Disequilibrium is a teleological experience indicating a need to change. Indeed, C.G. Jung referred to this process as the transcendent function (Jung, 1916; Miller, 2004). Accordingly, our Self has an innate self-correcting function. Actually, it is better portrayed as an alarm to inform us when our constructed Self can no longer function appropriately; it is not well aligned with our experience.

In healthy development, there is continuous interweaving (Gesell, 1939)[9] between assimilation and accommodation, equilibrium and disequilibrium, and trophotropic and ergotropic states. Our environments are not static. Contexts change, as do their constraints. Psychoadaptation is the process of moving through these interweaving states, building the self-concept to appropriate larger numbers of experiences.

When I first tried to start my car from the parked position, facing uphill toward M street, I was scared. I was afraid that I would not be able to maintain the car's position with the clutch. Naturally, my father didn't have control of the brake and steering wheel, so if I messed up, we were in trouble. At that time my self-concept included a conception about me as a driver. I had taken driving lessons in high school, so I knew how to drive an automatic. Thus, my conception of me as a driver wanted to assimilate driving a manual transmission. I knew I had to learn to drive a stick as that's the only type of car we had, but I was confident that I could learn pretty quickly given my recent experience in driver's education. The first failure I experienced, stalling the engine, was something I couldn't as easily

assimilate at that point, for I didn't know enough about driving a stick until I started learning to drive one. This naturally caused disequilibrium. My disequilibrium was heightened by learning to drive a car that could roll backward and crash or hurt someone. It was further heightened by my learning in a public setting (i.e., city street). Taken together, this made my disequilibrium very evident. Thankfully, I had a kind father to guide me through the process.

Self-concept is central to the adaptation process. Self-concept is the product of the Self's ego function (Masterson, 1985). The ego serves to organize the data of experience into a coherent self-concept, what Seymour Epstein referred to as the self-theory (Epstein, 1973). Epstein proposed several functions of the self-theory, including the maintenance of a positive pleasure–pain balance and the protection of self-esteem. His work played a critical role in my development of Psychoadaptation, particularly his hypothesis that even a dysfunctional self-theory is better than no self-theory at all, so long as it maintains self-esteem. When taken together with the unpleasant nature of disequilibrium, and the work required to change one's self-concept to accommodate the data of experience, is it any wonder that so many individuals desire to not change their self-conceptions? I wondered to myself why one would put oneself through so much discomfort when the self-esteem is fine as it is. This led to me understanding why some people do not change even if their adaptations are dysfunctional. Why should they change if they are fine the way they are? If one's behaviors served one well until this point, why change if one doesn't have to?

The last question is key, especially the qualifier "if one doesn't have to." The problem is that our self-conceptions do not occur in a vacuum. No matter how much we may try to isolate ourselves from those with opposing beliefs and criticism, isolation is hard, particularly in a world with social media. As there is this peculiar tendency to post views on public platforms like Twitter or Facebook, and people read these posts, there is bound to be disagreement and complicated attempts to assimilate the diverse views without changing one's self-conceptions.

Self-concept

I have mentioned self-concept quite frequently to this point without an adequate definition. Self-concept is a Self-constructed organization of our experiences in a hierarchical fashion such that each broader dimension encompasses lower and more distal experiences (Rodriguez, 2000). Figure 1.3 presents a general example of a self-concept, focusing on three dimensions of Self: Physical, Cognitive, and Interpersonal. At the highest (most distal) level is the Self. At the next highest level are specific facets of

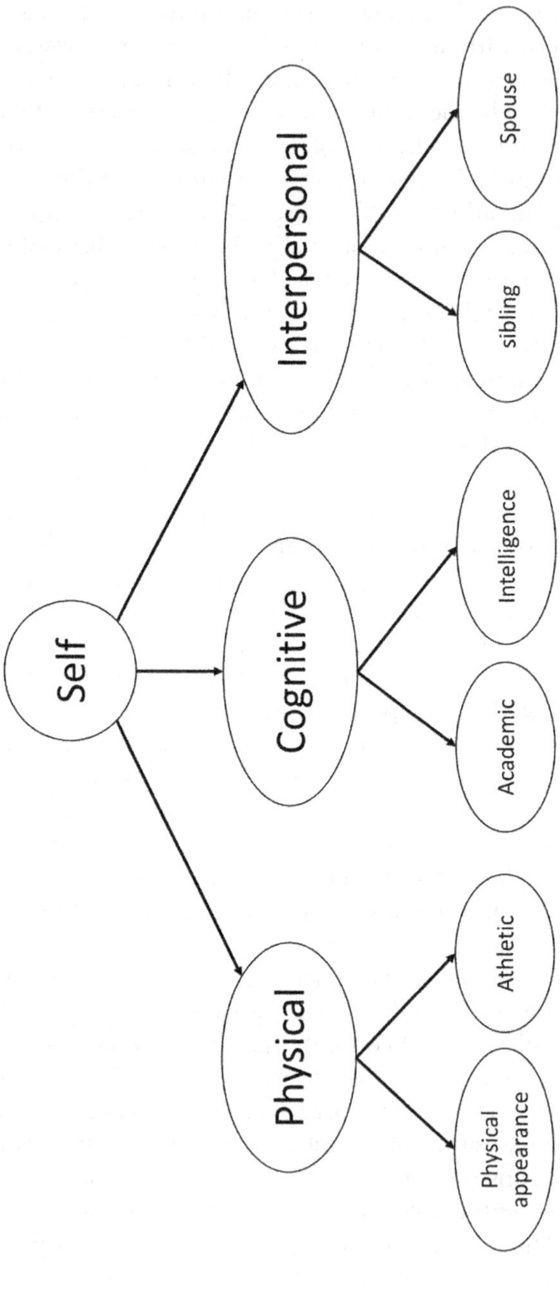

FIGURE 1.3 General example of self-concept.

the Self, including the physical, cognitive (intellectual), and interpersonal dimensions. At the lowest level are those facets that come to define the physical, cognitive, and interpersonal dimensions. Notice that arrows link the various levels, with arrows pointing from higher to lower levels. This is a *factor analysis* representation of the self-concept. As one moves from higher to lower levels, the dimensions become more concrete. Lower-level dimensions (factors) are indicators of the more abstract higher-order factors. Looking at the physical factor, it has two indicators in this figure, physical appearance Self and athletic Self. Figure 1.4 is an expansion of the physical factor and its two indicators. Notice also that I have changed the shape of the different dimensions. In factor analysis, ovals represent factors (latent variables) and rectangles represent measurable variables (Loehlin, 2004). In this case, I listed three (albeit non-exhaustive) indicators of the physical appearance and athletic self-concepts. I now shift terminology as well, with the physical appearance self-conception becoming Perceived Physical Appearance and Athletic self-concept becoming Athletic Competence Beliefs. I did this because our self-concept is Self-constructed. In other words, it is a product of our executive Self organizing experience. As such, our perceptions of our physical appearance are indicated by three factors in this model, one's weight, height, and the comments one has received or heard from others. Given that one cannot see oneself objectively, one relies on the reflected appraisals of others to understand the Self, what Charles Horton Cooley referred to as the looking-glass self (Cooley, 1992; Harter, 1988, 1998). Perhaps I should call Peer comments as Perceived Peer comments, given the role of one's interpretation of external cues (peer comments) on the construction of self-conceptions. Although initial responses may have played a critical role in the construction of one's perceived physical appearance, later interpretations may be influenced by those earlier experience and as such are a filter through which comments are appropriated. This too is a key part of the Psychoadaptation process. We aren't there yet, though.

Over time, one constructs a massive self-concept. Yet, not all self-concepts are equal. Individuals with greater experiences are likely to have more complicated self-concepts than those with fewer experiences. Individuals with primarily positive life experiences are likely to have different self-concepts than those with primarily negative experiences. Given that the self-concept is a repository of experiences, it comes to represent more than a psychological construction. *It is the person*. Thus, I am my self-concept. Because of this central role, there is a need to defend the self-concept against attack. This is precisely what Epstein meant when he proposed that a critical function of the self-concept is to maintain a positive pleasure-to-pain

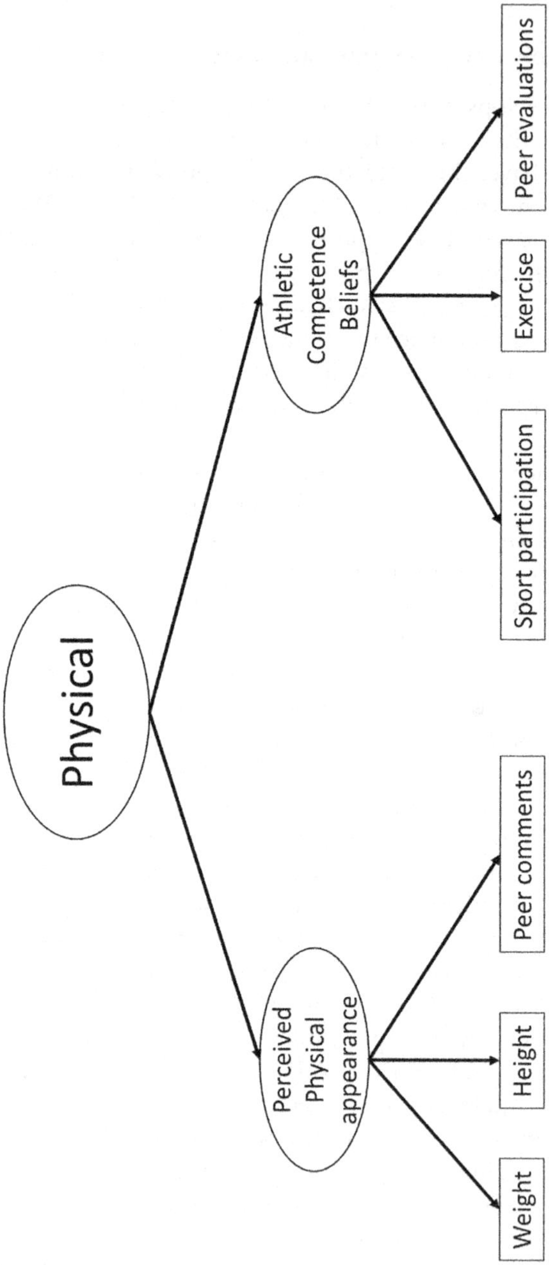

FIGURE 1.4 Physical self-concept.

balance (Epstein, 1973). This is done by defending the Self from external threats, with self-esteem as the primary indicator of Self health.

Self-concept, concepts, contexts, and disequilibrium

Self-concept develops through experience. The greater the breadth of our experience, the broader the self-concept. In other words, the more experiences we have, the more there is to appropriate into this structure. For instance, in my youth I was fortunate to travel a lot. With this travel, I experienced many different cultures and saw a variety of different living conditions, from tremendous poverty to great wealth. Those experiences helped me to understand who I am in relation to the greater world. Someone with less experience traveling would have a narrower self-concept. It's not that my self-concept is superior to the individual with less travel experiences than I had, but my self-concept will be broader because of those experiences.

You may notice that my discussion of self-concept is broader than claims made about the Self (e.g., me as a skier). Under the rubric self-concept, I include *all conceptions* one holds. For instance, my fandom for certain athletes, actors, or sport teams is just as much a part of my self-conceptions as my belief in my ability as a skier. Other self-conceptions I have include my political beliefs, my beliefs about public health, and my beliefs about religion. Thus, if I say "I think the Washington Commanders will win this week," this statement is a self-concept just as much as is me saying "I AM a Washington Commanders fan." The reason for this is traceable in a graphic description of one's domain-specific self-concept (Figure 1.5). Notice how I place sport fandom under physical self-concept, but not because cheering for my team is a physical activity. Rather, sport fandom falls under the leisure self-concept, since it's a leisure-time activity. If one visualizes a continuum with high physical activity at one pole and complete relaxation at the other pole, sport fandom would fall closer to the complete relaxation pole.

Leisure self-concept includes multiple dimensions beyond sport fandom. For instance, falling under this rubric, I also include travel self-concept and entertainment self-concept. Under entertainment, I have movies self-concept and reading self-concept. Although their placement under physical self-concept is debatable, the point here goes beyond the specific dimensions to how these self-conceptions affect one's beliefs and the impact of those beliefs on one's feelings of equilibrium and disequilibrium. For instance, if I claim that a specific movie is really good and someone counters my claim by saying that the film is horrible, this retort is more than another person's opinion, it can be taken as a direct attack on the validity of my movie self-concept. How one responds in such situations, however, depends on how

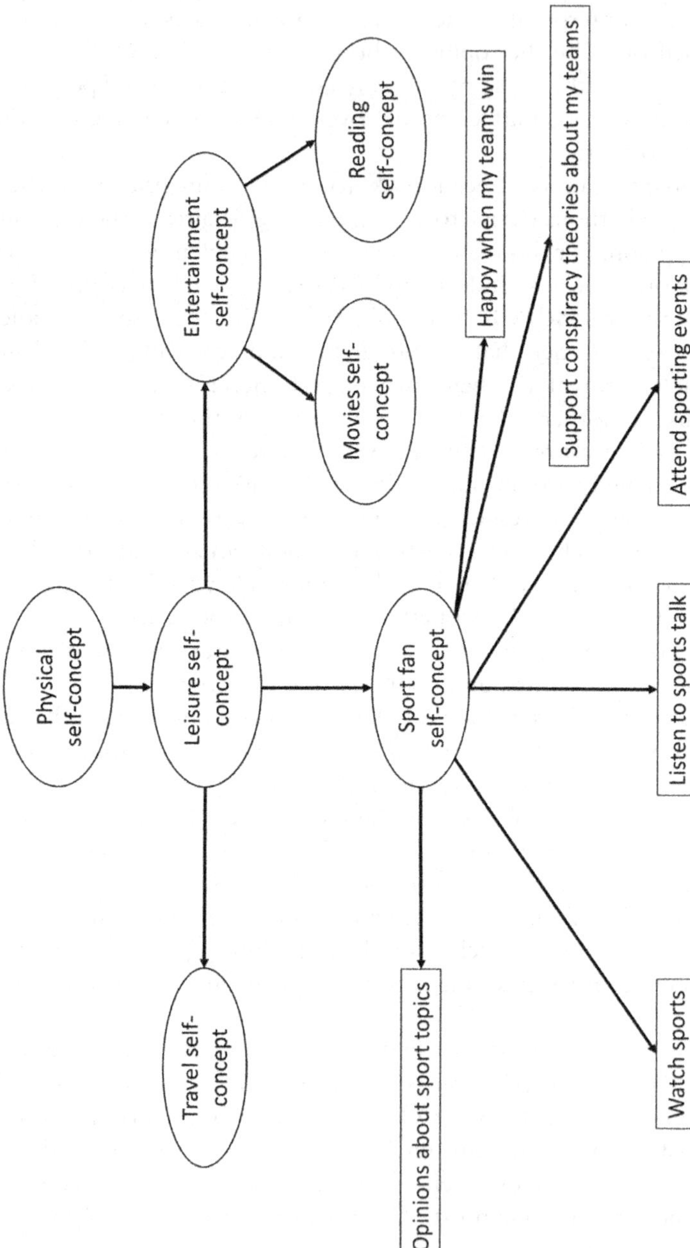

FIGURE 1.5 Physical self-concept in relation to sport fandom.

fluid is one's self-concept. If the individual is open to debate and listens to the opposing point of view, the self-concept may change. Thus, after hearing the counterpoint of view on the movie, a person with a healthier sense of Self may alter her opinion about the movie. If on the other hand, one has a less healthy sense of Self, any contradiction to her point of view will be taken as a direct attack on her overall sense of Self, and that may be too painful to bear.

All opinions can be traced back to higher dimensions of the Self. Eventually, all paths lead back to the core—the epicenter of the self-concept, "me" as a person. For this reason, we see so much defensiveness when others contradict one's beliefs. Indeed, individuals present beliefs proudly, as if these were the true Self (Bramer et al., 1993). Yet, they are only indicators of a deeper sense of Self that is more diverse and very vulnerable. However, these beliefs are real to their owners and therefore they are defended strongly, like a mother defends her newborn from threats.

Self is tied to context. The ego works hard to organize the data of experience gained through interacting with one's contexts. As experiences accrue, the consequences of our interactions with the environment are recorded (cognitively) and used to create new conceptions, or edit some and delete others. This psychological pruning is key to the development of a valid and functional self. To better understand the process, I'm going to assume a prototypical individual enters a novel context. For simplicity, I will use hiking as the context, and hiking a mountain trail more specifically. If we have functional legs, we walk. Hiking is a form of walking, although the terrain can be quite different than a sidewalk or a hallway. Indeed, hiking a mountain trail involves more variation than walking on a level sidewalk. We rarely encounter major obstacles walking on a sidewalk, excluding ice in the winter. Yet, when hiking a mountain trail, there are loose stones, holes, and protruding roots. Adding pitch to the hike increases difficulty, particularly when going downhill. I can remember many instances when walking downhill was far more treacherous than climbing uphill. My momentum alone was enough to make me slip if I stepped on a loose stone or some wet grass.

Entering a new context, the first goal is to identify the constraints. At times they are made explicit, such as a sign reading "No shoes or shirt, no service" on a restaurant door. Other times, they are inferred through the reactions of others. Although our inferences can be wrong, particularly if tainted by negative past experiences, it's not too hard to tell when we are an odd presence in a novel context. The reactions of others speak louder than their silence betrays.

Once the constraints are uncovered, the next step is to set goals. The most obvious goal is to adapt to the constraint. However, that's not always

possible immediately and may require some time, if adaptation is even possible at all. Some adaptations are beyond our means. If we assume, though, that adaptation is possible, setting a goal is the first step. The next is to read the context and begin one's journey.

I was hiking at a local ski area recently. The last part of the hike was a steep ascent up the most difficult ski slope. To the left side of the slope was a series of little steps, carved out by the shoes of other hikers climbing the same slope throughout the summer. My goal was to climb to the top of the mountain. This was my adaptation to the present context. The constraint was the steep slope rising before me. To master this constraint, I would simply need to hike up the slope. Very simple, right? Not so. The reality is that no context is as simple as one's perception allows. The first step was to find the best possible path up. This can change, depending on the time of day, lighting conditions, vegetation, and moisture, to name a few factors. Adaptation thus requires flexibility. Having a rigid approach works if the constraint remains constant. If it doesn't, rigidity is the easiest path to failure.

Adaptation requires goal flexibility. As you know from your personal experience, my good reader, not everyone adapts. As the constraints increase in difficulty, failure and quitting are far more common than success and persistence. Therefore, we can define successful adapters as those with goal flexibility. They change their goals to meet changing constraints. This does not mean, though, that the primary goal changes. The constraint remains the same; getting to the top of the mountain. However, the road traveled varies depending upon the conditions, external and internal (within the person). Goal flexibility means managing one's goals to meet these needs. It's about setting short-term goals to help one arrive at the long-term goal. In climbing this means finding the optimal path, with goals being as proximal as finding the safest path over the next three yards. As the primary goal remains adapting to the constraint, the hiker will continue progressing upward, although the path may no longer be a straight line.

To an outsider, goal flexibility can be misunderstood. Indeed, to some, it may appear weak or a sign of cowardice. Clearly taking more risks involves more courage. Yet, risks aren't always the most prudent course, particularly when one lacks skill. Climbing a steep slope when not prepared is not only imprudent but quite stupid. Sadly, many people are too highly influenced by social responses. Thus, to avoid looking bad in front of others, they will either perform acts that are beyond their ability or avoid them altogether. The truly superior adapter will adjust her goals to the changing constraints, including knowing her own mental and physical status. She will feel the sting of negative feedback but is apt to process it quickly and continue her path forward. Thus, the best adapters have what I call *adaptation competence*

because they read their environments and their minds and bodies well and adjust their goals to match the immediate constraints. They do this while never letting go of the ultimate aim, which is the adaptation to the primary constraint.

Adaptation competence and *goal flexibility* are two key ingredients to successful adaptation, in addition to *contextual competence*. Contextual competence is an understanding of a context. It may seem that one must have mastered a context to attain contextual competence. That is indeed one way to define contextual competence. For my part, I call that context-specific competence or adaptation. To master a context, one must adapt to its constraints. To adapt to its constraints, one must know the context well. Thus, the two are the same. Contextual competence is a broader competency. It's the ability to read a context and identify the best pathway to adaptation. This is an interesting mechanism I discovered while hiking down a steeper ski slope one Sunday afternoon. As I started down a dirt mountain-bike trail, I slipped but didn't fall. Losing my footing, I immediately felt that this could happen again and started a process of planning each segment of my remaining journey downward. I scanned the environment for the best path, adjusting my goals to the mastery of each segment, meter by meter. I made predictions for that segment using a vast amount of stored data, including data from that specific day and previous hiking adventures. These predictions were used to guide my progress downward in a probabilistic fashion, with my choosing the pathways down that had the highest probability of success.

Contextual competency is what differentiates those who persevere through a difficult context to attain mastery, from those who fail and give up their goals. In the current literature, some researchers like to refer to this perseverance as grit. Grit is the construct with ties to the learned helplessness and positive psychology literature (Duckworth et al., 2007; Duckworth & Quinn, 2009; Stix, 2011). Grit is this ability to withstand tremendous discomfort and succeed where others fail. Grit however is more of a psychophysiological trait than contextual competency. Although there is little evidence to suggest that people who succeed in difficult contexts don't possess grit (Duckworth & Gross, 2014), I submit that grit is not the mechanism responsible for their success. Successfully navigating a difficult context requires a special type of intelligence that allows one to process vast amounts of data and make very rapid and accurate predictions. This is contextual competency.

Like all prediction models, one makes errors, for there is rarely a perfect prediction. Borrowing from statistical terminology, error is the difference between the predicted and the actual outcome (i.e., residual). Individuals with contextual competency minimize this error. Their predictions result in what I like to call *residual parsimony*. What makes for a model that

minimizes residuals is the variables used in making the predictions. Thus, to have residual parsimony one must have access to an enormous storage of data to make good predictions. As you have guessed, no doubt, this refers to a vast but well-organized self-concept. It also requires the ability to read the context and look for clues. These clues are often processed at an exceptionally high speed, as the ability to relate clues to past experiences occurs nearly instantaneously. However, speed is not to be confused with automatic processing. For those without contextual competence, responses to cues within a context are often processed automatically; without thought. All humans depend upon schemas to a large extent to navigate contexts, especially new contexts. Schemas provide blueprints for responding based on the cues encountered (Crick & Dodge, 1994, 1996; Dodge & Crick, 1990; Markus et al., 1985). Yet, what differentiates the superior adapter from the average person is that the former doesn't depend solely upon these schemas. The superior adapter uses schematic responding only when it is the most efficient and prudent way to respond.

Returning to the mountain and climbing up involves identifying the best fitting model for the data, a model that minimizes error in prediction. Once the hiker reaches the top, she experiences equilibrium, for she has mastered the contextual constraint. At that moment she is at supreme peace, for she has no other goal. Goals involve the Self, and the contrast between the Self and the context. Goals are about adaptation, and adaptation—as I just explained—is a complicated process involving prediction, action, and the evaluation of results, with repetition. Yet, once the goal is achieved and before the next goal is set, the boundary between the Self and context shatters. The two are one, and she experiences this diffusion of boundary as pure peace, what is referred to as the Oceanic Feeling, the Zone, or Flow (Csikszentmihalyi, 1991; Freud, 2015; Stamatelopoulou et al., 2018).

In my younger years, I was bent on finding inner peace. Like many I read about this experience, intellectualizing something that is not intellectual. Of course, that's what we do in the western world. It's our way of understanding. Yet, to experience inner peace, one must fully adapt to one's context. Indeed, the better one gets at adapting, the more apt one is to lose the separation between the Self and not-Self, and the more likely is one to experience inner peace. It is ephemeral, however, as the moment one realizes one has it, it's gone. The superior adapter experiences the oceanic feeling more frequently than most people, although those who possess expertise in some realm do experience it during performance whether they are superior adaptors or not. Athletes experience flow when competing, being lost in their sport (Havlucu et al., 2022). Musicians experience it when in the throes of a favorite piece (Marin & Bhattacharya, 2013). Even nonexperts experience it at times, such as when a reader is lost in a story

and loses track of time (Thissen et al., 2018). The same goes for a music fan listening to her favorite song (Loepthien & Leipold, 2022). Unlike the rest, however, the superior adapter experiences it across more domains, whether walking to a store, driving, or writing a manuscript. It becomes a part of whom they are for they possess a healthy Self (Rodriguez, 2000).

The Psychoadaptation process is a lifelong endeavor. Each time we adapt to a context, new opportunities arise, and if we approach them, the adaptation process starts again. Yet, our previous experience adapting influences how we approach these new opportunities. It also influences how we deal with disequilibrium. Although never easy, disequilibrium becomes appreciated, and a welcome step in the development of adaptation. Indeed, some of us thrive on it, pushing ourselves in ways that enhance our discomfort, knowing full well that when we master the context, the feelings we experience will far outweigh the negative moments we have when in the throes of disequilibrium. This suggests that I encourage disequilibrium and mastering new challenges. Indeed, I do. Yet, some contexts are more difficult than others, even if mastery is attainable. Given dispositional differences in people, and differences in our upbringings, dealing with disequilibrium will be more difficult for some than others. That is why I recommend having a skilled mentor when approaching new contexts, ensuring the mentor is someone who truly understands the art of learning, and the reciprocal interweaving experienced between success and failure along the route to mastery. This will allow for an anticipation of roadblocks and learning the skills to ease one's transition through them.

Psychoadaptation is not the same as selling out. Psychoadaptation involves adapting to a context's constraints. I often ask myself if adaptation to a context is the best course for optimal development. If people adapt to a context, they become stereotypical members. At times, this means abandoning one's individuality for the collective norm. This is seen quite readily within the military, an institution that values collective behavior above individuality. The unit works better when individual goals are subservient to the collective good.

Social institutions have their constraints too. Full adaptation to these constraints is highly encouraged and rewarded. Given the influence of the macrosystem on microsystems, adaptation to the macrosystemic norms engendered within the microsystems ensures the developing person all the benefits the culture has to offer. However, like all contexts, macrosystems have their limitations. Once an individual has adapted to the most essential constraints and possesses mastery, flaws are magnified. It is how the individual responds to these flaws that differentiate the successful individual from the superior human being.

Adapting to contexts is the goal, and I strongly encourage everyone to adapt to the macrosystem's most coveted constraints. For it is only then that one reaps the full rewards society has to offer. *That is selling out.* However, contrast this to the individual who refuses to adapt to these constraints. This individual never receives any of the rewards a culture has to offer. What's worse from an optimal developmental perspective is that this individual never comes to see the system's flaws. Thus, rebellion against a macrosystem without adaptation is an illusion, for how can one rebel against something one does not understand. To understand, one must enter the context, buy into its constraints, see the flaws in the system, and attempt to repair the flaws. It is only if the system does not yield to these efforts, if the flaws indeed exist, that rebellion is possible. Now, just because one identifies flaws doesn't mean one has to seek to repair them. This is what distinguishes the most successful people from the superior human being, or what I once referred to as the healthy self (Rodriguez, 2000). Most successful individuals learn to master their contexts, attain a superior status, and then remain in the context. This is a sure way to reap all the rewards the context offers. A great example is in scholarship and grant writing. The best grant writers are those scholars who understand well how to navigate the system to secure funding. This funding provides scholars with power, as their institutions view them as essential. With this success also comes academic prestige, a high income, and a more lavish lifestyle. Yet, the system itself is flawed, as among the best predictors of receiving a grant is having received prior grants, and publication productivity, making it very difficult for newcomers to break into the vault of success particularly ethnic minorities (Fang & Casadevall, 2016; Kaltman et al., 2014). Most scholars once attaining this success tend to remain, even when they see flaws in the system. One such flaw is the nature of fundable ideas. In biomedical research, for instance, not all ideas are fundable, particularly those associated with low prevalence conditions. Even if the science behind the idea is strong, the idea is innovative and significant, if the grant application doesn't deal with a popular idea, the likelihood of funding decreases. As such, researchers chase grants in fundable areas instead of pursuing their true passions. This, my good reader, is classic selling out to maintain one's status.

The healthy Self sees these flaws and decides to rebel when appropriate. Do not mistake this for a flippant attitude whereby the individual curses the context and walks out leaving all possessions and accomplishments behind. The healthy Self is no fool. Instead, when the situation is appropriate, the individual confronts the flaws and makes plans for transcendence. Note that I wrote transcendence instead of departure. Departure is leaving, whereas transcendence is moving up to a higher personal plain.

Returning to the question of selling out, I again strongly encourage adaptation to the mainstream. Individuals who never experience its benefits are missing out on a great deal of pleasure. Indeed, after buying in, they may choose to never leave. That is an amazing advancement over living life as an outsider. For those who never experienced society's greatest rewards, I strongly encourage adaptation. However, once adapted, if one feels the pull to challenge or transcend, that is always an option. The healthy Self is indeed a unique individual. Although she may forgo the comforts of complete adaptation, this is irrelevant to her, as her life is a different sort; one that cherishes movement toward some personal aim, an aim that is more valuable than any luxury one's money can afford.

Psychoadaptation in the context of psychology. Reading this chapter may lead one to conclude that Psychoadaptation is a form of positive psychology. Positive psychology is a movement that was initiated in 1998 when Martin Seligman, then president of the American Psychological Association (APA), announced that there is too much focus on the negative in psychology, and that we need to return psychology to a balance in which psychological well-being and human excellence (nurturing talent) is pursued (Alex Linley et al., 2006; Seligman, 2002). Indeed, the goal is a happier individual, where happiness is defined by the happy trinity of a pleasant life, an engaged life, and a meaningful life (Lee Duckworth et al., 2005). While it is clear that adaptation to a given context and its constraints will make life pleasant and meaningful, and that being engaged in one's context will likely result in the oceanic feeling (or flow, to borrow from Csikszentmihalyi, a co-founder of the movement), Psychoadaptation is more than the pursuit of happiness. Indeed, as I expressed repeatedly throughout this chapter, to adapt, one must confront disequilibrium, and this is not a pleasant feeling. Further, in addition to this requirement, many individuals seek to transcend their contexts, challenging the systems governing constraints, even if that means sacrificing one's happiness. To quote Duckworth, Steen, and Seligman,

> We believe that positive traits and positive emotions flourish best in the context of positive institutions. Because meaning derives from belonging to and serving something larger than oneself, a life led in the service of positive institutions is the meaningful life.
>
> *(p. 636, Lee Duckworth et al., 2005)*

Unfortunately, not everything is as it appears, and what are positive institutions to some are unappealing to others, and perhaps even agents of oppression. Psychoadaptation coexists with both adaptation to the context and its transcendence. As such I believe that it has a broader reach than positive psychology. Further, there is a reason why psychology researchers

have focused more on disease than the pursuit of happiness. When people are happy, they are less likely to pursue treatment than when in the midst of mental suffering. Given the prevalence of violence (e.g., mass shootings, unprovoked attacks), war, poverty, social injustice, and disease in the past decade, positive psychology will likely again take a back seat to a focus on alleviating suffering.

Positive psychology is a movement, not a theory. One theoretical perspective that has similarities to Psychoadaptation is Prochaska and DiClemente's Transthoretical Model of Behavior Change (Prochaska, 2008; Prochaska & DiClemente, 1982, 1983; Prochaska & Velicer, 1997). Prochaska and DiClemente studied how individuals navigate the natural history of behavioral change, such as when quitting combustible cigarette smoking. They proposed a series of stages that include precontemplation, contemplation, preparation, action, maintenance, and termination, with possible relapse and a return to a prior stage. One could argue that the adaptation process occurs in these very stages as one confronts the constraints of a context to which one eventually adapts or fails to adapt. This model however is more clinical in nature than Psychoadaptation, which intends to explain change in general from within a human developmental perspective. As such, while the two are compatible and one can even argue that Psychoadaptation fits well within the context of the Transtheoretical model, and is perhaps even a model of how one progresses across the different stages, Psychoadaptation also accounts for individuals not desiring change. The Transtheoretical model accounts for this in its precontemplation stage. Yet, for individuals addicted to a substance such as nicotine, or enacting other maladaptive behaviors, precontemplation is a rebellion against positive change. In Psychoadaptation, people can be very comfortable and live healthy and well-adjusted lives without ever contemplating change. As such, Psychoadaptation is compatible with this theory and those falling within the rubric of positive psychology, yet it accounts for other processes that neither approach touches upon as thoroughly, if at all.

Notes

1 Farthest from the person.
2 I say range of behaviors because the normal probability distribution function is a probability density function, with the variable in question being continuous. For continuous variables, the probability of any one specific value is 0. Thus, we discuss ranges instead of specific points.
3 Perhaps a better probability representation is the cumulative distribution function (CDF), as moving from left to right one approaches mastering 100% of the constraint. However, I chose not to use the CDF because a key tenet of Psychoadaptation is that individuals chose not to leave contexts if there is an

advantage to remaining in a context one has mastered. Simply put, the praise one receives from the context may be too alluring to leave for new challenges.

4 Reinforcers are consequences that increase the likelihood a behavior will be reenacted. Tokens in a token economy are valuable because they can be exchanged for primary reinforcers, such as food.

5 You may be confused by my use of negative with reinforcement and positive with punishment as it doesn't seem that punishment can ever be positive, nor can reinforcement be negative. However, these adjectives are used to define the adding (positive) or removal (negative) of consequences. Positive punishment is the addition of a negative consequence, such as spanking. Negative reinforcement refers to the removal of a negative consequence, such as homework for good behavior. Negative punishment refers to the removal of a positive consequence, such as taking away recess for some behavioral transgression. Finally, positive reinforcement is the adding of a desired consequence, such as a dollar for completing a task on time.

6 I say "seasoned" because at times we can learn from younger individuals with greater expertise, such as learning to play tennis at an older age from a young-adult tennis coach.

7 Note the use of plus or minus. The standard normal distribution is centered at zero, and is symmetrical. Thus, values below it are negative, with the distance between the mean and any value equal whether one is above or below the mean.

8 Today's manual transmission cars have a cheat mechanism to prevent the car from going backward. My current car doesn't roll backward like the older cars did, making it easier to learn to drive a stick now than in the days of old. Still, the anti-roll mechanism isn't fail-proof, and the car does roll from time to time.

9 I borrowed interweaving from Arnold Gesell's term reciprocal interweaving to explain the back and forth nature of development.

References

Alex Linley, P., Joseph, S., Harrington, S., & Wood, A. M. (2006). Positive psychology: Past, present, and (possible) future. *The Journal of Positive Psychology*, *1*(1), 3–16.

Bramer, L. M., Abrego, P. J., & Shostrom, E. L. (1993). *Therapeutic Counseling and Psychotherapy* (6th ed.). Prentice Hall.

Bronfenbrenner, U. (1993). The ecology of cognitive development: Research models and fugitive findings. In H. Wozniak & K. Fischer (Eds.), *Development in Context: Acting and Thinking in Specific Environments* (pp. 3–46). Erlbaum.

Bronfenbrenner, U. (1994). Ecological models of human development. In T. Husten & N. Postlethwaite (Eds.), *International Encyclopedia of Education* (2nd ed., Vol. 3, pp. 1643–1647). Elsevier Science.

Bronfenbrenner, U., & Ceci, S. J. (1994). Nature-nuture reconceptualized in developmental perspective: A bioecological model. *Psychological Review*, *101*(4), 568–586. https://doi.org/10.1037/0033-295x.101.4.568

Cooley, C. H. (1992). *Human Nature and the Social Order*. Transaction Publishers.

Crick, N. R., & Dodge, K. A. (1994). A review and reformulation of social information-processing mechanisms in children's social adjustment. *Psychological Bulletin*, *115*(1), 74.

Crick, N. R., & Dodge, K. A. (1996). Social information-processing mechanisms in reactive and proactive aggression. *Child Development*, *67*(3), 993–1002.

Csikszentmihalyi, M. (1991). *Flow*. Munksgaard København.

Deci, E. L., & Ryan, R. M. (1985). Self-determination and intrinsic motivation in human behavior. Springer. https://doi.org/10.1007/978-1-4899-2271-7

Dodge, K. A., & Crick, N. R. (1990). Social information-processing bases of aggressive behavior in children. *Personality and Social Psychology Bulletin*, *16*(1), 8–22.

Duckworth, A., & Gross, J. J. (2014). Self-control and grit: Related but separable determinants of success. *Current Directions in Psychological Science*, *23*(5), 319–325.

Duckworth, A. L., Peterson, C., Matthews, M. D., & Kelly, D. R. (2007). Grit: Perseverance and passion for long-term goals. *Journal of Personality and Social Psychology*, *92*(6), 1087.

Duckworth, A. L., & Quinn, P. D. (2009). Development and validation of the Short Grit Scale (GRIT–S). *Journal of Personality Assessment*, *91*(2), 166–174.

Epstein, S. (1973). The self-concept revisited: Or a theory of a theory. *American Psychologist*, *28*(5), 404.

Fang, F. C., & Casadevall, A. (2016). Research funding: The case for a modified lottery. *American Society of Microbiology*, *7*, 00422–00416.

Freud, S. (2015). *Civilization and Its Discontents*. Broadview Press.

Gesell, A. (1939). Reciprocal interweaving in neuromotor development. *Journal of Comparative Neurology (and Psychology)*, *70*, 161–180.

Harter, S. (1988). The construction and conservation of the self: James and Cooley revisited. In *Self, Ego, and Identity* (pp. 43–70). Springer.

Harter, S. (1998). The development of self-representations. In W. Damon (Series Ed.) and N. Eisenberg (Vol. Ed.), *Handbook of Child Psychology* (5th ed., Vol. III, pp. 553–557). Macmillan.

Havlucu, H., Akgun, B., Eskenazi, T., Coskun, A., & Ozcan, O. (2022). Toward detecting the zone of elite tennis players through wearable technology. *Frontiers in Sports and Active Living*, *4*, 939641.

Jung, C. G. (1916). The transcendent function. *Collected Works*, *8*, 189.

Jung, C. G. (1970). *The Collected Works of CG Jung: Mysterium Coniunctionis, and Inquiry into the Separation and Synthesis of Psychic Opposites in Alchemy* (Vol. 20). Princeton University Press.

Kaltman, J. R., Evans, F. J., Danthi, N. S., Wu, C. O., DiMichele, D. M., & Lauer, M. S. (2014). Prior publication productivity, grant percentile ranking, and topic-normalized citation impact of NHLBI cardiovascular R01 grants. *Circulation Research*, *115*(7), 617–624.

Lee Duckworth, A., Steen, T. A., & Seligman, M. E. (2005). Positive psychology in clinical practice. *Annual Review of Clinical Psychology*, *1*, 629–651.

Loehlin, J. C. (2004). *Latent Variable Models: An Introduction to Factor, Path, and Structural Equation Analysis*. Psychology Press.

Loepthien, T., & Leipold, B. (2022). Flow in music performance and music-listening: Differences in intensity, predictors, and the relationship between flow and subjective well-being. *Psychology of Music*, *50*(1), 111–126. https://doi.org/10.1177/0305735620982056

Marin, M. M., & Bhattacharya, J. (2013). Getting into the musical zone: Trait emotional intelligence and amount of practice predict flow in pianists. *Frontiers in Psychology, 4*, 853.

Markus, H., & Nurius, P. (1986). Possible selves. *American Psychologist, 41*(9), 954.

Markus, H., Smith, J., & Moreland, R. L. (1985). Role of the self-concept in the perception of others. *Journal of Personality and Social Psychology, 49*(6), 1494.

Masterson, J. F. (1985). *The Real Self: A Developmental Self, and Object Reactions Approach.* Brunner/Mazel Publishers.

Miller, J. C. (2004). *The Transcendent Function: Jung's Model of Psychological Growth through Dialogue with the Unconscious.* SUNY Press.

Piaget, J. (1951). The biological problem of intelligence. In D. Rapaport (Ed.), *Organization and Pathology of Thought* (pp. 176–192). Columbia University Press.

Porges, S. W. (2011). *The Polyvagal Theory: Neurophysiological Foundations of Emotions, Attachment, Communication, and Self-regulation (Norton Series on Interpersonal Neurobiology).* WW Norton & Company.

Prochaska, J. O. (2008). Decision making in the transtheoretical model of behavior change. *Medical Decision Making, 28*(6), 845–849.

Prochaska, J. O., & DiClemente, C. C. (1982). Transtheoretical therapy: Toward a more integrative model of change. *Psychotherapy: Theory, Research & Practice, 19*(3), 276.

Prochaska, J. O., & DiClemente, C. C. (1983). Stages and processes of self-change of smoking: Toward an integrative model of change. *Journal of Consulting and Clinical Psychology, 51*(3), 390.

Prochaska, J. O., & Velicer, W. F. (1997). The transtheoretical model of health behavior change. *American Journal of Health Promotion, 12*(1), 38–48.

Rodriguez, D. (2000). Self and adaptation: Defining the healthy self. In R.G. Craven & H.W. Marsh (Eds.), *Self-Concept Theory, Research and Practice: Advances for the New Millennium: Collected Papers of the Inaugural Self-Concept Enhancement and Learning Facilitation (SELF) Research Centre International Conference* (pp. 355–365). SELF Research Centre, University of Western Sydney.

Rodriguez, D. (2020). *Core Statistics: Practical Knowledge for the Health Sciences.* Kendall Hunt Publishing.

Rodriguez, D., Tscherne, J., & Audrain-McGovern, J. (2007). Contextual consistency and adolescent smoking: Testing the indirect effect of home indoor smoking restrictions on adolescent smoking through peer smoking. *Nicotine & Tobacco Research, 9*(11), 1155–1161.

Seligman, M. E. (2002). Positive psychology, positive prevention, and positive therapy. *Handbook of Positive Psychology, 2*(2002), 3–12.

Stamatelopoulou, F., Pezirkianidis, C., Karakasidou, E., Lakioti, A., & Stalikas, A. (2018). "Being in the zone": A systematic review on the relationship of psychological correlates and the occurrence of flow experiences in sports' performance. *Psychology, 9*(08), 2011.

Stix, G. (2011). The neuroscience of true grit. *Scientific American, 304*(3), 28–33.

Thissen, B. A., Menninghaus, W., & Schlotz, W. (2018). Measuring optimal reading experiences: The reading flow short scale. *Frontiers in Psychology, 9*, 2542.

Vygotsky, L. S. (1980). *Mind in Society: The Development of Higher Psychological Processes.* Harvard University press.

PART I

Academia

2

SUCCEEDING AS A STUDENT

Being a student is one of the greatest pleasures in life. Imagine the ability to exercise the brain every day so that you can help fulfill humanity's destiny: intelligence. Our species is poorly equipped to deal with nature. We lack sharp claws and powerful jaws to snare and rip apart our enemies. We are weak compared to the other primates. We are not the fastest creatures either and are therefore unable to escape predators easily. Nor can we fly like birds to evade capture. Yet, what we lack physically we make up in our intellectual capabilities. Our brains provide for such spectacular potential that, if realized, allow us to make up for each of these limitations in ways to our knowledge[1] that no other animal can.

To realize our fullest intellectual potentials requires study. Fortunately, I live in a country that attempts to educate the entire population. The United States is the envy of other nations in this respect, particularly countries in which some children are either forbidden to learn or have limited access to schooling. Yet, primary and secondary school education in the United States has its limitations. Therefore, many individuals matriculate at universities or colleges to pursue higher education. Most who do attend an institution of higher learning do so with the hopes of securing a career. Very few individuals matriculate to pursue learning for its own sake. Yet, the benefits of a post-secondary education are amazing, like infinity in a mathematical equation. Thankfully, instead of focusing primarily on specific skills, colleges and universities[2] require students to pursue a wider curriculum, including liberal arts and sciences, and have learning outcomes including critical thinking. Such skills allow individuals to become true scholars despite students' desires to attain practical skills related to their majors. Critical

DOI: 10.4324/9781003460800-4

thinking and other institutional learning outcomes are practical skills too, as they help us exercise our brains and attain our fullest intellectual potentials.

Succeeding in college is not easy. Unlike secondary school, college students (students) have great freedom. For one, students can for the most part select their class schedules to fit their personal preferences. If one doesn't like attending early morning classes, one can take most classes in the afternoon or even at night. When I was an undergraduate, I didn't want classes on Fridays. I however liked early morning classes, so that's how I populated my schedule. Further, classes do not occur every day and are often in different buildings. On some campuses, one has to hike quite a distance to get to the next class. When I was at the University of Maryland, College Park, I'd sometimes have to hike a distance larger than many college campuses to get to my next class. With classes being in different buildings, there is no bell to warn students that class is about to start, and there are no hall monitors to ensure students get to class. Further, not all professors punish for tardiness or missed classes. Although some professors are strict about attendance, others leave it up to the student.

Freedom is a great gift, but it can be a booby trap of sorts. For the well-disciplined student, the autonomy is welcome, with time for additional study. However, for the less-disciplined student, freedom can result in missed classes, failure to maintain one's studies, and flunking classes. Unlike high school, professors generally provide a syllabus that they cover intensely at the start of the semester and then leave it up to the students to refer to and follow thereafter without additional prompting. It's quite the joke among my colleagues to say "see the syllabus" as we know students almost never look at the syllabus despite it containing every bit of information a student needs to know. Some students have a very difficult time adapting to this new freedom. As such, college is a ripe environment for the study of Psychoadaptation.

College is not high school. High schools differ in quality, and being the best in one's high school doesn't equate to being the best at another high school. This makes sense, as teachers adapt to their students. Our goal in educating students is to encourage their best performance. Students with limitations cannot be expected to perform as well as students with every advantage. The playing fields are not equal for all students. Thus, what is outstanding performance in one setting may be no more than mediocre performance at best in another setting. This means that an A in one high school does not necessarily equate to an A in another high school. Standardized tests are a better judge of relative performance. Standardized tests compare students to the entire population of students taking the test. Students are given percentile scores to compare their performance to others taking the same test. Yet, these tests are flawed as they fail to account for

environmental differences. Context means everything. A context filled with learning opportunities will provide a greater opportunity for adaptation than one that lacks cognitive challenge. Standardized testing is a better way to rank students on various competencies. However, the failure to account for the effects of one's learning environment, including perceptions of presumed performance and differences in preference for competitive settings, makes them less than ideal to judge capability (Niederle & Vesterlund, 2010; Walton & Spencer, 2009). For instance, it is widely believed that women and ethnic minorities, with the exception of Asian Americans, perform worse on standardized tests than non-minority men.

Given the importance context plays in academic achievement before college, neither Grade Point Average (GPA) nor standardized tests are ideal predictors of successful college performance. However, they can give us an indication of a student's preparedness (Jackson & Kurlaender, 2014; Marini et al., 2019). A student with a high GPA and a high standardized test score is better equipped to succeed academically in college than is a student with a lower GPA, a low standardized test score, or poor performance on both. Yet, high academic preparedness does not equate necessarily to success in college. The college environment is far more complicated than textbooks and exams.

For some, matriculation is a great achievement, particularly for those matriculating at highly competitive institutions. Yet, receiving an acceptance letter to a prestigious institution is not a guarantee of success. Like most achievements in life, there is always a next step. After the celebrations are done, it's time to get to work. Regardless of the college's ranking, most freshmen are greeted by faculty with higher expectations than what students encountered in high school. College faculty are diverse, coming from a variety of institutions and with a variety of degrees. Although in most colleges, faculty have PhDs and are full time, students will also have graduate student instructors, adjunct professors, and those with alternative doctorates (e.g., EdD, PsyD, or DrPh). Faculty will also differ in their expectations. In some colleges, faculty have enormous demands on their time, including writing grants and manuscripts for publication. Some faculty also run massive labs, consuming much of their time. All faculty have institutional duties as well, including sitting on committees, supervising doctoral students where applicable, and other forms of service. With all these demands, faculty tend to focus their teaching on what they know best. For some faculty, this means strong academic writing skills. Depending on one's major this can include writing as if one is writing for publication. This means that despite one's preparedness in high school and any accolades one received for high school scholarship, the standards for excellence are raised far above what one encountered previously.

With new standards for success, greater freedom, lower supervision, and differences in preparedness for academic success, the celebrations of acceptance can quickly turn into panic. Some students use their resources well and adapt easily to this new environment. For others, however, the stress becomes overwhelming and performance is far lower than what they experienced in high school.

Failure is a natural part of the learning process and is indeed required to attain success. Yet, despite this statement, I once proclaimed confidently (in a doctoral course I was taking) that there's no such thing as failure. I recall one of my fellow doctoral students was confounded by my statement. I heard her ask a peer, in response to my proclamation, "failure exists, right?" It was indeed an interesting moment for many reasons. I always liked throwing metaphorical wrenches into one's stream of consciousness, with the intent of breaking up formulaic thinking. When one's beliefs are fixed and a challenge is offered, confusion arises. That's indeed how disequilibrium works. Yet my goal at that moment wasn't to introduce disequilibrium. Indeed, I hadn't yet thought about the concept, although perhaps in my sessions with Dr. Hatfield. My purpose at the time was merely to discuss the importance of failure in the learning process. Nevertheless, my declaration had its intended effect. Thus, although I stated that there's no such thing as failure, my intent was to consider the role of failure in the learning process. It is as inevitable as the next moment.

When we set goals, we have a vision of the outcome. However, we rarely envision the process from the conception of an idea to its actualization. This is problematic because there is much work between the two, particularly when the objective is far away from the present. For instance, receiving one's PhD is a distant goal for a first-year doctoral student. It is even farther for a freshman undergraduate. Much takes place between the start of one's journey and its climax. I'll venture to say that those are some amazing years. Indeed, those were perhaps the best of my life. Then again, I love learning. If one only cares about the outcome instead of the process, these years can be rather tedious. For me, however, they were nothing short of amazing.

I found my years as a doctoral student invigorating because I love learning. Every time I walked onto the University of Maryland College Park campus, it was like an athlete walking onto the field for practice or competition. I came to enjoy every parcel of the experience, from finding a parking spot to walking to the library. I enjoyed my meetings with my advisor and the classes I took. Yet this wasn't new to me at the time. From my very beginning as a college student, I experienced bliss in being a student. I fondly recall my first class. It was an 8 AM linear algebra course. I remember getting a ride to campus from my father. He couldn't afford to buy me a car, and we couldn't afford me living on campus. My father,

however, was a kind soul and drove me a great distance to get me to class on time. We lived in Arlington, Virginia, so it was quite a way to College Park, Maryland, from home. I remember well the thrill I experienced walking into that classroom with a really cool textbook in the wee hours of the morning. I get chills thinking about it now. It was the start of an adventure that continues today as I type these lines.

I am a special case in that I found a love for learning. My goal in writing this book is for my reader to feel the same, or impart this feeling to a lucky someone. However, to enjoy learning one must understand failure. In academics, failure is inevitable. It's never an easy experience and is often very painful. It makes us angry and for some it may result in self-doubt and reduced effort (Kurtovic et al., 2019; Ojo & Owoyele, 2011). It certainly was that way for me. The failure process has several steps. It starts with a belief in one's supremacy in some realm. For instance, one may believe he is an outstanding writer. Perhaps he has some evidence to back up his claim. It may be that in high school he excelled in writing. Perhaps he wrote for the school paper, aced all of his writing assignments, and maybe even received an award or two for his writing competence. However, in college he receives a grade on his assignment that is below his expectations. What one considers a bad grade depends on the individual. For some it's an A-. For others, it is an F. For some, it's an A with lots of red marks and some comments suggesting ways to improve one's writing. The point is that the individual is unhappy with the result and disequilibrium steps in.

Disequilibrium is personal (Rodriguez, 2021). Some people cry. Some people get angry. Some people panic. Others are depressed. The initial reaction is disbelief, as if one says to one's self, "How is this possible?" Often this is followed by negative feelings about the instructor, including doubting the instructor's competence, or perhaps believing that the instructor dislikes the student. With time, if the individual is of the right mind, blame turns inward to the self. I wrote "right mind" because one can continue to blame others for failure, and that is not a sign of one having the appropriate makeup for academic success. Blaming others for one's failures may be adaptive to the individual at the moment, but its benefits are ephemeral and to hold on to such false beliefs is self-defeating in the long run.

Self-doubt is normal. Those who don't understand the learning process mistake it for a false belief, a belief that impedes successful progression to one's goal. From a Psychoadaptation perspective, it's inevitable and necessary, for it's an accurate perception of the relation between one's conception of the self and the data of experience. In short, one experiences self-doubt because one's beliefs about the self are wrong.

Up to this point, the process is essentially the same for everyone. What follows though differentiates those who are successful academically from

those who will likely fail to attain their goals. Self-doubt involves bargaining. One attempts to rationalize one's failure and decides to double down on one's efforts. The idea here is to maintain one's self-concept (Epstein, 1973; Rodriguez, 2000, 2021). From a Piagetian perspective, this entails attempting to assimilate the experience into one's current conception of one's self (Piaget, 1951). To assimilate an experience, one must fit the experience into one's worldview. For instance, in failing an exam one could say that she didn't study hard enough, ignoring the reality that her study method may be wrong. She may believe that she studied in the wrong place. Perhaps the library isn't the best place to study because of distractions from her peers. Although there may be some truth in all of these assertions, they do not tackle the essence of the problem, an overstatement of her competence. For those experiencing repeated academic failures, devaluating the context to maintain one's conception of self and self-esteem is a common process (Peixoto & Almeida, 2010).

The Psychoadaptation process is constructive in that one builds new structures in place of the older structure. One doesn't renovate the old. One takes a wrecking ball to the old structure, clears the debris, and builds a new structure in the same location. However, one doesn't forget the old structure. One merely archives the blueprints for posterity and reference if necessary. Yet destroying old structures isn't a quick process. It can take years or even an entire lifetime. For some, it never happens or occurs only in the face of death. Recently we've seen how some individuals faced with death from the Covid-19 started questioning their decision not to get vaccinated only to learn it may have been too late (Place, 2021). Fortunately, unlike those suffering from a debilitating disease, the most successful college students don't have to wait until their final breaths to build new structures. Instead of attempting to assimilate the negative experience into a faulty self-concept, they destroy the old one and construct a new self-concept.

When I first started college, I was on an emotional high for matriculating at the University of Maryland as a pre-engineering student. I was enormously excited and therefore attacked every course with the same vigor. Opening a book and smelling the newly printed pages was such a thrill. Reading every word was like running into a wave on a sunny beach day in the summer. However, it wasn't long before my enthusiasm hit a brick wall. I recall being lost in my philosophy course. It wasn't a pleasant experience, and my grade wasn't as high as I had hoped it would be. I couldn't understand the lessons and wasn't sure what to do. I had no choice but to alter my self-concept from this amazing college student I conceived myself to be, to a regular college student who struggled reading some text, particularly text written in older English or text that includes copious foreign words. Indeed, there is a part of me that is lazy when it comes to this type of reading. I've struggled

with this issue for years and even today. Yet I've learned to tolerate it when I cannot avoid such text.

Fortunately, at the time I was savvy enough to accept those weaknesses. I suppose that's why I didn't take a second philosophy course, and steered my electives in a different direction.[3]

Accepting one's weaknesses is not easy for some. In the American culture, admitting weakness has traditionally been seen as a failure. We are taught to be strong from our youth, and individuals who make it despite enormous struggles are viewed more favorably than those who quit in the face of challenge. Although there have been some changes in our cultural views of persistence under pressure over the past several years during the SARS Coronavirus-2 pandemic, the latent feeling is that those who quit are not the same as those who persist when challenged.

From a Psychoadaptation perspective, the most efficient approach is to abandon failed conceptions, however only after one tries to salvage them and all reasonable attempts are exhausted. I used the adjective reasonable here because one's failures may occur for many reasons. Although all failure is a sign of a weakness in the structure, some failures are minor and require only a tweaking of the Self. Thus, making new attempts through minor adjustments may be all that is required. When it's time to abandon a faulty self-concept, the signs will be clear.

In the academic realm, there is an easy equation for adaptation. Study until one attains mastery over the content, take the tests or complete the assigned projects, pass the courses, and move on to graduation. However, this equation does not work equally well for every student. Each student's history adds to the equation, making it very difficult for some to solve. It also changes the way one experiences emotion in completing different facets of the process. As I have noted frequently, for me the accomplishment of a small victory is very meaningful. For others, it may be an annoyance, and only becomes meaningful after the goal is achieved. Regardless of one's perspective, the aim remains the same: adaptation.

I am going to use my personal experience to demonstrate the process, as I have experienced the highs and lows of academic achievement along the way to my current state. I will start in my sophomore year of high school. I recall taking a mathematics course and being lost. Indeed, I didn't really pay much attention to anything that was going on. Most of the time I was infatuated with some pretty girl, and those thoughts eschewed any academic endeavor. In my junior year, I was taking a history course when my teacher assigned a book I fell in love with. I believe it was the Oregon Trail. I read voraciously. Never before had I sat so immersed in a book that I'd rather be there reading than doing anything else. Yet, that's what I experienced. Then, as if by magic, everything changed for me. Instead

of being lost in school, I was motivated and highly focused. I would have nothing less than an A.

Unfortunately for the purposes of matriculating into a competitive state school, my turnaround was too late. I applied to several schools I liked but was rejected. Fortunately, the admissions folks at the University of Maryland saw my potential and admitted me. Although I didn't get into the aerospace engineering program I applied to, I was admitted to pre-engineering and was on my way to the career I desired, or at least to a successful future.

I started college with a large chip on my shoulder. I was angry with myself for not being engaged early enough in high school and wanted more than anything to show those who doubted me that I was an excellent student. It was more than that, though, I wanted them to see that I was better than them. I became highly competitive and wanted to finish first in every course. I recall taking chemistry in a class with a couple of hundred students, and how our professor would post our exam grades outside her door, listed from highest to lowest. Looking up my social security number, I would find my score. If I wasn't in the top 10, I would be really angry. Indeed, I wanted to be number one. That wasn't always possible, but I soon became the student that I thought I should be. Yet, I had a flawed conception of academic achievement and what it meant to be successful. Although I excelled for the most part, I learned to value success instead of understanding the nature of the learning process. Indeed, I was so driven to show others that I am smart, that I left the University of Maryland and matriculated at George Washington University (GW) in Washington, DC. It was a university with a better academic reputation, and I felt that now I could show off my accomplishments to my high school peers.

Being motivated by showing up others is not a very healthy approach. I had defined my self-worth by someone else's ideal. There is an ideal that matriculating at a prestigious institution is a marker of success and intelligence (Campbell et al., 2019). Yet, that is an illusion. Such constructed selves will eventually collapse, as life will present lessons to wreck all pretensions. Indeed, it happened to me. Just before finishing my second year at Maryland and before I received the acceptance letter to GW, my father died. This was a devastating moment for our family for many reasons. Not only did I lose an important person in my life, but I lost all financial support. Fortunately for me, I received a full academic scholarship to study at GW. Unfortunately for me, our family needed financial help, and I had to go to work full time, and then some.

When one thinks of the college life, one often envisions parties, sport, and sitting in the quad reading a textbook on a sunny day. I did all of those, yet I also had to work. I got a full-time position as an assistant manager at Pier I Imports in Georgetown. That's 40 hours per week while

in school full time, taking five courses per semester. I then added to this by accepting a research assistant position at Western Union working for the cellular phone division. Yes, Western Union did dabble in cell phones early in the history of cellular communication. My job was as a statistics intern, as I was a statistics major at GW. For a time, I managed to hold on and keep my grades up. However, with time, the work became more intense, and fitting in homework, work, and my social life overwhelmed me. No doubt, I had serious fun during my time at GW, but I earned two Cs and that was forbidden for my scholarship. Thus, I lost the scholarship and had to leave GW. I had no way to pay the tuition. As it turns out, thus, my desire to prove to others that I was as smart as or smarter than they were by attending a more prestigious institution backfired badly. Instead of finishing school and getting a good job like many of my friends did, I was 22 and in need of another institution.

There is no such thing as failure. When I made that comment in graduate school, my intent was to say that every failure is a masked success. Without failing one cannot attain an ideal self. Failure means one is trying. However, my failure at the time did not feel like a success. I was very sad. I loved GW. I made so many friends there and still think fondly of them every now and then. As an individual who has now attained a PhD, I have learned to weave those failures into my narrative of success. That's why I say there's no such thing as failure. However, that's probably also why the student in my doctoral course was puzzled by my statement. Clearly, to the outsider, I failed at GW, for I lost my scholarship and didn't receive my degree there.

Times were hard indeed, and I thought about different ways to get back to college. I was hooked on learning, and I decided that I would do whatever it takes to get back to school. Life, though, had other ideas. When we make our goals and communicate them with others, they will receive some pushback, particularly if they contradict the reality of one's situation. First, I was poor. Unlike the general starving student, my family lost everything with my father's passing, and we were left homeless for a period of time. It was only with the help of a neighbor and a local Catholic church that we were able to salvage our lives until we could get back on our feet. Second, I was doing well in my job as an assistant manager and could easily succeed in retail. Yet none of that was enough. I had built this conception of myself as a student, and wouldn't give it up for anything. Indeed, the same neighbor who saved our family when we lost everything by letting us all live in a bedroom in her house became very frustrated with me that I was in school and threatened to dump our family's belongings in front of my store unless I gave up schooling and only worked. Our homelessness began while I was at GW, and for this neighbor, going to school instead of working full

time to support our family didn't fit her worldview. Thus, there was much pressure on me to adjust my worldview to fit reality.

Every story has a hero. In my story, I'm the hero. In your story, my good reader, you are the hero. Yet others may not have seen me as a hero, as I decided that to be successful, I had to leave the area and start my life over from scratch. Because of my hard work, I was able to move into my own place. I rented a studio apartment and then later a room in a high school friend's house. Shortly after, I left the DC metro area for good. While awaiting my shifts at Pier 1 Imports in Georgetown, I used to walk up the hill from M Street to Georgetown University and sit in the library reading. I read like a mad person. If I couldn't be in school, I thought, at least I could educate myself. I studied Eastern philosophy and read books on Psychology. Apparently, I could deal with these philosophical teachings better at the time than the European philosophers. In addition, I read through college catalogs.[4] As I loved travel, these idealized representations of academic institutions impressed me, and I decided that to attain my true academic self, I had to leave the area for good.

During this time, I also struggled with a chronic upper respiratory condition. As a child, I had asthma and was in and out of emergency rooms quite frequently. During my last years in DC, I visited specialists regularly and was on a wide variety of medications. Thus, when I found a brochure for San Diego State University and read that San Diego had the best climate for asthmatics, I decided that's where I had to go. I knew little about California and without the internet I didn't have information to learn more about the various colleges in California. I did read, however, that tuition was free or very low cost for California residents. I wasn't a resident, but living one year in California would make me eligible for the California tuition. So, that's what I did.

My dear reader, at this point you may be rolling your eyes and waving your arms urging me to move the story along and get to the Psychoadaptation point. If you are not happy with me telling my story, I understand. However, to understand the role adaptation plays in the learning process, one must understand how I developed into the academic I am. I promise I won't overindulge in this writing privilege as my main desire is to help readers understand the nature of a healthy self.

The year prior to moving was about making money for the move. Yet, I didn't stop learning. Once learning becomes a passion, nothing can stop it. I devoured everything I could. I particularly enjoyed reading psychological literature and the literature on Eastern religion. As reading costs no more than the price of a book, I spent little money on entertainment but filled my time beautifully. I also learned to live without much money and began to appreciate the beauty of my surroundings. Every walk through the old

streets of Georgetown was a mindful indulgence in the beauty of the old and historic. I especially enjoyed the later fall season and how the leaves contrasted with the red brick townhomes and sidewalks. Nothing heightens one's senses like meaningful poverty. I call it meaningful here because I made the deliberate choice to forgo luxuries for my goal of moving cross country to matriculate at San Diego State University. During my time at GW after I moved out on my own, by contrast, I indulged in the decadence of yuppiedom. Yuppies were a rather dull fashion set who believed in conservative yet elegant fashion, and spending on luxuries was meant to impress others. Is it any surprise that I went for that trend given I wanted to go to a college that would get me noticed? That fad did little for me except provide some good memories with friends and bills to pay for unnecessary things.

When I left for San Diego I went with nothing but a one-way ticket, a duffle bag filled with clothes, and $1,000 in traveler's checks. When I landed in San Diego, I caught a taxi to the YMCA and found lodging among sailors, and others like me seeking a new life. Imagine, moving across country with no more than knowledge of what was happening within the next few hours. What freedom! What stress! Yet, here was the origin of Psychoadaptation and its role in managing life so that one can excel academically regardless of one's circumstances.

I spent a year waiting and becoming a resident. I continued to read, but I also fell in love with cycling. I bought a bicycle to commute to work and started to ride her on my off days too. I loved her so much and christened her Sunship. In Southern California, the weather is pretty much always nice, so it's easy to be active. I cycled everywhere. I know San Diego well because I traveled vast distances on my bicycle. I frequently visited the local colleges, including San Diego State. However, now that I was in California, I also learned of the University of California (UC) system. Apparently, the UC schools have a reputation for being of higher quality than the Cal State system. I read about UC Santa Cruz and spoke to an admissions representative. Seeing my strong academic record, I was invited for an interview. I purchased the plane ticket but then, my first major shift in Self occurred. I was now completing my first year as a resident alone in a foreign land (to me). That year was quite lonely, and I had finally made some friends. I decided that I didn't need to go anywhere else and start again for a second time. I had all I needed in San Diego and SDSU. I returned the ticket and matriculated at SDSU.

One of the hardest acts one can do is to demolish one's current self-structure with all its self-concepts. The year spent in San Diego cycling up and down the hilly coast on Sunship provided a perspective on the meaning of education. I realized that everything I needed to become a master learner

was already within me, and whether I studied at UC Santa Cruz, SDSU, GW, or Maryland didn't make a difference. The goals were the same. I wanted to master content and if I have the books and the appropriate guidance, I could achieve everything regardless of where I do it. The need for prestige collapsed and now I had a new set of goals to navigate. From that point forward, including today, it has been easy to learn, and I have enjoyed every moment of the process.

I titled this chapter "Succeeding as a student." My personal story focuses on what I learned on my journey through my undergraduate studies. Yet, the lessons here apply to all learning, whether in high school or in one's doctoral studies. I will however cover learning at the elite levels in future chapters when I cover research and teaching.

My story is one of persistence and navigating barriers. I faced no shortage of barriers and climbed countless walls to return to college. Once there, however, I found it quite easy. Now, some of my readers may say that succeeding at a state school is much easier than succeeding at a highly competitive school like UC Berkley or Stanford. Those colleges are no doubt highly competitive. Yet, the competition generally ends upon matriculation. It's getting into the highly competitive institutions that is hard. Once there, learning is the same. First, there are far more doctoral-trained faculty than there are institutions to hire them. Indeed, if one peruses the peer-reviewed research one will find that some of the best and brightest authors are at institutions other than Harvard, Yale, or the like. Second, faculty at the most competitive institutions often do far more than teach. Indeed, the criteria for advancement in rank (i.e., movement from assistant to full professor) requires much publication and receiving major grants in some of the highest-profile institutions. With faculty focusing on publishing and grants, there is less time for preparing lessons. Thus, some of the best instructors are found in the institutions dedicated to teaching and not scholarship. Further, wherever one teaches, doctoral-trained faculty have high expectations of students, particularly faculty graduating from major research universities. Despite teaching for 25 years now, I still demand a lot from my students, particularly in academic writing. I was trained at a research institute, and the lessons learned there have stuck with me even with adjustments made for student competence.

Concerning student competence, students enter college as raw material. Although for some the raw material is better structured than for others, no student is complete. Molding students to become excellent learners requires faculty who are dedicated to teaching. Such faculty are found at all levels of higher education, most especially at institutions with less pressure on faculty to conduct high-level research. This was the case at San Diego State University. I had amazing faculty who were highly motivated for me to

succeed. As I too was highly motivated, we were a perfect match. I was so unconcerned with grades that I ate up lessons eagerly. This did not endear me among my fellow students who saw me as an oddball for asking so many questions in class and taking the focus away from more trivial matters. I'll save you all the details as they are irrelevant to this chapter. However, with my focus on learning, I was not only able to master content but to develop a system that ensured my success. I ended up mastering my environment perfectly. I adapted.

What I learned during my time at San Diego State may be unique to my personal situation, and perhaps it is useless to the reader's personal disposition both physical and mental. Yet, I doubt it as my years of teaching have solidified my understanding of the learning process.

On studying. Each semester starts with the syllabus. The syllabus communicates the course requirements. With time, syllabi have become standardized. Therefore, there is less idiosyncrasy in their development than in prior generations. Nevertheless, they are personalized by each professor and each course.[5] The syllabus is a contract, although there is generally a statement listing a caveat such as "The syllabus is subject to change …" We faculty do reserve the right to change the syllabus but do provide notice when doing so. That said, students must read the syllabus as the information is there, and faculty are bothered when students ask questions that are answered in the syllabus. The syllabus should be a planning tool for time management so that there are no surprises. Faculty don't want to surprise students for many reasons. First, it makes them look bad in their students' eyes and may result in lower evaluations. Second, changes introduce more work for faculty, and we don't want to add work to our already busy schedules.

With respect to planning, students should always read chapters before going to class. Thus, if I am covering chapter 2 today, and the student didn't read chapter 2, he will be less able to appropriate the content than if he did read it prior to class. The student may think that he is too busy to read all the chapters due in a given week, but I doubt it. In the work world, students will be asked to do far more than read a few chapters. I used to read chapters twice before class. The first reading was less intense. The second time I read the chapter, I would do so intently with a focus on mastering content.

Plan also to start projects early. The worst products are those done at the last moment. I spoke about this with class members last week. I told students to never wait until the last moment. One very good student told me that she waits until the last moment to produce products because that's how she works best. I retorted that despite what she believes, waiting until the last moment is flawed. First, unforeseen events can pop up and disrupt one's ability to focus on the project. Second, and perhaps most important,

there is less time for editing. All writers make mistakes, and one needs time to edit. Therefore, projects started at the last minute while perhaps ideal for one's personality style are not ideal in an academic environment.

On exams. In most colleges, grades are linked to one's performance on exams. There are a variety of testing modalities. Some professors use paper and pencil tests. Some rely on students filling in documents that are scanned for grading. Some professors administer tests on computers with live proctoring. Others may give students tests to take home and complete. For the purpose of simplicity, I'll use a paper and pencil test in a classroom setting as an example.

Preparing for tests requires intense study. But there is more to studying than reading and memorizing content. In fact, rote memorization is perhaps the worst way to study. There is a forgetting curve. Hermann Ebbinghaus conducted experiments on himself in which he memorized a series of nonsense syllables and explored his ability to remember them (Mazur, 2016). The further from learning in time, the more likely was he to forget. This makes sense given the nonsense syllables had little context. My suggestion is that instead of attempting to memorize content by repeating content and attempting to commit it to memory, find context. I would take new concepts out for a walk. As I walked (or cycled) around San Diego I would think of scenarios related to the concepts I learned in class. If the concepts are valid, I reasoned, they should apply to a variety of situations beyond textbook examples.

To take concepts out for a walk, I had to understand the content. This required me reading multiple times until I deeply understood it. In other words, I read until I could easily take my concepts for a walk and apply them to different scenarios in meaningful ways. This meant reading a textbook in my undergraduate years. Today, everything is far easier. With the internet, one can find information on any topic. For instance, many individuals post videos on YouTube, some of whom are excellent teachers. The problem is that some of these individuals know very little and may steer an eager learner in the wrong direction. I suggest that students navigate to videos produced by experts like professors when seeking sources.

Studying is done when one can apply the critical concepts to real life with ease. By the way, one can do this in every field of study, from mathematics to chemistry. For instance, when proving a statistics equation, I play around with it using different scenarios. Indeed, most statisticians apply their equations to cases pushing the boundaries of the equation. It's the "what if I do this?" scenario. That's a great idea.

With the completion of studying, it's time for the test. This is where I may diverge from many, and what I suggest may not be perfect for every student. However, it worked very well for me, and one can modify it to fit

one's personality style. First, I went at it alone. Although I loved sitting with people and talking about life in general, at test time I became extremely focused and refused to speak to anyone. I would find a place to sit away from everyone, making my desire to not be bothered quite clear. Some people try to reduce their stress by involving others in their misery. The less I spoke to others the better. Plus, other students would introduce possible scenarios that I may not have considered. This would increase my stress. Test time is not the time to think of new possibilities. To alleviate this, one can meet in a study group in the days before the exam.

Once I entered the classroom and found my seat, I began imagery. Imagery is popular with athletes and other elite performers, although research results are mixed on its efficacy (Di Corrado et al., 2020; Esplen & Hodnett, 1999; Finch & Moscovitch, 2016; Nguyen & Brymer, 2018). Nevertheless, it had the intended effect for me. I didn't know much about it then except from what I read in books covering Eastern philosophy. My imagery changed with time, but I settled on the following. I started by closing my eyes and taking some nice and slow breaths. Next, I visualized the exam before me, my hand, and pencil. I imagined I read the question and the answer would automatically flow like an electrical impulse from my brain to my hand and pencil. I would then fill in the correct response. I repeated this until I was interrupted by the test handed to me. I then began to work.

This imagery worked very well in my case, for when the exam started, my mind was clear. I often tell students that I prefer not to think when taking tests or writing. I just do. This may sound counterintuitive as academics is a cognitive pursuit, and how can one perform something cognitive without thinking? Yet, if one has the knowledge stored, it's merely a matter of accessing the stored information to answer the question (Kiefer, 2012). It's like opening a lock with a code. When one reaches for the lock, the code comes to mind as if by magic. Stress impedes retrieval (Sauro et al., 2003). That's why it's so important to be relaxed.

I used imagery a lot. It most likely worked for me because it distracted me from the task at hand rather than having any metaphysical properties. I also used a form of affirmation. I didn't tell myself that I am great. Instead, as I cycled Sunship on my way to campus, I used to go over why I am where I am and how it was my intense persistence that led me to my destination. I was setting up the context for the task at hand. The exam, I reasoned, was a validation of my progress and how one day I will have a degree because of the hard work I put in and my perseverance. Thus, when I took the exam, I was completely focused on the exam and nothing else.

There are of course situations in which automatic processing hits roadblocks. At times one encounters items that are complicated or

unforeseen. Yet, if one studies correctly and takes concepts out for a walk, as I call it, one is better prepared to deal with difficult questions. When I encountered one, the moment I realized it was difficult, I skipped it and finished the other items before returning to the difficult item. This ensured my momentum wasn't interrupted and that I wouldn't be thinking about something negative when there was so much more to do. Negative thoughts have a life of their own and are tied to complexes we have from past negative experiences (more on this in a later chapter). Thus, one thought leads to another, and so forth. As such, to reduce the likelihood of negative thinking, it was better to skip such problems and come back to them later. I would return to them.

Upon completing all the exam problems once, including the ones I had to return to, I would go back and review all items to ensure I didn't forget something. Earlier in my academic career, I was so nervous that at times I would forget to complete an item. That really made me feel ill afterward, once I realized I missed an item or more. I therefore assured myself that I would never let that happen again. Thus, I always made sure that I was the last person leaving the test session and only after I reviewed every single item for completion.

Exam results vary. First exams were always the hardest as I wasn't sure what to expect. Each instructor has her own set of constraints which she may allude to, but we don't necessarily understand until we encounter them. I studied hard for the first tests but knew that until I understand the professor's constraints it would be hard for me to adapt fully. With knowledge in hand, adaptation was easier, and I did better on subsequent exams. This approach worked so well that I was scoring as much as 20 to 30 points better than every student. I obliterated every curve.

Let me return to the idea of difficult problems and discuss how solving them relates to the Psychoadaptation process. One of the important tenets of Psychoadaptation is that the more one adapts, the easier it is to adapt to new challenges. Although our world is diverse and situations vary in complexity, there are similarities in all situations. The superior adaptor finds these similarities and applies them in solving new problems. This is why taking concepts out for a walk is so important. By applying the concepts learned in class to different situations, we stretch our understanding. Therefore, if a professor adds a complicated scenario to an exam, we are more likely to see similarity to what we have prepared for than if we have very basic understanding of the concept and never apply it broadly. Here's an example I use in teaching. There are many ways to solve problems in epidemiology related to sensitivity, specificity, interrater reliability (Kappa), and survival curves. These are different concepts covering diverse issues such as the validity

of screen tools, evaluations of testing results, and prognosis. Yet, each of these problems can be solved using what we know about probability rules. As such, before teaching about these different statistics, I cover probability. I make sure my students understand how the multiplication and addition rules of probability can be applied to these various situations. I use what I learned by taking concepts out for a walk and applied them to a diversity of problems which students would generally learn by memorizing equations that do no more than waste mental space. Knowing probability rules allows them to save that space for other information. Taking concepts out for a walk in the real world and applying them to a cornucopia of situations stretched my understanding. This prepared me to stretch my knowledge when I encountered purposefully obfuscating exam scenarios. The more we adapt, the more we are able to find communality among diverse situations.

My journey to graduation was long and difficult. I hope nobody reading these words has to encounter the negative experiences I had as I navigated the path from high school to being a college graduate. I do hope; however, other students apply the lessons I learned from these vast experiences to their own lives so that they may reduce the amount of stress they experience. Each journey has a beginning and an end. The superior adapter never shies away from challenge and moves forward until the goal is achieved. He accepts meaningful criticism, but the rest he allows in one ear and out the other. He is relentless and never quits until evidence tells him that further progress is not possible. I rarely ever quit a pursuit unless I know further attempts are fruitless. Realization of one's goals is possible if one transcends barriers and finds the best path to navigate based on his circumstances. Goals may take longer to achieve for some than for others, but no worthwhile goal is achieved without creeping over barriers.

Notes

1 We don't know what other animals can do because of our inability to communicate with them except in rudimentary ways.
2 I will refer to higher education as college from this point forward.
3 I have learned to embrace philosophy and now read it to learn the history of knowledge.
4 Prior to the public internet, one would browse brochures of colleges in libraries.
5 A likely exception is a course taught by an adjunct or a graduate student.

References

Campbell, C. M., Jimenez, M., & Arrozal, C. A. N. (2019). Prestige or education: College teaching and rigor of courses in prestigious and non-prestigious institutions in the US. *Higher Education*, *77*, 717–738.

Di Corrado, D., Guarnera, M., Guerrera, C. S., Maldonato, N. M., Di Nuovo, S., Castellano, S., & Coco, M. (2020). Mental imagery skills in competitive young athletes and non-athletes. *Frontiers in Psychology, 11*, 633.

Epstein, S. (1973). The self-concept revisited: Or a theory of a theory. *American Psychologist, 28*(5), 404.

Esplen, M. J., & Hodnett, E. (1999). A pilot study investigating student musicians' experiences of guided imagery as a technique to manage performance anxiety. *Medical Problems of Performing Artists, 14*(3), 127–132.

Finch, K., & Moscovitch, D. A. (2016). Imagery-based interventions for music performance anxiety: An integrative review. *Medical Problems of Performing Artists, 31*(4), 222–231.

Jackson, J., & Kurlaender, M. (2014). College readiness and college completion at broad access four-year institutions. *American Behavioral Scientist, 58*(8), 947–971.

Kiefer, M. (2012). Executive control over unconscious cognition: Attentional sensitization of unconscious information processing. *Frontiers in Human Neuroscience, 6*, 61.

Kurtovic, A., Vrdoljak, G., & Idzanovic, A. (2019). Predicting procrastination: The role of academic achievement, self-efficacy and perfectionism. *International Journal of Educational Psychology, 8*(1), 1–26.

Marini, J. P., Westrick, P. A., Young, L., Ng, H., Shmueli, D., & Shaw, E. J. (2019). Differential Validity and Prediction of the SAT®: Examining First-Year Grades and Retention to the Second Year. *College Board.*

Mazur, J. E. (2016). *Learning & Behavior* (8th ed.). Routledge.

Nguyen, J., & Brymer, E. (2018). Nature-based guided imagery as an intervention for state anxiety. *Frontiers in Psychology, 9*, 1858.

Niederle, M., & Vesterlund, L. (2010). Explaining the gender gap in math test scores: The role of competition. *Journal of Economic Perspectives, 24*(2), 129–144.

Ojo, A., & Owoyele, J. (2011). Causal attributions and affective reactions to academic failure among undergraduates in the Nigerian Premier University of Education. *European Journal of Scientific Research, 52*(3), 406–412.

Peixoto, F., & Almeida, L. S. (2010). Self-concept, self-esteem and academic achievement: Strategies for maintaining self-esteem in students experiencing academic failure. *European Journal of Psychology of Education, 25*, 157–175.

Piaget, J. (1951). The biological problem of intelligence. In D. Rapaport (Ed.), *Organization and Pathology of Thought* (pp. 176–192). Columbia University Press.

Place, N. (2021). 'That time has passed': Arkansas doctor shares anguish of telling dying Covid patients it's too late for vaccine. *Independent.* Retrieved June 6, 2023, from www.independent.co.uk/news/world/americas/arkansas-doctor-dying-covid-vaccine-b1890981.html

Rodriguez, D. (2000). Self and adaptation: Defining the healthy self. In R.G. Craven, & H.W. Marsh (Eds.), *Self-Concept Theory, Research and Practice: Advances for the New Millennium: Collected Papers of the Inaugural Self-Concept Enhancement and Learning Facilitation (SELF) Research Centre International Conference* (pp. 355–365). SELF Research Centre, University of Western Sydney.

Rodriguez, D. (2021). The art of learning and dealing with disequilibrium. In *Research Methods*. Kendall Hunt.

Sauro, M. D., Jorgensen, R. S., & Teal Pedlow, C. (2003). Stress, glucocorticoids, and memory: A meta-analytic review. *Stress*, *6*(4), 235–245.

Walton, G. M., & Spencer, S. J. (2009). Latent ability: Grades and test scores systematically underestimate the intellectual ability of negatively stereotyped students. *Psychological Science*, *20*(9), 1132–1139.

3

BEING AN EXPERT TEACHER

To be a great instructor, one must be a great learner. Great instructors take pride in their love for learning. They never miss an opportunity to learn something new. Nobody knows everything. Knowing that one knows so little about so much makes life far more enjoyable than if one believed one knows a great deal about pretty much everything. For with this self-awareness, one sees the world with wondrous eyes, like a child waking to a Christmas tree surrounded by gifts. Indeed, the great learner is easily excited by the novel, for with each novelty encountered comes another opportunity to expand knowledge and better the Self. Great instructors take great joy in learning.

Before moving to the academic realm, I will share a recent experience I had with a fellow ski instructor. Great instructors are found in every domain of learning. I was skiing on one of our few open trails at the start of the 2021–2022 season, and there were several fellow instructors there making some turns to break in their ski legs for the coming season. Naturally, as they love teaching as much as I do, the conversation quickly turned to teaching and learning. I asked a fellow instructor what I could do to improve my right turns. Without hesitation, he abandoned his own free skiing and made several runs with me to break down my technique and to show me how to improve my performance. What was most notable besides his selflessness in this circumstance was what he told me as we skied into the lift line. He noted that he takes every single moment when he's sliding, even when maneuvering into the lift line or disembarking the lift, to practice his technique, and he proceeded to show me how. Learning is everywhere, and good teachers never miss an opportunity to improve their own skills.

DOI: 10.4324/9781003460800-5

Good instructors know that learning never ends. Being a teacher myself, one of the most notable features of the teaching encounter is the novelty. I teach epidemiology, biostatistics, and grant writing, among other courses. The content in these courses changes regularly, especially epidemiology with new pathogens discovered frequently. With each novelty comes another opportunity to learn. Good instructors know that to be at one's best and to serve their students appropriately, one must continue learning. I'll use statistics as an example of my teaching and the importance of learning in the process. Although I cannot get inside the heads of all statistics instructors, I venture to suggest that many do not know a great deal about statistics.[1] Yes, they can teach a novice how to calculate a variance or a percentile. However, I wonder if they truly understand fully the more complicated concepts, such as *p*-values. It's easy to say that rejecting the null hypothesis is no more than demonstrating that the *p*-value is less than or equal to the alpha value, but what does that tell us about why a *p*-value allows us to reject a false null hypothesis?

As a good instructor, I never stop asking questions, especially when I see something that goes unexplained. A great example in teaching statistics is the standard error for a confidence interval surrounding an odds ratio. This equation is given to students without any explanation regarding its origin. Perhaps it's not important to know why we take the square root of the sum of the reciprocal of the cell sizes, but what if a sagacious student asks about it? Shouldn't an instructor be able to answer? The standard error in this example isn't perhaps the best example, as it may not be relevant to most reading this chapter. Perhaps a better example is the *p*-value. We use probabilities all the time, even when driving. The decision to take one path versus another on a given trip is related to the probability of arriving at one's destination safely. In statistics, it's used to determine the probability of a given value (or greater), assuming the null hypothesis is true. This isn't a piece about statistics, so I'll forgo the explanation here. However, it is important to note that for a student to become a consumer of research, and to work effectively as a researcher, this knowledge is key. Surface knowledge is not acceptable when teaching. Good instructors must dig deeper and know the origins of everything they teach.

Imagine that I am teaching an introductory lecture on statistical testing and say that the *p*-value is used to determine if one should reject or fail to reject the null hypothesis. In research, the null hypothesis is the hypothesis one seeks to reject in favor of the alternative hypothesis.[2] I note that the rule is to reject the null hypothesis if the *p*-value is less than or equal to the alpha. I tell my students that alpha is the probability of a false positive result, a Type I error. Responding to a raised hand, a smart student asks if there is a Type II error given there is a Type I error. Yes, I respond, praising the

student for her question, and note that this Type II error is failing to reject a false null hypothesis. Then, another student asks how are the two related. If I essentially repeat what I say, that may be good enough to appease the student. Yet, if the student asks for a deeper answer, it's my responsibility to know how to respond in brief but in sufficient detail.

This isn't a fictitious situation. It occurred to me once when I was teaching research methods to a cohort of graduate students in a Master of Clinical Psychology program. I repeated my explanation, but the student insisted that I explain exactly how the two are related. Saving face, I responded that I can't go into detail here about the relation now, but that I would respond to the comment in a couple of days via email. I did so because just like that student, I hated not having the answer to everything. I also realized that I failed in my teaching duties by not being prepared for every possible question a student could ask me. I recall going home and coming up with a beautiful piece on exactly how Type I and Type II errors are related. I brought it to class the next time we met and presented it to the student who was quite satisfied with what I taught him. The rest of the students, however, did not care one bit about what I had explained to the inquisitive student. They wanted to get the necessary content for the exam, pass the course, and move on with their studies.

That event took place a couple of decades ago, yet its ripples reach to everything I do. Nor was it the first or last such event to occur during my teaching career. Students come to learn. Faculty are supposed to be experts in the courses we teach. Failing to appropriate the necessary content to do our jobs exceptionally well is a failure of our duties. The good news, though, is that learning is addicting. Once one starts the process of learning new concepts, one gets the same rewards for mastering content that the addict does ingesting nefarious substances. Yet unlike drug or alcohol tolerance, one doesn't need to ingest greater quantities of the substance to experience the same highs one did previously. There is so much content to master that one never ceases to find something new to learn, and the rewarding processes start again. With drugs, there is tolerance (Peper, 2004a, 2004b). There is no such tolerance for learning academic content because the vast breadth of content makes it impossible for one to master everything.

In my quest for knowledge, I am thirsty. I have an insatiable thirst that is difficult to quench for long periods of time. In my journey to my current academic self, I have made many left turns to get where I am today. Along the way, though, there was always statistics. When I was younger, I was a statistics major at George Washington University (GW) in Washington DC. As I outlined in an earlier chapter, my family was homeless during my time at GW, and I had to work an unfathomable number of hours to make ends meet. This sadly affected my academic performance, and I earned two C

grades during my stint at GW, putting an end to my academic scholarship and my statistics degree. Years later, when I returned to college, I studied psychology. Although my love for statistics was always in me, not studying statistics impacted my knowledge drastically. While I was able to speak statistical language on a surface level, I no longer did proofs or studied novel methods. It wasn't until I was in my doctoral program that I began to dabble in statistics again, yet still only at a shallow level. It showed when I would discuss concepts with statistics graduate students and faculty. Nevertheless, I was on the road back to my true academic love again.

Let's fast forward a few years now to my teaching experience. During my postdoctoral fellowship, I became known as a structural equation modeling (SEM) expert. SEM is a statistical method that allows a researcher to model complex theoretical relations among variables pictorially, and then test the fit of this model to the observed data (Loehlin, 2004). I enjoyed doing this work, but I was no expert. I was like most of the individuals teaching statistics now, who know how to do something without truly understanding the why behind what they are doing. In other words, I had adapted to the constraints of the task. I knew how to do enough so that the experts were appeased, but not enough to push the field forward in any meaningful way. I recall one day that a student, who worked for me on a research grant I had, asked me to explain latent growth modeling (LGM) to him. LGM is an SEM method for modeling repeated measures data; data that are collected on multiple occasions from a cohort of people (Duncan & Duncan, 2004). My explanation was weak. I asked him how I did. Thankfully, he was honest enough to tell me that my explanation was terrible. That's because I knew how to do something but did not understand deeply the workings beneath the skills. Good teachers can explain concepts thoroughly because they understand the content they are entrusted with deeply. This is not an aim. It is a requirement for being a good instructor.

I started teaching statistics many years ago. I have always said to myself that teaching is the best way to ensure learning because one is motivated not to embarrass oneself in front of one's students by not knowing something. As I discussed in another chapter, I am motivated by negative possible selves. I visualize the worst possible outcome and use that to motivate my learning. Well, I don't do that as much now as I used to, but this motive is still there and plays a significant role in what I do. Thankfully, though, it's not a constant motive. For once learning starts, it is self-perpetuating. The rewards one experiences from mastering one event within the series of events required to master a skill, motivate one to seek the next reward, and so on thereafter. I had been teaching research methods for a few years before I taught my first statistics course. The course I taught was a year-long course at a local university that was a mix of statistics and research

methods; it covered both. The students were highly competent, and I knew it. I saw this as a significant challenge, and I wanted to succeed. Therefore, I studied hard, and I prepared for every lecture equally hard. I did not merely read the textbook, I read copious amounts of research literature to find additional content on what I was teaching. I was well prepared and felt good each time I stood in front of my students. Yet, the days before the lecture were filled with angst. I wanted to know everything. Each time I encountered something I did not know, I was afraid and then started searching for resources. I found good content and read a lot. I kept asking myself questions, sometimes waking up in the middle of the night to look for answers, falling asleep only when I was satisfied that I knew.

This process may sound terrible to some of my readers, but the reality is that I enjoy it. The extrinsic motive to not fail morphed into an intrinsic motive to learn new content. I did a good job teaching that full-year course and continued for several years before moving on to other endeavors. Nevertheless, those experiences took me to a higher level in my understanding of the art of teaching than I had previously when I attempted to teach LGM to my assistant. Yet, there was much more to come. Indeed, it wasn't until I left the research faculty track that I finally started the path to true teaching mastery.

As I started teaching full time, I realized how little I knew. Interestingly, teaching survey courses is harder than courses specializing in a specific topic. For instance, Introduction to Psychology is quite a vast course, covering every possible domain of psychology, from sensation and perception to psychoanalysis. Imagine how much one needs to know to be a successful teacher in psychology. The same can be said about epidemiology, research methods, and statistics. With statistics, there are different tests for different research designs and variables. Most statistics professors provide introductory statistics students with the basics, such as calculating means, medians, and variances. They also cover rudimentary statistical testing, such as the t-test, z-test, and correlations. Perhaps they also cover regression analysis. Like other introductory courses, the content is discussed at the surface level. Mostly, students want nothing complicated as they desire good grades. Yet, to teach this course well, and make learning easier for students, instructors need to be deeply familiar with what they are teaching. For instance, knowing that the *alpha* and critical value criteria are two different perspectives on the same thing makes teaching the two easy. Knowing that a one- and a two-tailed test are related to one's alternative hypothesis and alpha facilitates the teaching of decision making and the issue of power in hypothesis testing. Knowing what one is doing makes doing what one knows easier.

As I started teaching statistics regularly, I noticed which topics perplexed students. In my view, the concept students struggle with the most is the

idea of the *p*-value. They can learn equations of all complexities, but the *p*-value is as evasive as catching flies with chopsticks. So, I read much about probability values, which resulted in me needing to read more about distributions. Probabilities are based on distributions. Okay, so I needed to read about distributions. Distributions come in different forms, depending on the random process in question. Two common distributions are the normal distribution and the binomial distribution (Rodriguez, 2020). Given that what we discuss most is the normal distribution, I went into a deep study of this distribution. This was no simple endeavor, given that to understand the normal distribution one must understand calculus, and I hadn't taken calculus since I was 19 or 20 years old. So, I started by re-learning calculus. I started focusing on integrals since the normal distribution has a probability density function (pdf), and to integrate it one must use calculus. However, to integrate one must understand derivatives, and to understand differentiation, one must be able to use limits. The point here is that once I started upon this journey, instead of me getting closer to the end, I got further away from the goal. Frankly, the goal changed, with there no longer being a terminal point. I started down a pathway that led me to new questions requiring more complicated answers.

Bring us back to today, I now love doing proofs. My focus has been the normal distribution. However, I've also completed proofs on other distributions and other processes related to these distributions. As I have achieved these results, new doors have opened. More importantly, I've felt immense pleasure in this journey, and it's been low cost for the most part. I get access to proofs online from faculty members like myself who love teaching what they do to other eager learners. They too eschew profit for the personal satisfaction of mastery. Like the ski instructor who took me aside to help me better my right-turning skills, their love for demonstrating skills seeps through every pore of their being. I'll bet, like me, they spend hours of free time engaged in mastery. I do it whenever I can. It's not uncommon for me to have my mathematical statistics book with me in the car, get a thought, find a place to stop, and start reading until my thirst is quenched. What an amazing feeling it is to close the book and converse with myself internally about what I just learned. No money was exchanged. I didn't have to get people to like a post about it on social media. It's just the pure joy of mastery.

Psychoadaptation is about overcoming disequilibrium and returning the self to equilibrium. However, this new equilibrium is on a different plane, one that is the sum of all past experiences but qualitatively different than a mere sum. Teachers encounter new students each semester, and with new students come new microsystems and mesosystems. As such there are new constraints for adaptation. Moreover, because there is constant change in our

fields of study, constraints change, and we must adapt. The worst instructors are those who refuse to adapt and keep on doing what works best for them under a different set of constraints. Like all mastery, that adaptation may be enough to maintain their equilibrium while they frantically assimilate every datum of experience into their self-theories and theories about students and the teaching process. Unfortunately, what may appear to be good to them fails their students. Good teachers must have a fluid relation with the teaching environment, a Self that is capable of metamorphosing into a new Self. I like to refer to this as having a *liquid Self*. Although the core remains stable, the Self can change to fit its environment (Bramer et al., 1993). This will affect the core Self if the changes made become permanent. Whether temporary or permanent, the teacher's Self is malleable enough to meet the needs of his students because for the teacher, being his best at what he does is what is best for his students and for the betterment of all students he encounters. Teaching is a work of love, and good teachers are superior adapters because teaching is their vocation.

Notes

1 I am not referring to statisticians with PhDs in statistics. Often, faculty teach courses outside their immediate training out of necessity, not necessarily by preference. Although such faculty are fluent in data analysis and understand rudimentary statistical concepts better than many of their colleagues, they lack extensive training in statistics, including mathematical statistics.

2 I know this is related to null hypothesis significance testing, and there are many who do not subscribe to this practice. Yet, this isn't a statistics book, so I'll have to ignore the complexities of that debate here.

References

Bramer, L. M., Abrego, P. J., & Shostrom, E. L. (1993). *Therapeutic Counseling and Psychotherapy* (6th ed.). Prentice Hall.

Duncan, T. E., & Duncan, S. C. (2004). An introduction to latent growth curve modeling. *Behavior Therapy*, *35*(2), 333–363.

Loehlin, J. C. (2004). *Latent Variable Models: An Introduction to Factor, Path, and Structural Equation Analysis*. Psychology Press.

Peper, A. (2004a). A theory of drug tolerance and dependence I: A conceptual analysis. *Journal of Theoretical Biology*, *229*(4), 477–490.

Peper, A. (2004b). A theory of drug tolerance and dependence II: The mathematical model. *Journal of Theoretical Biology*, *229*(4), 491–500.

Rodriguez, D. (2020). *Core Statistics: Practical Knowledge for the Health Sciences*. Kendall Hunt Publishing.

4

CONDUCTING RESEARCH IN ACADEMIA

Teaching is a beautiful experience. Yet, it is but one function of an academic professional. We also conduct research. Research differs for every researcher. Some do qualitative studies in which data are collected on individuals or groups of participants and the results are conveyed without traditional statistical analysis (e.g., t-tests, ANOVA). Although I'm oversimplifying the nature of qualitative research here, my presentation serves my purpose in this chapter. For more detail on qualitative research, I suggest you obtain a good research methods textbook with substantial coverage of the discipline. Others do quantitative research. This type of research, in contrast to qualitative research, involves numbers and diverse statistical analysis methodologies. Still others combine the two in what has come to be known as mixed methods research designs. There are indeed a great variety of research types.

My research is quantitative. I do appreciate all forms of research, however. Yet, my love of mathematics and statistics led me to appropriating diverse statistical methods and applying them to assorted research questions. Becoming a good researcher has been quite the challenge, though, as mastering methods does not guarantee success. To be a good or even great researcher, one must do more than master one's chosen methods. Indeed, one must be able to identify good research questions and sell them to the peer reviewers gatekeeping access to high-impact journals and grant funding. That, my friends, is in my view the most difficult part of being a researcher.

Many of my students say they want to do research. It's a lofty and obfuscating proclamation indeed, as they often fail to realize what research is,

DOI: 10.4324/9781003460800-6

and can hardly communicate what they mean if probed for detail. I certainly do my very best to educate them about the nature of the endeavor. Research involves asking a research question, proposing hypotheses, identifying the ideal type and number of participants, and then finding the correct statistical method to analyze the data (Rodriguez, 2021b). Research also involves collecting data. These are the obvious steps in the process. The harder part is finding a question that is worth asking and then convincing stakeholders that it is important.

Finding good research questions necessitates a trained eye, for observation is key. The history of public health, for instance, highlights the importance of observation. When I teach epidemiology, I first discuss historical figures in the field. One such figure is Ignaz Semmelweis, a 19th-century Hungarian physician who observed deaths from childbed fever in Vienna, Austria (Best & Neuhauser, 2004). Childbed fever, also known as puerperal fever, is a bacterial infection that many women suffer after delivering the neonate (Loudon, 1987). At the time, there was a great disparity in death from childbed fever between two Vienna clinics, the first and second clinics. Medical students ran the first clinic, whereas midwives ran the second clinic. Deaths were more than twice as common in the first than in the second clinic. Semmelweis observed the difference and hypothesized that the disparity in deaths is due to unsanitary practices in the first clinic. Namely, medical students failed to clean their hands after performing autopsies on childbed fever victims before delivering babies. The cadaverous material therefore remained on their hands as they ministered to the delivering women, allowing for the spread of lethal bacteria to the mothers. Based on this observation, he instituted a hand-washing regimen, and the disparity in deaths between the two clinics was reduced drastically, saving countless lives.

Making observations is key to the conceptualization of a research idea. Not every observation, however, is as profound as that made by Semmelweis or will result in a publishable paper. Although interesting to the observer, not every intriguing observation is interesting to the scientific community. To publish research or attain the necessary funding to initiate a study, one's idea must appeal to more people than oneself. It must appeal to the scientific community one seeks to impress.

Impressing important others involves understanding what impresses them. It involves understanding the constraints of the context; contextual constraints. Luckily for the researcher, the peer reviewer embodies the generalized other of the scientific community of interest. The generalized other is the collected perspective of a given culture or subculture (Mead & Mind, 1934). Essentially, the generalized other is the embodiment of the collected perspective of others that allows one to anticipate what to expect in reaction to a behavioral enactment, such as the impact of our choice of

clothing when we dress in the morning. Peer reviewers are chosen from the community of researchers who are willing to review submitted content for quality, originality, and fit. Quality, originality, and fit are three indicators of adaptation to a set of constraints. Quality is a measure of the overall fit to a broad set of academic constraints. These include grammar and spelling, clarity and coherence, originality of ideas within broad constraints, and fit of the idea to the mission of the target journal or funding source, depending upon one's aim. Peer reviewers volunteer for this role. Indeed, they are not paid anything or much to engage in the peer review process. When reviewing scientific journals, they get nothing. When reviewing for grant funders, there is usually a stipend, albeit a small one.

The peer review process is a duty and privilege for the researcher. Among new researchers, it's a goal to become a peer reviewer. Indeed, it looks great on one's Curriculum Vitae (CV), the scholar's resume. For the seasoned researcher, we pick and choose when to review, as we get too many invitations to handle. For my part, I agree to review manuscripts if they look interesting to me, or if the editor is someone I know. I always want to help out my friends. However, if I have too many tasks on my desk at a given time, I reject invitations to review, for I want to do a good job. Juggling too many commitments precludes providing the effort the writers deserve when having their manuscripts reviewed. Nevertheless, when I reject invitations to review manuscripts, I always do so kindly as one never knows when one will need others for help. I don't like burning bridges.

I teach grant writing and graduate capstone courses. My grant writing course teaches students to write a National Institutes of Health (NIH) style grant application to a fictitious foundation. I also teach a two-course capstone sequence in which I have my students write a manuscript suitable for publication in a peer-reviewed journal. In both courses, one of the first lessons I teach is how to anticipate reviewers' comments. Thus, I teach my students to internalize the reviewer when writing. I tell them to imagine the worst-possible critic. Imagine that this critic is reading as you write, and is constantly picking on every word choice, sentence, or error. I tell my students that if they can't imagine a reviewer, they can picture me tearing apart their work, as I am the embodiment of the academic generalized other.

Researchers train to conduct research by taking a series of courses starting in their undergraduate studies, and even in high school. Actually, if students engage in science fairs in elementary school, the training starts much earlier. Research is about fit. We learn that to conduct a study, we must follow a very strict set of practices that aim to allow for causal inference. Causation is the aim. However, as one progresses up the academic ladder, one learns that causal conclusions are not always the end product of one's work. Causation requires quite of few conditions to be met. These include

meeting requirements such as temporal precedence, a dose-response relation, cessation of exposure, and replicability, among others. For instance, to be considered a cause, exposure to the putative cause must precede the effect in time. An example is cigarette smoking and lung cancer. Cigarette smoking precedes lung cancer. Although I suppose some individuals with lung cancer may pick up cigarette smoking after diagnosis, it's far less likely. A dose-response relation is one in which increasing the dose increases the effect. For instance, the more alcohol one drinks, the greater the intoxication. Cessation of exposure to alcohol would result in a lack of alcohol-related intoxication. Replicability means that the findings of a study are replicated by others. Without replication, findings may be no more than outliers. I'll return to the last criterion later, as it is key to understanding research and becoming an outstanding researcher.

As one learns to conduct research, the goal is to have the learner internalize the strict constraints of the research process. Researchers learn the scientific method, including which type of studies are useful in determining causation. They learn that laboratory studies are the best studies for ensuring the internal validity of a study. In other words, laboratory studies are best for proving that the independent variable is the one and only variable that causes change in the dependent variable. The independent variable is the variable under the researcher's control. Generally, it's the assignment to two or more groups of some treatment, such as drug and placebo, the placebo being an inert substance such as a sugar pill or saline. Randomization ensures that participants have an equal likelihood of being assigned to the various treatment options, reducing the potential effect of competing causes (i.e., confounding variables). Blinding the participants and the researchers is essential too, as it's important that neither the researcher nor the participant knows to which group the participant is assigned. These tight controls are more easily done in laboratory studies. Further, given the nature of the setting, researchers can control for other potentially confounding variables, such as temperature, humidity, and distractions.

The lab-based randomized controlled trial (RCT) is the ideal. Students always learn the ideal first, as that's what we should strive for. Ideally, we would end every study with the ability to make a causal conclusion. Otherwise, all conclusions are debatable, and in fields like public health, debatable findings are more difficult to sell to the public, particularly when seeking to initiate prevention practices. Yet, with time and education, students learn a variety of different research methods suitable for research questions that cannot be studied with RCTs. They also learn about historical research failures, particularly when researchers used unethical methods to conduct their desired studies. A notable example is the Tuskegee syphilis experiment. This experiment took place from 1932 to 1972 and was designed to follow 399

African American men with syphilis, and 201 healthy controls, through the natural course of the disease (natural history of the disease) (McCallum et al., 2006; Tobin, 2022). What was notable about this notorious study is that the information was withheld from the participants, precluding the right to refuse participation, what is called informed consent. In research, participants have the right to refuse participation and withdraw from a study at any time. Knowing what syphilis is and that there was a cure available (penicillin was available as a treatment in 1943 (Tampa et al., 2014)) may have dissuaded most if not all participants from involvement in the study. Thus, over time and with sufficient training, students appropriate the constraints of the research field and are well-equipped to produce products that align with the constraints.

Despite having knowledge of the constraints, including the ideals, and the skills necessary to conduct such studies, or at least where to find the information necessary to learn what is required, students struggle with the research process. Knowing how to is therefore necessary but not sufficient to ensure success. One must have the ability to withstand the tremendous disequilibrium experienced in the research process.

Disequilibrium is the norm in research (Rodriguez, 2021a). In my experience, very little works out the way we plan it. When I first attempted to publish, I was a haughty young man with an overinflated belief in my academic competence. Surely, whatever I did would be published immediately, I thought. Yet, what I failed to realize is that there are more constraints to adapt to than the ones I had believed I had mastered at the time. For, in addition to understanding how to write a research manuscript, researchers must know the aims of the different journals they submit their manuscripts to, how many other articles have been published on the topic of choice, and the overall importance of the topic. Although I felt that my tennis self-concept scale was something revolutionary, few others did. Thus, when I received the outright rejection, I was indignant. How dare they reject me and my work. Don't they see how great my work is? Those thoughts were circulating in my working memory like leaves in the breeze on a cool New England autumn afternoon. Yet, rejections are more common than acceptance. Indeed, in a recent industry study conducted for the publisher Elsevier, the average acceptance rate for 2,371 journals was 32%, with some journals accepting as few as 1% of all submitted manuscripts (Herbert, 2020). Thus, if we take the average as the best estimate of the probability of acceptance, this means that one is 53% less likely to be accepted than rejected when submitting a manuscript.

Over the years, I have adapted well to the publication process. I now understand the odds and plan accordingly. I also understand that the publication process is not homogenous, and that there is a diversity of

journals to which I can submit a manuscript, some of which better suit my work than others, and some of which better suit the stage of my career than others. More importantly, I have learned to appropriate the reviewer's *generalized other* when I write. I'm always asking myself if this makes sense. It also helps that I've had many interactions with reviewers and professional writers. I've also spent time reading. While I read for knowledge, I also study what works and what doesn't work. For instance, in writing grant applications, I have learned that showing one's knowledge of the field isn't as important as selling one's idea to the reviewers. Like journals, grant applications are reviewed by peer reviewers. However, their aims are different. While there is an evaluation of the science, much of the review centers upon the innovation of the idea, its significance, and its feasibility. I've known writers who are extremely intelligent, and it shows in their writing. However, I am more likely to use their writing to cure insomnia than endorse it for funding. These writers are like I was when I first submitted my tennis self-concept scale for review. They haven't yet appropriated the constraints of the process.

Stages in the development of an exceptional researcher

Having taught courses in human development, I have learned over time that people love stages, especially when the stages are easy to comprehend and apply to real-life situations. So here I present the stages through which I believe one must pass to become an exceptional researcher. **First**, one must become a great observer. Observation occurs in different ways. One can make an observation in the content found in the research literature. Yet, research is sterile. Researchers do what it takes to cleanse their work from the effects of possible confounding variables. In general, we do a poor job at it because it is impossible to include all potentially confounding variables without messy models. Indeed, research is governed by parsimony. Parsimonious models include fewer predictors than less parsimonious models. Thus, messy models are worse than models with few yet meaningful predictors. As such, focusing only on the literature is less useful than having a broader focus that includes non-scientific sources. This is an important point, as there is a tendency for researchers to believe that research ideas must come from the literature. The idea is that researchers look at the current state of the science, identify gaps in the literature, and then exploit those gaps. For instance, imagine a researcher assessing the relation between nicotine smoking (regardless of delivery mechanism) and depressive symptoms. After delivering the results, the researcher will likely write something like this. "Although these findings suggest a relation between the two, it is unclear whether smoking causes depressive symptoms or depressive symptoms make

one more likely to smoke. Future studies should focus on elucidating the nature of the relation." This is an open invitation for more research on the nature of the relation.

Relying on others to provide invitations for future studies is like hoping everyone will mask up in the midst of an airborne pandemic. It's not going to happen. Indeed, imagine if Ignaz Semmelweis waited for germ theory to take hold and for findings of carefully designed experiments to suggest the need for primary prevention measures to reduce the likelihood of transmitting pathogens. Imagine how many more women would have been lost to childbed fever. Today's insistence on handwashing and the use of hand sanitizers may have taken far longer to come to fruition than it did because science allowed for observation of all kinds.

The history of science is filled with profound discoveries made by simple observations. Vaccinations came about when some observers, including Edward Jenner, noticed that milkmaids infected with cowpox were immune to smallpox (Barquet & Domingo, 1997; Willis, 1997). John Snow observed that families living near the Broad Street water pump had more deaths from cholera than families living further away from the pump (Newsom, 2006). Yet, such observations have become less valued than discovering gaps in the literature. Clearly, with nearly eight billion people on earth, someone is bound to have thought of the same idea we are thinking of; the idea that we believe to be unique. Chances are, we'll find what we think is unique, already published in the literature. That is why every idea should be followed with a thorough search of the literature. Yet, one should not depend exclusively on the literature to generate ideas. The trained eye is strong enough to unlock mysteries in the world around us. Indeed, I have my epidemiology students look around them and tell me what they notice. Some of what they say is already in the literature, such as the link between poor food choices and obesity. Yet, there are some ideas that are quite novel. Thus, do not dismiss the ability to find something special in the array of events encountered in the normal course of events.

The **second stage** involves testing the novelty of one's idea. In addition to a thorough search of the literature, one must discuss the research idea with trusted colleagues, soliciting feedback. This is a key step for two reasons. First, one must structure the idea so that it can be communicated to others. When we keep ideas to ourselves, they are difficult to articulate. We often *feel* something and know it through our own unique cognitive processes. Yet, when asked to articulate it to an audience, we are as clumsy as a toddler learning to walk. Second, feedback allows us to judge the viability of our idea. The more people with whom we discuss the idea, the better. Some of my colleagues worry about others stealing ideas. That's certainly a risk. However, given the necessity to replicate findings, the more researchers

working on an idea the better. Thus, this shouldn't be a primary concern at this stage.

Sharing ideas with others comes with some risk, as we cannot anticipate the responses of others. The academic world is often quite cruel. Although we may hope for thoughtful responses, we may be greeted with less than savory comments, some even being downright nasty. Even if not distasteful, comments that contradict our ideas are painful, the pain experienced depends on personal factors, including one's history with negative interpersonal experiences. In short, one should expect a good dose of disequilibrium when sharing ideas with others. Yet, you should recall from the first chapter, my good reader, that disequilibrium is purposeful. In the case of sharing ideas, its aim is to strengthen the idea and eliminate those ideas that are worthless to pursue.

Passing through these stages, the research idea, if indeed viable, is strengthened. The **next step (stage)** is to write up a research question and hypotheses in preparation for action. Action can mean submitting a proposal for funding, or commencing analysis if the data are available. The course of action depends upon one's resources, the current position (job) one has, and the stage in one's career. For young faculty researchers on a research faculty track, ideas require grant funding. Grants provide the money necessary to conduct studies. Funds can be internal (institutional), foundation, or government grants. Thus, the researchers must prepare the idea for the target grant opportunity. For the scholar needing publications, with access to a sample or secondary data (i.e., data collected by others), the idea is targeted to a journal or perhaps a conference. To simplify the presentation, I'll focus on a grant submission.

In writing a grant application, the scholar has very strict guidelines to follow. This is good as the constraints of the application process are laid out in a very specific way, including what font the writer must use, the page length, the citation style, and line spacing. Nevertheless, those are only one set of constraints the writer must adapt to. More essential are the contextual constraints of the funder. It is essential that the grant writer must know the values of the funder. This is available in their mission statement and statement of funding priorities. Appropriating these aims will help the writer adapt better to the grant funder's constraints, improving the likelihood of funding. How much so is hard to know. Yet, not writing in a manner that is consistent with these constraints is a guarantee of failure.

The key in this stage is to prepare the specific aims section. In grants, the specific aims section is a grant in miniature. It is generally one page in length. It includes everything any researcher should include in a grant application. Actually, it includes almost everything a researcher would include in a manuscript submitted for publication, with the exception of

the results section and discussion. It includes an introduction covering the severity of the problem being studied. For instance, if one is writing a grant application to better understand the relation between cigarette smoking and depressive symptoms, one should cover the devastating effects of cigarette smoking on public health, as well as the impact of depressive symptoms on the population. Appropriating the constraints of the grant-writing culture, one should highlight the extreme nature of these problems so that the application impacts the reviewers reading it. The specific aims section must also include the link between the two variables, focusing particularly on the gaps in the literature. Recall how earlier I mentioned that researchers tend to exploit gaps in the research literature to generate ideas, and how I wrote that this was a limiting method. Well, that's for us to know. As for the scientific community as a whole, however, that's what the power brokers expect so that's what we must adapt to. As such, we discuss how the proposed project will fill the research gaps identified in the literature.

Identifying gaps is done carefully, for one never knows who may be reading one's application. The same goes for writing manuscripts for publication. The reviewer may be the very person whose work the applicant is criticizing. Thus, when identifying gaps, the good researcher is mindful not to insult others. You see, my good reader, this is why it is essential to appropriate the reviewer's perspective. When I write, I am always thinking about my reviewer. This is redundant. I've already written it several times. Yet, I do so because I want it to be at the forefront of your consciousness. You can imagine those old-school cartoons in which an individual is pondering some dilemma and a good and an evil Self is resting on one's shoulders, one on each shoulder. The reviewer persona is like these mythical little people on the author's shoulders. They are there to keep one's writing on the correct path so that authors do not stray too far off in an unwise direction.

The sections written provide the background for the research question to come. It should appear as a natural consequence of what was already written. Indeed, the best advice I have ever received about academic writing is to never allow the reviewer to think. The reviewer should be reading the application and nodding her head in agreement. The moment she starts thinking, the application starts losing points. In fact, I want you to imagine the reviewer now. It's a nice Sunday afternoon, and she has some family over for a festive occasion, perhaps a birthday. Yet, she has this grant application to review. It's your grant application. She's getting a small stipend to review it, but that's not enough to make it the number one priority in her life. Heck, she would much rather be enjoying the festivities than sitting alone in front of her computer trying to conclude the review before the meal is served. Imagine that she is reading through your application and everything

is flowing perfectly. I can only imagine that she's a happy person and will give you a great score, endorsing your hard work.

Now, let's imagine the alternative. The party is going on around her, and she's reading through your application and questions appear. She starts asking questions about your research idea with little desire to answer them with all the festivities going on outside her window. I can only imagine she would not score this grant too kindly. Even if the reviewers are secluded from family and friends reviewing grant applications, a poorly written grant application that generates more questions than providing answers will not make the reviewer happy. Reviewers are people with lots of stuff going on in their lives. The last thing they need is a bad grant application to read. Never insult the reviewer with poor work.

Once the setup is complete, the writer writes down the research question, the specific aims, and the hypothesis or hypotheses. Not too many of course, since too many aims will create questions about the feasibility of the study. This is also where the writer will explain, albeit very briefly, the methods being used, including who the participants are and what procedures are being planned. The writer can conclude with the research aims and hypotheses. However, the superior researcher leaves room to tie the project back to the funding source and the source's mission and priorities.

This single-page specific aims section is perhaps the most important part of any grant application because it may be the only section some reviewers read. Although reviewers can be experts, many are not. Indeed, some reviewers are non-scholars who have little knowledge of the science behind the proposed project. Yet, these reviewers have a voice on whether the application will be funded or not funded.

The **next stage** is perhaps the hardest, emotionally speaking. At this point, I return to the general research endeavor, as it's the same whether writing a grant application or a research manuscript. It is the response from the reviewers. We all await it with anticipation, and for some it's a quite fearful experience. We want to receive it to know the outcome of the process, with the hope of acceptance. Yet, we fear finding out that our product is rejected. Depending on one's mental state at the time of its receipt, an outright rejection can be taken lightly or be very painful. Imagine all the time one took researching and writing the manuscript. If rejected, does it mean that the applicant has to start from scratch and re-do the entire project? The answer is maybe. Thus, many are afraid of this outcome as it means what was once believed to be done, is on the table again, along with all of one's present commitments.

Rejection is quite normal when it comes to writing a manuscript or preparing a grant application. In the grant world, focusing on NIH grants, success rates hover about 20% (IMPAC, 2023). This means that only about

one in five grants is funded. What makes it worse is that unlike the blind peer-review process one expects, peer review is often anything but blind. Reviewers are supposed to act as if they are reviewing grants blind to the writers. However, skilled grant writers who have appropriated the constraints of the grant writing endeavor know how to unmask their applications. Here's an example. I could write, "Researchers have identified a link between x and y." I wrote this sentence to be anonymous. I could, instead, write it like this. "In our own work, we identified a link between x and y." The latter sentence betrays the researchers. I wrote it so that it maintains its integrity. However, I purposefully identified us as the researchers. This allows the reviewers to know who we are and that we are skilled researchers. This sentence is not blind.

Blinding in the grant review process aims to increase the likelihood that new researchers will succeed in securing funding. Otherwise, only the most successful grant writers will get grants. Unfortunately, that's what happens, making rejection more common for some researchers than others.

Rejection is never fun. Even if I expect it, reading the letter stating rejection stings. For some, the sting is so painful that they leave the field altogether. To be a successful researcher, thus, one must be able to withstand this pain. Disequilibrium is uncomfortable, yet being able to accept it, and allow it to manifest its symptoms, will result in a better ability to withstand future bouts of disequilibrium. Notice that I wrote, "allow it to manifest its symptoms." This is not an error, my friends. Part of being a successful academic writer is being able to deal with the pain of rejection. Indeed, if one looks at the most successful people on earth, they have dealt with failure often, although a casual observer is unlikely to see it. People tend to want outsiders to see their celebrations, not their tears and angry outbursts, although that has changed a little with the intrusiveness of social media. Nevertheless, when we think of the greats, like Rafa Nadal, Novak Djokovic, and Serena Williams in tennis, we mostly visualize their triumphs and debate about their Greatest of All Time (GOAT) status.

Failure is the key ingredient to the euphoria of success. Without failure, success would be as bland an emotion as ennui. For, how can one know the highs of success without knowing it's polar opposite. Just as one cannot know good without the presence of evil, success by itself is vacuous. As such, one must learn to endure failure and experience the concomitant emotional depths. Yet, one must not fall victim to it either. The idea is to embrace it, mourn the loss, but then figure out how to move forward. Understand that failure is inevitable. This understanding will prepare one for its punishing fury and may even lighten the bruising. However, do not forget that each of us experiences failure in our own unique ways. For some, traumatic experiences of the past will amplify the pain. Those experiences live within

us, appropriating other negative experiences into their complex webs. Next thing the victim knows, a failure in an entirely unrelated endeavor triggers the same negative experiences as the historic nuclear event that caused the trauma in the first place. Self-knowledge is key to success in any of life's endeavors, particularly those that involve tremendous disequilibrium.

Once the pain of failure subsides, the **next step (stage)** is to review the comments and reformulate the project if necessary. Now, this stage differs depending upon the nature of the failure in the prior stage. If one receives an invitation to revise and re-submit the project, and one desires to do so, the aim is to read through the comments and address each one carefully, and tactfully. If, by contrast, the result was an outright rejection, the aim is to read the comments and revise the project to submit elsewhere, or if the comments indicate a fatal flaw in the project, the best solution may be to drop the project entirely.

The last option seems in contradiction to everything I've written in this book so far. You, my faithful reader, may be discouraged to read such text from me. Yet, if you have been attending carefully, my aim is adaptation. Some constraints are impossible to overcome, even with the mightiest efforts and unyielding commitment. In such cases, one must evaluate the Self, carefully, and decide if further pursuit is justified. Failure is painful and worth enduring if success follows. If there is no success, the damage of continued failure to one's sense of self-worth can be hard to overcome. Indeed, I recall William James's (1892) advice to curing low self-esteem. Letting go of pretensions that cannot be realized is the quickest way to higher self-worth, as self-esteem is the ratio of successes to pretensions.

I have let go of projects before after reading reviewer comments, as what I thought of as being magnificent ideas ended up being mundane or not innovative to a seasoned reviewer. Letting go of those projects wasn't easy as any idea I generated is a piece of me and holds sway on my self-worth. However, the failures I experienced were painful, and instead of repeatedly trying to reason the negative feedback while attempting to maintain my faulty premises, letting go of these failed ideas brought tremendous relief. I am a better person for having tried those ideas, failed, and let go of them, than I would have become by continuing to fight an endless battle for nothing.

The decision to move on and resubmit a project with an invitation to revise and resubmit is an important moment. The key to success in this situation is appropriating the reviewer's comments and responding in ways to please them. Not everyone needs to please reviewers, and nobody should agree with everything the reviewer says. I certainly haven't at all times. However, the ability to disagree with a reviewer shouldn't be taken lightly. Disagreeing carelessly or angrily to a reviewer could anger them such that they'll attempt

to dissuade the editor (journal) from accepting the manuscript. Further, not everyone has earned the right to disagree with reviewers. For researchers with the highest standing and for whom publication doesn't mean career advancement, disagreements and their consequences are unlikely to impact the writer negatively. For a younger investigator (in terms of experience and standing), disagreements and failures to publish can be the difference between achieving and not achieving promotion and tenure. Thus, any disagreement must be done so tactfully.

I haven't disagreed often with reviewers in recent years, although I certainly did so naively early in my career. When I do disagree, now I do so tactfully. I always start every response by thanking the reviewer for the comments and noting how my manuscript is now stronger for the comments. If I disagree, I have a very explicit reason why and provide exhaustive evidence as to why I believe my point is correct. This may or may not appease the reviewer, however, but it may persuade the editor to accept the manuscript despite the reviewer's comments. Providing evidence in support of one's argument, and doing so in a tasteful manner, is an indication of the respect the writer has for the process and the adaptation to the constraints of the endeavor, and this holds weight in the eyes of the most important guardians of the context, the editors.

In the event that the project was rejected but the project itself has merit in the eyes of some of the reviewers, it is best to rework the project based on the reviewers' comments and submit elsewhere, for a journal, or even re-submit as a new application for a grant funding opportunity. In many cases, there isn't much to do to fix the project. This is not uncommon, as some journals are highly competitive in terms of manuscript submissions, and although good, the submitted project isn't viewed as the best from among those submitted. In that case, working one's way down to the next highest rated journal is the next step. If, however, the project needs a massive overhaul but doesn't have a fatal flaw, reading through the comments and answering them as if re-submitting is the best option, as those reviewers may be the same reviewers reviewing in the next journal or grant submission. The growth of the manuscript or project will show in the next submission, and regardless of who is reviewing it, the odds of success will improve.

As a final thought in this endeavor, I have appropriated the generalized reviewer to the extent that I am in tune with the way reviewers think. I know that all reviewers want to be heard. All human beings want to be recognized for whom they conceive themselves to be. One can read it in their comments. The way they formulate their sentences provides a window into their psyches. Thus, one can succeed by learning to appease them by appealing to their needs. For instance, if it appears that a reviewer wants a certain work or method to be recognized, do so. Appealing to this call

for recognition will make them very happy. Some people want and indeed crave praise. Although I may not give them the time of day in ordinary interactions, when I need them as I do in the submission of a manuscript or grant application, I will happily praise them. This isn't being disingenuous as our aim is to get published or receive funding for a worthwhile project, and if someone's ego needs are standing in the way of our success, I would rather appease them and make them feel happy for now than attack them and have my project fail. It's my hope that these individuals will one day learn to fix their personality flaws, but that's not our responsibility.

References

Barquet, N., & Domingo, P. (1997). Smallpox: The triumph over the most terrible of the ministers of death. *Annals of Internal Medicine*, *127*(8_Part_1), 635–642.

Best, M., & Neuhauser, D. (2004). Ignaz Semmelweis and the birth of infection control. *BMJ Quality & Safety*, *13*(3), 233–234.

Herbert, R. (2020). Accept me, accept me not: What do journal acceptance rates really mean?[ICSR Perspectives] (February 15, 2020). International Center for the Study of Research Paper No. Forthcoming, Available at SSRN: https://ssrn.com/abstract=3526365 or http://dx.doi.org/10.2139/ssrn.3526365.

IMPAC, N. (2023). *Research project grants: Competing applications, awards, and success rates*. https://report.nih.gov/nihdatabook/report/20

James, W. (1892). *Psychology: The Briefer Course*. Henry Holt.

Loudon, I. (1987). Puerperal fever, the streptococcus, and the sulphonamides, 1911–1945. *British Medical Journal (Clinical research ed.)*, *295*(6596), 485.

McCallum, J. M., Arekere, D. M., Green, B. L., Katz, R. V., & Rivers, B. M. (2006). Awareness and knowledge of the US Public Health Service syphilis study at Tuskegee: Implications for biomedical research. *Journal of Health Care for the Poor and Underserved*, *17*(4), 716.

Mead, G. H., & Mind, H. (1934). *Self and Society. University of Chicago*, 173–175.

Newsom, S. W. B. (2006). Pioneers in infection control: John Snow, Henry Whitehead, the Broad Street pump, and the beginnings of geographical epidemiology. *Journal of Hospital Infection*, *64*(3), 210–216. https://doi.org/https://doi.org/10.1016/j.jhin.2006.05.020

Rodriguez, D. (2021a). The art of learning and dealing with disequilibrium. In *Research Methods*. Kendall Hunt Publishing.

Rodriguez, D. (2021b). *Research Methods*. Kendall Hunt Publishing.

Tampa, M., Sarbu, I., Matei, C., Benea, V., & Georgescu, S. R. (2014). Brief history of syphilis. *Journal of Medicine and Life*, *7*(1), 4.

Tobin, M. J. (2022). Fiftieth anniversary of uncovering the tuskegee syphilis study: the story and timeless lessons. *American Journal of Respiratory and Critical Care Medicine*, *205*(10), 1145–1158.

Willis, N. (1997). Edward Jenner and the eradication of smallpox. *Scottish Medical Journal*, *42*(4), 118–121.

PART II
Sport

5

MAINTAINING AN EXERCISE REGIME

I love to exercise. I have never been the best athlete for a variety of reasons, but I sure am dedicated to my fitness. I engage in a variety of different physical activities, but my favorite has always been cycling. Although I no longer cycle on roads for reasons of safety,[1] I spend plenty of time on my indoor recumbent bicycle, building leg strength. I do whatever it takes to improve my fitness. With age, my activities have changed frequently, and with those changes came the need to overcome disequilibrium and adapt.

Sport requires tremendous commitment, including training with expert coaches and practicing what one learned from the experts; what Anders Ericsson refers to as deliberate practice (Ericsson et al., 1993). That said, being successful in sport is not guaranteed. One needs more than commitment to training and money to succeed. Genetics interact with environmental factors in complicated ways to create successful athletes (Davids & Baker, 2007). For instance, I started skiing regularly about 11 years ago, and then began to participate in Masters racing. The United States Ski and Snowboard Association (USSA) runs snow sport competitions at all age levels. Masters racing is for everyone but is generally populated by older racers who no longer can compete at the highest levels, along with racers who are good but not good enough to race on a professional circuit. Masters races are open to everyone, including people like me. Despite my desire to medal in one of these events in my age category, the probability of that happening is extremely low at this point in my skiing progression. Simply put, I may neither have the natural ability nor do I have the time spent training to compete with these athletes. I do it to learn from the competitions and hope to improve little by little, but I am not even a little competitive at this point.

DOI: 10.4324/9781003460800-8

I am dedicating an entire chapter to skiing, so I will not focus much on skiing here, with the exception of a few examples related to exercise. Unlike sport, exercise is not competitive. There are some exceptions, however, such as CrossFit that has competitions, and perhaps martial arts. For the most part, however, exercise is personal and involves no competition except for one's attempts to exceed personal bests. One can use this motivation to improve fitness. However, it's not the same competition as competing in a tennis tournament against another athlete. Interestingly, despite the personal nature of exercise and the lack of competition and overt social comparison, the success rate in exercise is low. Indeed, only about 53% of Americans engaged in recommended levels of physical activity (NHIS, 2018). The proportion is even lower when considering aerobic along with strength training activities, at 23%. Thus, something is keeping people from physical activity beyond competition.

Exercise is a learning endeavor that involves the same developmental processes involved in all other learning endeavors, whether learning to play the piano or sing, or ski, or do calculus. Some fitness activities are easier to learn than others, as they build upon the most basic human behaviors. For instance, hiking and jogging build upon walking and running, respectively. Weight training builds upon basic chores, such as moving furniture or lifting boxes. Pullups and pushups are exaggerations of childhood activities we did in the playground, or even simple maneuvers done at home, like lifting oneself off the floor. Cycling for exercise builds upon riding a bike for fun with friends, or riding one's bicycle to school. Inline skating and ice skating build upon activities we often did as children. The same goes for swimming. However, when we move basic activities into the realm of exercise, we now need to incorporate techniques to ensure we perform the activities in a way that incrementally increases the workload for fitness gains.

Further, some of the activities we did as children are hazardous when performed for exercise. For instance, engaging in sports like tennis and field hockey involves explosive movements that can place individuals at risk for serious injury (Cornelissen et al., 2020; Hess, 2010). When I started playing tennis again in my 40s after about 10 to 12 years of not playing, I thought I could play as hard as I did when I was in my 20s. Unfortunately, my body did not agree, and I injured both calf muscles pretty quickly. This continues to be a problem and affects how I approach the sports I do now. Other activities (e.g., inline skating, skiing, or snowboarding) involve the risk of accidents (Bigdon et al., 2019). When I wrote this chapter, my good reader, I was wearing a wrist brace from fracturing my left wrist while inline skating. I love finding exercise opportunities that fit my personality and strengths. My legs and endurance are my strengths. Thus, activities that require leg strength are my preferred activities. Further, since our lower body includes

some of the largest muscles of our body, working the lower body is a good way to increase aerobic fitness (Marterer et al., 2023).

Unfortunately, not every good idea starts off well. Inline skating, especially when the skates do not have brakes, can be tricky. Now, my sagacious reader may be wondering why I selected skates without brakes when most on the market have brakes behind the wheels. Well, one of my sport-related goals is to compete in a marathon skating event on ice, and the best equivalent from among the inline skates suitable for that purpose is the inline skate with larger wheels and no brakes. Still, though, given that I am newer to this type of skate and I have not skated on pavement for nearly 30 years, I probably should have purchased the easier skate to re-introduce myself to this type of skating. I'm getting better at it every day, though.

Accidents and illnesses are key elements of the Psychoadaptation process when it comes to exercise. We would like to believe that we will maintain the perfect repertoire throughout the year without interruption. In theory, we should never miss a day of exercise because that is how we would best attain our fitness goals. Yet, what is desired frequently differs from reality. Indeed, that is why Piaget noted that desirability is disequilibrium (Piaget, 1951). Failing to mentally prepare for the inevitable disruptions and an inability to adapt to such breaks in one's desired routine can be devastating for an exercise program. As such, the most important part of exercising is the ability to remain on the same course over the long haul including disruptions, instead of having perfect attendance.

Fracturing my wrist dented my exercise plans for that summer (Summer of 2022). My plan was to engage in a variety of activities, including re-kindling my pullups and pushups, as well as doing some cycling. With the fractured wrist, that was out of the question for at least six weeks. However, I have been exercising regularly since I was in my early 20s and have had many disruptions. Thus, even though I felt a bit deflated for not being able to achieve some of my exercise goals last summer, my self-conception of me as a fit person did not change. I appropriated the inevitable disruption into my exercise self-concept and therefore knew I would be exercising again after I recovered. This appropriation is no accident. Indeed, it stems from my experience with disruptions in my exercise routine, my immediate return to exercise after recovery or the disruption ends, and my continued aerobic and anaerobic health. Further, and perhaps more importantly, I know the challenges posed to the exerciser upon returning from an injury. Having fractured my right wrist about 15 years ago, I remember how weak I was after the removal of my cast. It was painful to start exercising again. Plus, I had some fears of further accidents. Yet, I was able to return and even exceed my prior exercise intensity.

The Self is built upon experience. Each experience we have, whether negative or positive, is appropriated into the structure we call our self-concept (Rodriguez, 2000). This self-concept is the cognitive library into which the ego, our executive self, descends to find historical examples when deciding upon the appropriate behavior for each situation (Masterson, 1985). With my fractured wrist, I had to wait to hear from the orthopedic specialist before I could decide upon the appropriate course of action. Unfortunately, I was not able to attain an appointment until a week after the injury and the x-ray confirming the fracture. Thus, my ego ("I") had to reach into my experience (exercise self-concept) to find answers to my most pressing questions. My first question was if I can exercise right now. My left wrist was swollen but not extremely painful. I had good wrist braces from past accidents, including the prior fracture, and they kept my wrist stable. My legs and core were fine, so I went on hikes. Unlike a respiratory infection that should preclude any such activity, this injury allowed me to exercise with my legs. Since I love hiking so much, I did not miss out on any leg activity. Once on the trail, however, I did fear injury at times, particularly when descending mountain trails. Stepping on loose rocks, I would slip frequently, and with each slip, my mind went to the thought of falling. That was scary, for I could imagine fracturing my other wrist and that would put me in a really difficult place. Our minds have a way of making us relive prior experiences, especially the emotionally painful sort.

Let me expand upon the last sentence of the preceding paragraph and discuss a fascinating concept in psychiatry introduced by Carl Gustav Jung, one of my favorite psychiatrists and theorists, that will help me better explain the interaction between the contextual constraints and our conception of Self. Some of you may be familiar with his work. I discussed him previously (Introduction and Chapter 1) in relation to his fascinating metaphysical work and its impact on my development as a scholar, and of course Psychoadaptation. One concept that is especially relevant to the current topic, and that I have taught about frequently in my courses, is the complex (Jung, 1969). Paraphrasing Jung, he said that people don't have complexes, complexes have people. Complexes are these constellations of events bound by an emotionally toned nuclear experience. This nuclear experience is generally some personally traumatic experience that an individual seeks to suppress and is repressed such that it lies within the unconscious. The event may be physical, such as an accident or physical abuse, or emotional, such as an embarrassing experience (Figure 5.1). For those of you not familiar with the language of psychoanalysis and analytical psychology (Jung's version), suppression is an active (conscious) attempt to remove a thought from consciousness, such as a desire to say something distasteful when talking to

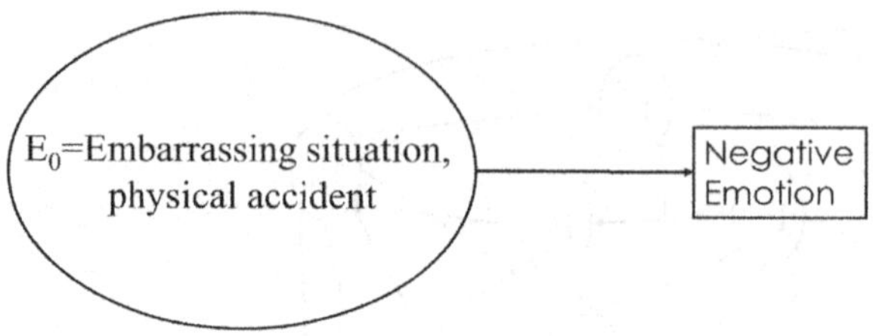

FIGURE 5.1 Formation of a complex.

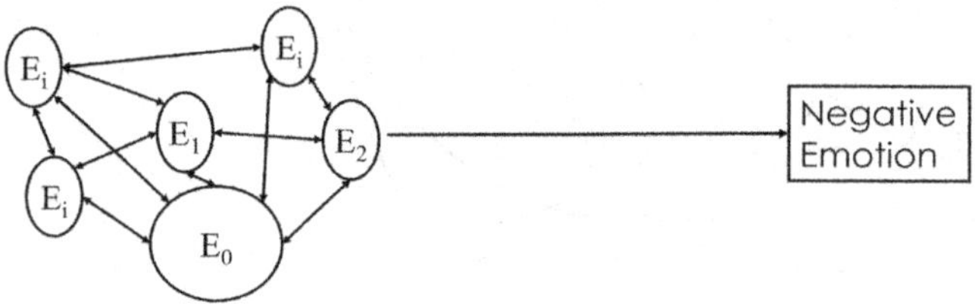

FIGURE 5.2 Complex appropriates similar events.

someone. Repression, by contrast, is the unconscious analog of suppression. It is being done outside one's awareness (Boag, 2010).

Jung proposed that complexes reside in the unconscious and play tricks on us frequently. Like Freud, Jung agreed that our ability to control unconscious content is in vain, and the content will slip into the open at inappropriate times. We see this scenario play out in movies or videos frequently, such as when a man standing near a woman says breast instead of best, or sex instead of six. This is known popularly as a ***Freudian slip*** (Bear, 1992). The idea of complexes, however, was detailed more extensively by Jung in my view than in any of Freud's work on the unconscious. The nuclear event is like a magnet, appropriating correlated events. I depict this graphically in Figure 5.2, with events E_1 and E_2 being most similar to E_0, and the remaining events (E_i) representing the other (i) related, albeit less similar events. The double-headed arrows represent the reciprocal relations among the events making up the complex. With time, the appropriated events are so dissimilar to the nuclear event that it takes a trained therapist to help the client to find the source. I depict a ***mature*** complex in Figure 5.3. The further the events (E_i) are from E_0, the more dissimilar they are to the nuclear event in nature and emotional potency. Nevertheless, these appropriated events come to have power over the person, creating anxiety whenever the individual is in their presence (Petchkovsky et al., 2013). All appropriated events, regardless of their distance from the nuclear event, trigger a response because they are associated with the nuclear event.[2]

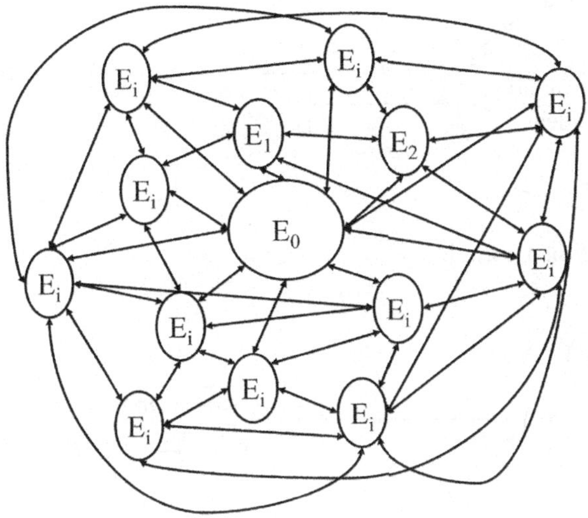

FIGURE 5.3 Mature complex.

The hiking scenario I am discussing here is an example of an unconscious complex affecting one's exercise. Indeed, I venture that complexes are a reason why so many individuals fail to commit to a lifetime of exercise. Each time I slipped on a rock, I felt a burst of anxiety. For me, that meant a little shiver and thoughts of falling and breaking something else. The nuclear event in this case was quite fresh, the fracture of my wrist. That fracture however is like the prior fracture and the many other injuries I have had that are related to my choice of physical activity. Fortunately for me, my experience dealing with complexes of all kinds, and overcoming them to a substantial degree, is enough to help me persevere their torment.[3] Yet for others it may not be the same.

When it comes to exercise in general, we make so many excuses for not exercising. It is raining outside. It is too hot. It is too cold. I'm too busy right now. I don't have the right clothing. It's too crowded. I can go on and on. The reality is, though, we can always find a way to exercise. Whether one has a broken wrist or leg, a cold, or another illness, or work commitments that preclude going to the gym, there is always a way to get in some exercise. Often, the reasons hindering our pursuit of health and fitness are so deep-rooted that it is very hard to identify the cause. Complexes may dictate why we feel the way we do when it comes to exercising, but do they really have to control us. While I agree to Jung's proclamation that complexes have us, I do not believe we are as helpless as that statement leads one to believe. Like the size of one's nose, the color of one's eyes, or one's height, we can

accept these features, but we shouldn't resign to them dictating our success and happiness. Even if one's lack of exercise relates to a complex about one's physical appearance stemming from a negative event in childhood, one can still exercise while acknowledging the fear and pain one experiences from the nuclear event. Here's where the practice of mindfulness comes into play (Kabat-Zinn, 2003).

Many years ago, while working at a tennis camp, I led mindfulness practice sessions with the campers during breaks from play. The kids loved it and referred to it as *deep thoughts* after a popular Saturday Night Live skit. Thinking, however, is farther from mindfulness than the campers imagined. Although not popularly referred to as mindfulness back in the mid-1990s, I taught them to keep their minds present on the task at hand. I did this by having them stretch and focus on the feeling they experienced in the muscles being stretched. I used guided imagery to help them visualize the stretch, creating an image of their own making that represented the muscle being stretched. It was like making a movie of a muscle stretching. Keeping their minds on the task at hand filled their minds and kept their focus off of distracting thoughts. When acting, thoughts creep into our minds. If we are vexed by a powerful complex, thoughts related to that complex tend to enter our minds at the least appropriate times. The solution from a mindfulness perspective is to acknowledge those thoughts and then let them go and then return to the task at hand, such as visualizing the stretched muscle. Guided imagery and mindfulness do indeed have much in common (Hamilton et al., 2013).

Exercising can be a private or public endeavor. For some, exercising around others may provoke social physique anxiety, as our bodies are on display for others to see and critique. With the proliferation of social media, there has been an increased propensity for people to comment anonymously yet harshly about physical appearance. The anonymity seems to have empowered bullying, and this frightens many, especially those who have endured a tremendous amount of bullying in the past. Women in particular are prone to experience bullying during exercise as our society is obsessed with the female form and any form that deviates from the contextual ideal. As such, for those women for whom their bodies are trigger points for a powerful complex, the gym and social exercise can be quite scary and could influence the propensity to exercise especially if they have higher body mass indexes (Auster-Gussman et al., 2021; Horenstein et al., 2021). Mindfulness and its consequences (e.g., self-compassion) can help to alleviate this fear by accepting the thoughts and physical sensations one experiences about being watched or critiqued and then letting go of them so that one can continue doing what she started (Magnus et al., 2010).

Mindfulness is not excusing the negative behaviors of others. It's not accepting them as okay either, nor is it encouraging them (Kabat-Zinn, 2003). When people enact negative behaviors, our responses either reinforce or punish them. Which one it is depends upon the person enacting the behavior, not the target. However, if our goal is to accomplish something positive for ourselves, like exercise, continuing our efforts is more important than punishing the transgressor. If, however, the actions become excessive or harassing, the response is likely to change and could result in appropriate action to alleviate the stressor, such as reporting the violation to the appropriate authority (e.g., exercise leader, management, or law enforcement). Yet, during the exercise, thoughts of being watched and critiqued are not abnormal, especially with those who've experienced bullying (Gattario & Frisén, 2019). These experiences are real and must be dealt with appropriately through counseling or psychotherapy.[4] During exercise, though, mindfulness may allow one to continue working out and finishing the tasks one seeks to enjoy. Interestingly, practicing mindfulness, if done so appropriately and consistently may alleviate the stressors altogether, precluding the need for additional therapy (Ghawadra et al., 2019; Zhou et al., 2020). Complexes gain their power through the appropriation of experiences. Imagine if one can break the process by placing an unsurmountable barrier before the complex such that the cycle of appropriation ceases. I equate complexes to these monsters that feed on our fears. Taking away its food starves the beast. Mindfulness is a complex's worst enemy, for one cannot feed on emptiness and still survive.

Exercising is a passion of mine. It's also a duty. We are obliged to maintain our health as long as possible to reduce the burdens associated with preventable illness to our families, friends, communities, and nation. Yet, building a lasting exercise program for oneself is challenging. Complexes run deep and play an important role in preventing us from achieving our exercise goals. Environmental hurdles exist too. For some, their community structure makes exercise difficult. For instance, crowded roads, lack of sidewalks, and crime can interfere with one's ability to exercise, even if an individual is willing to do so (Bonaccorsi et al., 2020; Tcymbal et al., 2020). Gyms are an option. However, their membership fees may be too much for some individuals to afford, particularly those with lower incomes. Plus, their structure can make attendance less desirable, particularly for women who notice male eyes on them. Although some gyms try to attract customers with stress-free environments, such gyms may not be convenient or are too expensive for all. Thus, other options are necessary.

Structural inequalities exist, and they interfere with health and fitness (Ogunwole & Golden, 2021; Sfm et al., 2020). Yet, the ultimate responsibility to live healthy lives resides within the individual, not with

others. This is a contentious issue, and one that I argue with others about frequently. In other words, should we blame the person or society for the inability of the individual to achieve certain goals? I always put the responsibility squarely on the person. This of course may be a result of my personal experiences, as you hopefully understand by now having read the prior chapters. I do acknowledge however the role of society in the imposition of barriers to individual success. For some, the barriers are more formidable than for others. For instance, if my neighborhood has a high crime rate, and I buy a bicycle for exercise, there is a greater chance that it could be stolen than if I live in a wealthy neighborhood and in a home with ample space to store my bicycle. If I live in a community with no sidewalks and limited transportation options, and I cannot afford a car, it will be very hard for me to take a walk for fitness or get to a gym. Structural inequalities are real, and changing them is slow and hard. Indeed, by the time some of them change, one may be too old to do the desired activities.

Structural inequalities place us at a crossroad. We must ask ourselves, should we give in to the structure or work around it. In my life, I have always chosen the latter. I look for ways to do what I can with what I have. For instance, if I have a car, I can drive to a park and walk. If I have the means, I can drive to a safer area to cycle. If I don't have a car but have sidewalks, I will walk. If there is a high school nearby, I can walk on their track or run the bleacher stairs. Indoors, I can do crunches and pushups. If I have the money and the appropriate framing, I can buy a portable pullup bar. If my neighborhood is unsafe in the evenings, I will walk or run earlier in the day. If I have to work, I can walk to work instead of taking public transportation. The point is that there is always a way to exercise. One must merely look for a way to adapt to one's environment. Give me a small opening, and I will squeeze my way through it to get what I want.[5]

Once the opportunity is there, the next step is to work meaningfully toward one's fitness goal. Our goals can be anything when it comes to fitness. For some, it may be controlling blood pressure. For others, it may be losing or gaining weight. For some, it may be looking good in a bikini or shirtless. Whatever the ultimate goal may be, one will not achieve it on the first day. Indeed, the first day will most likely be about managing pain, and the disappointment one feels upon realizing that one cannot do as much as previously thought possible. In other words, the biggest challenge to moving past the first day is disequilibrium.

Exercise isn't a bucket list item. Exercise is a commitment; a pact one makes with the Self to engage in a lifelong activity with many failures. On the first day of exercising, one may feel exhilarated about doing something new and good for the Self. Some people will invest in top-line clothing and equipment designed for comfort, performance, and safety. That is never

a bad idea, as exercise is a lifestyle that changes the self-concept from *me as someone who wants to exercise* to *me as an exerciser*. The more items one owns to identify one's Self with this self-concept, the better. I'm certainly not endorsing unwise expenditures, as not everyone has the resources to purchase the best clothing or equipment. Nevertheless, if one does, it is not a negative behavior.

Clothing and equipment are good for identification with the exerciser's self-concept, but they are not as important as how one manages the inevitable reciprocal interweaving between the feelings of success and failure that come with exercise. To simplify the presentation, I will focus on doing pullups, as this is an exercise that everyone has likely tried at some point, with the exception of individuals with a disability precluding using arms in such a powerful fashion. I love doing pullups! Unfortunately, after fracturing my wrist, I was unable to attempt a pullup. Nevertheless, prior to the fracture I was starting to do pullups again after about a year of not doing any at all.

As one ages, one often seeks to test one's abilities, particularly those that one excelled in at a younger age. I recall my father rowing hard on a pristine Northern Virginia lake one day to prove that he could still do it. As a younger man, he used to row on the Potomac near DC for exercise. However, in his early 50s, he was ill and dying from pulmonary fibrosis. I was about 16 at the time and recalled how happy he was to prove he still had it. I suppose it made him feel good at the time. Sadly, he died shortly after that, yet for at least that moment in time, he felt superior again.

My story isn't quite the same as my father's, but I used to do so many non-weight-bearing exercises. I figured that these exercises were better than those requiring weights because they were free (i.e., no cost), and I could do them almost anywhere. My love for pullups started when I took a rock-climbing clinic at San Diego State. We went to a local climbing spot and climbed all day. Climbing involves a variety of different muscles, but the ones that I remember most are those associated with the pullup motion. Although one isn't always doing massive pullups while scaling a rock face, at times the best way forward is to pull oneself up. Later in college, I discussed rock climbing and pullups with a friend with expertise in rock climbing. He told me that pullups are the primary exercise he does to ensure he's strong enough to manage any situation while climbing.

When my son was little, we used to go to the local playgrounds, and while he was learning to navigate the various structures, I spent my time doing pullups. If possible, I did a traditional pullup, palms facing away from my body. It wasn't always possible, though, as one needs a specific type of bar on which to do one's pullups. When not available, I of course adapted, using rings or monkey bars or climbing domes. I would use whatever I had at my disposal. To make my exercise more fun, I would imagine that I was

in quite the pickle and needed to use my upper body to get myself to safety. Leaving my feet hanging, I would pull myself up any obstacle. It was a fun way to exercise while adapting to the constraints of my environment.

At my peak, I could do about 20 pullups at a time. Yet, it didn't start that way. The first time I tried doing a pullup for exercise, I couldn't even do one. Indeed, the last time I tried, a week before fracturing my wrist, I again couldn't do even one. My first thoughts were like everyone else. I felt sad and thought of the long road ahead to do even one. I thought to myself, I will never get to 20 again. Should I continue or give up, I asked myself. Yet, I immediately tried again to no better conclusion. I still couldn't do one. Actually, I had little upward movement of my torso. It was more like I was hanging on the bar than doing a pull up. I had a long way to go.

There are many ways to do pullups. For me, a good pullup is the hardest type. My palms are facing away from my body and my legs are hanging. I have to start from a rested position and not jump to help myself up. Nor can I swing forward to help myself up either. If I'm going to do it, I want to do it right. Although I do not recommend this for everyone, it is my way of doing pullups, or at least it was when I could do them well.

With time, that feeling of hanging on the pullup bar went away, and I could feel myself inch upward. This could take a while, though. Indeed, it can take weeks before one achieves one's first actual pullup, with one's chin above the bar. In the meantime, many thoughts race through one's head, many of which involve self-doubt. Negative thoughts are exacerbated when one exercises around others, particularly those who like to critique performance. By the way, it is quite interesting how some individuals love to offer unsolicited advice or critiques. Such advice can, if one lets it, enhance one's disequilibrium, adding power to an already too-powerful complex. Nevertheless, it is these moments that are critical to one's progress. Giving up is okay if something is impossible. However, the ability to exceed a barrier adds to one's self-conception. If one is able to transcend the disequilibrium associated with the many failures on one's way to the first pullup, one can add this strength of character to the self-concept and deal a large blow to the complex.

I had many phases of doing pullups for exercise. The first was when I was a graduate student in college. I was young then and could do many interesting physical activities requiring strength. The second phase was in my late 30s to early 40s when my son was young. I was in quite good shape, so exercise was still quite a bit easier than now. My last phase, excluding the recent attempt, was about three years ago with me being in my mid-50s. Although I'm still in good shape, I was not doing much upper-body strength work at the time. Stuck at home at the start of the Covid-19 pandemic, I pulled out my portable pullup bar and placed it on the doorframe and started doing

pullups. Well, I actually could barely do one. I immediately recalled the days when I could do 20 and felt bad. Disequilibrium hit me. However, given my experience learning pullups in the past, I recalled how slow the process is. I immediately set myself some short-term goals that were far more realistic than doing 20 pullups.

We each set goals for whatever endeavor we pursue. In sport and exercise, we generally visualize ourselves mastering the activity like the best athletes we know. For me, it was my old self who could do 20 pullups. These goals are important motivators for success. However, they are of little value when one is struggling on the first day of exercise. As such, it is important to set short-term goals that are easier to achieve.

Setting achievable goals builds a history of success. It also teaches one to redefine success. At the lowest level, individuals compare themselves to superior athletes. Playing tennis, I can compare my backhand to Novak Djokovic's two-handed backhand. Given he has one of the best backhands in the game, he's a great model for my backhand. From a performance perspective, he's a great model. From a psychological perspective, he isn't. A better strategy is to find one facet of the backhand to focus on that is easy to attain with practice, and once attained will set me up for future success.

When I worked as a sport psychology intern at a tennis academy during my doctoral studies, I used to have athletes set goals. I asked them to set three types of goals: long-range goals, mid-range goals, and short-term goals. The belief was that the long-range goals were their ultimate aims, but it was the mid-range goals (six months or so) and particularly the short-term goals that were the ones they should be working on daily. I also taught them to evaluate their progress after each practice, focusing specifically on how they fared toward the short-term goals, and to update their goals once they were achieved. A typical example of a short-term goal would be to be in the correct stance for each shot. Another would be moving one's feet between shots. Achieving these goals gave the athletes a feeling of competence they could not achieve if they only focused on the long-term goal.

With time, exercisers start feeling competent as the body changes. With pullups, while the first day may result in nothing more than perhaps hanging on the bar, eventually one will feel one's torso move upward and eventually one's chin is over the bar. What an amazing feeling. Congratulations to the participant, for she earned it herself. This is motivation to move on to the next goal, a second pullup. Indeed, the reward experienced from this achievement is amazing. It's a feeling better I propose than any artificial substance ingested can provide.

Learning to exercise is about managing disequilibrium and becoming a stronger Self with each accomplishment. Like Psychoadaptation applied to writing, teaching, or peer relationships, one becomes a higher Self with each

achievement. It's not so much the ultimate success that is important in the process, though. It is the ability to withstand the disequilibrium and adapt. With time, the aims will change. As one adapts to diverse circumstances, one changes in relation to the world about the Self. Goals that were once important lose their potency as new aims emerge. The superior exerciser is born. Like other superior adaptors, the superior exerciser comes to understand the world isn't what was once perceived. Yet, without the numerous failures endured along the way, and the re-conceptualization of one's goals and one's Self in relation to the surroundings, this would not be possible. Given the proliferation of lifestyle-related diseases (e.g., Type 2 Diabetes), learning to deal with the pain of disequilibrium is indeed worth it, for the Self and for society. It is certainly better than fixing what's broken. Prevention is always better than cure. These aren't just words to place on one's social media to seek likes. These are words one must learn to live by.

Notes

1. Where I live, there is little room on the roads, and motorists get aggressive toward cyclists. Pennsylvania requires four feet between a cyclist and a car when a driver is passing the cyclist. There isn't that much room on the roads where I live, so tensions flare up frequently. I can live without that.
2. It is interesting to note the similarity between this model of complexes and classical conditioning. I used to teach learning and cognition, and the similarities are striking. All worldviews, regardless of what their proponents think, have similarities.
3. I don't mean to imply here that I am superior to others at dealing with complexes. Rather, I've had to deal with them so much that I have adapted.
4. It's sad to think that people who were victimized by others have to invest time and money to go to therapy for something not of their doing.
5. At work, my office is on the third floor. I rarely take the elevator up because I can get extra work done on my legs by taking the stairs. I urge my students to do the same.

References

Auster-Gussman, L. A., Crim, J., & Mann, T. L. (2021). The soulless cycle: Social physique anxiety as a mediator of the relation between body mass index and exercise frequency. *Stigma and Health, 6*(2), 192.

Bear, G. (1992). A Freudian slip? *Teaching of Psychology, 19*(3), 174–175.

Bigdon, S. F., Gewiess, J., Hoppe, S., Exadaktylos, A. K., Benneker, L. M., Fairhurst, P. G., & Albers, C. E. (2019). Spinal injury in alpine winter sports: A review. *Scandinavian Journal of Trauma, Resuscitation and Emergency Medicine, 27*(1), 1–11.

Boag, S. (2010). Repression, suppression, and conscious awareness. *Psychoanalytic Psychology, 27*(2), 164.

Bonaccorsi, G., Manzi, F., Del Riccio, M., Setola, N., Naldi, E., Milani, C., … Lorini, C. (2020). Impact of the built environment and the neighborhood in promoting the physical activity and the healthy aging in older people: An umbrella review. *International Journal of Environmental Research and Public Health, 17*(17), 6127.

Cornelissen, M., Kemler, E., Verhagen, E., & Gouttebarge, V. (2020). A systematic review of injuries in recreational field hockey: From injury problem to prevention. *Journal of Sports Sciences, 38*(17), 1953–1974.

Davids, K., & Baker, J. (2007). Genes, environment and sport performance: Why the nature-nurture dualism is no longer relevant. *Sports Medicine, 37*, 961–980.

Ericsson, K. A,, Krampe, R. T., &, Tesch-Römer, C. (1993). The role of deliberate practice in the acquisition of expert performance. *Psychological Review; 100*, 363–406.

Gattario, K. H., & Frisén, A. (2019). From negative to positive body image: Men's and women's journeys from early adolescence to emerging adulthood. *Body Image, 28*, 53–65.

Ghawadra, S. F., Abdullah, K. L., Choo, W. Y., & Phang, C. K. (2019). Mindfulness-based stress reduction for psychological distress among nurses: A systematic review. *Journal of Clinical Nursing, 28*(21–22), 3747–3758.

Hamilton, J., Fawson, S., May, J., Andrade, J., & Kavanagh, D. J. (2013). Brief guided imagery and body scanning interventions reduce food cravings. *Appetite, 71*, 158–162.

Hess, G. W. (2010). Achilles tendon rupture: A review of etiology, population, anatomy, risk factors, and injury prevention. *Foot & Ankle Specialist, 3*(1), 29–32.

Horenstein, A., Kaplan, S. C., Butler, R. M., & Heimberg, R. G. (2021). Social anxiety moderates the relationship between body mass index and motivation to avoid exercise. *Body Image, 36*, 185–192.

Jung, C. G. (1969). The structure and dynamics of the psyche. In *Collected Works* (Vol. 18; pp. 114–225). Princeton University Press.

Kabat-Zinn, J. (2003). Mindfulness-based interventions in context: Past, present, and future. *Clinical Psychology: Science and Practice*, 10(2):144–156.

Magnus, C. M., Kowalski, K. C., & McHugh, T.-L. F. (2010). The role of self-compassion in women's self-determined motives to exercise and exercise-related outcomes. *Self and Identity, 9*(4), 363–382.

Marterer, N., Mugele, H., Schäfer, S. K., & Faulhaber, M. (2023). Effects of Upper Body Exercise Training on Aerobic Fitness and Performance in Healthy People: A Systematic Review. *Biology, 12*(3), 355.

Masterson, J. F. (1985). *The Real Self: A Developmental Self, and Object Reactions Approach.* Brunner/Mazel Publishers.

NHIS. (2018, November 18, 2022). Figure 7.1. Percentage of adults aged 18 and over who met 2008 federal physical activity guidelines for aerobic activity through leisure-time aerobic activity. 2022, from https://public.tableau.com/app/profile/tina.norris/viz/FIGURE7_1/Dashboard7_1

Ogunwole, S. M., & Golden, S. H. (2021). Social determinants of health and structural inequities—root causes of diabetes disparities. *Diabetes Care, 44*(1), 11–13.

Petchkovsky, L., Petchkovsky, M., Morris, P., Dickson, P., Montgomery, D., Dwyer, J., & Burnett, P. (2013). fMRI responses to Jung's Word Association Test: Implications for theory, treatment and research. *Journal of Analytical Psychology, 58*(3), 409–431.

Piaget, J. (1951). The biological problem of intelligence. In D. Rapaport (Ed.), *Organization and Pathology of Thought* (pp. 176–192). Columbia University Press.

Rodriguez, D. (2000). Self and adaptation: Defining the healthy self. In R.G. Craven, & H.W. Marsh (Eds.), *Self-Concept Theory, Research and Practice: Advances for the New Millennium: Collected Papers of the Inaugural Self-Concept Enhancement and Learning Facilitation (SELF) Research Centre International Conference* (pp. 355–365). SELF Research Centre, University of Western Sydney.

Sfm, C., Van Cauwenberg, J., Maenhout, L., Cardon, G., Lambert, E., & Van Dyck, D. (2020). Inequality in physical activity, global trends by income inequality and gender in adults. *International Journal of Behavioral Nutrition and Physical Activity, 17*, 1–8.

Tcymbal, A., Demetriou, Y., Kelso, A., Wolbring, L., Wunsch, K., Wäsche, H., ... Reimers, A. K. (2020). Effects of the built environment on physical activity: A systematic review of longitudinal studies taking sex/gender into account. *Environmental Health and Preventive Medicine, 25*(1), 1–25.

Zhou, X., Guo, J., Lu, G., Chen, C., Xie, Z., Liu, J., & Zhang, C. (2020). Effects of mindfulness-based stress reduction on anxiety symptoms in young people: A systematic review and meta-analysis. *Psychiatry Research, 289*, 113002.

6

TENNIS

I love playing tennis. I have never been a very competitive tennis player, but hitting long rallies with heavy topspin is one of the true joys of my life. Picture this. It's a sunny morning, and the air is crisp. Under a cloudless blue sky, I'm standing barely behind the baseline with my Wilson Roger Federer Pro Staff in hand, the red and black older version. I can smell the city around me, and the aroma of a freshly opened can of tennis balls. If you are a tennis player, my good reader, you know that smell. It's as familiar and intense as the new car smell. My instructor feeds the first ball to me. I step rapidly but gingerly as if I'm walking on rice paper, while taking my racket back and down in a circular motion to meet the ball in front of me. When it works, I brush the ball from low to high as my racket moves forward toward the opposing backstop, making a unique whooshing sound that is a mix of power and spin. I watch the ball head toward the opposing backstop and then dip and bounce somewhere between the baseline and the service line, only to be returned with equal vigor and spin.

Writing this first paragraph, I stepped outside of my body and returned to a not-so-distant past when I practiced with coach K at Drexel University in Philadelphia. We worked out on these courts that are in the middle of campus, ensconced among high-rise dormitories, apartments, and office buildings. I always practiced early, as I'm an early riser. It's the best time, particularly in the summer when it gets hot and humid. Plus, this location had a good coffee shop across the street, and I always ended practice getting a large coffee to drink as I navigated my sweaty body back home.

Those days are memorable because they were the absolute peak of my tennis experience. My tennis history is indeed unique, not because I did

DOI: 10.4324/9781003460800-9

anything great in the sport but because I never stopped trying to improve, even when life got in the way of me playing. My initiation into the sport was not unlike that of most of my childhood peers in the 1970s. That era was perhaps the golden age of the sport in the United States. Although tennis remains popular globally, it makes barely a blip on the sporting radar in the States. A victim of perhaps the proliferation of media and competing rooting interests, or maybe it's because our country has produced few great tennis players since, with the exception of Venus and Serena Williams, and Sampras and Agassi, tennis has never again enjoyed the fandom it did then. Thinking back to my youth, we had the stoic Bjorn Borg, the fiery Jimmy Connors, the petulant John McEnroe, and the exotic Guillermo Villas on the men's side. Among the women, there were Chrissy Evert and Martina Navratilova, along with Gabriella Sabatini. Watching them compete in the finals of the majors[1] was like watching a heavyweight boxing event. One just had to see it. These matches were special events indeed.

After the majors, there was this phenomenon we don't see much today. People would flock to the tennis courts, rackets in hand, to play tennis. Perhaps they hoped to replicate the stoicism of Borg or the volleys of McEnroe. Perhaps they wanted to exhibit the grace of Chrissy Evert or the athleticism of Navratilova. In any case, they made it hard to get court time. As a child at the time, my friends and I played outside a lot. Believe it or not, we lacked video games, internet, or smartphones. We tended instead to use our imagination to come up with that which is now served to consumers by their smartphones: entertainment. We too had visions of ourselves competing in those big tournaments and winning trophies. This all played out on a tennis court by kids with no knowledge of how the game is played, and poor technique. We didn't care because we had fun.

My first memory of playing tennis was on one of those occasions with my friends on the public courts on 37th street across from Sidwell Friends school and near Phoebe Hearst Elementary School. Those were the closest public courts to my home in McLean Gardens. Armed with my orange wooden tennis racket, I would fling it at the ball not knowing what I was doing but loving the feel when I made contact. The framers (balls hit off the frame) might as well have been masterful topspin winners for all I knew. Indeed, when I dreamed about playing, that's what I saw, for I knew no better. I never even knew there was such a thing as a tennis lesson until later in life when I wanted to play for real. By then, it was a bit too late for me to do anything serious with the sport. Nevertheless, writing this chapter at 58, it is evident that I continued playing off and on for some 50 years now. Tennis is indeed a sport for a lifetime.

What memories I have. Tennis played such an important role in my life, especially when I got to high school. That was when I learned about the

difference between players receiving professional training and guys like me who taught ourselves to play using trial and error. There was a big difference indeed. I tried out for the tennis team, as what else would I do since that's the sport I loved. At Washington and Lee High School[2] in Arlington, Virginia, we had some really good tennis players. Being a suburb of the nation's capital meant that we had a wide variety of students, from the children of foreign service professionals, and immigrants, to locals. Among these were tennis players who received vast amounts of training from highly skilled professionals for years. So, when I first played a competitive match against other prospective team members, it wasn't much of a match. I clearly didn't belong on the same court as these kids.

All sport requires countless hours of training with skilled professionals for one to achieve elite performance (Ericsson et al., 1993). Yet, not everyone has the resources to do so. In some cases, one may not even know of the existence of training opportunities for a variety of reasons. That was my situation. Although my mother practiced sport as a young person, neither she nor my father planned for me to be involved in sport. I'm sure it had much to do with the cost. My father was a waiter and my mother a housewife. Although my sister and I were well cared for at home, extracurriculars, unless free, were off the agenda. However, I did spend much of my time after school and during the summer months in recreation centers. I did engage in sport that was free or low cost, such as little league baseball. Tennis, however, to the best of my memory, wasn't a sport offered in any of the recreation centers I attended. Thus, I didn't take formal lessons until after high school, when I had my own money to spend as I pleased.

My first recollection of tennis lessons was at a local YMCA that had a tennis center. The center offered drill sessions, and when I had money to invest in training, I enrolled in group lessons and drill sessions. This was fun. I recall one session when we were serving and I hit a few nice and strong first serves. One other participant commented on how nice my serve was. This made me feel quite good. I believe the instructor attributed it to my height. I am not very tall, but being 6' does make serving easier I suppose. Yet, as good as this lesson was, and as memorable as the experience, I was far behind other 18-year-old tennis players who had been playing since they were about five years old. No amount of training, I'd soon learn, can erase that experience gap. Further, learning as a young child isn't the same as learning as a young adult, and I couldn't change my developmental age either.[3]

When exploring sport performance, one must understand the athlete's history. People who started playing tennis early in life, who had regular training with a professional, and who experienced competing at the highest levels for their age have a big advantage over those of us who didn't do

the same. Sport is a cruel and unforgiving endeavor. It favors those who have talent, financial resources, and years of structured practice under the supervision of a coach, over those who are willing but lack the same experiences. Nor is the culture surrounding the sport different. The tennis culture is such that some individuals are seen as members and others as hackers. To be a hacker is an insult. It is the worst possible status one can have in a sport like tennis. Hackers are players who think they can play well but possess none of the necessary skills to succeed. Indeed, hackers often invent styles of play that give them success against other hackers and even some real tennis players who either lack confidence or have yet to refine their skills enough to defeat a hacker's challenge. The way I played tennis from childhood through my high school years made me a hacker. Once I realized that is what I was, I sought to change, and have worked decades to do so.

Awareness is key to success. If there is one lesson I hope you learn from this book, it is that there is no success without disequilibrium, and there is no disequilibrium unless one receives feedback (Rodriguez, 2021). Feedback is at times perceived as harsh, especially when it contradicts what we believe about ourselves (Fishbach et al., 2010). Like the difference in reception to feedback, delivery varies by the individual delivering the feedback. Some people are better at giving feedback than others. Not all feedback is necessary either, nor should be trusted. I am willing to listen to feedback from people from whom I can learn something. In those cases, I am in a hierarchical relationship with the individual delivering the feedback, with the messenger at a higher status than I am, at least in terms of the activity under scrutiny. This is an important point because status depends on accomplishment, not age or some other superficial characteristic. Thus, I can get really important feedback from someone much younger than I am. I can learn from a teenager perhaps better than I can learn from someone older than I am.

Good feedback, even when perceived as negative, is always constructive (Fong et al., 2019). As such, its aim is to help the recipient improve performance. It is never personal and as such focuses on the skill, not the individual. For instance, when assessing my footwork, good feedback would not merely indicate that I am not moving my feet well, but tell me how I can improve my footwork. As an example, coach K told me to hop five times between shots. In other words, after I hit the ball, I start hopping and attempt to reach five hops. He accompanied this feedback with reasoning. If I am moving, it's easier for me to get to the correct position when I meet the ball, instead of being flat-footed and late.

While good feedback is not personal and is instructive, most feedback we receive does not meet either criterion. Indeed, much of the feedback we hear is more likely given for the benefit of the person delivering the feedback

than the recipient. Thus, one has to learn how to distinguish between useful and useless feedback. Otherwise, we risk falling victim to our emotional lability. I have become really good at filtering out meaningless feedback and using good feedback to my advantage. Perhaps it is because of anxiety and my history of being bullied when I was a child that I learned to not trust what people say. Perhaps it is because I studied under some of the best professors in college, studied counseling, and came to know some of the finest instructors in sport one can know. It is hard to say where this skill comes from, but I think it's a mix of all these and my genetic personality traits. Nevertheless, I take in all feedback and do not dismiss any of it until I have received enough to determine their veracity. For even the worst intentioned feedback has some reality to it. For instance, I recall playing points with coach DH one day at a high school with the tennis courts located adjacent to a football practice field. One of the football coaches watched me struggle to get to any ball hit by DH and started laughing and making rude comments about my poor performance. Of course, I struggled that day. It was a very hot and sunny August day. I was in my early 50s, and DH was about 22 and a D1 scholarship tennis player who loved to play real tennis with me. Although the critic's delivery wasn't to my liking, his message was clear and accurate. My performance sucked against a true athlete.

I took the critic's feedback and stored it in my file of feedback regarding my tennis. Of course, I could have yelled back using some colorful metaphors to retort his comment, but it would not have done anything except ignite some incident. I could have pointed out that at his age he was likely half as fit as I was then. I could have commented on his appearance for while he could perhaps knock down a pass rusher, he'd likely faint if attempting to play as hard as I tried to. Still, even if those comments made me feel better, they wouldn't have changed the situation. I wasn't as good as I wanted to be at tennis, particularly when faced with a superior athlete. There are many levels to a sport, and my coach was standing on a peak looking down at me like a little ant.

I have a saying when it comes to feedback. I listen to all feedback, but with some feedback it goes in one ear and out the other. Yet, I am never cruel to the person delivering the message. Sometimes delivering feedback even when useless is not intended to be mean-spirited. I have received much unsolicited feedback from others who have seen flaws in my game and decided to approach me and tell me how they believe I can repair my game. I appreciate it because to these individuals, delivering that feedback is meaningful. They obviously love tennis and want to spread their love for the game with someone else who clearly loves it too. One time, a professor of mine saw me playing and told me I was too close to the ball when hitting. Although well-intentioned, that feedback was useless because it says

nothing about how to remedy the situation. Nevertheless, this professor of mine loved tennis and his intention was very good-hearted. I of course tried to comply but, without information on how to do so, I never did. I stored that feedback along with other such feedback I have received in my self-concept's tennis file, and because I have heard that feedback on other occasions from many, it is clearly an issue with my game. All feedback has some truth to it, no matter who is delivering it. Thus, one must have the ability to withstand the disequilibrium one feels from receiving the feedback and then find a way to correct the flaws.

Disequilibrium is the key to good tennis. Our beliefs about our ability in tennis are not always accurate. They depend on many factors. First, they depend on the people we play with. Tennis is a sport that requires a partner. Even if one is not playing a match or points, one needs a partner to hit with. At times one can play alone by hitting against a wall, using a ball machine, or practicing serves. Yet, that's practice and not tennis. Tennis requires a partner, someone to stand on the other side of the net to return balls. Second, tennis requires knowledge of ideal strokes. Third, tennis requires feedback that is instructive (Reid et al., 2007). Fourth, tennis requires receptivity to feedback and a willingness to improve upon one's flaws (Waples, 2015). Fifth, and not independent of the others, tennis requires fitness (Roetert et al., 1996; Ulbricht et al., 2016). While hitting two or three shot rallies isn't very taxing, hitting rallies of 20 shots and beyond requires stamina.

With all these demands, one must be able to deal with disequilibrium. With every happy moment for an achievement, one faces many moments of failure. Even the greatest tennis players of all fail. Indeed, as one improves in ranking and accumulates victories, the constraints change in different ways from prior constraints. One recent example was Serena Williams's quest to hold the all-time grand slam title of 24 currently held by Australian great Margaret Court. Although not necessary, and most Williams fans will agree with my assessment, Serena feels the pressure to win the 24th. Court's 24 came in both the amateur and open eras. Serena, of course being too young to play during the prior era, won all of her titles in the open era. Nevertheless, critics bring this up. Being human, Serena Williams appears to have fallen victim to the pressure. Constraints change. Beating Steffi Graf's record of 22 slams is in my view sufficient, yet people continued to bring up the 24th slam, adding unnecessary pressure to Serena. Constraints change, and even the best experience disequilibrium. One can seek to avoid it, but one can never completely escape it. Reporters ask about it and fans retort by providing the facts about Williams's amazing career, which only fuels her critics. Even if one buries one's head under pillows and screams to the top of her ability, one can never keep out all the *yeah but* thoughts. They create new complexes that may eventually take over one's life.

A second example was the 2021 grand slam run of Novak Djokovic and the run for the golden slam. Apparently, as if not enough to have to win all four slams in a calendar year, in an Olympic year one must win the gold medal too. Even if Novak avoided thinking about it, reporters came asking. Comparisons were made to Steffi Graf who is the only professional to ever win the golden slam. So, even if he won all four majors in a calendar year, that would not have been enough. Well, but he didn't win the golden slam, his critics would say. Novak couldn't keep his composure during some periods of poor play and succumbed to the pressure. Worse yet, after saying that pressure is a privilege, he was slammed by critics for making this comment during the Olympics in which U.S. gymnast Simone Biles withdrew from events after experiencing psychological symptoms gymnasts call the twisties. Although I doubt that Biles was on Djokovic's mind given that he's not American, and may for all that matters not even know who Biles is, he was slammed as being insensitive. I believe his comment was actually a statement that he experiences pressure because he's in a unique situation, and that's a privilege. Nevertheless, the *yeah but* folks jumped on him and made a bully out of an athlete. Is it any wonder that tennis player Naomi Osaka eschewed interviews for a bit? Disequilibrium, however, finds its way into our consciousness. Novak failed to win the Olympic gold, and then completely limped through the U.S. Open final, admitting that he was relieved the ordeal was over when it ended. Constraints always change, and nobody is immune to them.

There are so many other examples in tennis. Indeed, like figure skating, gymnastics, and golf, tennis is a sport in which all eyes are on one athlete. This magnifies mistakes, especially when they are made on the highest stages. Yet, not one of us is immune to the destructive force of disequilibrium, regardless of our level. It is how we process it that counts. For recreational tennis players like myself, there are no majors, but there is competition. Even if we are not playing matches, we may experience competition when striking a ball or practicing serves. Each skill we practice has its constraints, and mastery means adapting to those constraints. Like the changes occurring to champions, as situations change so do the constraints. With each change, we must adapt again.

To understand fully the psychological adaptation process in tennis, I'll walk us through a tennis skill I've worked on a lot, the one-handed backhand. Tennis players tend to struggle with backhands more so than forehands, although this isn't universal. More of an issue for recreational players than experts, the backhand is challenging because of the muscles used to strike the ball, especially with a one-handed backhand. So much goes into hitting a good one-handed backhand. First, one must set one's feet such that they are essentially perpendicular to the ball's flight line. This

means that if one draws a line from heel to toe and extends this line to infinity, it should be approximately perpendicular to the ball's flight line, making about a 90-degree angle. This also means, of course, one has to read the ball's flight line correctly and be light enough on the feet to set oneself up in this position to meet the ball.

Simultaneously, as one is moving one's feet to the appropriate position, one brings the racket back (i.e., the backswing). If done correctly, the racket will essentially loop from high to low, in a circular motion, to meet the ball without hesitating a moment. Hesitation reduces power, and given for most of us the one-handed backhand is a weaker stroke, we need every advantage we can. To facilitate this process, the good tennis player holds the racket's neck with the non-dominant hand, using this motion to help guide the racket back as he rotates his torso away from the ball's flight path to create the tension necessary for an explosive shot. Focusing on the approaching ball, the player stands ready to meet it in flight, before the ball reaches its apex. Uncorking his torso, the racket is released, and its head drops, facilitating the rising motion necessary to create the low-to-high brush required to generate topspin. The ideal is to meet the ball in front of the body and as the ball is rising. If the entire sequence presented here is done correctly, the stroke will be swift and smooth, producing a beautiful and powerful shot. In addition, the tennis player should stay grounded, with both feet planted firmly on the ground, but knees bent so that the tennis player can extend into the shot. Feet should also be wide enough apart to ensure a strong base of support. Coach K used to demonstrate this by shoving me when my feet were close together, and then again when they were set the correct distance apart. He'd note correctly that it's easier to knock one down when one's feet are closer together than farther apart. A strong base produces a strong shot.

Two final pieces of the picture are the eyes and follow-through. For the outstanding tennis player like Roger Federer, the eyes are locked on the contact point rather than moving one's gaze and head upward to follow the ball's trajectory once struck. The racket would follow-through forward in a straight line until it could go no further, and then would move upward with the upper body's rotation adding power to the strike. When all is done perfectly, the one-handed backhand is in my view the most beautiful stroke in tennis, and perhaps also one of the most beautiful actions in all sport. Indeed, one should watch a video of Swiss star Stan Wawrinka hitting the one-hander. It's pure art.

I broke the one-hander down into a series of steps as I know them. Naturally, a good tennis coach could add more to what I described. Perhaps the coach would note that the player should look over his front shoulder as he anticipates the ball. This would facilitate rotation, adding tension to the

torso as it winds up before releasing into the shot, increasing rotation and power. The coach could also add the need to ensure appropriate distance between the racket and the body. It's a lot. Yet, if one watches Federer or Wawrinka hit the shot, one gets the impression it's learnable with practice. Unfortunately, when one gets out on the court and tries this backhand, it's very difficult if not impossible to replicate their strokes. Instead of the ball leaving the racket and traveling high over the net and then spinning back down inside the baseline, the ball will likely fly off the frame or out onto the parking lot, if one doesn't miss the ball altogether. What Federer, Wawrinka, and other one-hand backhand professionals do is the ideal. Their execution is the prototype that sets the optimal constraints to which we all must adapt if we are to use the one-hander. It's a lifetime process indeed, and it is highly probable that all but the elite will fail to attain it. This doesn't mean, however, that we shouldn't play with the one-handed backhand and go straight for the two-hander. It merely points to how difficult it is to adapt to this set of constraints. As such, if one chooses this option, it must be done in a sequential fashion, under the guidance of an expert instructor, and without concern about winning points over mastery.

I am really starting to enjoy writing down steps or stages in relation to some desired outcome. I'm not writing a book on tennis per se, but rather a book about the Psychoadaptation process. As such, I will not discuss what one should do to attain the ideal form. Instead, my goal is to ensure my reader understands what must occur mentally to achieve one's best possible performance and personal satisfaction. When training with expert instructors, the instructors feed balls to the student in an ideal fashion, ensuring that the student has the best opportunity to strike the ball clean. Instructors do this so they can evaluate the student's progress, and will not change the feeding style until necessary. When necessary, though, they either increase or decrease the complexity of their feeds depending on the student's mastery. What the instructor does is adapt to the student. Instructors are master adapters in the context of their sport. Constraints constantly change, with students improving over time but having setbacks. With each such change, the instructor's tactics change. What differentiates a great instructor from an average instructor is the latter's inability to modify instruction for the student.

When learning new skills, we must adapt too. We go through many changes with each attempt to strike the ball. Sometimes we hit the ball with near ideal form. We differ in our abilities to replicate what we see, with some learners having a distinct advantage over others. Yet, even if we do hit the ball nicely in our first few attempts, flaws become evident the more shots we attempt, for we have yet to develop the neuromuscular memory to consistently hit the ball with similar mechanics (Wulf & Lewthwaite,

2016). With time, failures become more frequent. Muscles fatigue, and when they do, our strokes return to their baseline (no pun intended). For every learner, this causes disequilibrium, as we realize we are far from the ideal stroke. However, some manage disequilibrium better than others. The instructor will provide feedback, and the best instructors will find ways to help students feel encouraged by the performance. How we deal with the disequilibrium, however, depends on our personal histories with learning. Complexes invade our thoughts, and they can be pretty intense for some. Nevertheless, if one can manage the complexes and listen to the instructor's feedback, everything is provided to help the student learn the skill with practice.

Managing complexes is hard. I discussed them in relation to exercise in Chapter 5. They invade our working memory, leaving little room for constructive thoughts. Thus, to move forward one must halt their progress. Imagine, for clarity, some nefarious competitor in a bicycle race taking his portable pump and jamming it between the spokes of another rider's wheel. That would put an abrupt stop to the cyclist's ride and likely cause serious injury. Similarly, the complex is like the bicycle wheel that spins along on its own, and its progress can only be halted by some abrupt intervention. One of my favorite theories that applies well to this scenario is Dodge and Crick's social information processing theory (Dodge & Crick, 1990). In their model, the process from a cue (such as a spoken word) to the enactment of a behavior flows automatically, particularly in socially maladjusted individuals, such as those with a propensity for violent behavior. This makes the behavior seem inevitable, especially for the individual enacting the behavior. It's as if the enactor has no control over the process once it starts. Yet, we control all behaviors we enact. For instance, some tennis players bounce their rackets off the ground when angry. To them, they may feel that the behavior is out of control, perhaps with some embarrassment afterward. It's not. At any moment the tennis player can impede the behavior's processing by jamming a mental pump in the spokes.

When learning new skills, particularly if we believe we cannot perform them due to some historical failures, and reactions to our failures, we often feel like our reactions are inevitable and unstoppable. We may even feel that we cannot continue as our ability to replicate the ideal is not possible, and no further effort or monetary investment in training is warranted. I venture that this is how most people end their adventures with new sport. Actually, this likely happens prior to taking lessons. Like my early days playing tennis, most individuals get excited about playing after seeing a professional or other high-level competitor play. Perhaps after watching the 2021 Williams sisters' movie, King Richard, a young woman runs out to the tennis courts with a shiny new racket and the best tennis outfit thinking she can replicate

what Serena and Venus accomplished. Then, after making a few attempts at hitting the ball and realizing how difficult tennis actually is, she gives up. Out of these individuals, only a few will take the next step to register for lessons. Many are lost from the sport there too. Only the smallest proportion move on to make tennis a significant part of their lives. Like a great sieve, only the select few remain after sifting.

Sieves keep the most desired elements. When I write desired here, however, I am not considering skill but rather mental toughness; the ability to withstand disequilibrium. It doesn't have to be this way, though, as learning to jam a metaphorical pump in one's mental spokes is easy. For my part, I use mindfulness. I love mindfulness but find the traditional teaching style a bit cumbersome. What Jon Kabat-Zinn created in Mindfulness Based Stress Reduction (MBSR) is beautiful and has had a tremendous impact on my life (Kabat-Zinn, 2003). Nevertheless, I feel that intense training isn't necessary for everyone. I thus practice what I like to call *practical mindfulness.* Years ago, I coined this term when discussing a mindfulness program with someone interested in creating a mindfulness program with me. At the time, I was an assistant professor at Brown University in Providence, Rhode Island. I was also spending much time around tennis players and thinking sport psychology. Indeed, at the time, I was volunteering for a local tennis coach who coached a women's USTA league team. I would come to their practices, and we would work on various mental skills they could take onto the court during their league matches. I introduced my form of practical mindfulness to them, as it was something I had been using for years when working with tennis players. Now I could finally link it to a name, as Mindfulness and MBSR were catching on in popularity.

The idea behind mindfulness is to remove thoughts that cause distress when allowed to run their course. It also involves the unconditional acceptance of one's thoughts (Birrer et al., 2012; Foroughi et al., 2020; Wolkin, 2015). This is hard for some, as our thoughts can be quite unsavory at times. Yet, our thoughts are part of who we are as a person. We are complex beings, and at times we have very negative thoughts about ourselves and others. The wisest person understands this and allows for them but does not act upon them. Allowing one's Self to be human is a key step in the mental health process. Ignoring all of one's complexities, especially the most gruesome of thoughts, is a breeding ground for complexes.

I love the idea of mindfulness and the retreat-like training. I unfortunately could not afford to spend so much time away from work and other family duties at the time to attend a workshop. Funny, shouldn't I have given myself the luxury of mental health and eschewed all commitments. I suppose one could argue that by not attending workshops that I desired to attend, I am not being truthful to my desire to educate one about mindfulness and

its benefits. Fortunately, though, there is much literature on mindfulness. Further, in my youth I spent much time reading about eastern philosophy and practicing Taiichi and attending other retreats, such as the Whole Being Weekend in Southern California. I therefore had a great deal of experience with mindfulness and felt that although it would have been very beneficial to attend an official mindfulness training, I could do much of the practice on my own. I did. However, I found ways to incorporate mindfulness into what I already do; I made it practical.

Unconditional acceptance required work. Whenever a thought invaded my working memory, I verbally acknowledged and accepted it. I said to myself quietly, "I accept this thought and let it go." It took quite some time before this self-talk was no longer necessary. Now when I have unacceptable thoughts, regardless of their nature, I let them go. I rarely pull out the saying unless a situation occurs that is beyond my ability to do so unconsciously. These do occur, but they are far less frequent than previously. Now, when I get stressed it's usually when I take the initiative to challenge something that I deem as unfair to me or others. In those cases, I do get stressed, and multiple thoughts race through my head. Sometimes, I do get as stressed as I was when I was at my worst. That stress, my friends, is the kind that seems to fill one's body with unescapable tension. At my worst, it results in stomach pain. Thankfully, I have non-chemical remedies for that, such as autogenic training, another psychological practice for dealing with stress (Seo & Kim, 2019).

In addition to accepting thoughts, one must let them go. Letting go of thoughts is the mental equivalent of jamming a pump in the spokes. The severe stress symptoms I discuss come from the release of stress hormones. Hormones have lasting effects. Once they are released one will feel stressed for quite some time. The human stress response is the workings of the Hypothalamic-Pituitary-Adrenal (HPA) axis (Leistner & Menke, 2020). The goal of the HPA is to allow us to respond appropriately to environmental stressors, such as being confronted by a predator. Ideally, when faced by danger, we respond quickly to eliminate the threat, and then our bodies return to homeostasis. The changes we experience, often referred to as the fight-or-flight response, are designed to help us fight if necessary, or escape to safety. For instance, changes such as dilating pupils and blood diverted away from the periphery and to the large muscles, prepare us to assess our environment fully and run or punch an enemy if necessary. Of course, time has changed our environments. For the most part, we are not living in dangerous spaces. However, wars, structural inequalities, political violence, sexual assault, and bullying result in some people experiencing the fight-or-flight response too frequently, even after the danger ceases (Adam et al., 2020; Chen et al., 2018; Morris et al., 2020). Negative thinking linked to

negative experiences maintains the power to trigger the HPA axis and the release of stress hormones (Thomas & Larkin, 2020). Designed as a short-term response, repeated and prolonged responses to stress can have negative effects on one's health across the lifespan (Krushas & Schwartz, 2022) and can even be transmitted across generations (Parade et al., 2019). As such, learning to short-circuit self-effacing thoughts is critical to good health and good performance, including sport performance.

Practical mindfulness means incorporating mindfulness in conventional activities. I practice it everywhere. I give myself permission, borrowing a phrase from the teachings of Dr. George James, to pause my thinking when walking or waiting in line at the grocery store, for instance, and accept and let go of all thoughts entering my short-term memory space. It's an amazing feeling to free one's mind of thought. Thinking is a unique human mechanism designed to help us master our environments (Heyes, 2012). Thinking has its place though, such as when we are planning, or identifying an escape route. Other than that, we need to have breaks from thought. Thinking is, after all, ergotropic (Porges, 2011). It is meant for problem solving: work. Practicing mindfulness regularly provides these breaks. I practice everywhere.

In addition to letting go of thoughts, I also focus on replacing incongruous thoughts with task-appropriate cognitions. For instance, I practice mindful driving. While driving, my focus is on scanning my environment for threats, such as drivers attempting foolish maneuvers, potholes, and pedestrians. I am always on the lookout for anomalies. Imagine if my mind was focusing on something inappropriate at the time instead of driving. I recall one particular incident during my graduate school days when I was thinking about theory while driving somewhere in Fairfax county, Virginia. The next thing I noticed was me bumping into the car right before me. Thankfully, nothing bad happened. Yet, task-inappropriate thoughts can lead to undesired consequences.

Tennis is ripe for practicing practical mindfulness. Returning to the backhand, the tennis player finds a specific point of focus, and all thinking should aim at that focal point. For instance, it can be the preparation, such as rotating the torso or taking the racket back to the desired position in anticipation of the ball. It can be moving forward into the shot. It can be finding one's appropriate position behind the baseline. It can be the follow-through. Notice, though, that it must be *one* focus only. If an instructor tells the learner to focus on too many facets of the swing, this may be too much for the student to achieve, overwhelming the student's working memory capacity. When I work with athletes, I tell them to focus on the most fundamental skill, the skill that has the most profound impact on their performance. I tell them that their coach will let them know what to focus

on, even if not stating it directly. Indeed, for any person ever taking a tennis lesson, coaches focus on the skills in which the athlete is most deficient. For me, it was generally being late in my preparation, which resulted in a very weak backhand. Early preparation results in meeting the ball early, maximizing my power.

It is interesting though, as one improves performance, one's focus can change while still promoting the development of a specific skill. For instance, since I tend to be late in meeting the ball when playing very good tennis players, telling me to focus on meeting the ball on the rise works well. This is effective because I have taken enough lessons and practiced enough that my body knows what to do. Focusing on one point, such as hitting the ball before it reaches its peak, frees my mind from the extraneous thoughts that complicate tennis for me, and I hit the ball better. Indeed, one of my favorite feelings in tennis is when I hit the ball just as it starts risking. It feels so good.

One of the benefits of practical mindfulness is experiencing the oceanic feeling. I discussed this in Chapter 1 when I introduced my theoretical perspective. As the mind is freed of extraneous thoughts and all focus is on specific tasks, such as hitting the ball on the rise, one begins to merge mentally with the game. One loses the Self in the moment, as if the separation between the person and the racket and the ball disappears. Athletes like to call this flow (Csikszentmihalyi, 1991). It is not a religious moment. Indeed, there is nothing metaphysical about it, even if it feels like there should be. It's as if for that one moment one transcends the material self and is living in heaven. Although ephemeral, it is indeed a beautiful feeling. What makes it even more special and motivates me and others to pursue mindfulness is that one cannot will the oceanic feeling into existence. It comes on its own when it wants to. It occurs when one least expects it. I love this feeling and indeed I just felt it as I was writing this paragraph. Friends, there is nothing more rewarding.

Tennis is a beautiful sport. Some of my most wonderful experiences in life took place on or around tennis courts. I frequently think back to the days my friends and I practiced with our coach on the San Diego State University courts, when everything still seemed possible. I was naïve but realistic. Visions of me winning tournaments in my 30s, 40s, or older raced through my mind while the stable master (as our coach liked to be called) fed us balls and made funny sounds. We spent hours on the courts with him, playing and dreaming.

I have trained with so many people and have learned so very much from each one. Yet, what has hindered me from progressing beyond where I am today is my mind. While I have been successful using mindfulness in so many ways, the complexes I have related to performance have caused me

havoc in the sport. I can escape much, but the fears I had as a child never left, and despite my best efforts they still invade my mind at the wrong times, like when I need to finish off a match. Nevertheless, I have found a place for tennis in my life. I still experience the joy of being on the court and mastering new skills. When I hit a ball right, it's as if I feel the topspin in my heart as the ball arcs above the net. Indeed, writing about it now is filling my body with joy.

I started this chapter with a memory of playing tennis with coach K on the Drexel University courts. Those were indeed beautiful days. On a perfect day, I'd find a parking space right next to the courts, and they would be empty so that I could pick the court I liked the most, the one furthest from the busy street. I would sit on the court and stretch. When finished my stretching, I would grab a tennis ball and bounce it on my frame. Maybe if I was feeling good that day, I could achieve 30 without the ball hitting the ground. I would watch people as they drove to work or walked to class, and wait for Coach's arrival and hopefully a good day of practice. When I was in the zone, I would meet balls early, and we would hit some long rallies. "Let's see if we can now go 20 shots," coach K would yell out. When I could, I was in heaven. I felt every ball leave my racket and I felt like a puppet master, able to dictate where it went, its depth and pace. God, I love this sport.

Notes

1 For those not in the know about tennis, there are four major tournaments: The Australian Open, the French Open, Wimbledon, and the US Open. Unlike other events, these are five-set tournaments on the men's side, with massive prize money.
2 It was renamed Washington and Liberty High School in 2018.
3 There are some exceptions, though. I know of two individuals who took up skill-intensive activities as adults and now excel. That will have to be in my next book.

References

Adam, E. K., Hittner, E. F., Thomas, S. E., Villaume, S. C., & Nwafor, E. E. (2020). Racial discrimination and ethnic racial identity in adolescence as modulators of HPA axis activity. *Development and Psychopathology, 32*(5), 1669–1684.

Birrer, D., Röthlin, P., & Morgan, G. (2012). Mindfulness to enhance athletic performance: Theoretical considerations and possible impact mechanisms. *Mindfulness, 3*(3), 235–246. doi: 10.1007/s12671-012-0109-2.

Chen, G., Kong, Y., Deater-Deckard, K., & Zhang, W. (2018). Bullying victimization heightens cortisol response to psychosocial stress in Chinese children. *Journal of Abnormal Child Psychology, 46*(5), 1051–1059.

Csikszentmihalyi, M. (1991). *Flow*. Munksgaard København.

Dodge, K. A., & Crick, N. R. (1990). Social information-processing bases of aggressive behavior in children. *Personality and Social Psychology Bulletin, 16*(1), 8–22.

Ericsson, K. A., Krampe, R. T., &, Tesch-Römer, C. (1993). The role of deliberate practice in the acquisition of expert performance. *Psychological Review, 100*,: 363–406.

Fishbach, A., Eyal, T., & Finkelstein, S. R. (2010). How positive and negative feedback motivate goal pursuit. *Social and Personality Psychology Compass, 4*(8), 517–530.

Fong, C. J., Patall, E. A., Vasquez, A. C., & Stautberg, S. (2019). A meta-analysis of negative feedback on intrinsic motivation. *Educational Psychology Review, 31*, 121–162.

Foroughi, A., Sadeghi, K., Parvizifard, A., Parsa Moghadam, A., Davarinejad, O., Farnia, V., & Azar, G. (2020). The effectiveness of mindfulness-based cognitive therapy for reducing rumination and improving mindfulness and self-compassion in patients with treatment-resistant depression. *Trends in Psychiatry and Psychotherapy, 42*, 138–146.

Heyes, C. (2012). *New Thinking: The Evolution of Human Cognition* (Vol. 367, pp. 2091–2096). The Royal Society.

Kabat-Zinn, J. (2003). Mindfulness-based interventions in context: Past, present, and future. *Clinical Psychology: Science and Practice, 10*(2), 144–156.

Krushas, A. E., & Schwartz, J. A. (2022). An examination of the components of toxic stress in childhood and biological markers of physical health in emerging adulthood. *Journal of Child & Adolescent Trauma, 15*(1), 105–119.

Leistner, C., & Menke, A. (2020). Hypothalamic–pituitary–adrenal axis and stress. *Handbook of Clinical Neurology, 175*, 55–64.

Morris, M. C., Bailey, B., Hellman, N., Williams, A., Lannon, E. W., Kutcher, M. E., ... Rao, U. (2020). Dynamics and determinants of cortisol and alpha-amylase responses to repeated stressors in recent interpersonal trauma survivors. *Psychoneuroendocrinology, 122*, 104899.

Parade, S. H., Newland, R. P., Bublitz, M. H., & Stroud, L. R. (2019). Maternal witness to intimate partner violence during childhood and prenatal family functioning alter newborn cortisol reactivity. *Stress, 22*(2), 190–199.

Porges, S. W. (2011). *The Polyvagal Theory: Neurophysiological Foundations of Emotions, Attachment, Communication, and Self-regulation (Norton Series on Interpersonal Neurobiology)*. WW Norton & Company.

Reid, M., Crespo, M., Lay, B., & Berry, J. (2007). Skill acquisition in tennis: Research and current practice. *Journal of Science and Medicine in Sport, 10*(1), 1–10. doi: https://doi.org/10.1016/j.jsams.2006.05.011.

Rodriguez, D. (2021). The art of learning and dealing with disequilibrium. *Research Methods*. Dubuque, IA: Kendall Hunt.

Roetert, E. P., Brown, S. W., Piorkowskil, P. A., & Woods, R. B. (1996). Fitness comparisons among three different levels of elite tennis players. *The Journal of Strength & Conditioning Research, 10*(3), 139–143.

Seo, E., & Kim, S. (2019). Effect of autogenic training for stress response: A systematic review and meta-analysis. *Journal of Korean Academy of Nursing, 49*(4), 361–374.

Thomas, S. J., & Larkin, T. (2020). Cognitive distortions in relation to plasma cortisol and oxytocin levels in major depressive disorder. *Frontiers in Psychiatry, 10*, 971.

Ulbricht, A., Fernandez-Fernandez, J., Mendez-Villanueva, A., & Ferrauti, A. (2016). Impact of fitness characteristics on tennis performance in elite junior tennis players. *The Journal of Strength & Conditioning Research, 30*(4), 989–998. doi: 10.1519/jsc.0000000000001267.

Waples, C. J. (2015). *Receptivity to Feedback: An Investigation of the Influence of Feedback Sign, Feedback Specificity, and Goal Orientation*. Kansas State University.

Wolkin, J. R. (2015). Cultivating multiple aspects of attention through mindfulness meditation accounts for psychological well-being through decreased rumination. *Psychology Research and Behavior Management, 8*, 171–180. doi: 10.2147/PRBM.S31458.

Wulf, G., & Lewthwaite, R. (2016). Optimizing performance through intrinsic motivation and attention for learning: The OPTIMAL theory of motor learning. *Psychonomic Bulletin & Review, 23*, 1382–1414.

7
SKIING

Every day I see pictures or videos of skiing on my social media accounts. It's summer now, and I'm sitting on my porch in a short-sleeved shirt wearing one of my many vests. It's a bit chilly this morning. Yesterday was hot and humid. It rained a lot. I guess that weather brought with it the cooler temperature, making me think of the fall and the coming ski season.

I don't need cooler temperatures or social media posts to keep me thinking about skiing. Skiing is always on my mind. Every time I walk out to my car, I pass my skis and my boots. Most of my t-shirts are ski-themed, or from towns in which I ski. I'm wearing my *Tacos Tacos* t-shirt from Ludlow, Vermont, now. Every time I ski Okemo or Killington in Vermont, I stop by *Tacos Tacos* for one of their legendary chicken burritos. Indeed, my mouth is watering right now as I'm writing these very words, and the sensory memory of their famous hot sauce is making my cheeks and gums tingle as if I was eating a burrito right now.

Skiing wasn't always a passion of mine. In my youth, I wanted to ski but going skiing was beyond my family's means. Neither of my parents grew up around skiing, and growing up in Washington, DC, skiing wasn't exactly within easy reach. There are ski areas around DC, but not close enough to make it enticing to parents, unless skiing is in their blood. If I lived in DC now, I'm sure I would drive to the closest ski areas every weekend. For my parents, though, it wasn't on their minds. Nor could they afford it. My father was a waiter and my mother didn't work; she was a housewife. They had other expenditures to tackle beyond extracurriculars. Unless it was community-organized and low-cost or free, I wouldn't be doing it.

DOI: 10.4324/9781003460800-10

Nevertheless, there were magazines at the drugstore. For young people today, magazines are meaningless. Everything one wants to see is on social media, within easy access. However, when I was young, if it wasn't shown on broadcast television, I would have to see it in print. I used to go to the drugstore regularly and hang out by the magazines. My favorite magazines to look at were the ones with pictures of travel, outdoor activities like hunting and fishing, skateboarding, and the ski magazines. I recall clearly the pictures of ski boots and skis advertised by the manufacturers, and how staring at them was like looking at a beautiful painting. Instead of analyzing the motivation behind the art like scholars do when discussing a masterpiece, I was imagining what it would be like to wear those boots and a colorful ski outfit as I walked to the slopes. I knew nothing of the sport and its culture, but I had an active imagination and could conjure different mountain scenarios.

Skiing was on television too. The legendary program Wide World of Sports was in its prime during my young life, and skiing was among the sports shown frequently. My fondest memories were watching Phil and Steve Mahre compete in the 1970s and 1980s. Watching them was truly inspiring. I wondered what it would be like to compete like them on the circuit, traveling to exotic Alpine destinations in Europe and winning medals. I also remember the Susie Chapstick commercials with former Alpine skier Susie Chaffee, peddling lip balm. Skiing had an appeal similar to other exotic sports belonging to the wealthy, including golf and Formula 1 racing. With their beautiful backgrounds, is it any wonder a young person would desire to be involved? I dreamed hard of one day being able to see those amazing sites and feel the ambiance of the ski lodge with the crackling fire and cozy couches surrounding it.

Life has a way to divert our attention from our dreams, though, especially when the activities we covet are outside our regular experiences. Nevertheless, skiing remained close in mind, and as soon as I started working for pay, I invested in a ski trip. Fortunately for me, I was around the local YMCA frequently. Our YMCA had a tennis club associated with it, and my small income was enough to get me tennis lessons. Although I cannot remember the exact circumstance, I found my way onto a ski trip to a Pennsylvania ski area, Ski Roundtop, just outside Harrisburg, PA. I recall us driving up in a van. It was in January of 1983. I recall this month and year because it was on the same day the Washington football team was playing in the playoffs against the Minnesota Vikings. It must have been very important for me to go skiing, as I was and remain a strong football fan, and the Skins being in the playoffs was indeed a momentous event for me. Nevertheless, there I was on the bunny slope wedging my way down happily as I finally got

to ski. Although I wasn't Phil Mahre that first day, I was skiing, and it was absolutely beautiful. I was having the time of my life.

Interestingly, I was outside Harrisburg recently and decided to drive to Roundtop to sit and read. One of my favorite summer pastimes is pulling out my portable chair and sitting in the shade looking at some beautiful mountain scenery or lake while reading a good book. Wow, Roundtop looked really small to me. It's not because I have grown so much since my teenage visit to the mountain, as I'm probably the same weight and height as I was then. Rather, since that first experience in January of 1983, I have skied in so many different places around the country and have been to some very high and large ski areas. That said, it was quite beautiful to see the mountain and to walk to the bunny hill on which I first learned to ski.

Skiing is an expensive sport, and I knew little about the ski culture except what I imagined in my daydreaming. Had I known what I know now, I could have moved closer to the mountains for college, had a job at the ski area to cover my season pass, and dedicated my free time to learning to ski for free. Instead, though, I lived off of the memories of that first trip and a couple of other trips I took during college with my friends. Fortunately for me, I had friends who wanted to try new things and had cars, and so we went on a few trips to Pennsylvania to ski. Among these were a day trip to Ski Liberty and a weekend trip to Jack Frost and Big Boulder. Once those days were gone, however, so was my skiing until I was in my 40s. Life had taken its turns, and skiing was once again beyond my reach.

My real life as a skier started when I was about 48 years old. My son was a fourth grader, and in Pennsylvania we had a program through which fourth and fifth graders ski for free. One of my neighbors told me about it, and I signed up my son the moment registration was open. Of course, I would go too. I wanted to get back into skiing, and crossed my fingers and toes that my son would love it so we could do it together. Over the prior five years, I tried skiing with him on several occasions. This included a family lesson for my son and me, a children's lesson for my son, and another time when the two of us went to a local bunny slope, we did a run and gave up when my son didn't know how to stop and ran into the b-netting, the netting designed to keep skiers from running off course and into trees and other obstructions. The experiences we had during those earlier attempts were discouraging, but I kept trying because I saw promise, and my son enjoyed it when he was moving.

The fourth- and fifth-grade skiing initiative included a free lesson. We went to Camelback Mountain in the Poconos. I left my son at the lesson and went off to the more advanced bunny slope to practice. To my pleasure, when I returned, my son was so excited that he didn't want to stop. That

had to be one of the happiest days of my life as a father. I had finally found something we could do outside together. Parents seek the ideal activity for their children and go through great pains to find it, not to mention the costs. Thus, when we do find something they love, it's a true joy.

There is a saying among ski instructors that skiing is easy to learn but hard to master, whereas snowboarding is hard to learn but easy to master. Both activities are amazing, and I don't want to take anything away from snowboarding, for some of my most memorable sliding experiences involved snowboarding. However, I have to agree that skiing is a truly difficult sport to master, with new levels emerging whenever we feel we have mastered the art.

When I returned to skiing, my primary aim was assuring my son succeeded in the sport. I wanted him to become an expert skier. I also, however, desired for us to one day travel to exotic ski resorts and enjoy all the amenities associated with the ski experience. Yet, I wasn't aware of what becoming an expert skier meant. Indeed, the first time we skied together down a short green slope, I was frightened. My son flew down the trail as kids do, with me lagging behind.[1] Despite my fear, though, I vowed to myself that I would not allow my fears to show, as I worried that showing how scared I am would make him anxious and ruin his ability to progress. My decision had its moments, as my son kept on pushing the limits. At times he was scared, and I would march forward as if I hadn't a care in the world. I was scared but went anyway. It paid off enormously, for both of us.

Progressing up the skiing ladder should be done with the guidance of a good ski instructor. One problem with skiing is that lessons are quite expensive, especially private lessons. Group lessons are more affordable. However, there is no guarantee that a student will attain what he desires, particularly if there is diversity in skill within a group. Teachers generally teach to the lowest ability skier. This is good, as we all need to improve upon our basic skills. Nevertheless, one's progress slows if group members can't ski together. That said, ski instructors ensure students do not ski trails or slopes above their ability level and use the best available terrain to teach fundamentals. With those fundamentals in hand, one is ready to move up the mountain to more advanced terrain.

Knowing the signs and symbols

Given my penchant for Jungian psychology, you may be thinking I'm going to delve into the collective unconscious here, with some archetypes about skiing. Not so. I'm referring to signs and symbols on ski trails, as seen on one's favorite ski trail map. Ski trail ratings vary among mountains.[2] In the United States, green trails are the easiest trails. Blue trails are intermediate

trails. Black diamonds are advanced trails, with double and triple black diamond trails increasing the difficulty many times fold. There are also trails labeled extreme. Yet, what is a green trail on one mountain may be a blue or even black diamond on another. For instance, I ski at Snowbird in Utah whenever I can. One of the slopes, Big Emma, is blue for about a half (top half) and then green for the bottom half. This slope would be a black diamond in some smaller ski areas. Indeed, some of their blue trails would be double black diamonds on a Pennsylvania mountain. Still, most skiers treat these trail ratings as if they were universal. We see skiers expect that all green trails are easy and accessible to a beginner, even a first-time skier. This is not the case. In my home mountain, Blue Mountain Resort, our two long green trails on the mountain are far more difficult than our bunny trails. Bunny trails are meant for absolute beginners. One of our green trails, Burma Road is winding with many short but relatively steep curves. Further, Burma Road gets very busy as it's not merely a beginner trail; it's also a transit route from the summit lodge to the base lodge. Our other green trail, Paradise, is much wider but also has some steepness. Absolute beginners and novices don't belong on these trails until they know how to turn confidently and come to a complete stop without falling. Nevertheless, we find absolute beginners on these trails all the time, as their friends told them they could learn without an instructor. That's a big mistake and a sure way to make skiing nothing more than a bucket list item.

My strategy with my son was to not let him be afraid. I also signed him up for lessons frequently. Indeed, he's 21 and in college now and I still gift him lessons, although now he and his instructor work on refining his skills and tackling more interesting terrain. Yet, in those early days, while I helped him deal with discomfort on steeps and other obstacles, I didn't do myself any favors. I would go down the trails but pizza my way along. He kept getting better, while I struggled to make it to the end of the run, and the day. After a while, skiing became a chore for me. Despite the ambiance of the amazing ski areas we visited, each time I was on a run, I was awaiting the end of the day, hoping I would make it without getting hurt. I wasn't having the fun I imagined I would have.

Fearing for my safety, as I did, while evolutionarily adaptive, does not make for safe skiing. To ski safely, one must have the correct balance. Fear contradicts good balance. When we are afraid, we tend to move our weight back, as we seek to avoid going headlong into what seems like a blazing fire. Skiing is about approaching the slope, not retreating to flatter ground. If one wants to avoid a slope, one shouldn't ski. Skiing is about navigating one's way down a gradient (slope) and having fun doing so. Indeed, when I'm teaching absolute beginners who show fear, and fall, I point out the reason they fell. It's as if they fell on purpose because they are more comfortable

being on the ground than on their skis. Their weight is over their heels rather than the center of their feet, with their weight pushing backward the further they travel down the slope. I tell them that skiing is about going down the hill and to be a good skier one has to want to go down the hill. Good balance makes skiing safer. Falling, by contrast, although relieving the fear of an uncontrolled descent can result in severe injury or even death. I would rather stay on the trail than have someone find me in pieces among the trees.

Lessons help students learn how to balance. As a ski instructor, I have taken many lessons. I attend multiple workshops to improve my skiing, and I listen to feedback. I also practice everything I learn, including balance drills. This wasn't the case in my first five years of skiing with my son. During that period, I skied on my own or with him. I paid for his lessons but did nothing to improve my own skiing. I mostly skied on my heels as I was afraid. Verbally and behaviorally, I refused to show fear in front of my son. Yet, to an expert my scared skiing style must have been as evident as it is now to me when I watch novices ski down trails on which they don't belong. As a result, I had plenty of falls. I didn't fall every time I skied, but when I did it was quite painful and memorable. It created complexes that affected how I skied every run and especially how I skied sloppy snow.

Skiing sloppy snow

In the east, snow varies in its consistency, from ice to mashed potatoes. Mashed potato snow is snow that is thick, heavy, and piles up into skier-made moguls. At times, the moguls can be so high that one can scarcely see other skiers. It's especially common when we have a streak of milder weather. Naturally, one must have good balance to remain stable across varying conditions. Given my history of falling, I came to fear snow conditions in warmer temperatures. My fear was so strong that I would do my best to avoid skiing when it got warmer than 32 degrees, if possible, or would ski extra cautiously as the temperatures rose. Unfortunately, as one cannot control the weather, and my son has no such fear, I skied quite often in these conditions and I hated it. I recall one day we were skiing on Loon Mountain in New Hampshire. It was a beautiful warm day and I was having a great time being there, but I was afraid to get on the mountain. Yet, I couldn't show my fear to my son, so I skied with him. I had a miserable time wedging my way through the rutted snow and couldn't wait for the day to end. That wasn't what I wanted out of skiing and I never spoke of it to my son. He was having a great time and was becoming better with each trip. I was essentially becoming worse with each trip.

Overcoming fears

Four years ago, I passed my Professional Ski Instructors of America (PSIA) level-one ski instructor test. For good skiers, the skiing portion of the test is not much of an accomplishment, and they are right. If one can ski and has a good attitude about teaching, one will likely pass the test. Receiving my pin, I felt amazing though. To me, it was a validation of my efforts to improve my skiing. I was in my third year of teaching. I waited to take the test in order to ensure I had improved my technique enough to pass a basic skiing part. With the help of the many lessons I took during my time as an instructor, I had improved. However, my balance remained an issue, and as a result I still fell in difficult snow conditions. Perhaps it was fate or good luck (from a Psychoadaptation perspective), but our two-day certification process took place in 60-degree weather. We were at Bear Creek Mountain Resort, a small mountain with a beautiful lodge in Macungie, PA. It was so warm that I skied in a t-shirt and vest. The testing took place over two days, Sunday and Monday. The first day was crowded. In addition to fearing mashed potato snow, I also came to fear crowding. Think about how complexes appropriate circumstances and grow. I feared bad snow and falling. Seeing people around me triggered the thought of accidents when falling, including hurting others. Indeed, on one such day skiing down Great Northern in Killington, Vermont, an absolute beginner snowboarder slid across my path, and I couldn't stop. Instead, I flew over him and landed hard on my left shoulder. It took months of physical therapy to repair that injury. Crowded conditions were now as fear-provoking to me as was rutted snow.

It was crowded on that Sunday, and the snow was rutty. Great for me, I thought. Despite my fears, I of course understood the nature of learning and the importance of disequilibrium in the learning process. The conditions created disequilibrium, and when I had my druthers, I would avoid them. In those situations, disequilibrium won. When I couldn't avoid doing so, I had to confront the disequilibrium and I won. Actually, I could always avoid conditions I feared. However, that goes against my mission to become the best possible skier I can be. To do so, I must challenge myself and do so correctly. By correctly I mean with the help of experts.

The level-one certification process is educational as well as an assessment. The first day, the examiner analyzed our skiing. The second day was about our teaching. Monday was warmer than Sunday, and the snow was extra sticky. This was ripe for overcoming my disequilibrium. Indeed, the examiner showed us how to ski in these conditions. He told us to carve more to reduce the friction from our skis on the snow. My skis were sticking and adding wax didn't help much. Yet when I started carving more, I cruised down the hill

faster. He also told us that to maximize our carving, we should act as if we were about to make a hockey stop but don't, carve instead. The lessons in these conditions increased my sense of competence tenfold. Moreover, the fact that we were on the snow all day, despite my wish at times to call to quit for the day, was a major victory over my disequilibrium. Defeating complexes is like fighting a war. There are many battles, and we often lose. Yet, if we persevere we can win the war. Those two days and all the skiing we did were essential to my long-term development as a skier. I can now stay on the mountain all day and be happy doing so. That was indeed a watershed moment for me. Sadly, though, it wasn't long after that the skiing season ended due to Covid-19. My son and I had a trip planned for Utah and like everyone else, our plans were squashed. Still, I dealt a major blow to my complex, and I felt for the first time that I was on the path to victory against this demon I had been fighting against for years.

My PSIA Level I testing experience was important to me. I skied several times after that until we could ski no more due to Covid-19. I recall the last day of the season. It was a Sunday, and I went to Blue Mountain Resort for a few last turns. I was feeling sick to my stomach about the whole pandemic situation. I lost my motivation and fun skiing, and after one run down the mountain, I packed up my skis and left. The mountain closed early that day too, as the world began shutting down for a long time.

Heavy snow

The following year was the Covid-19 skiing year, and perhaps the best snow year I have experienced as a skier in Pennsylvania. It snowed a great deal, and there were some deep snow days indeed. The rules were different because of Covid-19, but people skied a lot. People worked from home, which meant that they could go skiing on weekdays. So, the mountains were crowded, even if ownership attempted to limit attendance for public health reasons. Conditions weren't always groomed. As I was learning to deal with challenging conditions, the increased snow and the crowds were a mixed site for me. Yet, when the season ended, I felt as though I had progressed greatly from a mental perspective. I was forced to adapt to so many different conditions that I became a better skier. The more one goes skiing, the more comfortable one gets with different conditions. To overcome disequilibrium, therefore, one must welcome variations in conditions and persist through them.

Some days were difficult in the 20/21 season, and there were many times I hesitated due to my disequilibrium. Yet, at no time did I stop skiing. I gathered myself and continued down trails with varying snow conditions. Listening to the advice of better skiers, I appropriated the information and

practiced it. One key moment was on a heavy snow day at Blue Mountain. I was skiing one of my favorite runs, Switchback, and the trail was filled with what appeared to be the dreaded skier-made moguls. I stopped in the middle of a run. One of my favorite ski instructors, TB, was leisurely skiing down the trail, making it look so easy. He stopped by me and I told him I don't know how to ski in these conditions. He told me not to make so many sharp turns, as that only increases the moguls by pushing more snow into piles. Instead, he noted, I have to ski right through them. These moguls were not of the solid kind made by skiers in warmer conditions, nor were they machine-made moguls. Instead, one could ski right through them. I followed what TB said and made it down fine, and faster than I would have with my fearful skiing style. I listened to someone with greater knowledge and skill than I had. More importantly, though, I followed his advice and continued practicing. In my prior skiing experience, particularly in the early years, I would have left the mountain after that run, without additional practice. For the first time now, I had the urge to continue. The negative thoughts were there, urging me to stop. However, there were more thoughts urging me to ski on and practice what I had learned. I followed the latter. Listening to pros who have a skier's best interests in mind, and trusting what they say, is one of the most important ingredients to becoming an expert skier.

Skiing is about taking what one learns from a lesson and practicing it. It's about dedicating time to practice. For a while, skiing becomes like a chore, as one works on drills that are not necessarily fun at the time but have the benefit of making the skier better. Best of all, when done correctly, the fun will come, with tenfold power, if not more. I spent many days working on drills. Yet, one cannot practice drills unless one gets drills to practice. Sadly, it's not enough to watch YouTube videos to learn drills, at least until one has mastery. As such, unless one is an advanced skier, one needs to have drills taught face-to-face by an instructor who can evaluate the skier's ability to perform the drills correctly.

Another very important day in my development as a skier also came during the 20/21 season. I took a workshop from a young instructor, IR, who was practicing for his PSIA Level III alpine exam. I signed up for a workshop on short turns. Fortunately for me, I was the only person attending. Thus, I got a two-hour private lesson on short turns. My complexes were playing games with me that morning. First, it was snowing, meaning that the conditions weren't going to be groomed. Relatedly, the mountain would likely be crowded, as people chase powder in skiing, at least they do if they can reach the mountain. Third, although I like having lessons, I've never had one lasting that long. These fears were mixing around in my head like disequilibrium soup. Then, coach IR was late. I waited and waited at the

meeting location, and he wasn't there. I kept wanting to leave as that was the perfect excuse to satisfy my complexes. Yet, I didn't. For as I knew, the only way to get better would be to confront and overcome my disequilibrium. I stayed and had one of the most amazing experiences of my skiing career.

Coach IR and I skied a lot that day and practiced on our steepest terrain. This was important because of my displeasure with messy snow. What better way to defeat disequilibrium than to charge into it headlong, embrace it with a massive hug, and then walk it to the trash heap where it belongs. That day we practiced short turns one after another, and coach IR critiqued my style and made sure I was mastering the correct stance. As usual, balance was an issue. As the gradient increased, I tended to fall further into the back seat, precluding my ability to control my skis well. He gave me many drills to work on, including a drill I now do regularly, which starts by skating on my skis and progresses to making short turns. Also important is having a separation between the skis and the upper body, such that the upper body points down the fall line as much as possible, while the skis move side to side (rotation) (Coffey et al., 2014). If done correctly, there is little skidding and smooth skiing on the edges.

By the end of the season, I was feeling comfortable with these drills and making better short turns. Although I'm sure I am not where I should be technique-wise on my short turns, I made great progress from that point to now. Indeed, I use them regularly, especially on steeper terrain as short turns control speed. One of my favorite experiences using short turns was skiing in Snowbird, Utah later that season. I was skiing down a blue run, Bassackwards, which has a very steep but short section somewhere after the middle of the run. I didn't hesitate at all because I felt so much control using short turns. Even though I was skiing for fun that day, each turn I made was a practice turn. Further, having the lesson helped me to critique my performance, as if I were watching myself from above. Without the lesson, I most likely would have been struggling down the run. Instead, I felt like I was Mikaela Shiffrin. Lessons mean a lot.

Practice and experience are key. Yet, it's not always easy to hit every possible condition in every lesson. Some conditions are unlikely to happen in the mid-Atlantic region. Although we do get powder days, when there is a lot of fresh snow, and it's deep, they are rare. Further, with the population density in the region and the small size of our mountains, powder disappears like fresh scones from the bakery shelves in the morning. In the same season, I encountered powder on several occasions. In the movies and on social media, skiers post these amazing images of skiing deep powder, and they seem to be having the time of their lives. Truthfully, though, it's not easy to ski powder. For one, a skier must have the right skis to do so effectively. Although skiers like Lindsey Vonn can ski powder with their racing skis,

most skiers need wide skis, and the skis we use for navigating ice in the east aren't ideal for skiing deep powder, where floating is more important than carving. Second, one must regulate pressure correctly to float on snow.

Our trip to Utah was a powder fest. Traveling to Utah or Colorado is best for me in the latter season, March to April, as there's a lot of snow and fewer people. When my son and I skied Alta, it was snowing hard. Indeed, we were lucky to be able to get to Alta at all with all the snow. I always rent four-wheel drive vehicles when traveling west in anticipation of snow, as travel can be treacherous or illegal without the appropriate traction, tires, or chains when there is snow. I decided I would work on my powder skiing, having heard what one should do in such conditions. I learned to bounce up and down as I was skiing to keep light on the snow. I did that, as well as centered my weight back a bit to prevent my skis from sinking tips first into the snow. My son and I tried a few easier powder runs, and I was having fun. On one such run, as we were heading from the Sunnyside to the Supreme lift, we took a nice little powder run that merged onto Dipsy Doodle, a green path to our next lift. I recall how beautiful it felt with the fine powder spraying around my skis. I didn't turn for I wanted to allow myself to feel what it was like to enjoy what is widely believed to be the world's finest powder. It was beautiful indeed. Powder does, however, occlude obstacles, so one knows not what lies below. I recall that instead of skiing smoothly onto Dipsy Doodle as I expected, we hit a bump of sorts, and jumped. Fortunately, I was able to turn quickly enough to stay on the green trail instead of hitting some unfortunate trees.

Skiing powder requires lessons. As I was doing my last run of the day before leaving, I again skied down an easier powder run, either Bluebell or Race Hill. Now, as I felt comfortable skiing in some easier powder runs, I was making a right turn when without warning I flew and landed face-first in the snow. Some very kind skier came over to check if I was alright. I told her yes and wondered if there was something in the snow I hit. She said probably not, and that everything looked fine to her. Discussing this event with fellow ski instructors later that year and the next, I learned that the most likely reason for the fall was my stance and my ski width. The powder, though fine, was deep. If one has the wrong balance for powder, given a narrower ski width, one's tips can dig into the snow and eventually trip the skier. Thankfully, because the powder is so fine at Alta, falling means nothing more than a face full of powder. Nevertheless, falling in deep powder can have some negative consequences. For instance, one can lose equipment. I lost one of my beloved ski poles. I've had these poles since I first started skiing again, and losing the one I lost made me a bit sad. Second, if one is not careful, one can lose skis in the deep snow. One of my skis came off during the fall and buried itself quite deep. It took some fine detective work

on my part to find it. I did and skied down to meet my son, who as usual was waiting for me. What an important learning experience. As Piaget noted, life is adaptation (Piaget, 1951). One continues to meet new constraints as one progresses from a novice to expertise, and with changes in constraints comes disequilibrium. Despite our best efforts to do so, disequilibrium never leaves us, like a good friend with an obsession.

Becoming a good skier is harder than one can imagine when one first puts on a pair of boots. First, one must have a lesson. I have seen absolute beginners[3] try to learn on their own, and although some can make their way down a hill through sheer perseverance and a willingness to take many falls, I would guess the vast majority fail and then quit. Having the basics is a requirement to progress. Indeed, one gets much of the information necessary to become a good skier in the first lesson, including discussions of balance, pressure, and edging, as well as feedback to improve performance (Coffey et al., 2014; Marshall, 2001). I wish that was enough, but one needs additional lessons to get the feedback necessary to prevent the formation of bad habits and injuries (Wojtyczek et al., 2014). One may learn quickly, as I did the first time I put on skis, but without additional training, one gets locked into skiing like a beginner. Beginners do not ski like experts. Beginners use rotation more than edging. If you, my reader, imagine a vertical line piercing the center of the body from top to bottom, rotation is spinning the body around that axis.

Rotation has its place in advanced skiing, such as when one skis mogul runs or needs to brush off speed. However, good skiers use their edges to turn. While edging is always present even with pizza skiing (wedging), it's secondary to rotation among novice skiers. The problem is that once someone gets comfortable wedging and rotating down a mountain, it's hard for them to disengage and French-fry ski. I love using ski vernacular, such as pizza and french-fries, as that's the way we speak when teaching. French-fry skiing is also known as parallel skiing. This is more difficult to achieve for some, as French-fry skiing results in going faster, and that can be quite scary. For others, body alignment issues may interfere with good form. It's really difficult for one to learn parallel skiing on one's own because once one skis fast, one must stop, and stopping isn't intuitive when skiing. Most beginners stop with either a braking wedge or by falling. A braking wedge is an extreme pizza, where the angle between the ski tips increases dramatically. This forces the ski-tip edges to dig into the snow and reduce speed. I teach the braking wedge for lift lines. I tell my students that in general we don't like to teach the braking wedge because it doesn't promote good skiing form. However, at times one needs to stop in tight spaces, such as a lift line, so as to prevent touching others' skis or boards. Some people are very protective of their equipment and can get angry if one touches their

skis or boards. With some equipment costing well over $1,000, I see their points.

The braking wedge isn't comfortable either, at least for adult skiers, especially on steeper slopes. A better strategy is to J turn, coming to a complete stop (Coffey et al., 2014). Done at high speeds, the J turn stop essentially becomes a hockey stop. The hockey stop is an efficient way to come to a complete stop. The skis are pointed perpendicular to the fall line, and pressure is disproportionately applied to the downhill ski (Komissarov, 2021). That's my favorite way to stop. One needs guidance and practice to learn these skills. Organized programs provide for this experience. Importantly, the learner receives performance feedback. Sadly, we cannot see ourselves skiing unless someone videotapes us. Thus, having someone to critique us will provide the necessary feedback to become a better skier.

The 21/22 ski season was my best ski season to that point in time. The following year, 2022/2023 was even better. Because of my motivation to one day become an expert skier, I continue to challenge myself. I seek out feedback when possible, attend organized programs, and practice what I've learned. My motivation to progress and my willingness to listen to others' feedback makes me an ideal student. Further, because I don't discriminate against younger instructors, I can learn from anyone, for when it comes to learning, experience isn't judged by age; it's judged by time spent on the task.

Learning to race

I always wanted to race. From my days watching the Mahre brothers on Wide World of Sports, I imagined myself running gates. It looked so beautiful and effortless. Surely, I can do that, I thought, if only I had the opportunity. Well, finally I had the opportunity, but it was not easy. Indeed, I venture to say that ski racers are the best skiers on the mountain. Not only do they have the best form, but they can handle difficult conditions. Unlike a tennis court that doesn't generally change from day to day,[4] snow conditions vary by the hour. Unless one has people slip a course between runs,[5] prior skiers affect what subsequent skiers will face when running the gates. Weather changes too. While skiers crave powder, if it's snowing, racing becomes difficult if not impossible. These differences are magnified for skiers with anxieties about bad conditions, like myself.

My first experience running gates came through an adult ski-racing program at Blue Mountain Resort in the 2014/2015 season, my third year of committed skiing. This program ran once weekly and provided two-and–a-half hours of gate running and organized practice, as well as lots of feedback. I recall one day watching a video taken of the participants.

The head instructor was critiquing our performance, then he watched me and said nothing. I was slow and couldn't navigate the turns without wedging. My edge angle was probably less than 10%. I looked out of place. Interestingly, as I was running the gates I felt as if I was a skier just as good as the Mahre brothers or Mikaela Shiffrin. Without the feedback, then, I wouldn't have known how far away I was from even being a bad ski racer.

I continued running gates in the program yearly until the pandemic forced an end to adult training. Finally, it returned in the 2022–2023 season, but on a day that I couldn't attend due to my work schedule. Yet, I continued to train wherever possible and participate in Mid-Atlantic Masters ski racing each year. Despite the training, I'm not even close to being competitive. I marvel at how easily the athletes run gates. Good racers know how to manage all facets of their skiing, and running gates well requires mastering balance, pressure, edging, and rotation, as well as knowing exactly where to initiate the turn before the next gate for the best line around it (Spörri et al., 2012). In the 2021–2022 season, for the first time I attended a PSIA alpine race clinic. It was another watershed moment in my skiing career, for it was the first time I attended a two-days event for training purposes. The event is held several times yearly at different locations. I attended the clinic at Ski Butternut, a small ski area in Great Barrington, Massachusetts.

The days I attended the clinic were very cold and windy, although it was sunny; the temperature never went above 10 degrees Fahrenheit. In the first half of the day we did high-performance skiing. In the second half, we ran gates. Our days went from 8:45 AM to 4 PM. By this time, many of my fears related to injury and snow conditions faded. Although the conditions were ideal for my skiing preference (i.e., cold), there were ice spots and some obstacles in the snow that made skiing a bit less easy than I would have expected for cold weather. The steps we took to ensure safety are ideal, and they are the reason I love PSIA events; health and safety come before performance. Nevertheless, as this is a performance clinic, the focus was on high-performance skiing.

When our leader said we would be doing high-performance skiing, my mind flashed back to the day when the Blue Mountain Racing coach watched me wedge down through our gates. "Wow," I thought to myself. Imagine me skiing high performance. I was sure I'd not do well, but at least I'd be around caring professionals who would help me through any problem areas. Indeed, as much as I love free skiing and learning, I long for skiing better through gates. As such, I craved the type of feedback that would improve my performance.

We started by doing a couple of warm-up runs. A big mistake many skiers make is trying to ski fast and hard on their first run. It's critical to take time to warm up. We went down a nice blue run from the summit. I felt that

I skied well. After those first runs, we started going full tilt. We were given skills to work on to improve our performance, including ankle flexion. It's key to flex hard when skiing hard, and relaxing one's ankles means keeping them flexed, but not as flexed as when navigating a turn. We also focused on the inside ski. Our leader told us that we already focus a great deal on the outside ski in training, but not enough attention is given to the inside ski. It too should be active.

The first part of the day was hard work. Then came the gates. The team of instructors set up slalom gates. Slalom is something I really want to master. It's the most technical of the technical ski events (slalom and giant slalom). Gates are close together, allowing about one second between turns, and then there are interesting gate combinations that I've yet to master cognitively. Makes sense for now, as my mind's focus is on mastering the skiing required to navigate the gates. I will learn the gate combinations later.

The instructors set up two sets of gates, one for those wanting to run through traditional gates, and one with brushes. As much as I desire to knock down gates, I am clearly not there yet, so I stuck to the brushes. Knocking down gates is actually skiing through gates. As the saying goes, the shortest distance between two points is a straight line or the fastest line, and it generally does not involve a massive turn radius (Spörri et al., 2012). Good skiers get their skis around the gates, allowing their bodies to smash through the gates. Gates hurt, though, so slalom racers protect their bodies with armor. They wear chin bars on their helmets, shin guards, and hand protectors, among other protective equipment. When done correctly, skiers knock down gates with their hand guards. The hand guards are attached to the ski poles and are likely the first surface hitting the gates as the skier advances. I have been told by race coaches that the skier does not punch the gate, as some racers do, but rather the skier's position forces the hands to meet the gates as the skier advances.

Brushes by contrast to gates are short, and rise inches above the snow. Yet, with the distance between brushes being so short, turning correctly and without skidding is key. My biggest issue in ski racing is that I skid my turns. To an outsider who knows nothing about skiing, I'm sure I look fine when I ski through gates, and far better than I did when I started. Yet, to other skiers who race, the skidding is evident. My big issue is that I don't get enough of an edge angle when running the gates. Edge angle is important as it locks the ski into the snow and allows the ski's engineered performance to flourish (Coffey et al., 2014). Skidding, by contrast, increases friction. Friction decreases speed. As skiers with the fastest times win races, skidding is counterproductive to race performance.

Thus far, I've focused primarily on giant slalom (GS) Masters events. I have yet to try slalom. I struggle to get through the slalom gates because

I over turn. There is a critical zone in ski racing in which the skier must initiate a turn to minimize time through the gates (Spörri et al., 2012). I'm always late. Perhaps it's because I started skiing so late in my life that I can't react quickly enough, or perhaps it's some deficit in my physio-cognitive processing. It could also be that I get so happy that I make it through a gate that I neglect to start the next turn as I perseverate on my prior success. The problem is that if one messes up timing on one turn, it's highly unlikely that one can recover thereafter. As such, many of my slalom runs end with me washing out of the course. Interestingly, this past season (2022–2023) I tried a Super G race for the first time. The race was held at Gore Mountain in New York, on Echo, a blue trail with some steep turns. I loved it! I was a bit nervous at first, having seen how close some of the gates were to the edge of the run. However, a Super G involves less turning and more speed, so I thought I would enjoy that, and I did. I ran it with GS skis, so that wasn't a plus for me. However, since it was my first time, I thought it wouldn't matter. I wanted the experience to see how it would feel, and I accomplished that.

Perseverance is key to learning. Being able to accept one's desire to quit but let it go is critical to success (Rodriguez, 2021). Returning to the PSIA training event at Ski Butternut, we spent a good two to three hours at the gates, and there were many times that I wanted to quit. However, quitting has never been a characteristic of mine. Hopefully, my good reader, I've made this abundantly clear by now. I feel the desire to quit and I could make an easy excuse to do so, but for some reason I never allow myself to quit. I keep moving forward. As time advanced, I started having some success through the brushes. I didn't feel good because I struggled, but I felt sated because I never quit. I stayed until the end and was satisfied with a good day's work. Plus, the next day would be GS training, and for me GS is easier than slalom. So, I looked forward to a nice meal and a good glass of wine to finish my day.

I arrived early on the second day of the alpine race clinic. I hung out in the lodge a bit. Ski Butternut has an old-fashioned lodge that harkens back to the days of old, when the skis were narrow and prices were low. I was excited for another day of skiing. I kept my mind calm like a New England frozen pond in February. My mind likes to wander, imagining the most negative outcomes. I'm not sure why I am like that, but I tend to think of all the worst-case scenarios first. I guess that helps me prepare to be my best. In academics and teaching, it comes in handy. Although I have to deal with the physiological consequences of anticipatory anxiety at the time, I also prepare to ensure the worst case doesn't come to be. At times though, nothing can be done other than wait out the anxious thoughts. At those times, I fall back into my mindfulness practice, and the thoughts flush down some psychological drain to nowhere land and I feel at peace.

I was excited about doing GS gates, but then thought about the possibility of doing poorly there too. It was training, though, and knowing the way PSIA instructors teach, I felt more at ease. It's interesting that ski race coaches ignore bad skiers. Indeed, if one isn't a top performer, one virtually doesn't exist. I have seen this with youth ski racers, where coaches do all but hand-feed their star racers. Yet, when it comes to the mediocre racer, the individual is isolated. This happens despite racers and parents (juniors' programs) paying the same amounts of money for training. I respect ski racing and the coaches, but I disagree with their treatment of the less gifted or newer skier. I guess it's a meritocracy, but it shouldn't be when one pays for training. At the World Cup or college level, where athletes are sponsored by companies, institutions, and countries, unequal treatment based on merit is acceptable. Yet, in training where families invest large sums of money for coaching, this treatment is in my view unacceptable.

We don't see this in PSIA, and that's why I prefer PSIA over other training. I can afford to go to summer camps, as many individuals I know in masters racing do so. One racer I know has been suggesting I attend training on a glacier in the summer. He does it every year. Sounds beautiful but I'm not quite there yet to benefit from it, nor am I convinced I would receive the attention I would pay for. I want to be the best my body will allow me to do, but until I have the competence to match my desire, investment is likely futile.

On the second day, like the first, we started with high-performance skiing. I was feeling good and skied well. We were on a different side of the mountain, focusing primarily on the blue and black diamond trails, Freewheeler and Downspout, respectively. These runs were beautiful that morning. The temperature leaped out of the teens to the low 20s. With the sunshine, I felt nice and toasty warm. We focused on our feet and keeping our legs active while our upper bodies were relaxed. We made many runs, and with each run I gained confidence in my performance. I was skiing my 170 cm Head Supershape i.Titan skis. I bought these to learn to carve and I am not disappointed with their performance. They are advanced skis though. Equipment is important in sport, but just because one has the money doesn't mean one should purchase the best equipment. I learned that on the first day of skiing with my Supershapers. The first run down an easy slope at the start of the 2019/2020 season, I caught an edge and fell. Yet, with time, I have come to love these skis. Nevertheless, they are not the best option for training GS. Still, given my focus on learning to ski correctly, they are a good option. I do have a pair of GS skis that I purchased the year before, thinking that somehow the equipment would make me the skier I wanted to be. I have a pair of 2016 176-cm Volkl Racetiger skis that I could have brought with me, but I feared skiing all day in them as they are faster

and narrower than my Supershapers. Remember, complexes have people, and I guess I allowed my old snow-condition complex to usurp my mind the day I was packing my equipment to go. Interestingly, though, another skier at the event discussed her trepidation about using her GS skis on that day, so perhaps I'm not the only one with such a complex. Nevertheless, since then, I have skied much with those skis, even on a warm day in sticky snow. Complexes may have us, but a good strategy and perseverance can begin to tear down even the most stubborn complex.

We spent the second half of the day back on the race course, adjacent to Main Street. Conditions were perfect like the day before. With time and all the skiers running down the course, the ice began to show. It is said that Eastern skiers are born on ice. I suppose that's because our conditions vary greatly, and ice is always involved at some point. Ice is not ideal for individuals unable to carve well. Thus, I had to focus more heavily on carving mastery. One of our instructors videotaped me running the gates. This was the first time since the Blue Mountain Racing coach videotaped me years earlier that I would be able to see myself running gates on film. After I completed my run and then a few more, and the coach finished filming every skier's run, he rode the lift up with me and shared what he saw. I saw where I failed to grip the snow, as my edge angle wasn't high enough. Low edge angles mean poor ski performance and a propensity to skid and lose time (Coffey et al., 2014). I told him that my biggest issue is that I lose time in skiing gates. I'm not afraid of the gates and want to attack them but I can't seem to get faster. The video was helpful. He told me about the negative facets of my skiing the gates, such as me skiing too upright and not using my polls correctly, and the low edge angles. However, he pointed to the positive facets of my skiing as well, such as when I initiated the turns correctly. He also told me to use the video to improve my skiing, and as a baseline for comparing future performance.

I ran gates as many times as I possibly could that day. I even worked with one coach independently on a cowboy turns drill to improve my carving. For this drill, I essentially made a wide stance, as if straddling a horse. As I skied, the aim was to ski completely on my edges. It was hard, so we worked on calmer terrain. I loved the effort to help me improve upon my deficit. Yet, the best moment of the entire trip came when one fellow participant came to me and told me that he and one of the instructors celebrated when they saw the bottom of my skis during one of my runs. It was funny, but I was elated. This means that I was on edge enough that they could see the bottom of my skis. I often tell others that the only time I'll be happy in my learning is when a ski instructor or a very good skier tells me that I am skiing well or doing something correctly. I am a tough person to please when it comes to my own personal development.

Technology in skiing

I wish every day skiing would include feedback. Unfortunately, feedback is expensive. Skiers must have someone follow them to get feedback on their skiing. That means one needs a fellow skier to ski slower than the person being observed, and one must either pay for that or have good friends willing to do so, perhaps taking turns being the observer. I ask my son to observe me from time to time and am thankful when he does it. Yet, I ski more by myself than I do with others, and that makes it hard for me to judge my performance. I suppose I can burry my phone somewhere in the woods, ride the lift uphill, and then film myself skiing downhill. I know one skier who does that, but I don't trust my battery to last that long, or that my phone wouldn't be stolen. Then came ski technological advances like Carv.

I thought a great deal about getting private lessons but the price is too high. Although I can count on others to help me out with new drills and to watch me ski periodically, I want momentary assessment and feedback in real-time. I can't ask others to do that for me, as it is neither realistic nor fair, as they ski for their own reasons. Nevertheless, it is important to note that one of the greatest benefits I have received from being a ski instructor is having other ski instructors share their wisdom with me. Others have critiqued my performance, providing valuable feedback. I am eternally grateful for this, as despite the timing and my mental state when I receive the feedback (i.e., readiness for disequilibrium), I need to hear feedback from other professionals. However, none of this compares to continuous real-time feedback. Luckily, there is technology to do that.

Over the past several years, I have read about the development of technology that provides real-time skiing feedback. As a PSIA member, I am fortunate to receive membership discounts on different equipment and technologies. One such technology is the Carv system ("Carv," 2023). Given the role feedback plays within the Psychoadaptation process (Rodriguez, 2021), and my belief that the best feedback is in real-time, I decided to invest in Carv. The system relies on insoles with pressure and motion sensors that submit information to an app. Data generated from these sensors (36 pressure sensors and one motion sensor) provide information on one's balance, rotation, pressure, and edging performance. Within each of these areas, one can view one's performance after a run and analyze it on different facets of these four domains. Within the balance domain, Carv assesses skiers on the start and end of the turn, and topple. Toppling, according to the description on the Carv app, initiates what I believe my instructor colleagues like to call *forangular* movement. As one initiates the next turn, the body should move forward and diagonally into the new turn as if toppling. This toppling is then countered by one's

upper body, the result being that the pressure is on the inside of the outside ski. Ideally, this means a banana-shaped body while carving. Using your imagination, my eager reader, visualize your body like a banana, with your legs being the neck (the part you pull to peel it) and your torso curving to the flower tip ("Bananas, 2023").

For edging, there are four skills: early edging, edge angle, edge similarity, and edge smoothness, along with a graph showing where edging is best during the turn for left and right turns. For pressure, there is outside ski pressure, pressure smoothness, and turn comparison, the latter comparing one's ability to transfer pressure to the outside ski when turning left and right. There's also a graphic that shows when pressure is ideal for both turns. Rotary assesses parallel skiing and turn shape, with C-shaped turns scoring higher than Z-shaped turns.

Based on the data accumulated on these four domains, along with one's goals set when one registers (e.g., carving like a racer), one receives a ski IQ score. There are seven levels of IQ (with names), ranging from 50–90 (Green Guru) to 150+ (Grim Ripper). One is assigned an IQ after each run and can evaluate one's IQ for each turn on each run. Using GPS (Global Positioning System), one also receives other information, including speed and distance skied. I am currently a level 5 (Carv Connoisseur), with my highest IQ to date being 131. Although I don't always ski at that level, and my IQ depends on the terrain, I was happy to achieve that level by the end of the ski season. I scored much lower, below 100 when I first started using Carv.

Receiving data after one completes a run isn't real-time. Although extremely useful, I wanted data during my run. Thankfully, that's available too. Wearing headphones during a run, one receives feedback, particularly when training. Carv provides training modes, with suggested drills based on one's weaker points. Balance has been an issue of mine, so I tend to do balance practice. In my favorite drill, I receive a chime each time I complete a turn with the appropriate balance (positive reinforcement) and no chime (negative punishment) when I don't complete a turn correctly. I also receive verbal feedback when my balance is not correct. For instance, a friendly voice will tell me if I'm in my back seat (balance is too far back). This positive punishment is helpful because I can make an immediate adjustment and receive a chime in my next turn. One also receives IQ scores on training runs, and because one is focused on specific tasks, it's common to receive higher IQ scores on training runs than free runs.

In another drill I like, I am asked to complete as many turns as possible in a minute. I love this drill because it keeps my legs active. As an older skier who desires to ski slalom, this drill is ideal. During the run, one receives feedback on how many good turns one completes; bad turns do not count.

Thus, when I don't get credit for a turn, that negative punishment motivates me to do better on the next turn. I have found that if I focus on making as many turns as possible, I ski better because my balance, pressure, edging, and rotation come together. Focusing on a specific aim, such as making as many turns as possible, keeps one's mind away from irrelevant thoughts, and learned performance flows as it should. We appropriate every lesson learned, and it takes focus on the present to allow these skills to emerge from our vault of lessons.

There are other interesting drills too. For improving parallel skiing, there is a slipping drill in which one rotates one's skis down the fall line. I once did this drill on one of our intermediate trails, Lazy Mile. It was interesting doing that for such a long distance. Yet, it is this type of training that allows one to ski one's best when one is out recreational skiing on steeps (steeper runs) or running gates.

Technology like Carv is relatively new, and research is just beginning to be conducted to assess its efficacy, and the results are promising (Adesidaet al., 2019; Lee et al., 2017; Snyder et al., 2021; Snyder et al., 2022). With time, however, all the kinks in these systems will be worked through, and I can imagine a world where most skiers will be wearing monitors and skiing will improve for everyone willing to learn. For me, I use Carv to evaluate my performance but supplement it with evaluations from other experts, especially when I attend PSIA certification events. We get evaluated a great deal. That's what makes teaching skiing such a joy for me; there is always room for growth.

Skiing changed my life. When I was younger, one of my goals was to travel the world. Indeed, one day I was with a career counselor at San Diego State University when my counselor asked me what I would like to do with my life. He said that I should visualize the ideal job I desire, not worrying if it's possible or not, and then use that image to shape my career path. The idea was to find a career that most closely approximates my vision. I think I had done a good job living out my vision, as my career does allow me to travel to conferences and other meetings in some very beautiful places. Skiing, however, has allowed me to visit some of the most beautiful destinations possible. I am hoping to expand my destinations in the coming years before I age out of skiing fun terrain. Age tends to do that to skiers, but I still have some time.

When I started writing this chapter, I endeavored to find an ideal image to convey what skiing is like for me. I have so many, but I think the most beautiful for me are those bluebird days out West. I think one of my favorite scenes was looking down into Mineral Basin at Snowbird. Mineral Basin is a bowl in the back of Snowbird (back bowl). One reaches it either by a massive Tram or smaller lifts. When we ski Snowbird, we always park at

the Creekside Day Lodge. I am what people call a creature of habit. Once I find a place to park, I tend to stay there and use that lot each time I ski in the area. Taking the Gadzoom lift, and then the Little Cloud lift, one reaches the summit. It's an interesting place that I do not recommend for anyone but a seasoned skier. It can be quite windy up top, and there isn't a lot of room to hang out and sightsee. Indeed, when crowded, it can be quite intimidating, especially if one fears heights. To get to the area where I wanted to ski, we took Path to Paradise, a catwalk above a very steep area. For those of us with some fear of heights, it gets quite intimidating, especially since the seasoned skiers are flying by on both sides. Interestingly, the right side heading from the Tram outward is sloping upward. Thus, if people want to pass a slower traveler, they do it at an angle. We reached an area that I wanted to ski, a black diamond trail ironically named White Diamond. It was steep, but there was far steeper terrain around. Yet before sliding down, I took a moment to survey the surroundings. The snow was beautiful, and I could see for miles. The sky was a deep blue that I find hard to visualize at the moment as I am writing this chapter. It was a weekday in April, and less crowded than other times of the year. For one moment, I was lost in the oceanic feeling. I didn't fear the run, as I generally don't fear skiing down steep terrain. Thus, my mind was free to release all possible thoughts, negative or positive. For that brief moment, I felt what it was like to live the vision I had when speaking to that career counselor at SDSU or looking through those ski magazines at the drugstore when I was a child. Fleeting as it may have been, and three years removed from where I am now as a skier, I felt that I was where I belonged. I am the mountain, for it is in me all the time.

Notes

1 Interestingly, ten years on, I still chase after my son. However, there are times, rare as they may be, that I catch him. Those times are worth celebrating for me. He's surprised.

2 I will use trails and slopes interchangeably from this point forward, even though trails and slopes differ. Slopes are wider and ideal for making nice wide turns. Thus, slopes are ideal for learning. Trails differ in width and difficulty. They can also be quite long, but are usually scenic.

3 I use the term "absolute beginner" to distinguish between the individual never having skied before the lesson from the individual who has taken lessons and is working on advancing beyond beginner status. Skiing is complicated indeed.

4 Of course, this isn't absolutely true. Grass and clay courts do change with time and weather conditions. Indeed, a little moisture can make grass courts dangerous. With time too, as the grass is eaten away by tennis shoes, the surface speeds up.

5 Slipping a course means clearing ruts and leveling the snow on the course to make skiing easier for the next skier. One generally side slips down the course to do so, or one can use a wide braking wedge to clean up the ruts.

References

Adesida, Y., Papi, E., & McGregor, A. H. (2019). Exploring the role of wearable technology in sport kinematics and kinetics: A systematic review. *Sensors, 19*(7), 1597.

Bananas. Retrieved 6/22/2023, from www.usfoods.com/great-food/great-food-resources/produce-resources/bananas.html

Carv. (2023). Retrieved 6/21/2023, 2023, from https://getcarv.com

Coffey, K., Post Foster, E., & Sogard, R. (2014). *Alpine Technical Manual*. American Snowsports Education Association.

Komissarov, S. S. (2021). Mechanics of side-slipping in alpine skiing. Braking and skidded traversing. *Sports Engineering, 24*(1), 20.

Lee, S., Kim, K., Yoon Hyuk, K., & Lee, S. s. (2017, 5–8 Oct. 2017). *Motion analysis in lower extremity joints during Ski carving turns using wearable inertial sensors and plantar pressure sensors*. Paper presented at the 2017 IEEE International Conference on Systems, Man, and Cybernetics (SMC).

Marshall, E. K. (2001). *Effects of verbal feedback on skier efficacy, skier performance, skier technique, and intention to take another ski lesson in first-time skiers*: The University of Utah.

Piaget, J. (1951). The biological problem of intelligence. In D. Rapaport (Ed.), *Organization and Pathology of Thought* (pp. 176–192). Columbia University Press.

Rodriguez, D. (2021). The art of learning and dealing with disequilibrium. *Research Methods*. Kendall Hunt.

Snyder, C., Martínez, A., Jahnel, R., Roe, J., & Stöggl, T. (2021). Connected skiing: Motion quality quantification in alpine skiing. *Sensors, 21*(11), 3779.

Snyder, C., Martinez, A., Strutzenberger, G., & Stöggl, T. (2022). Connected skiing: Validation of edge angle and radial force estimation as motion quality parameters during alpine skiing. *European Journal of Sport Science, 22*(10), 1484–1492.

Spörri, J., Kröll, J., Schwameder, H., & Müller, E. (2012). Turn characteristics of a top world class athlete in giant slalom: A case study assessing current performance prediction concepts. *International Journal of Sports Science & Coaching, 7*(4), 647–659.

Wojtyczek, B., Pasławska, M., & Raschner, C. (2014). Changes in the balance performance of Polish recreational skiers after seven days of alpine skiing. *Journal of Human Kinetics, 44*(1), 29–40.

PART III
Health

8

OBESITY

Weight has been on my mind daily ever since I can remember. Ideally, not one of us should focus on something so superficial unless there is a medical reason to do so. Yet, I do. I guess one wouldn't be surprised if one went through the same difficulties I did being an obese child in the late 1960s to early 1970s. In today's world, I feel that people are kinder. Of course, nobody escapes the social media trolls whose aims are to elicit a reaction from others. With the empowerment movement of the present, people post pictures of themselves regardless of weight and receive supportive comments for putting themselves out in public. Yet, for every 100 positive comments, there are at least 10 to 15 offensive comments from trolls. Despite the overwhelming support people seem to receive today for stepping into the light with their bodies exposed, it's the negative comments that likely provoke the greatest response and have the strongest psychological impact on the individual and the individual's supporters.

Weight concerns go in two directions, high and low, with the worst outcomes being obesity and anorexia, respectively. Obesity at present is one of the leading causes of death and disease in the United States. Conditions associated with obesity are Type 2 diabetes, heart disease, hypertension, sleep difficulties, osteoarthritis, and mental health complications, among other conditions (Koenen et al., 2021; Powell-Wiley et al., 2021; Sarma et al., 2021). The most widely accepted and present classification of weight defines obesity using Body Mass Index (BMI). BMI is kilograms per meter squared. Using BMI, individuals with a BMI < 18.5 are considered underweight. Individuals with BMIs ranging from 18.5 but less than 25 are considered normal weight. Individuals with BMIs from 25 but less than 30

DOI: 10.4324/9781003460800-12

are considered overweight. Individuals with BMIs ≥ 30 are considered obese (Timothy Garvey, 2019). Alarmingly, the findings of a recent study using the National Health and Nutrition Examination Survey (NHANES) with 2017–2020 data indicate that 41.9% (95% CI=39.4%, 44.3%) of American adults (≥ 20 years old) are considered obese. For children and adolescents ages 2–19, the prevalence of obesity was 19.7% (95% CI=17.9%, 21.6%) ("National Health and Nutrition Examination Survey 2017–March 2020 Prepandemic Data Files Development of Files and Prevalence Estimates for Selected Health Outcomes," 2021). If your jaw isn't touching the floor now, mine is. Although many argue that BMI is a poor measure of weight as it is calculated using height and weight, ignoring lean body mass (e.g., muscle, bone, and connective tissue), these estimates are staggering. Perhaps this is why I believe people are kinder to individuals with obesity today; there are far more obese individuals now than there were during my youth.

It is hard to say why the prevalence of obesity is so high. Factors proposed include proliferation of technology, resulting in a greater screen time which can result in a reduction in exercise and sleep quality, reductions in cigarette smoking,[1] and medications (Davis et al., 2018; Fang et al., 2019; Haghjoo et al., 2022; Hall, 2018). With this greater prevalence has come an insistence on accepting different body types. As a victim of peer punishment during my more obese days, I would have welcomed sympathy. Indeed, I am thankful for the people who did support me during those difficult times. However, as an adult I have learned to take charge of my mental health in relation to weight without falling into false movements that hurt rather than help people struggling with weight. It is wonderful that people post pictures of themselves online wearing revealing clothing despite their body shapes. However, it is also important to realize that obesity isn't an uncontrollable condition, and tackling obesity is critical to one's own physical and mental health. Living with the effects of obesity into old age would not be fun.

Obesity is but one side of the weight continuum. At the other extreme is anorexia. Anorexia is a serious condition involving extreme weight loss. Using the BMI cutoffs, individuals with values below 18.5 are considered underweight. Individuals with values below 16.5 are considered severely underweight, with those with values ≤ 17 considered anorectic (Reas & Rø, 2017; Weir & Jan, 2021). The lifetime prevalence of Anorexia Nervosa is 4% for females and 0.3% for males (van Eeden et al., 2021). Although there are many hypotheses for the genesis of this disease within an individual, including genetic factors (Johnson et al., 2022), anorexia nervosa is a serious condition that cannot be ignored when discussing weight maintenance as I am here. Thus, I caution you, my reader, to keep in mind that this chapter includes my personal journey with weight, which can invoke disequilibrium, and my weight maintenance strategy, a strategy that is not ideal for everyone.

Although I hope it can work for others too, there are some individuals for whom their weight-related pathology can take even the most benign approach and turn it into something destructive.

Being abused by others leaves lasting marks. My abuse came because I was obese in a non-accepting climate. My family lived in a lower-middle-class garden apartment complex located in the midst of an upper-middle-class section of Washington, DC. Although there were obese individuals around, most people I saw were normal weight. Therefore, I looked different from others. Not only was I obese but my father, a native of northern Argentina, was very dark brown. I was, by contrast, somewhere in between my father's and mother's skin tones, my mother being quite white. Plus, my curly black hair made me stand out from the rest of my neighbors. I won't focus on my entire childhood though, as that's not the focus of this chapter. I will instead focus on a couple of incidents that created the complexes I deal with even now, over 50 years later, and how I dealt with those struggles from a Psychoadaptation perspective.

One day, I recall, playing football in the field outside Annunciation Catholic School on Massachusetts Avenue. Annunciation is a beautiful little school. I'm not sure why I went there, but I know that my father couldn't really afford it. I suppose that's why I attended Annunciation for only two or three years before returning to public school. I know that my mother always wanted to pretend that we had more money than we did, and that we were somehow in a higher socioeconomic status than we truly were, so I suppose she pushed my father to matriculate us, and he gave in.

Playing outside was of course the highlight of my day, as it was and probably still is for most kids in grade school. Our field was adjacent to Massachusetts Avenue, so people driving by could watch as we played. Most days I enjoyed myself, especially when we played football. We played tackle football. No equipment, just our bodies. I being obese and taller than many kids seemed indestructible to the others. As much as the experience was physically painful to me, I was strong and could carry several potential tacklers on my back when I had the ball. That part was fun. What wasn't fun was what happened when I was tackled. All the kids would jump on me like they were jumping onto an airbag in a funhouse. They laughed heartily as they landed full-force onto my belly. Obviously, to them it wasn't an issue because they sincerely believed I couldn't be hurt with all that fat. It hurt and did so badly. I remember some onlookers watching us as this happened. I'm not sure what they were thinking. I remember an ambulance driver, in particular, watching from the window of his emergency vehicle. For years, the vision of his eyes peering at me filled me with ideas about what he was thinking. Was he concerned about me or just curious about what was

going on? Perhaps he wasn't thinking about anything at all and just looking mindlessly in my direction, but I was hurting and I hoped others knew.

I was obese as a child. When I was an adolescent, however, I was within normal weight range. I stayed that way until my early 30s. I suppose this was the result of my propensity to walk. I love walking, especially in cities. In DC, I used to walk around the entire city. I walked to work and back as well. For instance, I would walk from my home in North Arlington, Virginia, to the Smithsonian Air and Space Museum, and back home. This was a round trip of about 10 miles. I did this or similar walks frequently, and on nearly a daily basis when I had free time. Even after moving west, my propensity to exercise continued. When I was in college in San Diego, I cycled a lot. A favorite trip of mine was from my home in Pacific Beach to Encinitas and back, about 40 miles in total. Other days, I would continue up to San Clemente, via Camp Pendleton, a round trip of about 125 miles. I burned a lot of calories. Even eating like a garbage disposal after a feast, I went down to around 155 lbs. My high school weight was 176 lbs. The activities I did during those years really kept my weight in check, and me in great physical shape.

When I was in the doctoral program at the University of Maryland, I continued to exercise. However, I changed to working out at a gym and doing weight training. I followed the best practices at the time, working out about 30 minutes on aerobic equipment (e.g., stationary bicycles). I also changed my eating habits as I started gaining weight. I ate lots of carbohydrate-rich foods and ignored foods heavy in fats. I reasoned that given the calories per gram of fats (9 calories per gram) versus carbohydrates (4 calories per gram), eating foods rich in the latter would help me maintain weight. This was not the case, though, as carbs not required for energy are stored in the body as fat. Activities like cycling help one become an efficient fat burner, but I was no longer riding hours per day, or going on long walks about the city. Most of my time commuting was spent in a car, sitting on the beltway between campus and home in Falls Church Virginia. So, I gained weight. Eventually, I topped out at about 210 lbs. I didn't really notice the weight gain as I also gained a great deal of muscle. Muscle weight is fine, but it doesn't affect one's waist. I recall one day going to buy a new pair of jeans and finding that my usual pant size didn't fit. I was confused and thought I had done something wrong shopping. I was a 38. I'm usually a 34. Disequilibrium is indeed one's friend. I had received a message, and it told me I was fat.

Learning that my pant size isn't what it used to be was only one of the watershed moments in my weight journey. Another occurred when my grand aunt looked at my legs as I sat at the kitchen table eating breakfast. I was on one of my many international trips as a younger person, visiting

my family on my mother's side in Belgrade, Serbia. My family was never shy in over-feeding me. They also weren't shy about telling me the truth. My grand aunt told me that my legs were huge. For many, that wouldn't be an important comment. It was an old woman making a spontaneous comment. For me, though, it was important as it triggered my weight complex. I relived all the personal horrors of being obese as a child. Thus, I immediately sprang into action, not eating the same from that moment forward, despite being goaded to eat by my family.

The Balkans are rich in history. Serbia, for instance, was controlled by the Ottoman Empire for 500 years. That's a lot of time, during which it appropriated many Turkish cultural practices, including food and its preparation. One of my favorite food items is Burek. There are many styles of preparing this amazing dish. My mom was a master of preparing cultural cuisine. Burek can be made with feta cheese or meat. It's lined by many layers of filo dough. It's greasy and delicious. When coupled with drinkable yogurt, there's nothing better. Indeed, my mouth is watering just thinking of it now.

Whenever I visited my family, we'd buy breakfast daily. Unlike my current practice of shopping for the week, my aunt would send me out on a daily bread and breakfast run. I would go out and purchase what was necessary for our meal. Thus, the food was extra fresh and optimally delicious. I ate it up and it showed. Thus, when my grand aunt commented on the size of my legs, I knew exactly what to do. I had to stop eating so much and go back to exercising the way I did in the earlier years.

While still in Serbia, I went for massive walks, like I used to in DC. I also restricted my diet to the best extent I could, given the circumstances. It's not uncommon in other countries for families to confuse food for respect. My aunt would offer me food, and if I refused, she would take it as an insult. I learned to deal with that somehow, as I am strong-willed but empathetic. It worked well enough for me to manage my way back home where the real dieting began.

At home, I was free to do as I pleased without worrying about anyone's feelings. I was smart, and read voraciously. I also took exercise physiology during my master's studies at San Diego State University, so I understood the relation between calories consumed and expended. I knew that to gain weight one had to expend fewer calories than one consumed. To lose weight, one had to consume fewer calories than one expended. To maintain weight, one had to consume about the same number of calories one expended. I also knew that there was a magic number of calories for healthy living, 2000 per day. So, I figured since I needed to lose weight I'd decrease my calories consumed to something less than 2000. Since I'm a go-getter, I decided that I'd restrict my calories to 1200 per day,[2] while continuing to exercise.

By now, my faithful reader, I hope you realize how dedicated I am to achieving the goals I set. This goal, however, was hard on me, as I love food. Thus, there was a competition between me as a goal achiever and me as a hedonist who loves to eat. My goal-achiever-self won. I had no problem eating less. I started learning the calories of different foods and soon was able to calculate calories consumed as quickly as a banker can calculate the interest she'll earn off our money. The weight came off quickly. I went from 210 to about 160 in a very short period of time. To make things more dramatic, I cut off my long hair. Until that point, I wore my hair long. Indeed, some friends of ours used to call me Tarzan for my physique and long hair. That was no more. I showed up at my College Park office (research assistant office) a new man. I am sure some wondered what happened to me, but nobody said anything. Perhaps they didn't care, but I did. From that point forward, I've kept my weight within limits. Today, for instance, I weighed in at 170.4 lbs. That's consistency, my friends. This ability to maintain weight, and the experiences surrounding my weight journey, are key reasons I began developing my worldview and am writing this book. I learned how to deal with disequilibrium in the most obvious and easy way, by reading the scale.

My weight-maintenance practice

Every morning upon waking up, after getting the coffee started, I head into the bathroom and onto the scale. I have a smart scale, one that is connected to an app and provides information on weight, BMI, body fat percentage, percent muscle, and percent water. I weigh myself nude. I want to eliminate any possible means of questioning my results (confounding variables). Thus, I weigh myself in the same exact way every single time I step onto the scale. By the way, as you are by now likely aware of my good reader, the weight you get at your healthcare provider's office is flawed. You are weighed in clothing and perhaps after eating or drinking. That weight is unreliable, although I suppose if you know how much your clothing weighs you can estimate your weight. When I weigh myself, I do so without eating anything, and after using the toilet. This is the best possible scenario for weighing oneself and attaining a relatively accurate reading.

Now, weight varies daily because of what we eat and drink, and whether we have been able to evacuate our bowels. Nevertheless, over time, we can get a good picture of trends. When I weigh myself, I am especially interested in my weight and my body fat percentage. I am also interested in getting a picture of my lean body mass (particularly muscle). My goal is not to lose weight but to maintain a healthy weight and body profile (% body fat; % muscle) for my age. This should be everyone's goal.

The readings I get on a given day are not as meaningful as the observed trends. I should write this twice because it is the most important advice I can give anyone desiring for a healthy weight program. Over the long haul, the daily fluctuations wash out, and what we see is the real story of our body composition. This is key information as it hints at what we should focus on in our eating patterns. Note that I did not mention exercise. Exercise is a given for me and for anyone desiring to be healthy, especially as one ages. As I wrote in a prior chapter, I exercise regularly and have been doing so for decades. As such, I am able to add routines to my practice that many others couldn't likely do for fear of injury or a cardiac anomaly. For instance, I have recently started running stairs again. This is not easy for older individuals who are not used to exercising. For me, it's not an issue because I am always doing aerobic exercise.

There is no agreed-upon theoretical understanding of weight management, yet it is clear that genetics and environmental influences play a role in one's weight and whether one becomes obese or remains within a healthy range for one's age (Müller et al., 2018). Understanding what is considered healthy requires some research from reputable medical sources. I turn to the Centers for Disease Control and Prevention (CDC) or the National Institutes of Health (NIH) for my information, or other professional diet and fitness organizations. According to guidelines published by the American College of Sports Medicine (ACSM), an excellent body fat percentage for a man of my age is between 17% and 19.4%. Today I was at 15.6% (Liguori & Medicine, 2020). Lower values, such as mine, are indicative of athletic status for a man of my age, but I'm sure there are many top-level older athletes with far lower body fat percentages than mine.[3] So, that's where I want to be as I train to compete in sport.

Trends are key when focusing on weight, since we can't simply accept our readings as our actual weight. Weight, however, if taken appropriately is likely to be within some small margin of error. Perhaps it's a five-pound margin. Thus, if my weight is 167, my actual weight is likely to be between 167-5=162 (lower bound), and 167+5=172 (upper bound). This isn't a scientific assessment; it's my personal observation. That said, the weight we see on the scale can shock us, especially if one hasn't looked at the scale for quite some time. Imagine, if you will, that today after reading this text, you decide to weigh yourself. Imagine that you assume you are within a healthy weight range for your age and biological sex. Yet, when you get the reading it is much higher than you thought, and outside what is considered healthy for your age. Your response is key. For some, there are the immediate rationalizations to account for the discrepancy. In other words, for some the first step is to attempt to assimilate the information to fit one's view about one's weight. Rationalizations include but are not limited to time of

day, water retention, muscle weight, faulty scale, and genetics. Returning to the first chapter of this text, the shock created by the discordant reading is disequilibrium.

Disequilibrium is the unpleasant feeling one experiences when one encounters information that contradicts one's conceptions. In the case of the scale and my example, the weight seen differs from what the individual believed about the Self (physical self-concept). However, this uncomfortable feeling is the recipient's best friend, as unlike sycophants, disequilibrium is part of what C.G. Jung once referred to as the transcendent function (Jung, 1916; Miller, 2004). It's teleological in that its aim is to help one correct something wrong within one's self-concept. The goal of this psychological gift is to help us improve our adaptation and physical health in this specific case. Disequilibrium is speaking to us and telling us that we are wrong and that we must correct our view, otherwise it will continue to visit us and cause us stress.

There are many ways to rationalize weight. In my time as an obese child, there was no choice but to adapt, as the world was unkind to the obese. In today's world, however, obesity is accepted and is seen as cultural in some cases, as if being unhealthy is valued in some cultures. Although being overweight does not mean one is an open target for ridicule, it shouldn't be accepted as a given. As I know what it feels like to be obese, I accept everyone for the person they are at a given moment, but I will encourage them to become a better person. In the case of obesity, this means losing weight the right way and re-gaining one's health. Instead, what we are seeing now is obesity being used by individuals with strange complexes about physical appearance, for their own personal gain. Thus, some individuals who are not obese but have views about the physical body will champion obesity. This is seen mostly in women as too much emphasis is being placed on women's bodies. Although standards of beauty change, this focus has severe repercussions for women as many women struggle to attain what is considered perfect, or maintain it once age starts to decay the body. It's interesting, but browsing the web every morning, I inevitably come to an article on some older woman showing her body and how it's so empowering. I don't get it, as what we look like changes, and people's views on beauty differ as much as their fingerprints. I suppose it's some editor's agenda to tell us what we should feel. Perhaps it's that editor's own complex that is seeking to make us assimilate their reality. Sadly, it doesn't work and is as transparent as a clean glass window. One only needs to read the comments to see how effective the agenda is.

Disequilibrium is our friend. However, like any information, one needs verification to trust it. Although our psyches have our best interests in mind, our complexes occlude the content. Thus, opening one's senses

to information is critical. Listening to what others say is important, as is looking at ourselves in the mirrors objectively. Reading the information on a smart scale and looking up criteria associated with health is crucial. Without this, we allow ourselves to be governed by forces without our best interest in mind.

Becoming one's healthiest self is key to a lifetime of enjoyment. If one is burdened with lifestyle disease, one's enjoyment is limited to the younger years. Life should be fulfilling to the very end. That's certainly what I am striving for. Neither obesity nor anorexia are outcomes that are consistent with a healthy life. Yet, too many individuals allow others to dictate their lives and the choices made. Today, with the ubiquity of social media, it has become even more difficult to escape outside influences. I entreat you to put down your phones for a moment and observe how others enslave themselves to social media. Recently, as I was driving north in New Jersey along the coast from Island Beach State Park to Point Pleasant, I noticed a girl riding her bicycle with her face down looking at her phone. As a former cyclist, I find that odd, as attention to one's surroundings is required to ensure safety. Yet, for most, social media has become more important than safety. Social media is addicting, as one can never know what's coming next. The problem, though, is that most of what we see on social media is highly manufactured. Social media influencers spend countless hours perfecting images to portray moments as if a moment were an entire lifespan. Moments are no more than moments and are no substitute for a lifetime of fulfillment. A perfect picture, albeit beautiful cannot substitute for an earned accomplishment. I subscribe to the advice one of my cousins, Nikola, once told me. He said that I should put away the camera and enjoy the moment. The memory of the moment is more important than the snapshot taken.

I will end this chapter with my prescription for healthy weight. **First**, nobody should hate the person they are at the moment. Life's circumstances brought them here, but where they are now does not define the whole person they are. Whether obese or anorectic, that's what they are at the moment, but they can change. Moments are ephemeral. Like the bubbles in soda, they rise to the top of the glass and disappear. **Second**, when one weighs oneself, they must remember that it's no more than one reading. In itself, it means nothing. They should look at it in relation to the ideal for their personal health. **Third**, one should not concern the Self with one's BMI. While it's an amazing tool for research, it doesn't do much for the individual. One should always look first at their weight and body fat percentage. They should then find what is their ideal by appealing to a reputable source. I suggested what I believe is the best. However, if one does a search, one will find the ideals. When reviewing the research, one should look for consistency. If one site reports a specific standard but all

other sites contradict it, the reader should go with the majority. Consensus is key when reading health-related research and standards.

With the ideal in place, if one's outcome is highly inconsistent with the ideal, either being above or below, one should start making the required change (**Fourth**). Regardless of what theoretical perspective one follows regarding weight, calories in should equal calories expended if one aims to maintain weight. Thus, if one is eating far more than one is expending, one needs to reduce caloric consumption. If, on the other hand, one's goal is to gain weight, one should follow the opposite approach. Eat more, but keep the food healthy. Not all calories are equal, with some being more detrimental to health than others. **Fifth**, one should stay consistent on how one weighs oneself. I suggest following my approach, weighing oneself first thing in the morning and naked. Once there are enough data, at least seven days, one will see if there are any trends, either increasing or decreasing. This will provide the necessary information to either decrease or increase caloric consumption. The biggest concern is one's ability to deal with disequilibrium, especially if reality contradicts perception. If, for instance, one believes one is doing well at maintaining weight, but then the data tell them otherwise, how will they deal with it? The best strategy is to accept the disappointment and make the adjustment. Soon, and with much practice, one will be able to dismiss the disappointment like one does an inconsiderate driver at an intersection, or a rude person one encounters accidentally in one's journey.

With practice, adaptation becomes easy, and what was once considered impossible becomes reality. I have had a tremendous journey with weight. I could have either ballooned into a morbidly obese person with a reality television show, or starved myself. I am happy that I instead learned to deal with disequilibrium through adaptation. Indeed, this is where my worldview was crafted, if not born. Psychoadaptation came from the sum total of my life experience living, and appropriating what I read in the literature. Yet, it wasn't until I forced myself to listen to what I was experiencing that I was able to turn my health around. Since first starting this practice, I have continued to maintain my weight within a healthy range, even after the emergence of the Covid-19 pandemic. It was a challenge though, as staying inside reduced the amount of exercise I did. I did gain weight, but only into the 180s. I was however able to turn it around quickly once I saw that my earlier practices were not working. I suppose that is why we have so many theories about weight. With age, our bodies change, and what we used to be able to do no longer works. Nevertheless, the relation between calories consumed and expended does not change. Our aims may alter, as age changes what is considered healthy. However, the practice of collecting

and reading the data, adjusting our eating and exercise habits, does not change. We react to our new realities.

Being one's healthiest Self should be everyone's goal. However, we cannot achieve this alone. We need others to help us see that which we cannot see, to be the mirrors in which we see our reflected Selves (Cooley, 1992). Often, though, the individuals we hope to guide us have personal agendas that interfere with our desires to live healthy lives. When that happens, we receive false information, and we are worse for it. It is important that we learn to question what we read and see, critically examining information before choosing to follow. Most individuals making outlandish claims do so for their own personal benefit, protecting their self-esteems (Epstein, 1973). Health is a personal responsibility. It's only with the guidance of reputable sources or certified and trusted professionals (e.g., nutritionists, counselors) that we can attain the Selves we deserve to be.

Notes

1 Cigarettes are stimulants, and stimulants help people stay thin.
2 This approach is not recommended for anyone. I wouldn't do it again in the same way. Losing weight should be a slower process, and consider all factors, including how much one exercises. I restricted my calories but did not change how much I exercised. Thus, my weight loss was very fast. It's better to consult a nutritionist to find the optimal number of calories to consume daily.
3 Note that male and female differ in body fat for biological reasons (Sansone et al., 2022).

References

Cooley, C. H. (1992). *Human Nature and the Social Order*. Transaction Publishers.

Davis, R. A., Plaisance, E. P., & Allison, D. B. (2018). Complementary hypotheses on contributors to the obesity epidemic. *Obesity, 26*(1), 17–21.

Epstein, S. (1973). The self-concept revisited: Or a theory of a theory. *American Psychologist, 28*(5), 404.

Fang, K., Mu, M., Liu, K., & He, Y. (2019). Screen time and childhood overweight/obesity: A systematic review and meta-analysis. *Child: Care, Health and Development, 45*(5), 744–753.

Haghjoo, P., Siri, G., Soleimani, E., Farhangi, M. A., & Alesaeidi, S. (2022). Screen time increases overweight and obesity risk among adolescents: A systematic review and dose-response meta-analysis. *BMC Primary Care, 23*(1), 1–24.

Hall, K. D. (2018). Did the food environment cause the obesity epidemic? *Obesity, 26*(1), 11–13.

Johnson, J. S., Cote, A. C., Dobbyn, A., Sloofman, L. G., Xu, J., Cotter, L., ... Huckins, L. M. (2022). Mapping anorexia nervosa genes to clinical phenotypes. *Psychological Medicine*, 1–15. doi: 10.1017/S0033291721004554.

Jung, C. G. (1916). The transcendent function. *Collected Works, 8*, 189.

Koenen, M., Hill, M. A., Cohen, P., & Sowers, J. R. (2021). Obesity, adipose tissue and vascular dysfunction. *Circulation Research, 128*(7), 951–968.

Liguori, G., & Medicine, A. C. o. S. (2020). *ACSM's Guidelines for Exercise Testing and Prescription*. Lippincott Williams & Wilkins.

Miller, J. C. (2004). *The Transcendent Function: Jung's Model of Psychological Growth through Dialogue with the Unconscious*. SUNY Press.

Müller, M. J., Geisler, C., Heymsfield, S. B., & Bosy-Westphal, A. (2018). Recent advances in understanding body weight homeostasis in humans. *F1000Research, 7*.

National Health and Nutrition Examination Survey 2017–March 2020. (2021). Prepandemic Data Files Development of Files and Prevalence Estimates for Selected Health Outcomes, http://dx.doi.org/10.15620/cdc:106273.

Powell-Wiley, T. M., Poirier, P., Burke, L. E., Després, J.-P., Gordon-Larsen, P., Lavie, C. J., ... Sanders, P. (2021). Obesity and cardiovascular disease: A scientific statement from the American Heart Association. *Circulation, 143*(21), e984–e1010.

Reas, D. L., & Rø, Ø. (2017). Investigating the DSM-5 severity specifiers based on thinness for adults with anorexia nervosa. *International Journal of Eating Disorders, 50*(8), 990–994. doi: https://doi.org/10.1002/eat.22729.

Sansone, P., Makivic, B., Csapo, R., Hume, P., Martínez-Rodríguez, A., & Bauer, P. (2022). Body fat of basketball players: A systematic review and meta-analysis. *Sports Medicine-Open, 8*(1), 1–21.

Sarma, S., Sockalingam, S., & Dash, S. (2021). Obesity as a multisystem disease: Trends in obesity rates and obesity-related complications. *Diabetes, Obesity and Metabolism, 23*, 3–16.

Timothy Garvey, W. (2019). Clinical definition of overweight and obesity. *Bariatric Endocrinology* (pp. 121–143). Springer.

van Eeden, A. E., van Hoeken, D., & Hoek, H. W. (2021). Incidence, prevalence and mortality of anorexia nervosa and bulimia nervosa. *Current Opinion in psychiatry, 34*(6), 515.

Weir, C. B., & Jan, A. (2021). *BMI Classification Percentile and Cut Off Points*. StatPearls Publishing.

9

SMOKING AND VAPING

Smoking was never a big part of my life as a child. However, my mother did smoke on occasion. I believe she felt that it made her sophisticated in some way. My father smoked cigars from time to time. The smell of a cigar still conjures strong memories of my childhood back when my father was a taxi driver in Washington, DC. I can visualize him holding a stogie out the window of his cab on a hot summer day. I never tried one, but I tried a cigarette or two in my life. Cigarette smoking never caught on with me though, as I have asthma and I have a hard time being around cigarettes. I don't like the way they smell either. Unlike cigars, there's nothing pleasant for me in a cigarette.

As a Ph.D. student, I focused on sport psychology and the mental processes involved in athletic performance. I visualized myself one day working with elite athletes. However, with time and continued study, I became intrigued by the effect of mental processes in all performance domains, including those outside of sport. My first job after graduate school was teaching sport and health psychology as an Assistant Professor in Psychology at Widener University in Chester, Pennsylvania. Although I enjoyed the sport psychology course, I found health psychology even more interesting because of the diverse topics covered. Indeed, health psychology includes exercise and its psychology. Not all people are equal when it comes to exercise motivation, so we see diversity in how people respond to exercise opportunities. For the most part, they make excuses to keep themselves from engaging in this health-promoting behavior.

Over the next four years of my life, I taught health psychology and sport psychology and conducted my own research, when possible, on the

DOI: 10.4324/9781003460800-13

reciprocal relation between physical activity and self-concept. Unfortunately, it was hard to conduct much research as my teaching load was four and four, meaning I taught four courses in the fall semester and another four courses in the spring semester. As such, I turned my attention away from teaching to research in the following years. I was fortunate to attain a position as a postdoctoral fellow at the University of Pennsylvania, in the School of Medicine, Department of Psychiatry. Landing a postdoctoral fellowship (postdoc) is not easy, as there is a great deal of competition, especially when one seeks a postdoc at the most coveted institutions. However, my focus on exercise and sport, along with my love for structural equation modeling (SEM), made me an attractive candidate for the researcher with whom I worked. Dr. Janet Audrain-McGovern (JAM) is as intrigued by sport and physical activity as I am, but has adapted her research to fundable research aims such as cigarette smoking and now vaping in adolescents. Although there is a great diversity of nicotine delivery systems today, at the time of my hiring (2002) the prevalence of cigarette smoking was quite high in adolescents (around 20%). Yet, even with the increase in nicotine delivery modalities today, cigarette smoking remains the leading preventable cause of death and disease. Sadly, despite its declining prevalence, the consequences of smoking combustible cigarettes continue to be devastating.

For the remainder of this chapter, I will refer to combustible cigarette smoking as smoking. When I discuss electronic cigarette (e-cigarette) smoking, I will refer to it as vaping. With respect to any other form of smoking I may discuss, such as cigar or marijuana, I will make sure to clarify the substance as necessary.

I have learned a great deal about human behavior by studying smoking. At one time, smoking was considered a fashionable behavior. The most sophisticated people smoked cigarettes. Even physicians promoted it. Today, smoking is a behavior that is pursued primarily by people with lower socioeconomic status (Drope et al., 2018). Indeed, if one reads any data source on smoking, cigarettes are more likely to be smoked by individuals with a high school education or less, or individuals with lower incomes. They are also consumed by individuals with any mental illness, with those individuals suffering from schizophrenia and bipolar disorder smoking the most cigarettes (Drope et al., 2018; Faith Dickerson et al., 2018; Lipari & Van Horn, 2017). The bottom line is that people still smoke, with the current prevalence greater than 11% among adults 18 and older (Cornelius, Loretan, Wang, Jamal, & Homa, 2022; Schiller & Norris, 2023).

Much less is known at this point about vaping, although the data suggest that the prevalence is rising, particularly among high school adolescents and young adults aged 18–24 (Tehrani, Rajabi, Ghelichi- Ghojogh, Nejatian, & Jafari, 2022; Walley, Wilson, Winickoff, & Groner, 2019). Vaping is

now the leading tobacco-consumption modality in youth (Cooper et al., 2022). An estimated 14% of high school students are current vapers (having vaped at least once in the past 30 days). Of those, about 30% vape daily. By contrast, current vaping is lower among adults in general (4.5%), as smoking remains the preferred nicotine delivery mechanism (Cornelius et al., 2023). However, compared to adults of all other ages, the prevalence of vaping is highest in young adults (aged 18–24) at 11%. This suggests that vaping is more popular among younger individuals, particularly those around high school and college age, whereas smoking is more prevalent in older adults.

Researchers are beginning to understand why individuals initiate vaping. Indeed, researchers have found that adolescents tend to believe vaping is a less dangerous alternative to combustible cigarette smoking and are therefore motivated to vape for the purpose of harm reduction (Audrain-McGovern, Rodriguez, Pianin, & Testa, 2021; Audrain-McGovern, Rodriguez, Testa, & Pianin, 2022). There are shared and distinct risk factors (e.g., peer use, family use) related to vaping and smoking initiation. In some cases, these shared risk factors result in the dual use of smoking and vaping (Audrain-McGovern et al., 2021), what one may consider a worst-case scenario. One such factor is depressive symptoms, which increases the risk of smoking and vaping in adolescents (Moustafa, Testa, Rodriguez, Pianin, & Audrain-McGovern, 2021; Rodriguez, Moss, & Audrain-McGovern, 2005), suggesting that nicotine may have a role in self-medication for depression; people consume nicotine to alleviate depressive symptoms. Unfortunately, unlike the case of smoking, it is too early to conclude definitively whether vaping is safe, or at least a safe alternative to smoking for those who smoke but want to quit. Further, from what we have learned from research on smoking, it takes quite some time for one to progress from the initiation of smoking to the inception of diseases like lung cancer and emphysema. As such, it may take years, if not decades, for us to know the real consequences of vaping. That said, given that there is some overlap in chemical compounds found in vaping and smoking beyond nicotine, including carcinogens, the safest conclusion for now is that vaping is not safe, even if it may be safer than smoking (Walley et al., 2019).

Health safety aside, unless one is vaping a nicotine-free product, smoking and vaping involve nicotine, and both are therefore likely to result in nicotine dependence. With respect to Psychoadaptation, the processes underlying adaptation to the vaping and smoking contexts are the same, just as it is the same for all the behaviors I have discussed in this book. Although the specifics of the contextual constraints may differ from behavior to behavior, the impact of context on behavior will not differ; one still must adapt to the contextual constraints to gain acceptance and become a true smoker or vaper. As we know far more about smoking and its consequences than

vaping and its consequences to this point, I will focus more on smoking than vaping in the remainder of the chapter. Nevertheless, I suggest you, my good reader, interchange vaping and smoking when conceptualizing the adaptation process. It will be our way of taking the concepts discussed here out for a walk and assess how well Psychoadaptation applies to both forms of nicotine consumption. That's what I always do.

Smoking is a hard behavior to quit. However, many current smokers do want to quit. Indeed, a full 68% of adult smokers reported wanting to quit, with 55% making a quit attempt in the past year (Babb, Malarcher, Schauer, Asman, & Jamal, 2017). Of those, however, only about 7% were considered quit for not smoking in the past 6 to 12 months. There are unquestionably major benefits to smoking cessation in improving overall respiratory function, and reducing the risk of lung cancer and chronic obstructive pulmonary disease (COPD) (Jobst et al., 2018; Wu et al., 2019; Zhao & Du, 2022). Thus, quitting smoking is critical to reducing the burden of disease for those addicted to smoking, and their loved ones.

It is interesting, however, that with all the funding provided for research, so little has been accomplished to help smokers quit for good. A whopping 56 million dollars was spent on tobacco-related research in 2016 (Merianos, Gordon, Wood, & Mahabee-Gittens, 2019). While smoking cessation products exist and are helpful to the few smokers succeeding to abstain from smoking, I would think that more should have been accomplished by this point with all the investment. It's as if the money spent on smoking cessation research was wasted, except to make some researchers famous and increase their retirement portfolios. A major problem with current research in smoking cessation is the dependence on medication or technology (e.g., quit smoking apps) to help smokers quit. There is far less focus on the psychological processes of maintaining smoking than possible quick fixes that generally do not last beyond a month or so.

Having read my book to this point, you, my faithful reader, are likely familiar with my support of mindfulness practices. They do indeed help, but here too the results are not likely to last unless one has the discipline to maintain the practice. I will go further and say that all cognitively based practices including Cognitive Behavioral Therapy (CBT), mindfulness, and other like methods will work only if one has the discipline to maintain the practice. As such, it's not the technique that is faulty, it's the belief that one can maintain practice across time. This is a psychological issue that must be addressed if we are to turn our investment in smoking cessation research into something more than a benefit to the researchers.[1]

In my own research, I have sought to address the psychological nature of smoking. I seized upon my personal observations of smokers to develop a measure that captures the subjective **im**portance of smoking, the SIMS.

In this measure, I ask smokers many questions most people would find ridiculous if not having an addiction to cigarettes and smoking. However, I felt that smokers would endorse them as what is ridiculous to the non-smoker is within the realm of normality to the smoker. Questions in this measure include items such as "I would feel really empty without smoking, like I lost an important part of my life," "Smoking is a big part of who I am," and "When I am holding a cigarette I feel really competent, like I can do anything." I won't spend much time discussing the results of my research on the SIMS except to say that it does show promise as a predictor of smoking cessation and the psychological burden associated with smoking (Rodriguez et al., 2019). If you are interested in reading more about it, see the reference. You could also read my chapter on the making of an assessment instrument in which I describe the process of developing the SIMS (Rodriguez, 2020). However, my main focus here is to explain what I believe are the barriers to successful smoking cessation and the role of Psychoadaptation in the process.

Quitting should be simple with the availability of nicotine replacement therapy (NRT), including skin patches, lozenges, and gum. One can include vaping too I suppose, although we are still learning about its health consequences. The key addictive substance in cigarette smoking is nicotine. Even if one replaces cigarettes with NRT, one still receives nicotine. The story is not that simple, though, as much of the addiction to cigarettes is psychological, including the reward experienced from smoking cigarettes with peers. Smokers also come to associate cigarette smoking with specific locations, and being near or at those locations comes to trigger cravings. Cravings are a key component to addiction. Indeed, DiFranza and colleagues (see Contreras, O'Loughlin, Rodriguez, Wellman, & DiFranza, 2010) define nicotine dependence as a three-stage process, starting with wanting a cigarette, even if just once a week, to craving cigarettes, and finally needing cigarettes. This geographic trigger is known as a conditioned place preference, and when interacting with a genetic propensity to nicotine dependence, is associated with developmental changes in the brain's reward centers in response to nicotine (Brunzell, Mineur, Neve, & Picciotto, 2009; Sharp & Chen, 2019). As such, smokers are vulnerable to cues that trigger withdrawal symptoms. As withdrawal symptoms can be quite intense, including impatience, anhedonia (i.e., inability to experience pleasure), reduced cognitive function, depressive symptoms, and low positive affect (Klemperer et al., 2021; Martin & Sayette, 2018), any cue that triggers such symptoms makes the smoker vulnerable to lighting up a cigarette. Thus, we can see a smoker passing by a location where she regularly smokes, lighting up a cigarette even when there is no need for the nicotine. Nicotine has a half-life of about two hours (Xue et al., 2020),

so smoking more frequently is more likely a response to psychological cues than a real need for nicotine.

Nicotine is a primary reinforcer (Caggiula et al., 2009; Mazur, 2016).[2] Like food (another primary reinforcer), it provides direct reinforcement when ingested by those vulnerable to its addictive potential. However, when a particular location triggers withdrawal symptoms, it's acting as a higher-order reinforcer. Higher-order reinforcers attain their strength through pairings with primary reinforcers (Mazur, 2016). Thus, when one smokes a cigarette at a specific location, that location comes to be associated with nicotine. Nicotine is the primary reinforcer, and it is paired with the cigarette (secondary reinforcer). The cigarette is a nicotine delivery system (Gray et al., 2005). As such, the sight of a cigarette triggers withdrawal symptoms. When the cigarette is smoked in a specific location, like a designated park bench for smokers, that bench comes to trigger the same withdrawal symptoms the cigarette does.

There are indeed many reinforcers activating withdrawal symptoms in smokers and former smokers. This makes quitting a difficult task, even with NRT. Yet, people do quit. What follows is my view based on my personal observations and the scientific literature I have consumed, about the route from smoking to quitting and the barriers to quitting.

Like all of us, smokers live within contexts. The smoking context involves cigarettes, and the cigarette sits on an ornate throne in the center of the context. Like all contexts, the smoking context has its set of constraints, the most obvious being smoking. As such, smokers affiliate with other smokers. Peer smoking is perhaps the strongest predictor of smoking initiation, particularly among adolescents (Audrain-McGovern et al., 2004). Given that the vast majority of adults smoking cigarettes initiated smoking in adolescence or young adulthood (18–23), peer influence is key (Barrington-Trimis et al., 2020; General, 2014). Smokers are like all other people with the exception that they smoke. Smokers work, exercise, vary in wealth and marital status, and gender identification. However, there are some commonalities among smokers, including activities that smokers are less likely to participate in. For instance, smokers tend to be lower in socioeconomic status and less likely to exercise regularly than non-smokers (Pampel, Krueger, & Denney, 2010; Schultz et al., 2018). Such characteristics are critical to one's mobility outside the smoking context.

Adaptation is about changing one's view of one's Self based on the data of one's experience (Rodriguez, 2000, 2021). Despite being surrounded by cigarettes and cigarette smoking, smokers receive information about the perils of smoking. It's hard to escape from public health advertising promoting smoking cessation. In some countries, cigarette packs contain disgusting images of the physiologic ravages caused by cigarette smoking,

including diseased lungs, although the effect of such ads on risk beliefs is questionable (Noar, Rohde, Barker, Hall, & Brewer, 2020). Thus, smokers do receive the messages, but they do not necessarily heed the warnings and quit.

Changing behavior is a complicated process. As you now likely know, I am writing this book to explain why some people succeed in making grand changes to their life course, and others do not. Quitting smoking involves a great many adaptations. More importantly, though, it requires the person seeking to quit to endure tremendous disequilibrium. While nicotine plays a role in this process, I suggest that it is the adaptations to the smoking context and the preparation required to adapt to the mainstream context that make it most difficult to go from being a current to a former smoker.

I remember coming up with a slogan that I hope one day catches on with former smokers. It is a play on the saying that quitters never win and winners never quit. I changed it to, quitters win and winners quit. This should make sense from a former smoker's perspective. Yet, beyond being a catchy slogan possibly printed on a t-shirt, my aim was to provide former smokers with a sense of identity outside the smoking context, along with a new norm to bond former smokers. Given that smokers affiliate with one another, and this affiliation is the fodder for the smoking context, non-smokers need to come together as a unit, bonding around their status as former smokers. Then, they too can define a context that creates its own constraints, including support when quitters feel lost and want to return to the comforts of the smoking context. Something as small as a t-shirt that can identify a former smoker may be all that is needed to stimulate a conversation, and perhaps a friendship.

Smoking is about comfort. Smokers, I propose, are very comfortable in the smoking context. They share so much in common, beyond SES and other health habits. They also share experiencing discrimination. Smokers are discriminated against. They are seen as lesser beings than non-smokers. One day, I was at a Society for Research on Nicotine and Tobacco (SRNT) conference and overheard a representative of some research company talking to a man who asked a question about his wife's smoking habit. This man was a researcher who happened to have a wife who smokes. The representative asked him, aren't you ashamed of being a researcher and having a wife who smokes? I couldn't believe I heard that. How can, I ask, one work in an industry attempting to help smokers quit (whether directly or indirectly), yet be ashamed of the very people one is paid to help, as this representative clearly was by asking the question?

I don't believe any human being on earth wants to experience discrimination. The easiest way to prevent the experience is to not venture outside one's primary context. The context provides protection. Yet, hiding

in one's context to prevent experiencing disequilibrium precludes successful adaptation to new contexts. While the smoker has adapted to the smoking context, the healthy Self can adapt to many different contexts, with the emphasis being on adapting to the healthiest contexts in the macrosystem. Let's walk through an example as I see the adaptation process in quitting smoking. Imagine a man, Dave, in his later 50s who desires to quit smoking. This individual works as a construction contractor. Dave is well off after many years in the profession, although he came from a lower socioeconomic status family. Imagine also that his work left Dave with little time for exercise and other extracurricular activities outside of some hobbies like fishing and cars. He also had a propensity to engage in risk-taking behaviors as an adolescent and young adult. As an older adult, Dave no longer does such activities but still enjoys drinking alcohol at a local bar with his friends after work.

My good reader, this characterization seems like I am stereotyping a smoker. In my research, I am a big fan of assessing heterogeneity in behaviors and characterizing behavioral outcomes. One of my favorite methods is latent variable mixture modeling (LVMM), a method that allows a researcher to identify hidden (latent) subgroupings of individuals that regular statistical methods do not allow for, and then to characterize the latent subgroups on select characteristics (Audrain-McGovern et al., 2004; Muthen, 2001; Rodriguez, Carlos, Adachi-Mejia, Berke, & Sargent, 2014). Characterizing latent classes gives researchers a method to profile the prototypical member of each class. In the right hands, this permits one to generate targeted intervention initiatives to help prevent negative health behaviors. In the wrong hands, it facilitates discrimination. I am using it here to profile a prototypical smoker and discuss how Psychoadaptation works within the smoking context.

Returning to Dave, imagine that he desires to quit smoking. As such, he visits his healthcare provider and the provider recommends the use of a nicotine patch to replace the nicotine attained through smoking. At first, he wasn't sure and asked if he could vape instead. Not being sure about the long-term impact of vaping, the healthcare provider could not in good conscience endorse vaping. So, they went with the nicotine patch instead. The patch works for Dave and he is able to successfully abstain from cigarette smoking. To facilitate his success, the healthcare provider also recommends a phone counseling quit line, which Dave calls to discuss the experiences he's having quitting, and for guidance when he experiences withdrawal symptoms. All goes well at first, and Dave is able to remain abstinent for a full month. Yet, the situation begins to change as Dave's behavior changes. First, as most of his friends outside of work are cigarette smokers, he finds affiliating with these peers awkward. He tries to stay away

from them which creates resentment. "It's like Dave thinks he's better than us now that he's not smoking," one of his friends says to another friend. Dave feels the resentment and discusses it with his phone counselor who recommends other activities, including exercise or various hobbies not affiliated with cigarette smoking.

Moving outside one's context is a difficult journey, especially when most if not all of one's friends belong to the context one seeks to escape. First, changing one's behavior means that one is no longer accepting one's adaptations as adequate. Failure to enact behaviors considered critical to the context is the contextual equivalent of breaking a law and is met with punishing consequences, such as social isolation. Yet, expecting members of the new environment to welcome one with open arms, beyond the first polite greetings is fraught with danger. Soon, members of the new context will expect full adaptation, and for those unable to adapt or slow to adapt, sanctions await. Dave is excited when he begins his new journey. Soon, however, he realizes he isn't close to being a prototypical member of this new non-smoker context. First, many of the actors he desires to befriend are different from him in terms of education, with nearly all completing college. Dave, on the other hand, dropped out of high school and received his General Education Diploma (GED) in his mid-20s. The very question, where did you go to college, elicits anxiety whenever it's asked. "It's as if my heart jumps into my face," Dave tells his counselor when discussing his physiological response to that question. Thus, he started to avoid situations in which the question may be asked.[3]

Another difference he has come to find is the extracurricular activities non-smokers engage in. Many are heavy exercisers. Others engage in activities he never even tried, including skiing and ecotourism. Further, he meets relatively few former smokers, and although he feels pride in his ability to quit smoking, he becomes weary of discussing it with others as the mere topic of smoking elicits poorly veiled sympathy for his success. "I feel so alone being a former smoker in a non-smoker's world," Dave tells his phone counselor. "It's as if I'm an alien. Everyone reacts to me funny, and I can't even do any of the things they do. I'm trying, but it's so hard. I miss my old friends," he continues.

The feelings Dave experiences are difficult for him, and he feels the burden psychologically. Losing one's friends hurts. Even the smell of cigarette smoke evokes memories of his time standing outside a building with other smokers just chatting about anything or nothing at all. Dave relapses. He's welcomed back into his former life with open arms. His friends laugh it up with him, particularly when he talks of all the odd experiences he has with non-smokers who seem to him to think they are better than smokers, and for no real reason except they do not smoke.

This was a hypothetical example, of course, but Dave's experience fits in with Psychoadaptation in that it involves the context, the contextual constraints, equilibrium and disequilibrium, and assimilation and adaptation. Dave mastered his context. Yet, he was able to see its flaws. This led to his desire to depart the context to attain a higher level of Self. However, in departing his context, he experienced tremendous disequilibrium, including the loss of support from his peers. In entering the new context, his hope of immediate acceptance was dashed. It reminds me of veterans returning from Vietnam after the war. Instead of being greeted with open arms, they were forgotten and even hated for participating in an unpopular war. Further, the adaptations required of Dave to become a member of this new context were large, many of which he was ill-prepared for, and some of which are impossible to change. For instance, while he could go to college and earn a degree, this would require night classes and a tremendous investment in time and money. Further, at his age, he may find it difficult to get some jobs he would desire, even with a degree. Still, he could get the degree. He cannot, however, change from where he came from and his birth family's socioeconomic status.

What happens to people quitting, I posit, is they enter a context as if they were aliens from a distant galaxy. They see the smiles but read the disdain underneath them. This is likely true for anyone entering a new context as an older person. I explained it when I discussed my entering the skiing context in my chapter on skiing. It happens anytime one desires to try something new. One has to hurdle many obstacles to gain acceptance, and there are some who will never accept the alien, no matter how much he does right. Disequilibrium is the norm when quitting smoking. One has to be strong to manage the multiple hurdles, and one has to have the ability to find reinforcement that is personal. I suppose that's why I came up with the *winners quit, quitters win* slogan. It's a way, in my view, to bind people together the way smoking did. It provides a force field of sorts to deflect the disequilibrium until the former smoker has the internal strength to reverse it and achieve equilibrium.

Changing health behaviors is extremely difficult. Even when there is a tool available to help one change, such as NRT, one has to deal with all the remaining obstacles to quitting. The ability to withstand the disequilibrium associated with the new context is critical. Unfortunately, most researchers are so concerned with demonstrating success that they focus only on the easiest outcomes, and those are the outcomes assessable early in the cessation process. Psychoadaptation is about the long haul. Success occurs only when one stays quit for a lifetime. It is not enough to quit for a week, a month, or even a year. Quitting is a lifelong process, and one will most likely experience some withdrawal symptoms for the rest of her life. Yet, if

one remains on course, and learns to experience these withdrawal symptoms without yielding to them, they will be no more than an acceptable annoyance. Unfortunately, there is not enough emphasis on keeping smokers quit for a lifetime. Part of this negligence is due to the constraints of science and the research career. Science needs results, and the easiest way to attain a large number of results is through the publication of studies. The more studies one can publish, the better. In one's career, though, one can only work on studies for so long before one must move ahead to the next study. One needs to receive grants and publish papers to attain promotion and tenure (i.e., academic career advancement). Spending time following one group of research participants for an entire lifespan is not only impractical, it's almost career suicide. The result is neglecting the very participant one desires to help. It's not that people are doing this for nefarious reasons. Rather, it's the way career paths in research are structured. Success at all costs.

Smokers are not bad people, they are merely people who smoke. Quitting smoking is nearly impossible for a person who is addicted to nicotine and cigarettes. The barriers are formidable. However, it is wonderful to hear about those individuals who have quit and stayed quit for years, without transitioning to another tobacco product. The willpower required to confront and overcome all the barriers one faces, from dealing with withdrawal symptoms when walking by a specific location to dealing with the negative reactions of non-smokers, is far above what most people have. Perhaps by highlighting how hard it is and meeting with those making quit attempts regularly for years after quitting, quitters will feel that they are appreciated and proud of their new status as former smokers. For they will know that quitters win, and winners quit.

Notes

1 To smoking cessation research, I can add research designed to reduce the likelihood one will initiate smoking in the first place. The savvy research will point to the great decrease in cigarette smoking over the past several decades, claiming it's a victory for research. However, a closer look at today's nicotine consumption data shows that while cigarette smoking has decreased, the use of at least one nicotine delivery system is quite high, at 14.5%, for a smoked tobacco product (e.g., e-cigarette, combustible cigarette, cigars), while this proportion increases to 18.7% when including any tobacco product. So, the situation remains far from where we'd like it to be. It appears that people moved away from smoking but found another system to attain their nicotine. It's a rather empty victory.

2 Caggiula and colleagues suggest nicotine may also act as a reinforcement enhancer, impacting the potency of environmental stimuli to affect cravings.

3 You should be thinking complexes here.

References

Audrain-McGovern, J., Rodriguez, D., Pianin, S., & Testa, S. (2021). Conjoint developmental trajectories of adolescent e-cigarette and combustible cigarette use. *Pediatrics, 148*(5). doi: 10.1542/peds.2021-051828.

Audrain-McGovern, J., Rodriguez, D., Tercyak, K. P., Cuevas, J., Rodgers, K., & Patterson, F. (2004). Identifying and characterizing adolescent smoking trajectories. *Cancer Epidemiology Biomarkers & Prevention, 13*(12), 2023–2034.

Audrain-McGovern, J., Rodriguez, D., Testa, S., & Pianin, S. (2022). The indirect effect of cigarette smoking on e-cigarette progression via substitution beliefs. *Journal of Adolescent Health, 70*(1), 140–146. doi: https://doi.org/10.1016/j.jadohealth.2021.07.007.

Babb, S., Malarcher, A., Schauer, G., Asman, K., & Jamal, A. (2017). Quitting smoking among adults—United States, 2000–2015. *Morbidity and Mortality Weekly Report, 65*(52), 1457–1464.

Barrington-Trimis, J. L., Braymiller, J. L., Unger, J. B., McConnell, R., Stokes, A., Leventhal, A. M., ... Goodwin, R. D. (2020). Trends in the age of cigarette smoking initiation among young adults in the US from 2002 to 2018. *JAMA Network Open, 3*(10), e2019022–e2019022.

Brunzell, D. H., Mineur, Y. S., Neve, R. L., & Picciotto, M. R. (2009). Nucleus accumbens CREB activity is necessary for nicotine conditioned place preference. *Neuropsychopharmacology, 34*(8), 1993–2001.

Caggiula, A. R., Donny, E. C., Palmatier, M. I., Liu, X., Chaudhri, N., & Sved, A. F. (2009). The role of nicotine in smoking: A dual-reinforcement model. *Nebraska Symposium on Motivation, 55*, 91–109. doi: 10.1007/978-0-387-78748-0_6.

Contreras, G. A., O'Loughlin, J., Rodriguez, D., Wellman, R. J., & DiFranza, J. R. (2010). Measures of nicotine dependence in adolescents: An update of the evidence 2000–2010. *Journal of Pediatric Biochemistry, 1*(02), 143–164.

Cooper, M., Park-Lee, E., Ren, C., Cornelius, M., Jamal, A., & Cullen, K. A. (2022). Notes from the field: E-cigarette use among middle and high school students—United States, 2022. *Morbidity and Mortality Weekly Report, 71*(40), 1283.

Cornelius, M. E., Loretan, C. G., Jamal, A., Lynn, B. C. D., Mayer, M., Alcantara, I. C., & Neff, L. (2023). Tobacco product use among adults–United States, 2021. *Morbidity and Mortality Weekly Report, 72*(18), 475.

Cornelius, M. E., Loretan, C. G., Wang, T. W., Jamal, A., & Homa, D. M. (2022). Tobacco product use among adults—United States, 2020. *Morbidity and Mortality Weekly Report, 71*(11), 397.

Drope, J., Liber, A. C., Cahn, Z., Stoklosa, M., Kennedy, R., Douglas, C. E., ... Drope, J. (2018). Who's still smoking? Disparities in adult cigarette smoking prevalence in the United States. *CA: A Cancer Journal for Clinicians, 68*(2), 106–115.

Faith Dickerson, Jennifer Schroeder, Emily Katsafanas, Sunil Khushalani, Andrea E. Origoni, Christina Savage, ... Robert H. Yolken, (2018). Cigarette smoking by patients with serious mental illness, 1999–2016: An increasing disparity. *Psychiatric Services, 69*(2), 147–153. doi: 10.1176/appi.ps.201700118.

General, U. S. (2014). The health consequences of smoking: 50 years of progress. A Report of the Surgeon General. Atlanta (GA): US Department of Health and Human Services. Centers for Disease Control and Prevention. *National Center*

for Chronic Disease Prevention and Health Promotion, Office on Smoking and Health, 17.

Gray, N., Henningfield, J. E., Benowitz, N. L., Connolly, G. N., Dresler, C., Fagerstrom, K., ... Boyle, P. (2005). Toward a comprehensive long term nicotine policy. *Tobacco Control, 14*(3), 161–165. doi: 10.1136/tc.2004.010272.

Jobst, B. J., Weinheimer, O., Trauth, M., Becker, N., Motsch, E., Groß, M.-L., ... Wielpütz, M. O. (2018). Effect of smoking cessation on quantitative computed tomography in smokers at risk in a lung cancer screening population. *European Radiology, 28*(2), 807–815. doi: 10.1007/s00330-017-5030-6.

Klemperer, E. M., Hughes, J. R., Peasley-Miklus, C. E., Callas, P. W., Cook, J. W., Streck, J. M., & Morley, N. E. (2021). Possible new symptoms of tobacco withdrawal III: Reduced positive affect—A review and meta-analysis. *Nicotine and Tobacco Research, 23*(2), 259–266.

Lipari, R. N., & Van Horn, S. (2017). Smoking and mental illness among adults in the United States. *The CBHSQ report.*

Martin, L. M., & Sayette, M. A. (2018). A review of the effects of nicotine on social functioning. *Experimental and Clinical Psychopharmacology, 26*(5), 425.

Mazur, J. E. (2016). *Learning & Behavior* (8th ed.): Routledge.

Merianos, A. L., Gordon, J. S., Wood, K. J., & Mahabee-Gittens, E. M. (2019). National Institutes of Health Funding for Tobacco Control: 2006 and 2016. *American Journal of Health Promotion, 33*(2), 279–284. doi: 10.1177/0890117118779013.

Moustafa, A. F., Testa, S., Rodriguez, D., Pianin, S., & Audrain-McGovern, J. (2021). Adolescent depression symptoms and e-cigarette progression. *Drug and Alcohol Dependence, 228*, 109072. doi: https://doi.org/10.1016/j.drugalcdep.2021.109072.

Muthen, B. (2001). Latent variable mixture modeling. *New Developments and Techniques in Structural Equation Modeling, 2*, 1–33.

Noar, S. M., Rohde, J. A., Barker, J. O., Hall, M. G., & Brewer, N. T. (2020). Pictorial cigarette pack warnings increase some risk appraisals but not risk beliefs: A meta-analysis. *Human Communication Research, 46*(2–3), 250–272. doi: 10.1093/hcr/hqz016.

Pampel, F. C., Krueger, P. M., & Denney, J. T. (2010). Socioeconomic disparities in health behaviors. *Annual Review of Sociology, 36*, 349.

Rodriguez, D. (2000). Self and adaptation: Defining the healthy self. In R.G. Craven & H.W. Marsh (Eds.), *Self-Concept Theory, Research and Practice: Advances for the New Millennium: Collected Papers of the Inaugural Self-Concept Enhancement and Learning Facilitation (SELF) Research Centre International Conference* (pp. 355–365). SELF Research Centre, University of Western Sydney.

Rodriguez, D. (2020). *Navigating the Many Hurdles in Creating a Self-Report Measure.* SAGE.

Rodriguez, D. (2021). The art of learning and dealing with disequilibrium. In *Research Methods.* Kendall Hunt.

Rodriguez, D., Carlos, H. A., Adachi-Mejia, A. M., Berke, E. M., & Sargent, J. (2014). Retail tobacco exposure: Using geographic analysis to identify areas with excessively high retail density. *Nicotine & Tobacco Research, 16*(2), 155–165.

Rodriguez, D., Goulazian, T., Strasser, A. A., O'Loughlin, J., Dugas, E. N., Kuoiloi, C., ... Schnoll, R. (2019). The role of the subjective importance of smoking (SIMS) in cessation and abstinence. *Journal of Smoking Cessation, 14*(1), 1–11.

Rodriguez, D., Moss, H. B., & Audrain-McGovern, J. (2005). Developmental heterogeneity in adolescent depressive symptoms: Associations with smoking behavior. *Psychosomatic Medicine, 67*(2), 200–210.

Schiller, J., & Norris, T. (2023). Early release of selected estimates based on data from the 2022 National Health Interview Survey. *National Center for Health Statistics, Hyattsville, MD.*

Schultz, W. M., Kelli, H. M., Lisko, J. C., Varghese, T., Shen, J., Sandesara, P., ... Harold, J. G. (2018). Socioeconomic status and cardiovascular outcomes: Challenges and interventions. *Circulation, 137*(20), 2166–2178.

Sharp, B. M., & Chen, H. (2019). Neurogenetic determinants and mechanisms of addiction to nicotine and smoked tobacco. *European Journal of Neuroscience, 50*(3), 2164–2179.

Tehrani, H., Rajabi, A., Ghelichi- Ghojogh, M., Nejatian, M., & Jafari, A. (2022). The prevalence of electronic cigarettes vaping globally: A systematic review and meta-analysis. *Archives of Public Health, 80*(1), 240. doi: 10.1186/s13690-022-00998-w.

Walley, S. C., Wilson, K. M., Winickoff, J. P., & Groner, J. (2019). A public health crisis: Electronic cigarettes, vape, and JUUL. *Pediatrics, 143*(6). doi: 10.1542/peds.2018-2741.

Wu, X., Huang, Q., Javed, R., Zhong, J., Gao, H., & Liang, H. (2019). Effect of tobacco smoking on the epigenetic age of human respiratory organs. *Clinical Epigenetics, 11*(1), 1–9.

Xue, Y., Zhou, H., Jiang, C., Liu, X., Zhou, Z., & Wang, J. (2020). Two-hour tobacco abstinence has no effect on cognitive control in male patients with nicotine dependence: An ERP study. *Front Psychiatry, 11*, 604684. doi: 10.3389/fpsyt.2020.604684.

Zhao, X., & Du, C. (2022). Effect of smoking status on spirometric lung age in adult Chinese Men. *Health & Social Care in the Community, 30*(4), 1384–1390.

10

PSYCHOADAPTATION IN THE MODERN WORLD

I wrote this book to explain Psychoadaptation, my worldview. Reading through the chapters, you know that I believe the key to a successful life is allowing for disequilibrium with all its harshness, but then overcoming it to build a new and higher Self. I remember this saying from when I was an undergraduate and visited Nicaragua on a summer vacation volunteer experience: "construction, not destruction." This referred to the war at the time in which the Sandinistas were fighting against the Contras. Our goal was to help build an addition to a school in Matagalpa, Nicaragua. In that case, of course, we didn't want to see destruction. Psychoadaptation is, however, about destruction. It is about tearing down the old and ineffective ways for something new and better. The new, however, includes the old, as one can never destroy completely that which once was. One can only build upon the wreckage, using the old as fertilizer for the new. In that way, the old feeds the new.

In this final chapter, my aim is to discuss Psychoadaptation in the modern world. It was one thing for me to develop my worldview in a time without the same access to the internet and social media we now have. Today's world, however, is far more complicated. We are being bombarded by information from so many different sources. Everyone has a say, even the least significant person's comments can weigh as heavily as the highest-ranking individual. As such, I believe Psychoadaptation is needed today more so than at any time in our history. Disequilibrium is everywhere. Indeed, it's nearly impossible for one to make a simple statement, post a picture or a video, or go out with friends without reading a negative comment online. Further, with the focus shifting to the online world, crafted comments found on social media sites

DOI: 10.4324/9781003460800-14

like Twitter[1] and Instagram, and the decrease in social interactions in face-to-face settings, people are less prepared to deal with social distress than individuals raised in earlier times. Therefore, guidance is needed. My hope in this chapter is to provide such guidance.

Social media

Like most of you reading this book, I use social media. I check Twitter and Facebook once daily in the morning. This may not be the normal amount of time spent on social media platforms, but it's all I can afford with my schedule. I also check Instagram, but even there I only use it when I have nothing else to do, which is quite rare. Every morning I also go through various news sites of interest to me. I love looking over the Washington Post, not so much because I believe it is a great newspaper, but because I was born and raised in DC, and it's my hometown source. I also scroll through Yahoo. I'm especially interested in reading user comments, particularly surrounding controversial topics. I am intrigued by the responses some individuals write to articles. I know there are bots that can learn to mimic the worst in people, but I believe most of the negativity spewed by users is real. It is often said that people feel protected when they can hide behind a keyboard. I suppose that is true, but it takes quite a sense of freedom and a very warped understanding of reality to write some of the angry nonsense I read online.

Long ago, I said in a graduate psychology classroom that *the internet is the sum total of human consciousness*, and I coined the term *internet consciousness* to reflect it. I was responding to this unending desire to create lifelike robots using artificial intelligence that would allow them to think and act like humans do. Imagine these autonomous robot beings conversing with us and having the same kind of feelings we express, and without looking fake. I thought, why do that when we have the internet. The internet represents every facet of human consciousness, from the vilest to the heavenly. We even have a dark web, which from what I can surmise is the internet equivalent of the psychoanalytic unconscious. It holds all of the darkest secrets we want to disappear but cannot destroy for they are part of who we are. That said, there is no need in my view for a robot being. Use the internet instead. Indeed, why not build this robot being and install Google in it? Perhaps it can be like the little Alexa devices many of us have in our households. Whenever I ask Alexa something, she interacts with me like a smart human being, providing me with a variety of options. She stays away from negativity though. Our autonomous internet robot, however, would do whatever it wants once we ask it, even delving into the worst places.

Human beings do what they like, or at least they do what is adaptive to their contexts. Evidently, on social media, it's adaptive to insult others when responding. Post anything on one of these platforms, assuming it's open to public comment, and there will be a mix of supportive and negative comments. The negative comments are especially likely if one posts something that is deemed *innovative positive* (sounds like a good term for this), such as an older or obese woman in a bikini. While these posts are perhaps meant to inspire others like the individual doing the posting, it's probable that the photo will receive a number of negative responses. It is expected and completely normal within the mainstream social media context.

Desirability is disequilibrium (Piaget, 1951). I never liked this quote's structure in that I think it should be desire is disequilibrium. Nevertheless, desirability is a quality given to something coveted. To covet is to want something one doesn't possess. We all covet. This recalls a line from the film *Silence of the Lambs* when the cannibal psychiatrist Hannibal Lecter, referencing Marcus Aurelius, questions his protege Clarice Starling about what it is that the villain Buffalo Bob covets. He covets what he sees, says Hannibal. That's indeed the problem here, we covet what we see instead of coveting that which we create in our minds. In our mainstream context, we see much and are conditioned to desire social media likes; to covet that which we see. Social media is the mainstream context's most valuable tool to gain disciples. The desire for reinforcing likes makes one like other individuals' social media pictures and then mimic what the social media influencers do so that we too can get likes. The worst examples of this come from the social media sites of self-created celebrities. These social media influencers, as they are called, perform like marionettes, with the context's overlords manipulating the strings. They post pictures that are intended to depict an idealized lifestyle, usually in an exclusive location, to which we should all strive. Imagine me, lounging at a pool in the Mediterranean with a drink in hand and having some assistant take this picture of me as if I spent my entire life in such a blissful relaxed state.

Idealized images are not real but for the moment. They are ephemeral with the next moment being different, perhaps even filled with stress. Repeating again what my cousin Nikola once told me, he doesn't waste time taking pictures because it takes away from his enjoyment of the moment. Those words have influenced me greatly. Although I take pictures, I do so less than I could because I too want to enjoy the moment. Pictures are great because they evoke memories. However, it's the memory itself that is more valuable than the picture. Words can evoke the memories as strongly as pictures.

Social media influencers are important in Psychoadaptation because they represent a context's ideal. If one adapts perfectly to the context, one will be like the influencer. In fact, isn't it ideal to adapt to the contextual constraints? Doing so will ensure one receives the context's rewards, that is, likes. Unfortunately, most of what we see on social media involves constraints that are not easy to attain. For instance, for the idealized body pictures we see, most of us cannot attain them. Social media influencers peddling their images generally attain their influencer status because they have ideal bodies, with the most coveted proportions. When one of us posts a picture of the Self with less than ideal (per context) attributes, we'll get some nice comments, but we are likely to also receive some or many negative comments.[2] This will of course cause disequilibrium. In that way, desiring to be something that we cannot necessarily attain would cause us to feel bad about ourselves, which is disequilibrium. Desirability does indeed result in disequilibrium.

Living in a world in which one strives to attain the unattainable is ripe for anxiety and depression. Thankfully, disequilibrium exists to help us see the errors in our actions and to reduce the likelihood we are in pain for too long. Although we tend to eschew disequilibrium at first, and often relish in our ignorance during our youth, my experience leads me to conclude that most people begin to recognize disequilibrium as we age. We can only fool ourselves for so long. There's a common saying in sport that age is undefeated. With age, we tend to realize that what we could do once, we can no longer do, or do as well as we did earlier in life. The way we looked as young people isn't the same as we look now either. Thus, trying to be what someone half our age is will result in nothing but more pain from disequilibrium. One way or another, disequilibrium will have its way, until we change or run away to oblivion.

Negative comments are there to help us, but only if we can escape their potency. The negative comments one experiences when posting pictures of oneself, or videos of their activities online, or commenting on news articles trigger responses within that are teleological (Jung, 1916; Miller, 2004). They frustrate. They embarrass. They enrage. They tell individuals that there is something wrong with their attempts to adapt to the context. Even the most vile comments do so. They represent the vilest part of human consciousness (or internet consciousness), but they are part of the context to which one strives to adapt. For instance, if one posts a photo of one's self in a bathing suit but has a small gut instead of a toned midsection, someone will undoubtedly comment about the gut. If someone posts oneself at an event but is wearing a mask to prevent spreading a pathogen, someone will likely comment about why the person is wearing the mask. To truly become one's healthiest self within the context, one must be able to appropriate

those comments and then respond correctly. There will be disequilibrium. Individuals will tell us that they do not pay attention to those comments, but I believe that's a lie. No human being is immune to negative comments. Even if one shuts off comments, the comments will get to the person posting, for our unconscious knows what others know and feels what others think. We have a strong generalized other too (Mead & Mind, 1934), and it has appropriated the context's norms. Hiding comments doesn't help those making posts escape them.

A better strategy is to allow for the comments, expect the worst type, and respond to the individuals with whom one can have a conversation. Individuals posting negative comments have an agenda. Like everyone else, they too experience disequilibrium. The pictures or comments posted trigger their own worst fears, causing them disequilibrium. Instead of attempting to understand their feelings and adapt, their aim is to assimilate what is posted into their current worldviews. For instance, if an obese or overweight woman posts a picture of herself on the beach, and an observer feels it's not appropriate for a heavy person to post a body picture because in the context that's not normative, and comments in some negative fashion, the picture triggered disequilibrium in the observer. It does so because it contradicts a contextual constraint on posting, and that causes disequilibrium in those adapting fully to the contextual constraint. To counter this disequilibrium, the individual making the negative comment attempts to assimilate it into what he knows about the context. Channeling the contextual constraint, perhaps he'll say something to himself like, "she's fat and is trying to pretend it's okay to be fat in that bikini. Nobody wants to see that. People only like the image to push an agenda. The likes she's getting are from other fat people or snowflakes." Snowflake is of course the term for liberal individuals coined by some conservative-leaning individuals because according to the individuals using this term, liberal individuals think they are unique, like snowflakes.

The reality is that the individuals making negative comments on a posting are experiencing disequilibrium themselves. The people reading the comments on their posts are experiencing disequilibrium too. One option, as I demonstrated in the last example, is to assimilate the experience into one's worldview. This is what most people likely do. At times, though, one twists and bends so much to assimilate something into their worldview that they end up more knotted than a Philadelphia soft pretzel sold by a street vendor on Roosevelt Boulevard. Disequilibrium is a hard state to deal with, though, so I sympathize with them. Empathy tells me, however, that they truly desire to escape to a world of earned equilibrium. They can, but only if they attend to the comments they so much desire to dismiss. As for the individuals making the negative comments, people will respond

to their negative comments with counter comments. When there is an overwhelming outcry against the negative comment, it means that the comment is not acceptable within the context, and the commenter should adapt. I must note that at times one will make a comment that is truthful but nevertheless receives collective outrage. The mainstream context does have its limitations, and for the few who can see its limitations, the limitations are magnified. In such cases, comments contradicting the status quo can be greeted harshly. However, that is an issue of collective disequilibrium, as the sum total of the collected consciousness needs adaptation.

When commenters make negative comments, they also do so for nefarious reasons, such as to cause enragement. There are indeed a variety of human propensities within any context. As the normal curve shows, while most are around the mean (average), there are individuals at each extreme end. Some individuals love to make others feel pain and will therefore make negative comments as bait. If one engages with these trolls whose only aim is to hook others for their own entertainment, the trolls are successful. This is where adaptation experience is critical. One must know the difference between a person with whom one can engage in debate, and one who seeks to offend for one's own pleasure. Thankfully, internet trolls aren't usually intellectually or emotionally deep, and one can spot a troll by the lack of adaptation in the comments. Trolls tend to repeat insults. In my experience, once I spot a troll, I stop engaging with them. Others though, I will engage with, as both of us can learn from one another. Perhaps there is something within me that needs to adapt, and the person making the negative comment has something useful to say. Perhaps they respond in a way that shows there is growth if I make a helpful comment. In either case, there is something to be learned from people commenting on social media and other sites. Experience helps to build a thick skin and allows us to adapt more easily.

Politics

Over the past decade, we have seen a great deal of discord. With time, our nation has become more open, with people feeling greater freedom to express themselves for who they are. We have also seen an increase in opportunities for marginalized people. Our planet is diverse, with as much diversity as there are people living on the land. Unfortunately, it's easy to lump people together into discrete categories and attribute personality and behavioral characteristics based on superficial differences. Indeed, in the chapter on cigarette smoking, I mentioned how I conduct a type of data analysis involving profiling. People do indeed share some characteristic behaviors and personality dispositions. Even so, no two people are alike. A brief discussion with each person reveals the individual's uniqueness.

Unfortunately, it is human nature to profile. It makes sense from an energy-preservation perspective. It takes effort to get to know a person deeply, and most people prefer not to take time to do so. Stereotyping people is more energy efficient. Unfortunately, with stereotyping comes a lost opportunity to identify gems in the billions of people on earth.

I recall a couple of decades ago the intense discussions on immigration, particularly the crossing of undocumented workers over our southern border with Mexico. As a native Washingtonian, I stay in touch with the news by browsing the Washington Post's website every morning. At the time, it seemed that every discussion topic turned to illegal aliens crossing the border and causing crime in the United States. I'm sure most people then passed off these comments as the words of some uneducated people with nothing better to do than stir up emotions online. Yet, I worried. What would happen, I thought to myself, if one of the proponents advocating an anti-immigrant policy won power. Now, you may say that I shouldn't write immigrant, as the individuals to whom I'm referring were peddling policies against undocumented workers crossing the border illegally, not legal immigrants. I kindly disagree. Reading the comments, I refer to, they had a distinct anti-Hispanic stench to them. Indeed, if there was news of a Hispanic-American individual, whether documented or third generation, the comments were still negative. It was evident to me that these individuals felt the way they did toward Hispanics in general, at least those of mixed racial origin.[3]

Fast forward to 2016, Donald Trump won the election by defeating Hillary Clinton. I'm sure most Americans remember that night vividly. It appeared that Hillary was on her way to victory when the tide changed and before we knew it, Donald Trump was president. It was a victory for the advocates of an America first policy. Not merely that, but an America that shifted values back to perhaps the 1950s. Indeed, Trump's famous red Make America Great Again (MAGA) baseball cap symbolized his belief that we had somehow lost our way and needed to return to an earlier time when there was less discord, but less freedom as well.

It is interesting how human beings need a target on to which they can project their failures. There is always someone worse, and when things are not going our way, let's blame others for it. We see this often in times of war, when we endow the worst possible characteristics to our enemies. That is done to justify killing them. Nobody wants to hurt good people, but bad people get what they deserve, so the reasoning goes. Donald Trump ran his campaign on an anti-illegal alien platform. Indeed, who could ever forget the massive wall he started building along the Mexican border. This wall, although largely ineffective in keeping out determined migrants, was symbolic. It divided North America into an Us and Them, a good and an

evil. On the north side of the border were the good people. South, behind the massively expensive wall were the bad people, those whom if let in, according to its proponents, would steal, rape, and murder good Americans. Indeed, if one read all the hateful rhetoric spewed by the anti-immigrant proponents, one would believe that all crime in this country was caused by undocumented workers. Of course, if an undocumented worker committed a crime, it was enough evidence to condemn a whole ethnic group to the lowest level of hell.

In the time since, we have seen a drastic change in American culture, with the emergence of two separate Americas, it seems. Of course, there are never just two of anything. The world is multidimensional, and there are many subcultures within the American culture. However, politically speaking, there was a seeming divide between those who wanted to send America backward culturally and those for whom progress was the only option. These are extremely diverse groups, though, and to paint each with such broad strokes is not accurate, but I am using it as a starting point.

I am enjoying watching America change. Donald Trump's election did more than elect a common person to office, it triggered a massive movement to diversify our country. Wait, what, you may be asking yourself. I am discussing the movement on the other side of the sociopolitical spectrum. Human nature is predictable. When people in power seek to deny rights, those affected will rebel. We saw this. Although diversity has existed during my entire life, many hid their uniqueness outside the public eye for fear of reprisal. This is justified, as marginalized people are often victimized for who they are. Three of the far too many notable examples include Matthew Shepard who died in 1998 after being beaten and tortured for being gay; Robert Bowers's 2019 massacre at the Tree of Life synagogue in Pittsburgh, PA, in which he murdered 11 worshipers and wounded 7 other people; the 2015 mass murder of 9 African American worshipers by Dylann Roof in a bible study session in Charleston, South Carolina. With these tragedies in mind, people don't give up. There has never been such an expression of diversity in the United States as we see today. In the media, for instance, people in ads are extremely diverse. Movies and shows have a greater diversity of characters than at any time in our country's history. Even in politics, we've had the first BIPOC (Black Indigenous People of Color) president and vice president. People do not want barriers except to climb over them and shout proudly "I'm here."

While we've seen this progression forward, those opposing change are equally motivated by their desire to regress to a former state. The rhetoric coming from opponents to change is strong. It's no surprise, though, as change causes disequilibrium, and nobody can hide from it. It is interesting to observe how advocates of the status quo attempt to assimilate experiences

into their dying worldviews. We have seen the rising of conspiracy theories that rival the imagination of Dr. Seuss. Whether attributing the Coronavirus to 5G networks, or Bill Gates, or aliens in Area 51, conspiracy theories help their perpetrators and believers make sense of events that their psyches cannot readily assimilate into their worldviews. However, instead of seeking to change their worldviews and adapt based on the overwhelming data against them, these individuals choose to preserve what they have by conceptualizing vaguely plausible scenarios. It's not hard for them to attract others, as people do not enjoy disequilibrium, and for some the pain experienced is far too much to bear, not to mention the work required to change the faulty worldview.

The human mind is complex. I know many people do not subscribe to their being an active unconscious as Freud proposed. It cannot be debated, however, that there is content that exists outside of consciousness, only accessed when the appropriate cues stimulate us such that they become conscious. Phone numbers are an example. You, my good reader, aren't thinking of a phone number constantly. When you desire to make a call, and if you've memorized the number, it's there.[4] The nation has its own psyche, and it too is split. It is hard to say, though, which is the equivalent of consciousness and which represents the unconscious. However, what we see is forces making their presence known and a rebellion against that which we find difficult to assimilate. Like our personal psyches, our nation is diverse, with many different selves. Some of these selves have been hidden from the light of consciousness for generations, only known in secret. If we imagine a drag club, for instance, where drag queens perform, these locations are less public than secret. Of course, anyone can attend a drag show. However, they are likely harder to find than a football game because they are less popular to the general public, and there are relatively few drag queens. Nevertheless, they do exist in our nation's collective Self. Thankfully, with the increased openness in our society, we are seeing more such diversity, and in contrast to what many of the more conservative-leaning pundits proclaim, these individuals are not corrupting our nation. As a straight man, I have no desire to dress up as a drag queen. However, I accept that other people do and would gladly go to an event just because I can.

Despite the increased diversity, the next few decades will be hard, becoming a stronger nation requires individuals to adapt. Because adaptation means building the new on the wreckage of the old and wrecking the old entails disequilibrium, we are in for a fight. Unfortunately, this may mean violence. Sadly, there are people who are willing and capable of perpetrating violence in the name of assimilation. Yet, I believe what we are seeing is a last stand. Progression will not lose. It never does. However, as the pain of change is so strong, we can expect a battle until the last of the holdouts is defeated. This

isn't a battle between people and their armies. Rather, it's a battle within the Self as the current Self tries to maintain its dominance. We can help reduce the ravages by teaching others to manage disequilibrium. Collectively, we can cry about the old until it's nothing but a pleasant memory. Yet, by holding each other's hands, we can walk together into the new. It shouldn't be one person who becomes a super adapter. We should all do it together. If I had it my way, that's what I would see. We would create a healthy nation in which everyone experiences the oceanic feeling because we have all adapted. Think of the beauty of that world. Imagine a world with less stress. We would probably be lost in our thoughts much of the time, but the thoughts would be pleasant instead of ruminating on something too difficult to bear. We would accomplish so much, and likely lose our taste for the useless. We would eliminate prejudice and inequalities because those are created by minds fearing the unknown and by people unwilling to let go of the past. There would be no need to make America great again because we would be great. Instead of one nation, though, we would be a planet of people working together for the betterment of all living creatures. It's a dream, but a plausible outcome. It starts with one person learning how to manage disequilibrium and finding a higher equilibrium, and a new Self. It starts with you.

Notes

1 I guess Elon Musk is changing the name to x. However, most of us will always know it as Twitter. I'll continue to refer to it as Twitter here for sake of clarity as many haven't adapted to this change yet. It's only days old at the time of this writing.
2 If we limit who can view our images, we may be able to prevent negative comments. Yet, for some this contradicts the desire to have likes.
3 There is much diversity in Latin America. When I wrote "mixed race," I was referring to the mestizos, Hispanics of mixed European and Native American origin.
4 Today, most people let their smartphones act like the unconscious, keeping the phone number in its memory instead of wasting cognitive space on remembering 7 or 10 digits.

References

Jung, C. G. (1916). The transcendent function. *Collected Works, 8*, 189.

Mead, G. H., & Mind, H. (1934). *Self and Society. University of Chicago*, 173–175.

Miller, J. C. (2004). *The Transcendent Function: Jung's Model of Psychological Growth through Dialogue with the Unconscious*. SUNY Press.

Piaget, J. (1951). The biological problem of intelligence. In D. Rapaport (Ed.), *Organization and Pathology of Thought* (pp. 176–192). Columbia University Press.

INDEX

Note: Endnotes are indicated by the page number followed by "n" and the note number e.g., 159n2 refers to note 2 on page 159. Page numbers in *italics* indicate figures.

Made in the USA
Monee, IL
13 September 2026

62980174R10103